1990

Interfacing and Scientific Computing
on Personal Computers

Interfacing and Scientific Computing
on
Personal Computers

J. N. Demas

University of Virginia

S. E. Demas

Allyn and Bacon
Boston   London   Sydney   Toronto

Library of Congress Cataloging-in-Publication Data

Demas, J. N.
    Interfacing and scientific computing on personal computers / James N. Demas, Susan E. Demas.
        p.   cm.
    Includes bibliographical references.
    ISBN 0-205-12368-6
      1. Microcomputers--Programming.   2. Pascal (Computer program language) 3. Turbo Pascal (Computer program) 4. Computer interfaces.   I. Demas, Susan E.   II. Title.
QA76.6.D455   1990   89-49413
005.26--dc20   CIP

ISBN 0-205-12368-6
ISBN 0-205-12551-4 (International)

Printed in the United States of America

10 9 8 7 6 5 4 3 2 1—95 94 93 92 91 90

In Memory of

Elsie F. Demas

and

John W. Conlon

CONTENTS

Preface

The microelectronics revolution has given low cost, very high performance computing power to virtually anyone. Scientists and engineers in all areas are in the position to use these general purpose microcomputers to control experiments, gather and reduce data, and optimize measurements—if they can determine what to buy, how to interface it, and how to acquire and manipulate data.

In *Interfacing and Scientific Computing on Personal Computers*, we present a highly applied, experimental approach to computer interfacing and data acquisition and reduction. We demonstrate basic concepts, clarify jargon, provide powerful software subroutines and complete programs, and present problems and experiments designed to develop skills for efficiently interfacing and automating many instruments and systems. This material is designed for those who are reasonably familiar with any computer language. We assume no knowledge of electronics, and sophisticated electronic hardware descriptions are avoided, although enough digital and analog background is provided to understand important hardware interfaces. This book forms the basis of our upper division undergraduate and graduate interfacing course that is taken by physicists, chemists, biochemists, physiologists, and engineers.

We generally utilize commercial high-performance, low-cost hardware and software. We build around software and hardware that is compatible with IBM Personal Computer (PCs) and work-alike clones because of their high performance-cost ratio, and the ready availability of scientifically useful peripherals and software.

Our main software language is Pascal, which is a structured high-level programming language that teaches good programming skills and prepares students for languages such as the government standard Ada. We use Borland's Turbo Pascal which is inexpensive, powerful, and convenient. Its wide availability makes Turbo Pascal the *de facto* microcomputer Pascal. Turbo Pascal compiles and executes extremely quickly, and for interfacing applications has extensions for direct hardware control and graphics.

Interfacing the new equipment is made easier with our detailed sections on input and output devices such as analog-to-digital converters (ADCs), digital-to-analog converters (DACs), parallel interfaces, RS-232 serial interfaces, keyboards, video displays, digitization tablets, and real time clocks (RTCs). Concepts are introduced in the context of laboratory automation and on-line data reduction of scientifically useful experiments. Emphasis is placed on understanding fundamental principles and avoiding the numerous subtle problems that can arise.

In addition to showing how to acquire data, we demonstrate how to improve its accuracy and precision using a variety of signal-to-noise (S/N) enhancement techniques, and data reduction and fitting techniques, especially nonlinear fitting. Pitfalls such as false minima and the blind use of smoothing in many commercial instruments are explained.

For those interfacing problems that require the exquisite control and speed of machine language programming, we devote several chapters to assembly language. In particular, we show how to marry high-level and assembly language routines to gain the benefits of both.

We emphasize understanding underlying principles, avoiding pitfalls, and using experiments and programming to develop skills. Thus, even though readers might not end up using specific hardware or software, they will understand the principles of commercial instrumentation and be able to probe the manufacturer to find out what the instrument can actually do rather than blindly accept any exaggerated or misleading claims.

Acknowledgments

We thank the many students who have contributed their time and energy to this course. Their comments, unfavorable as well as favorable, were considered heavily in the evolution of this material. I especially thank my teaching assistants, Nelson Ayala, Elizabeth R. Carraway, and Seth Snyder for invaluable assistance—indeed, the first year of the PC version of this course would have been an unmitigated disaster without their unflagging efforts and abilities. We also thank Richard Ballew for his software skills (which made many of our projects possible) as well as a number of students who patiently debugged many experiments. We thank our son, David, for writing and debugging some of the software, for reading and commenting on the manuscript, and for checking many of the experiments. Our daughter, Stacy, receives humble gratitude for giving up some of a well-earned summer vacation to decipher handwritten additions. Dee Irwin in Academic Computing was the UNIX troff guru who smoothed the rough spots on the typesetting of this book. Karen Mason's able editing of this book clarified some points and imposed a consistent format. We thank the University of Virginia's Division of Academic Computing for a grant that allowed us to upgrade the course to its current level, and the Chemistry Department for its continued support. We thank Borland International for permission to use part of a copyrighted program. Finally, special thanks to David G. Taylor who originally got one (J.N.D.) of us interested in microcomputers in the 1970s—that led to our purchase of one of the first Altair 8800 microcomputers, which, as it turned out, was the beginning of the end!

Interfacing and Scientific Computing
on Personal Computers

1

Logic, Numbers, Arithmetic, Software, and Computer Architecture

1.1 INTRODUCTION

In this chapter we introduce a number of important concepts and supply an overview of computer hardware and software. While much of what we say applies to computers in general, this text is based on IBM Personal Computers (PCs) and their clones or work-alikes.

We begin with basic digital logic because all computer operations are built on these logic elements and many computer interfaces utilize such logic. Then follows a description of the basic ways of representing numbers in computers, different number bases, and conversions between bases. This information is necessary to appreciate the resolution and range of numbers as well as to understand how they are stored in memory.

A brief overview of microcomputer architecture gives an idea of some of the capabilities and limitations of these machines. This is followed by a discussion of the driving force behind computers, software. Finally, there is a section on different types of computer languages with a description of the advantages and weaknesses of the more common languages.

1.2 LOGIC

In order to understand how a computer works and how many interfaces are constructed, we must understand basic logic and the corresponding electronic symbols. We describe here the basic building blocks of any computer system. These consist of NOT or invert, AND, OR, and exclusive OR functions as well as the basic counting element—the flip-flop. In addition, we show how the essential shift register can be built from flip-flops. We will not go into the electronic construction of the logic elements.

We first establish a convention. Symbolic logic has two states: true and false. However, in electronic logic, two other conventions are used. These are "0" and "1" or "L" (low) and "H" (high). Both alternatives are widely used but we prefer the more common 0–1 convention.

H and 1, being true states, correspond to "positive true" logic. Positive true is the most likely. The other convention is "negative true" logic where the true and false states of positive true logic are reversed. That is, a true is low or 0 and a false is high or 1. Certain computer (DEC 11 series) and communications buses (HPIB or IEEE-488 instrument bus) use negative true logic. Unfortunately, some systems mix positive and negative true logic and do not tell you which is used where, or bury this information in an appendix.

One widely used logic family is Transistor-Transistor-Logic (TTL). The high state is 2–5 V, while the low state range is 0–0.8 V. Any voltage in the 0.8–2.0 V range is ambiguous to the logic devices. Many devices that are built with other technologies are TTL compatible; that is, they recognize and generate TTL level voltages. Most logic devices in PCs are TTL compatible.

Logic functions are commonly described by a truth table, which is a complete list of the output states for all possible input states. We turn now to different logic functions.

1.2.1 NOT Gate or Invert Function

The NOT function is the inverse of the input. The NOT function of input A is written as $\overline{A}$ and is read NOT A. The truth table and logic symbols are shown in Figure 1–1.

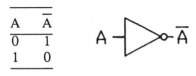

A	$\overline{A}$
0	1
1	0

Figure 1–1. NOT function truth table and logic symbol.

1.2.2 AND Function

The AND function is true if the inputs are all true. For a two-input AND function of A and B, it is written as AB and read as A AND B. The truth table and symbol are shown in Figure 1–2.

A	B	AB
0	0	0
0	1	0
1	0	0
1	1	1

A ⟩ AB
B ⟩

Figure 1-2. AND function truth table and logic symbol.

Logic devices such as the AND are called gates because they can be used to control or "gate" the flow of information. Consider a two-input AND. If B is the control input, then the A input can be transmitted or blocked by the setting of B. If B=1 then A is transmitted directly to the output, or the gate is transmitting. Conversely, if B=0, the gate is off and the input is fixed at 0 regardless of what A is.

A related function is the NAND or NOT AND denoted by $\overline{AB}$ and read NOT the quantity A AND B. The symbol and truth table are shown in Figure 1-3. An "o" at an input or an output of a logic symbol stands for the NOT or invert function.

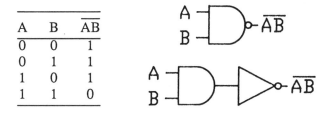

A	B	$\overline{AB}$
0	0	1
0	1	1
1	0	1
1	1	0

Figure 1-3. NAND truth table and logic symbol.

1.2.3 OR Function

The OR function is true if any input is true. The OR of two inputs is denoted by A+B and read A OR B. Similarly, there is a NOR or NOT OR function. The truth tables and symbols for the OR and NOR are shown in Figure 1-4.

A	B	A+B	$\overline{A+B}$
0	0	0	1
0	1	1	0
1	0	1	0
1	1	1	0

A ⟩ A+B
B ⟩

A ⟩ $\overline{A+B}$
B ⟩

Figure 1-4. OR and NOR truth tables and logic symbols.

1.2.4 Exclusive OR Function

The exclusive OR (XOR) is a two-input function that is true if and only if one or the other input is true. The truth table and logic symbol are shown in Figure 1–5.

A	B	A⊕B
0	0	0
0	1	1
1	0	1
1	1	0

Figure 1–5. Exclusive OR truth table and logic symbol.

An exclusive OR can function as a controllable inverter. If A=0, the gate transmits B unchanged. If A=1, then B is inverted at the output.

1.2.5 Flip-Flops (FF)

Flip-flops are the basic counting elements of digital logic. Their name arises since their output can flip-flop or toggle between different output states. In contrast to the static logic devices described thus far, flip-flops change state in response to a clock pulse. The changes are dependent on the states of the control inputs. The clock pulse can be a complete $0 \to 1 \to 0$ transition or the edges of a $0 \to 1$ or negative $1 \to 0$ transition. The first is called level triggered while the latter two are positive and negative edge-triggered respectively.

There are numerous types of flip-flops and we restrict our current discussion to a positive edge-triggered JK flip-flop. The truth table and symbols are shown in Figure 1–6. Q_n is the state of the Q output before the clock pulse and Q_{n+1} is the state after the trigger clock. The flip-flop has two outputs Q and $\overline{Q}$ where $\overline{Q}$ is the complement of Q (i.e., NOT Q). As we will see, having the complement available greatly simplifies certain types of logic design.

To read the table we consider different state changes. If J=K=0 and there is a clock transition, the outputs remain unchanged. That is, Q at time n+1 is equal to Q at n or $Q_{n+1}=Q_n$. If J=1 and K=0, Q goes to a 1 after the clock transition regardless of its original state. If J=K=1, then Q is complemented or toggled after the clock pulse. This last

J	K	Q_{n+1}
0	0	Q_n
0	1	0
1	0	1
1	1	$\overline{Q}_n$ (toggle)

Figure 1–6. JK flip-flop truth table and logic symbol.

mode is the normal flip-flop mode where Q will toggle between two possible states for each clock transition.

To make a divide by 4 counter, consider the circuit shown in Figure 1–7A where Q_A and Q_B are the outputs. Q_A and Q_B respond to the clock as shown in Figure 1–7B.

Note that after four clock edges, Q_A and Q_B return to the original state. Further, Q_A changes at exactly half the rate as the input clock and always changes on a positive clock edge; this is the simple divide by two or flip-flop mode. Q_B changes at half the rate of the Q_A output or one fourth the clock rate. Thus, we get a divide by four. The divide by four works because the outputs of the first FF are tied to the inputs of the B FF. The necessary condition for the B FF to change state occurs only on every other output state of FF A.

One subtle point requires comment. On clock edge 2, Q_B goes to a 1, but its input seems to be changing at the same time. Why does it not become confused? In reality, the JK inputs of B are derived from Q_A. Flip-flop A sees the clock pulse at the same instant as B does, but it takes a finite length of time for Q_A to change. Thus, B changes states based on the original inputs. It is for this reason that counters of this design must use edge-triggered flip-flops.

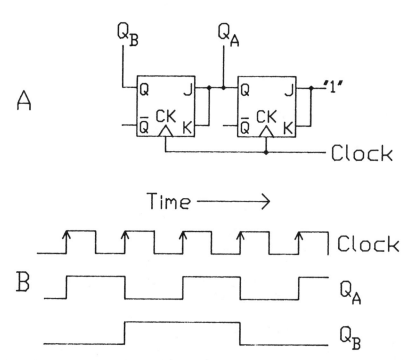

Figure 1–7. Schematic representation of a divide by 4 counter built on flip-flops. A) Circuit. B) Waveforms in response to clock pulse.

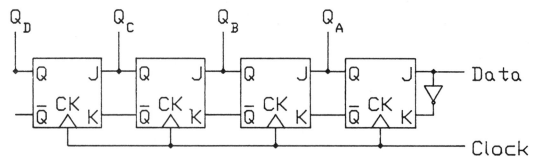

Figure 1–8. Four-bit shift register built from JK flip-flops.

1.2.6 Shift Registers

Shifting strings of binary numbers is an essential arithmetic and logic operation. In particular, computers (and humans) do multiplication and division by repeated shift-add or shift-subtract operations.

A 4-bit shift register is shown in Figure 1–8. While seemingly complex, its operation is straightforward. Q and $\overline{Q}$ from the previous stage are applied to the JK inputs of the next. For the first stage, the input datum is applied directly to the J input, then inverted and applied to the K input. The FF truth table shows that on each clock transition Q and $\overline{Q}$ information from the previous stage gets loaded or shifted into the next FF.

To load four bits of information, apply each bit in turn to the data input and clock it in by a single clock pulse. Thus, four clock pulses are needed to fully load a 4-bit shift register. This is called a serial input or serial load shift register. For very high speed circuits, the time overhead of a serial load can seriously degrade system performance.

To overcome the slowness of a serial load, there are parallel load shift registers where all bits are presented in parallel. A single load pulse loads all the FFs at once. Because of the large number of external connections involved, parallel load devices are usually limited to 4 or 8 bits of data.

1.2.7 Memory

Memory is necessary for storage of program and data. It comes in two basic forms: random access (RAM) or read only (ROM). Random access memory can be written to (altered) as well as read back, while ROM has permanent or semipermanent data or programs in it and can only be read. Actually, both RAM and ROM are random access in that you can access any location in any order by changing the address. A more accurate term for RAM is read/write memory, but this is not in common use.

ROM comes in several versions. There is real ROM, which comes from the factory with the information built directly on the chip. Only if the information is cast in concrete and you plan to use thousands of this program is ROM attractive; the semiconductor manufacturers will only make these in quantities of hundreds to thousands. However, for small users there is PROM or programmable ROM, which is field programmable. Some of these are erasable either electrically or with ultraviolet (uv) light; you can tell the latter by the clear window over the chip. You will see PROM or ROM within most computers and on many peripheral boards that use dedicated microprocessors to implement their function and where the microprocessor must know what to do as soon as the system is turned on.

In it simplest form, RAM consists of a two-dimensional array of flip-flops with a means for selectively storing data in a specific flip-flop and reading it back later. This configuration is called static since the information is statically held in the flip-flop and will stay there until you explicitly change it or turn the power off.

Much more prevalent is dynamic memory in which the data are stored as micro-charges on capacitors; charged corresponds to one state while uncharged is the other. Since the charge on a capacitor will leak off and disappear after a while, you must refresh the charge periodically. Typically, this refreshing must be done a thousand times a second, which is generally a problem for the designer, not the user.

The prevalence of dynamic memory over static arises from its much lower power consumption, higher memory densities, and lower cost. Dynamic RAM is generally not as fast as static memory; this is getting to be a problem in many of the very fast new microcomputers in which computation is being limited by how fast the data can be fetched or stored in memory.

Memory chips come in a variety of sizes, but with increasingly memory-intensive software, the bigger the better. About the smallest size useful chip is 256K, with 1M chips rapidly coming into prominence. Four megabyte chips are in production. A K in computer notation is 1024 (2^{10}) and M or meg is 1,048,576 (2^{20}).

1.2.8   Three-State and Open Collector Logic

There are two additional types of logic that are used in computers. These are three-state logic and open collector logic. Three-state logic is also known as Tri-State logic, which is the copyrighted name from National Semiconductors. Other manufacturers are limited to the term three-state logic, although in spoken usage Tri-State and three-state are used interchangeably.

Three-state and open collector logic are what make modern computer architecture possible. While open collector has been replaced by three-state logic for new computer construction, open collector devices still find wide use in the IEEE-488 instrumentation interface bus.

As the term implies, three-state logic has three possible output states. These are high, low, and "not there." That is, the device can have the usual high and low or it can be disconnected from the circuit. The not there state, which is referred to as the high impedance or off state, is controlled by an additional input to the device. This control is called the enable. The truth table and schematic of a simple, straight through, noninverting driver is shown in Figure 1–9. The Z in the output indicates the high impedance or not there state. The enable input in this case is active high; the device is turned on (i.e., connects the circuitry to the output) with a high enable signal. Active low circuitry is also common. The notation on the IC is the invert or circle symbol on the input.

Of what use is this three-state function? The answer is that it allows multiple devices to sit on a common line, but have only one of them active at a time. Consider Figure 1–10. For simplicity we show only two inputs on a common line, but in a computer many devices may share a common line. Assume that there are two input signals that

A	E	B
0	0	Z
1	0	Z
0	1	0
1	1	1

Z = high impedance state

Figure 1–9. Three-state gate truth table and logic symbol.

you might like to look at, one from each input. By changing the Select line to the circuit, we can turn on either device and look at its signal on the bus line. The decoder circuit in this case is responsible for selecting which of the two devices will be connected to the bus or information line. In this case it is particularly simple, since we assume only two inputs and one of them will be on all the time. Thus, the single inverter suffices. When the Select is low, device #1 is turned on and when it is high, device #2 is on.

Note that it is impossible for both devices to be connected to the bus line if the circuitry is working. When device #1 is enabled, device #2 is disabled and vice versa. More complicated decoders are readily developed for selecting one of many devices.

Consider a more realistic example. Suppose you have a computer with 512K of memory made up with two 256K memory boards where 1K=1024 words of computer memory. In an old style computer, there would be one slot specially wired to accept the board for the first 256K board and a second one for the second 256K board. The difficulty of this configuration becomes obvious when someone introduces a single board with 512K of memory. You would then like to upgrade with two 512K boards in these two slots to give you 1024K of memory. Unless it was very carefully designed with an eye to the future, the old configuration would not accommodate the new boards at all.

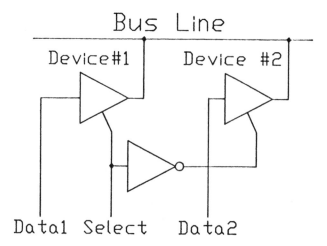

Figure 1–10. Simple two-input bus (signal) line with three-state gates.

Another example is if you wish to put in several data acquisition boards and would like to install them in the slot for one of the memory boards, but have already used up all the other slots—assuming that the manufacturer had the insight to include slots that were adaptable to your design at all. How can you put a data acquisition board with its completely different address requirements into a slot designed for memory?

The three-state solution is shown schematically in Figure 1–11. We show a computer bus with data lines (typically 8, 16, or 32) with associated address and control lines. If we had 20 address lines we could select up to 1024K of memory. In contrast to the narrow design of the previous example, all board slots in this configuration are identical. Each has all data lines, 20 address lines, and the control lines for regulating activity. Every bus line goes to a common connector pin on each connector slot. The bus is the set of lines that join the different connectors together. Generally the bus is laid out on a single printed circuit board and very regular sets of lines tie the connectors together.

Control lines serve many functions. They set whether the CPU is inputting or outputting data and whether input/output involves memory or ports. Ports are a special PC configuration used for input and output; we discuss and use ports in later chapters. Control lines also match the speeds of the devices. For example, many CPUs are faster than their memory, and the control lines inform the CPU when memory data are successfully written or ready to be read.

The CPU sets the address lines to locations of information that it wants or destinations to which it sends data. Each board, which has a unique address, must determine whether it is addressed and the function requested. A board decoder determines whether these conditions are met and only then enables the board. This is done by comparing the address set by the CPU to the board's address and checking the control line states (see Problem 1–2). Board addresses are generally set with little multiple section dip switches.

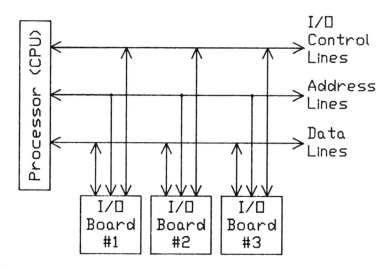

Figure 1–11. A computer bus with several input/output devices connected to a multiline bus.

Three-state logic isolates every device from the bus until it is supposed to put data on the bus. Each line that can apply a signal to the bus is isolated by a three-state gate. If each board has a separate address, only one device is activated at a time and imposes a bus signal. This prevents multiple devices from simultaneously trying to assert bus line control, which would garble information or destroy devices.

A bus architecture has enormous benefits. Wiring is simple; all card connectors are the same. Thus, you can put any type of card into any slot although every card must have a unique address. This generality makes it less likely that you will run out of slots. Manufacturers have great design freedom; their boards only have to understand the addressing and communications scheme.

An example of the utility of the bus is the first IBM PC. The early PCs had 64K of memory and few expansion slots. Each IBM function, including the video adaptor, the serial communications, and the parallel printer port required a separate board. In short, users could not populate a system to a reasonable level. In response to this need several manufacturers introduced single slot, multifunction boards that included a serial port and parallel ports, up to 384K of memory, and a real time clock. Since all signals were available at every slot, these boards could be plugged in anywhere and free additional slots.

Open collector logic is functionally quite different from three state but was also used to generate a bus structure at one time. The DEC 8 and 11 series computers used an open collector rather than a three-state bus. Open collectors rest on the switching properties of transistors.

Figure 1–12 shows an NPN transistor. For our purposes the transistor can function as a simple off-on switch with the base-emitter connection being the control and the emitter-collector connections being the switched lines. In the absence of a control voltage on the transistor base, the transistor is off and there is a large resistance between the emitter and collector leads. If a positive voltage greater than about 0.6 V is applied between the base and emitter, the emitter-collector connection becomes a low resistance path or the transistor is on. The on state is not perfect. The on emitter collector voltage drop is about 200 mV, but for TTL logic this is a perfectly respectable logic low.

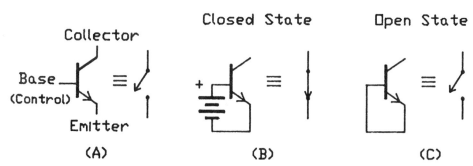

Figure 1–12. NPN transistor showing how it behaves as a switch in response to different base control signals. (A) Equivalent circuit. (B) On (closed) state. (C) Off (open) state.

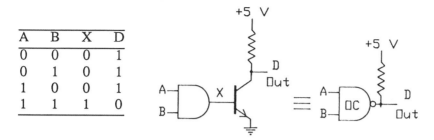

A	B	X	D
0	0	0	1
0	1	0	1
1	0	0	1
1	1	1	0

Figure 1–13. Open collector NAND gate truth table and symbol. The pull up resistor is external to the gate.

A critical point is that the transistor output is not a source of voltage. If a logic high is to be generated some external voltage source must be applied. Figure 1–13 shows an open collector NAND gate with a powering voltage source as well as the truth table. The gate is derived from a standard TTL AND and a transistor. The reason for the term open collector becomes apparent; the output of the gate is internally unconnected within the logic device. That is, the collector is open. The external voltage source is necessary for generating a logic high and is derived by pulling up the open collector output with a resistor, which is known as a pull up resistor. The resistor limits the transistor current flow when it is on. If the collector were connected directly to the power supply, the transistor would draw large currents and burn itself or the power supply out; it is equivalent to connecting a wire directly across the 110 VAC line. In this circuit, when the transistor is off, the resistor pulls the line up to 5V or a high. When the transistor is on, the line is pulled down to <200mV or a low.

It is clear that the combination of a two-input AND with an open collector output is functionally logically equivalent to a normal two-input NAND. The difference comes when we generate a bus. Figure 1–14 shows a simple single bus line with two separate

D1	D2	E	E'	B
0	0	0	1	1
0	1	0	1	0
1	0	0	1	1
1	1	0	1	0
0	0	1	0	1
0	1	1	0	1
1	0	1	0	0
1	1	1	0	0

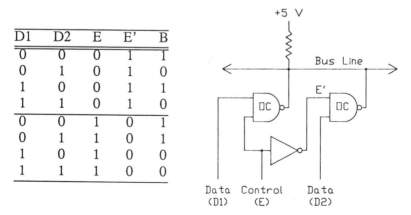

Figure 1–14. Simple open collector bus and truth table.

input devices and a simple decoder along with its truth table. The table is more complicated, but it is easily understood when you recognize that if either D1 or D2 had a zero output, the output of the line would be pulled down to a logic level low regardless of the output state of the other gate. The reason is that the outputs are just switches. If one of the switches is closed to ground then the line is pulled to 0V or a logic low. From the standpoint of busing, the important point about this truth table is that if D1 is enabled with E=1 then the output B equals $\overline{D1}$, while if D2 is enabled with E=0, then the output equals $\overline{D2}$. In other words, the bus line is the inverse of the selected input.

Thus, an open collector bus achieves the same bus function as three-state logic. It is no longer used in computer buses, however, because it is slower and does not have the large expansion capability of three-state. Open collector logic does form the basis of the common IEEE-488 instrument bus.

1.2.9 Logic Examples

We turn now to the design of simple but important logic circuits. Specifically, we will design a half adder and a full adder. Later, when we discuss subtraction, we will also design a single circuit that will do both addition and subtraction.

A half adder takes two bits and adds them together to get a sum and a carry. If the two input bits are A and B, the truth table is shown in Figure 1–15.

The logic implementation is obvious. The sum bit is the XOR, and the carry is the AND. Therefore, a half adder is shown in Figure 1–15.

A half adder is inadequate if one needs multibit addition. There you need a carry in from the previous stage. From a conceptual standpoint, rather than a logic minimization standpoint, the easiest way to implement this is with two half adders as shown in Figure 1–16.

The OR is needed because there are two conditions that generate a carry out. A carry out arises if the A and B sum generates a carry or if the A and B sum plus the preceding carry (carry in) generates a carry. Note that it is impossible to have a carry from both sources simultaneously. Verify this by making a full adder truth table. It is tempting to connect the two carry outs together rather than use the OR. With a few special exceptions, one cannot connect outputs together. If the two outputs disagree, they fight over the line and large, potentially destructive, currents flow. One or both devices may burn out or, at the very least, the state can be improperly set and the logic fails.

		Sum	Carry
A	B	(Σ)	(CY)
0	0	0	0
0	1	1	0
1	0	1	0
1	1	0	1

Figure 1–15. Binary half-adder truth table and implementation.

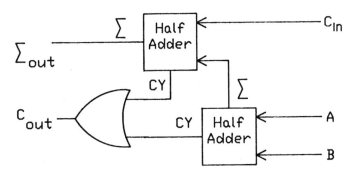

Figure 1–16. Implementation of full adder using two half adders.

One could easily construct an n-bit full adder. Merely connect the carry out from the p-1 stage to the carry in of the p stage. The carry in to the first stage is set to 0.

We defer the problem of subtraction. As we will see it is easily possible to generate a subtractor using almost the same circuit as is used for the adder.

1.3 BITS, NIBBLES, BYTES, AND WORDS

A single binary digit is called a bit. Larger numbers are built up by stacking bits together. In practice, a byte is a collection of 8 bits. A word is usually the width of the central processing unit's (CPU) internal data size. Most older micros used 8-bit words. Most modern micros use 16-bit, and some use 32-bit words. The meaning of a word can be further confused because the internal and external word widths can differ. For example, in the standard IBM PC that uses the 8088 CPU, the internal CPU word width is 16 bit, but the external memory width is 8 bit. Clones and IBM AT style machines using 8086 or 80286 CPUs have external and internal 16-bit paths. The 80386 and 80486 CPUs use 32-bit external and internal data paths; even though the basic instruction set width is still 16 bit it is enhanced with 32-bit instructions and registers. The 80386sx is an 80386 with 16-bit external data paths.

Each processor has a math coprocessor or floating point accelerator. The 8087 is used with the 8088 and 8086, the 80287 with the 80286, the 80387 with the 80386, and the 80387sx with the 80386sx. The 80486 has the math coprocessor built in.

Intel's registered trademarks for these processors are the 386, 387sx, 387, 387sx, and i486, although much of the Intel literature uses the 80– designation. Since most of what we say is generic to the entire series of chips, we will frequently refer to them as the 8086 family of CPUs or the 80X86 series and the 80X87 math coprocessors.

If a bit of data is too small and a byte is too large, what falls in between? The answer is a nibble, which is 4 bits wide. A nibble is frequently used to represent one numeric digit. Thus, a byte of memory could hold two numeric digits.

1.4 NUMBER BASES AND NUMBER REPRESENTATIONS

While we are familiar, and fluent, with decimal representations of numbers, computers are much less at ease with them. Indeed, standard logic circuits directly handle only binary numbers since the basic building block circuit can only represent a 0 or 1. Thus, computers must reasonably think in binary. Humans, on the other hand, dislike long strings of zeroes and ones. To make computer numbers more manageable to humans, they are frequently displayed as hexadecimal numbers. Finally, a hybrid representation binary-coded decimal (BCD) is frequently used by devices and software to bridge the human-machine gap. We discuss how to convert between the different bases. Another major problem that arises in computers is the representation of signed numbers and of floating point numbers. We discuss some of the more common representations.

We begin by pointing out what a given representation of a number means. For example, if we write 375 decimal what we are really saying is that we have three hundreds, seven tens, and five ones. This can be written:

$$3 \cdot 10^2 + 7 \cdot 10^1 + 5 \cdot 10^0$$

1.4.1 Binary

Similarly, we can have an n+1 digit binary number given by the following sequence:

$$b_n \, b_{n-1} \, \ldots \, b_2 \, b_1 \, b_0$$

where each b represents a digit and b_0 is the least significant bit (LSB) and b_n is the most significant bit (MSB). Then the decimal equivalent of the number is:

$$b_n 2^n + b_{n-1} 2^{n-1} \ldots b_2 2^2 + b_1 2^1 + b_0 2^0 \qquad (1-1)$$

where all arithmetic is done in decimal.

Thus, it is a simple exercise to convert a binary number into its decimal representation. For example, 101101 binary is:

$$1 \cdot 2^5 + 0 \cdot 2^4 + 1 \cdot 2^3 + 1 \cdot 2^2 + 0 \cdot 2^1 + 1 \cdot 2^0 =$$

$$1 \cdot 32 + 0 \cdot 16 + 1 \cdot 8 + 1 \cdot 4 + 0 \cdot 2 + 1 \cdot 1 = 45 \text{ decimal}$$

Somewhat less obvious is the inverse case. The simplest procedure is a brute force or "bull moose" approach. Suppose that our number is represented by Equation 1–1. Find the largest n such that 2^n is less than or equal to our number. This means that $b_n=1$ where b_n is the MSB. Subtract $b_n \cdot 2^n$ from the original number. This yields:

$$b_{n-1} 2^{n-1} \ldots b_2 2^2 + b_1 2^1 + b_0 2^0 \qquad (1-2)$$

We now repeat the process of asking if 2^{n-1} goes into this number. If a given power of 2 is larger than the remainder, the coefficient on that power is zero. If the power divides into the number, that coefficient is 1 and you subtract that power from our current remainder. Repeating this process yields the coefficients on successively smaller powers until the difference is reduced to zero.

For example, convert 131 decimal to binary. The smallest power of two that is less than 131 is 2^7(128). So $b_7=1$. Subtracting 128 leaves 3. 64, 32, 16, 8, and 4 are all larger than 3, so $b_6=b_5=b_4=b_3=b_2=0$. Since 3>2, $b_1=1$. Subtracting 2^1 leaves a remainder of 1. Finally, since $2^0=1$, $b_0=1$, and the final subtraction reduces our remainder to zero. The binary value is 10000011.

1.4.2 Hexadecimal Numbers

Hexadecimal (commonly called hex) numbers are numbers expressed to base 16. There are 16 individual digits. By convention they are 0 through 9 and A, B, C, D, E, and F. To convert the hexadecimal number $h_n h_{n-1} \ldots h_1 h_0$ to decimal, we write:

$$h_n 16^n + h_{n-1} 16^{n-1} \ldots h_1 16^1 + h_0 16^0$$

where we use the decimal equivalent of h for values greater than 9. For example, F08B hex is equal to:

$$15 \cdot 16^3 + 0 \cdot 16^2 + 8 \cdot 16^2 + 11 \cdot 16^0$$

Similarly, we can convert decimal numbers to hexadecimal by a procedure analogous to that used for binary. For example, 37948 decimal is 943C hex.

1.4.3 Alternative Conversion from Decimal

A tidy general way of converting a decimal number to any base is to repeatedly divide the decimal number by the base. As an example, consider a decimal to binary conversion. Assume that the decimal number is expressed by Equation 1–1. Divide the number by 2, the binary base. We obtain an integer part and a remainder given by:

Integer Part $b_n 2^{n-1} + b_{n-1} 2^{n-2} \ldots b_2 2^1 + b_1 2^0$
Remainder b_0

The remainder is b_0, the LSB. Divide the integer part by 2 to obtain:

Integer Part $b_n 2^{n-2} + b_{n-1} 2^{n-3} \ldots b_2 2^0$
Remainder b_1

The new remainder is b_1, the next LSB. Division by the base is repeated until the integer part is zero. Then assemble the remainder bits to form the binary number.

As an example, consider conversion of 343 decimal to binary:

343/2	=	171	+	remainder of 1	=>	$b_0=1$
171/2	=	85	+	remainder of 1	=>	$b_1=1$
85/2	=	42	+	remainder of 1	=>	$b_2=1$

$$42/2 \quad = \quad 21 \quad + \quad \text{remainder of 0} \quad => \quad b_3=0$$
$$21/2 \quad = \quad 10 \quad + \quad \text{remainder of 1} \quad => \quad b_4=1$$
$$10/2 \quad = \quad 5 \quad + \quad \text{remainder of 0} \quad => \quad b_5=0$$
$$5/2 \quad = \quad 2 \quad + \quad \text{remainder of 1} \quad => \quad b_6=1$$
$$2/2 \quad = \quad 1 \quad + \quad \text{remainder of 0} \quad => \quad b_7=0$$
$$1/2 \quad = \quad 0 \quad + \quad \text{remainder of 1} \quad => \quad b_8=1$$

which yields a binary representation of 101010111.

A similar strategy can be used for decimal to hex conversions. The decimal remainder is converted into the equivalent hex digit.

1.4.4 Miscellaneous Conversions

Conversion from binary to hex or from hex to binary could be made by converting to decimal and then to the final number base. A more direct procedure is possible because 16 is also 2^4. To convert any binary number to hex, mark off the digits into groups of four starting at the decimal point. Then replace each group by equivalent hex digits. For example, to convert 101011110:

1 1011 1110 (binary) = 1BE (hexadecimal)

Similarly, to convert hex to binary, replace each hex digit by its corresponding 4-bit binary equivalent. For example, to convert 3FA to binary write:

3FA (hex) = 0011 1111 1010 (binary) = 1111111010 (binary)

Many binary, decimal, or hex numbers can look valid but be quite different. For example, 11 is a valid binary, decimal or hex number but in each case it has a completely different value. Its decimal equivalent is 3, 11, or 17 depending on its base. To avoid ambiguities, conventions are used to differentiate the base of numbers. However, the conventions are not always consistent among different pieces of software.

For example, assembler programs use the suffix B to indicate binary numbers (e.g., 11B). Decimal numbers may be differentiated by a D suffix (e.g., 11D) or frequently by no suffix, since decimal is the default value. Hex numbers can have a trailing H (e.g., 3FH). In addition, hex numbers must begin with a leading number to differentiate a hex number from a label. Thus, F40H is an invalid hex number, but 0F40H is acceptable. Octal base numbers have a suffix Q. This may seem strange until one sees how hard a letter O and a number 0 are to distinguish on some systems.

Microsoft BASIC uses another convention in which decimal numbers are the default values. For hex numbers the value is preceded by &H. Thus, F40 hex is expressed as &HF40. Octal base numbers are preceded by &O.

Turbo Pascal uses another convention. Again the default is decimal. Hex numbers use a prefix $. Thus, $E000 is a valid hex number.

1.4.5 Binary Coded Decimal (BCD)

A common way of representing decimal numbers is to replace each decimal digit by its 4-bit binary equivalent. Thus, 98D becomes 1001 1000. For conversion of BCD to decimal, merely mark off groups of 4 binary bits starting at the decimal point, and convert each group to its equivalent decimal digit. If one of the digits was greater than 9, then the number was not a valid BCD digit.

1.4.6 Signed Binary Numbers

Several important methods of representing signed binary numbers are sign plus magnitude, offset binary, 1s complement, and 2s complement.

Sign plus magnitude appends a leading bit to the number that denotes whether it is positive or negative. A leading 0 is a positive number while a leading 1 means a negative number. We indicate 4 bit sign plus magnitude representations for the possible values -7 to $+7$ in Table 1–1. The most interesting anomalies are that even though 4 bits are used and we should be able to represent 16 different values, we can express only 15. Also $+0$ and -0 are different values.

Offset binary gets around these problems. One makes the most negative value 0 and adds 1 for each higher value. This is shown in Table 1–1, but we can start at -8 and run through $+7$. Note that we have 16 different values and no ambiguous 0.

Another way of representing negative numbers is with 1s complement. To make a positive number negative bitwise negate (NOT) each bit. This is shown in Table 1–1. Several problems exist with 1s complement. There are only 15 numbers represented by

| | Sign Plus | Offset | 1s | 2s |
Decimal	Magnitude	Binary	Complement	Complement
7	0111	1111	0111	0111
6	0110	1110	0110	0110
5	0101	1101	0101	0101
4	0100	1100	0100	0100
3	0011	1011	0011	0011
2	0010	1010	0010	0010
1	0001	1001	0001	0001
0	0000	1000	0000	0000
−0	1000	1000	1111	0000
−1	1001	0111	1110	1111
−2	1010	0110	1101	1110
−3	1011	0101	1100	1101
−4	1100	0100	1011	1100
−5	1101	0011	1010	1011
−6	1110	0010	1001	1010
−7	1111	0001	1000	1001
−8		0000		1000

Table 1–1. Comparison of Different Signed Number Types

the 4 bits (1111 is not valid). Thus, −8 would be the same as +7 in a 4-bit representation.

Another weakness in all of the previous methods is that the arithmetic is complicated. One would hope that adding a positive number to its negative value would be zero. Simple addition in any of the previous representations yields incorrect values.

We turn now to 2s complement. The 2s complement is formed by adding one to the 1s complement of the number. This is shown in Table 1–1. Note that a 4-bit 2s complement can represent 16 different numbers and there is no ambiguity about zero.

An important aspect of 2s complement is its arithmetic characteristics. Adding any number to its 2s complement negative equivalent gives zero. That is, for number A:

$$A+(-A)=0$$

where −A is the 2s complement of A. Similarly, to compute A−B:

$$A-B=A+(-B).$$

This important result shows that subtraction of one number from another can be performed merely by forming the 2s complement of the second and adding it to the first. Since NOT and addition are the only functions required to form a 2s complement, a separate subtraction circuit is not required.

We point out one less obvious feature of 1s and 2s complements. Both are actually extended to the left an infinite number of digits. Thus, −7 is actually:

$$...1111001$$

where there is an infinite number of ones to the left. This is not really bizarre since for positive numbers there is an implied infinite number of zeroes to the left. However, for the current issue we are dealing with the computer's finite bit number representation.

We now consider several examples of 2s complement arithmetic with 4-bit representations of the number (i.e., Table 1–1).

$$
\begin{array}{lll}
7_{10} & 0111_2 & 0111_2 \\
-3_{10} & -0011_2 & +1101_2 \\
\hline
4_{10} & & 0100_2=+4_{10}
\end{array}
\qquad
\begin{array}{lll}
3_{10} & 0011_2 & 0011_2 \\
-7_{10} & -0111_2 & +1001_2 \\
\hline
-4_2 & & 1100_2=-4_{10}
\end{array}
$$

Clearly the results are correct in both cases. However, using finite digit representation in 2s complement has hazards. Consider the following examples:

$$
\begin{array}{ll}
-7_{10} & 1001_2 \\
-7_{10} & +1001_2 \\
\hline
-14_{10} & 1|0010_2=2
\end{array}
\quad
\begin{array}{ll}
-7_{10} & 1001_2 \\
-6_{10} & +1010_2 \\
\hline
-13_{10} & 1|0011_2=3_{10}
\end{array}
\quad
\begin{array}{ll}
4_{10} & 0100_2 \\
+6_{10} & +0110_2 \\
\hline
+10_{10} & 1010_2=-6_{10}
\end{array}
$$

where all three examples yield incorrect results in a 4-bit 2s complement representation. The problem is called overflow—we have overflowed the dynamic range of our representation; −14, −13, and 10 are invalid 4-bit 2s complement numbers. Adding two numbers of opposite sign can never yield overflow. Overflow can be detected when the sign of the result of an addition differs from the signs of the two numbers added. As we

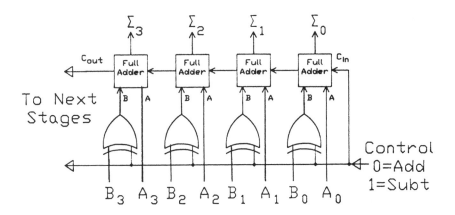

Figure 1–17. Four-bit adder-subtractor circuit.

see later, the 80X86 processor automatically detects overflow on addition or subtraction.

We return now to our earlier promise of showing how to build a single circuit that will perform both addition and subtraction. Our earlier full subtractor design required an entirely different logic block for subtraction and our signals would have had to be routed to the different blocks depending on the desired operation.

Fortunately, using 2s complement arithmetic solves this problem. Remember that to form the 2s complement of a number we bitwise complement each bit and add one to the resultant 1s complement.

The adder/subtractor circuit is shown in Figure 1–17. For purposes of example we consider only a 4-bit system and use full adders. We take advantage of a special characteristic of the XOR to switch between the add and subtract modes using a single control bit. Remember that an XOR can function as a direct transition gate or an inverter depending on the state of a control bit. If the control bit is 0, the XOR transmits the data bit without change, but if the control bit is 1, then the data bit is inverted or NOTed.

If the mode bit is 0, the circuit adds the A and B words normally; the B bits are passed through the XOR without change since the control bits are 0. If, however, the mode bit is 1, a 1 is applied to the control bit of each XOR. This inverts each B bit (forms the 1s complement) and adds it to A. If we could now add 1 to the final sum we would effectively form the 2s complement of B and add it to A, which forms A–B. Merely by applying the mode bit to the carry in on the adder string, we add the necessary 1 and form a proper A–B difference.

1.4.7 Large Numbers

The common way to increase the dynamic range of integers is to increase the number of bits. Some software (e.g., BASIC and Turbo Pascal) uses 16-bit 2s complement integers. The PCs 80X87 provides expanded integer formats: 32-bit short and 64-bit long integers. The approximate number of decimal digits and the dynamic range of these integer types are given in Table 1–2.

Type[1,2]	Number of Bits	Resolution Decimal Digits	Approximate Dynamic Range
Byte (Turbo [*byte*])	8	2	0–255
Turbo Shortint (Turbo [*shortint*])	8	2	−128 to 127
Turbo/BASIC Integer (BASIC, Turbo [*integer*])	16	4	−32,768 to 32,767
Turbo Word (Turbo [*word*])	16	4	0 to 65,535
Integer (80X87, Pascal, FORTRAN, C)	32	8	-2×10^9 to 2×10^9
BASIC/Turbo Long Integer (BASIC, Turbo [*longint*])	32	8	-2×10^9 to 2×10^9
80X87 Long Integer (80X87, Turbo [*comp*], C, FORTRAN)	64	18	-9×10^{18} to 9×10^{18}
Short Real (80X87, Turbo [*single*] Pascal, FORTRAN, C)	32	6–7	10^{-45} to 10^{38}
Turbo Real (Turbo [*real*])	48	11–12	10^{-39} to 10^{38}
Long Real (80X87, Turbo [*double*], Pascal, FORTRAN, C)	64	15–16	10^{-324} to 10^{308}
Temporary Real (80X87, Turbo [*extended*])	80	19–20	10^{-4951} to 10^{4932}

Table 1–2. Characteristics of Different Number Representations

[1] Turbo means Turbo Pascal; Pascal means other Pascals.

[2] Turbo types are in italics.

Unfortunately, there is no consistent nomenclature between different pieces of software. For example, Turbo Pascal 4/5 calls a 32 bit 2s complement a long integer, while for the 80X87 math coprocessor and FORTRAN this is a regular integer. The 64 bit 2s complement integer of the 80X87 is called a long integer, but since Turbo Pascal has exhausted this name, it is given the name "comp." Other discrepancies exist in the floating point numbers. However, in spite of these problems Turbo Pascal has a wide and very useful range of different numeric types such as byte, shortint, word, integer, and long integer. You will make use of many of these types later.

1.4.8   Floating Point Numbers

The relatively limited dynamic range of straight binary numbers forces us to adopt other strategies for representing floating point numbers. A very logical floating point scheme is to normalize all numbers in a fashion similar to scientific notation. For example, in scientific notation we write 3742 as 3.742E3 where we adopt the computer notation of the number following E being a power of 10.

A similar strategy is used in computers where a floating point number is given by:

$$(-1)^{sgn} * S * 2^{E}$$

where sgn is the sign bit of the number, S is the significand (mantissa in logarithms), and E is the exponent value. Implementations of this method follow.

The 80X86/80X87 system has three important ways of representing floating point numbers. These are 32-bit short, 64-bit long, and 80-bit temporary reals. The short and long reals are also referred to as single and double precision.

The dynamic range and number of significant digits of each of these is summarized in Table 1–2. Excluding the Turbo Pascal Real type, each of these number representations is expressed as:

<sign><exponent><significand>

An important question is how many bits to use for the significand and the exponent. Using more bits in the exponent gives a wider dynamic range while using more bits in the significand gives more precision. The generally accepted tradeoff is shown in Table 1–3.

One other important issue is how to handle the exponents since they can be both positive and negative. The obvious answer, which is wrong, is 2s complement. What is used is a biased exponent. The exponent has a constant called the bias added to it before it is stored. To convert it back to the correct value, the bias is subtracted off. The biases for the different representations are shown in Table 1–3.

The significand is treated as a number with one non-zero digit to the left of the decimal. For example, 11101 is represented as 1.1101E100.

Table 1–3. Bit Usage in 80X87 Floating Point Numbers					
	Number of Bits	Sign	Exponent	Significand	Bias (Decimal)	Hidden Bit
Short Real	32	1	8	23	127	Yes
Long Real	64	1	11	52	1023	Yes
Temporary Real	80	1	15	64	16383	No

Finally, to make life even more interesting, one additional trick is used. When we write a binary number in scientific notation, the leftmost digit is always one. The exception is the number zero, which is handled in a special manner; the exponent and the significand bits are all set to zero. However, if the one is always there, why waste one of our few precious bits of significand with it? Thus, for short and long reals, this bit is dropped and its presence is implied. This hidden bit is used in many single and double precision representations of floating point numbers.

The temporary real, however, does not hide the most significant bit of the significand, but leaves it intact. The reason is that the temporary real is the floating point representation of the 80X87 math coprocessor, which is designed for high speed arithmetic. If the 80X87 had to keep track of the hidden bit, it would slow arithmetic. Since we already have 64 bits of significand, the loss of one bit here is not serious.

For example, we convert -15.25_{10} into short, long, and temporary reals. The binary equivalent is -1111.01. In scientific notation this is $-1.11101E11$. The exponent is 3_{10} and the biased exponent is 130_{10} (short real). The representations are:

	sign	biased exponent	significand	
short real	1	10000010	11101000000000000000000	
long real	1	10000000010	1110100....	0
temporary real	1	100000000000010	1111010....	0

where we indicate the rightmost zeroes in the long and temporary reals by "....."

We turn now to one important characteristic of Turbo Pascal 4 and 5. These have floating reals of type Real but as shown in Table 1–2 Real is not compatible with any of the 80X87 types. If you declare any variables in Turbo 4/5 as Real (and you must if you want direct compatibility with any other Pascal) your reals will be stored as the 6 byte format. If you have a math coprocessor, you will find that Turbo must switch these reals back and forth between the Turbo reals and the 80X87 reals before processing them with, or reading results from, the 80X87. The implications of this are that the use of Real variables in a Turbo 4 program will cause it to execute more slowly than if you declare the same variables as type single, double, or extended since these types match directly what the 80X87 requires and no conversions are needed. You will demonstrate this fact in a later experiment. Turbo 5 does have a mode that makes all reals 80X87 reals.

1.5 COMPUTER ARCHITECTURE

Figure 1–18 shows the overall organization of a computer. The CPU is the central processing unit, which is responsible for fetching instructions, decoding them, and executing them. In the IBM style personal computer (PC), the 8088 CPU has 30,000 transistor equivalents while the i486 has over a million.

Memory is generally organized in bytes. It may be all or part of an instruction, a byte number value, a character, part of an integer or floating point numbers, or garbage. A 256K computer is minimal. With PC machines 256–640K is standard, up to 16M are addressable in AT style PCs, and up to 4 gigabytes ($2^{32} = 4,294,967,296$) are addressable by the 386 and i486. Remember that $1K=2^{10}$ (1024) and $1M=2^{20}$ (1,048,576).

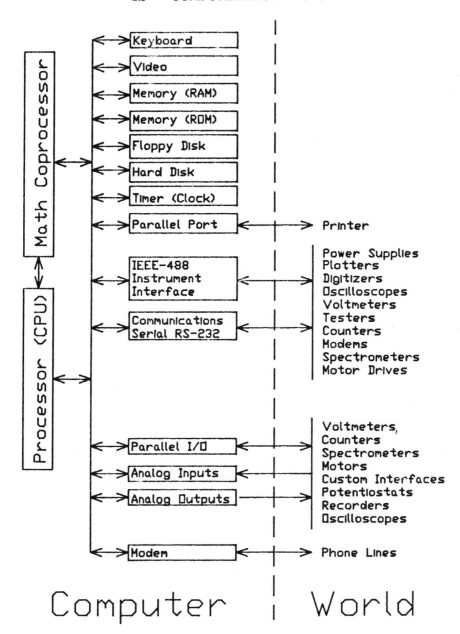

Figure 1–18. Overall organization of a computer.

Peripherals will invariably include some type of disk system. Disk systems may use floppy disks or hard (fixed) disks. Occasionally, tape back-ups are used to protect the data on the hard disks against catastrophic failures.

Floppy disks, or floppies as they are most commonly known, are flexible disks of magnetically coated media. The diskette is grabbed by a shaft or spindle that comes up through the center and spins the diskette much like a record player. The disk drive has read/write heads that permit magnetizing domains on the disk and reading it back like an audio or video cassette. The information is organized in concentric rings rather than as a spiral as on records. Each ring of data is called a track. Typically, 35, 40, or, on high density drives, up to 96 tracks are used. Each track is divided into sectors where the data are stored. Current 5.25" diskettes on IBM style machines have 40 tracks with 9 sectors of 1024 bytes of data each or 360K of storage.

Floppies come in several styles. The old 8" diameter disks are widely used on old micros and some current minicomputers, but are rarely used on modern microcomputers. Currently the most common size is 5.25" diameter floppies on IBM PC style machines. However, with the widespread adoption of the PS2 series and laptops, these are being steadily supplanted by 3.5" floppies. The 8" and 5.25" diskettes come in a protective paper envelope and must be removed before insertion into the disk drive. The 3.5" diskettes have their own protective plastic shell so the entire diskette is inserted into the drive. A little door on the shell is opened automatically on insertion to expose the magnetic medium.

If only one side of the diskette is used, the disk is called single sided. If both sides are used it is double sided. A typical IBM style 5.25" diameter diskette stores 360K bytes double sided or 180K single sided. The 1.2M double-sided diskette is common on AT class machines. Access time on most floppies is typically 250 milliseconds (ms). The very compact 3.5" floppy typically holds 720K or 1.44M—you can carry several megabytes in a vest pocket.

In a floppy system the read/write head actually rubs against the surface and will eventually make it unusable. Therefore, the heads are lifted off the surface except when read/write operations are in progress. To further reduce wear the drive is stopped several seconds following the last use. Because of potential failure of diskettes due to wear or other reasons, regularly make back-up copies on another diskette.

Hard or fixed disks use a quite different approach. The magnetic medium is on rigid (hard) platens with read/write heads that skim over the surface on a cushion of air. The heads never (except during catastrophic failure or when the drive is off) contact the surface. Capacities of 20, 30, and 40 M bytes are common and larger ones are available. In addition to the much greater storage capacity, hard disks are much faster with average access times of 25–80 ms. Unlike floppies, fixed disks cannot be exchanged (which is the reason for the term fixed). Once the disk is full, material must be cleared off to make room for more.

The video display adaptor can be either straight text or text and graphics. For scientific purposes, a graphics adaptor is essential. Resolution of the standard IBM color graphics adaptor (CGA) is 640x200 in monochrome mode or 320x200 in the four-color mode. The enhanced color graphic adaptor (EGA) can have higher resolution. This is also true of the newer VGA with 640x480 sixteen-color resolution. EGA and VGA require more expensive monitors than does CGA but give improved resolution.

Another very important element in the figure is the numeric data processor, which is also called a math coprocessor or floating point accelerator. These devices can frequently be added at little cost (about a hundred dollars on an IBM PC) and yet will accelerate math intensive calculations by tens to hundreds of times—if the software supports them. It is like supercharging a Ford and making it perform like a Maserati. The omission of such a device on a scientific computer is a grave tactical error. We will demonstrate the advantages of a math coprocessor in the next chapter.

Other input/output devices would be printers, analog-digital data acquisition subsystems, modems for phone communications, plotters, and so on. These accessories can be either cards that plug in directly or something that interfaces to the computer through external buses or communication lines.

Figure 1–19A shows a 1969 vintage Digital Equipment Company PDP-8I computer. The 10 character per second Teletype was the primary output device. Keyboard input or a fast paper tape reader were the primary input devices. Memory was only 8K! Two hard disks gave less than a megabyte of disk storage. There was no video display and a digital plotter was used for figures. System cost was about $35,000. The laptop is a modern 16 MHz 80386/80387 micro with 2M of memory, a 40M byte hard disk, and a plasma display with high resolution graphics.

A vintage IBM PC is shown in Figure 1–19B. The machine with the toggle switches is the classic Altair 8800, the first widely used 8-bit microcomputer. The PC came with 64K of memory. Our original 1975 Altair had a mere 256 bytes of memory and had to be programmed from the front panel.

In all respects the modern IBM style PCs run circles around the 8I, yet the prices with digital plotters and 200 characters per second printers are a fraction of the cost of the mini. The point is not to compare manufacturers' technologies, but to emphasize the enormous, incredibly rapid technological advances.

1.6 SOFTWARE

The most powerful computer is expensive junk without software to run it. There are several different types of software with quite different operating characteristics. These include machine language, debuggers, assemblers, interpreters, and compilers.

The fundamental operating instructions in computers are in machine language. These are the binary instructions that the CPU fetches, decodes, and executes. In many early computers, programs were entered from front panel toggle switches. Fortunately, only primitive loader programs were generally entered in this tedious way. The loader program then gave the computer enough intelligence to load the remainder of the operating system from paper tape or a disk drive.

Debuggers were a step up. The human mind relates poorly to long strings of ones and zeroes. Debuggers permit machine code to be entered in octal, decimal, or in mnemonics that give some idea of the actual nature of the instruction.

Assemblers are a still more rational way of programming in machine language. English-like mnemonics replace the hex or binary numbers. A simple assembly language program is shown below:

```
          mov bx,3
          mov ax, partialsum
loop1     add ax,bx
          cmp dx
          jnz loop1
```

(A)

(B)

Figure 1–19. (A) PDP 8I computer with 8K of memory, 1M of hard disk space in two drives in the upper right half. The keyboard/printer is a 10 character per second Teletype. The Toshiba laptop computer is a 16 MHz 80386/80387 based system with a 40M byte hard disk (courtesy of Dynabyte Computers, Charlottesville, Virginia). (B) Original style IBM PC with color monitor next to an MITS Altair 8800 8-bit microcomputer (less Teletype). The 6.5 pound Toshiba laptop has 512K of RAM, one 720K floppy, and a monochrome CGA compatible liquid crystal display.

While they are not English, the mnemonics give some idea of what the program does. The mov transfers data from one place to another, the add does an arithmetic add, the cmp does a comparison, and the jnz is a conditional jump when the result of the comparison is not zero. Note that data (partialsum) and branch destination loop1 are assigned symbolic labels or names that further increase readability and ease of program writing. However, the CPU does not understand assembly language. A special machine language program called an assembler translates the assembly language listing into machine language code.

Well-written machine code generates the fastest, most efficient, and compact code, but it is very tedious to write. Further, machine language code is completely machine specific. That is, code written for one type of CPU will not run on any other type of CPU. Indeed, differences in hardware configurations can make programs fail on different types of computers even if they have the same CPU. The result is poor portability of software.

To ease the difficulty of writing software and to improve portability, a number of high-level languages have been developed. These languages provide a convenient English-like, algebraic language with the support of sophisticated arithmetic and character-oriented features. They are immeasurably easier to write in than assembly language. Programs written in these high-level languages are converted into runnable machine language by a CPU-specific program. However, unlike assembly language, the same high-level language program will run on any CPU for which the translation programs are written. Once the translation program is written, the large body of available high-level language programs can be promptly transferred and run on the new CPU. Since only the translation program need be written in machine language, this is clearly a much simpler task than having to rewrite every machine language program from scratch.

The three basic types of translation programs are interpreters, compilers, and throw-away or incremental compilers. In the following discussion the **source code** is the original high-level program. The **object code** will be the machine code program derived from the source code.

Interpreters keep the entire source code available in computer memory at once. As the program is executed, the interpreter converts the source code one command at a time into executable machine code and then executes (i.e., interprets) it. The next command to be executed is interpreted, and so on.

The translation step is quite wasteful of time, and the penalty becomes even more severe in loops or repetitive structures where the statement must be interpreted over and over again. Counterbalancing this slowness of execution is the simplicity of debugging. When an error is encountered, the interpreter knows exactly which line of the source code the error was on and flags it with a, hopefully, meaningful error message. Application of a built-in editor allows correction of the error, and the program can be tried again immediately.

Compilers, on the other hand, take a very different tack. The entire source code is converted *en masse* into a monolithic block of machine code, the object code. The object code is a separate program and can be executed at any later time.

Compilers have advantages over interpreters. Compiled code generally executes much more rapidly, and the compiled program is more compact since the interpreter and source code need not be present at the same time. Also, unlike interpreted programs, compiled ones have a high degree of security; it is very hard to see how a program was written from the machine code. Counterbalancing these advantages are the typically cumbersome debugging steps needed with a compiler. The compilation step can be quite time-consuming and there is generally no obvious relationship between where an error occurred in the object code relative to the source code. Many computers, in addition, require not only a separate compilation step but also a linking step where the object code is connected to all the necessary library routines. Thus, a simple error correction might take several minutes. The editor and source code must be loaded, the error corrected, and the program recompiled and relinked.

Several things can blur these rules. Several languages are available that have both compiler and interpreter versions (i.e., BASIC, Pascal, and C). Thus, the program can be developed efficiently in the interpreted mode. Once all the bugs are fixed, it can be compiled. Also, some very convenient compilers keep the source code, the editor, the compiler, and the machine code all in memory simultaneously. Compilation is very fast, errors are found immediately and easily corrected with the built in editor, and no linking is required. Turbo Pascal and QuickBASIC are examples.

Finally, a hybrid interpreter-compiler system called a throwaway or incremental compiler has been developed. Similar to an interpreter, an incremental compiler keeps the entire source code in memory. When you try to run the program the compiler begins translating the statements into machine code and executing them. Rather than discarding each translated piece of machine language, however, the machine code is kept in memory. For loops or subroutines which are frequently used, the machine code is available for execution on subsequent iterations or calls, and no translation penalty is accrued. The term "throwaway compiler" comes from the fact that if the size of the machine code exceeds the size of memory, early converted machine code is discarded to make room for more. Since loops tend to be short, loop structures will generally all be available as required. QuickBASIC in its interactive mode is actually an incremented computer without the throwaway feature.

Thus, incremental compilers have many of the advantages of interpreters and compilers. When errors are discovered, the compilers can point to the offending statement in the source code. Therefore, debugging is easy. Computational speed can approach that of a compiler since most programs spend much of their time in loops, and the computer only pays the translation penalty on the first pass through a structure. Further, since most programs tend to perform groups of actions repetitively, the throwaway feature generally costs little.

1.7 LANGUAGES

We turn now to the subject of specific languages. We discuss several common high-level languages. These include BASIC, FORTRAN, C, Pascal, Modula-2, and Forth.

BASIC (Beginners All-purpose Symbolic Instruction Code) is available on virtually every microcomputer. Microsoft BASIC is the most common form. BASIC exists in both interpreted and compiled forms. It is quick and dirty. It is simple to learn, easy to write small programs with, and lends itself to unstructured spaghetti code that is a mess of intertwined code. It frequently lacks many of the refinements of other languages, such as localized variables and true subroutines. This makes it very easy to have side effects, where a change in one portion of a program affects what other portions do. Even advanced forms still allow the writing of unstructured spaghetti code.

FORTRAN (FORmula TRANslation) is one of the most widely used scientific languages. It is only a compiled language. In the early forms it lacked structured language control features that simplified program writing and minimized side effects. Newer versions, not available on many micros, provide good control structures, but sloppy spaghetti code can still be easily written.

C is a powerful structured language. It was developed at AT&T as their system programming language. The compiler form is most common but interpreted versions are available. It is the darling of system programmers and forms the basic language of the AT&T UNIX operating system. Unfortunately, it allows for great brevity in writing code and obscure ways of doing things. In the hands of extremely knowledgeable programmers, this can lead to virtually unreadable programs.

Pascal is a powerful language developed by Nicholas Wirth to teach good programming. Its original intent was solely as a teaching language. In its idealized form, it made no concessions to the operating system or hardware and was unable to do graphics and many important system operations. Because of the beauty and the power of the language, however, extensions have been added onto the basic language to minimize these shortcomings. Many versions of Pascal are now capable of doing most of the things that a scientific or instrumentation programmer requires. Turbo Pascal is the primary language of this text. Pascal is available in interpreted and compiled forms.

Modula-2 was written by Wirth to correct some of the deficiencies of Pascal. In particular, Modula-2 allows very large programming problems to be broken up into modules with well defined points of contact and interaction between modules. Thus, it particularly lends itself to problems that are being attacked by teams. Pascal and Modula-2 are so similar that a good Pascal programmer can quickly learn Modula-2. Also, Pascal to Modula-2 translation programs are available.

Forth was developed by Charles Moore while he was working at the University of Virginia radioastronomy department. He was working on antenna control programs, which were traditionally written in assembly language. He is alleged to have said that he wished to write more than two or three major programs in his lifetime, so he developed Forth. Forth is a quasi-compiled language. As the programmer enters strings of operations, they are compiled. Then, at a future time, the programmer can invoke the operation by using its name.

Forth generates enormous heat from its advocates and detractors, probably more heat than any other language. The biggest problem is that Forth is basically a stack-oriented language, much like the reverse Polish notation used in Hewlett-Packard calculators. However, in Forth, the stack is essentially unlimited in size, and the stack orientation makes it hard for a reader of a program to keep track of where everything is on the stack as it grows and contracts. Documentation, then, is especially difficult. Further, Forth lends itself to very compact, poorly documented, and opaque programs. The ease of writing and debugging Forth programs coupled with the ease of poorly documenting them has led to the claim that Forth is an excellent write only language.

Forth is particularly well suited for micros. Most of the Forth language is written in Forth itself and only a relatively small number of primitive operations must be written in CPU-specific machine code. Therefore, it has been ported to virtually every microcomputer made. It is the primary language of video arcade games. Its speed varies enormously on different CPUs since it assumes a specific CPU architecture. The more closely the CPU matches the ideal CPU and the fewer contortions the programmer has to go through to implement the functions, the faster Forth will be.

In the authors' opinion, Forth was important in the days of tight memory, slow machines, and sluggish, memory-hungry high-level languages. Cost and improvements in hardware and software have eliminated much of the need for Forth except on very small systems. There is at least one public domain version.

1.8 REFERENCES

For general information on computer architecture and number bases, Wakerly is excellent. Lemone is good for a description of number bases. Startz gives an excellent overview of the 8087 math coprocessor and number bases. Crawford and Gelsinger give a good update on the differences between the 8087 and the 80387. For information on IBM style architecture, the latest version of Norton's "Inside the IBM PC" is essential reading.

Problems[1]

1–1 [1.2.4]. (A) Show that a two-input NAND also gates a signal off and on with the same control levels as for the AND but it inverts the input and has an off output of 1.

(B) Using a truth table show how an OR and a NOR can gate a signal off and on. Is the gate transmitting or blocking with a control level of 1?

(C) Can an off/on gate be made from an exclusive OR? If not, why not?

1–2 [1.2.4]. A common use of the exclusive OR is as an equality (actually an inequality) detector. Only if A≠B is the output true. Thus, the output is true if the two bits are unequal.

A more common problem is a multibyte comparison. Consider the comparison of two two-bit words a_1a_0 and b_1b_0 where the a's and b's are individual bits. Devise a circuit that combines two XORs with any additional gates that you need to give a true output only if $a_1=b_1$ and $a_0=b_0$. Do not connect two or more logic gate outputs together; this will not work and may burn out the gates.

1–3 [1.2.5]. Using two positive edge-triggered flip-flops and any additional logic that you wish, design a divide by 3 circuit. Its count sequence for Q_BQ_A will be 00, 01, 10, 00, . . . The trick here is to feed the outputs into the JK inputs in such a way that when the outputs are 10, the FFs are forced to change to 00 on the next clock transition.

---

[1]In square brackets following each problem number is the section to which the problem applies. Problems are designed to demonstrate key points and should be routinely examined and worked out.

1–4 [1.2.8]. Design a circuit that takes a 2-bit input address (i.e., 00 . . .11) and four outputs labelled 0 to 3 decimal. If the input address is 00, output 0 is low and all other outputs are 1. If the input is 01, then output 1 is low and the other outputs are high, and so on. This circuit is called a decoder where the different outputs are used to enable or activate a single board or memory chip out of a large number.

1–5 [1.2.9]. Write out the truth table for a half subtractor. Include the difference bit and the borrow bit outputs. Implement its function using standard logic gates.

1–6 [1.2.9]. Using half subtractors implement a full subtractor circuit.

1–7 [1.4.3]. The elegant method described for converting decimal numbers into binary numbers works only for integers. Modify the algorithm so that it works for numbers less than 1. How would you handle numbers that were greater than 1 and contained a fractional part? Using your algorithm convert 361.875 decimal into binary.

1–8 [1.4.5]. Convert 375D to octal (base 8), hexadecimal, and BCD.

1–9 [1.4.5]. Convert $FEC9 (Turbo notation) into binary and decimal.

1–10 [1.4.5]. Add 0E00F0H and 111011110111B (assembler formats). Give the result in hex, decimal and binary.

1–11 [1.4.8]. Express 375.1875 decimal as as pure binary, as an 80X87 short real, an 80X87 long real, and an 80X87 temporary real.

1–12 [1.4.8]. Express 0.1 decimal as an 80X87 short real. Convert this short real back into decimal. What is the error (percentage) in the storage of the exact 0.1 decimal when we convert it into binary? Approximately how many significant decimal digits does this correspond to?

1–13 [1.4.8]. In 1–12, what would be the percent error in 0.1 if a short real did not use the hidden bit but kept all bits including the most significant in memory?

1–14 [1.4.8]. Suppose that we had 0.1 decimal stored as an 80X87 short real. What would be the error in raising this value to the tenth power if all the arithmetic were done in binary? You do not have to multiply this out. Assume that all the error in the result is due to the error in representing 0.1. Then take advantage of the relationship:

$$[N\,(1+x)]^n = N^n\,(1+x)^n$$

$$(1+x)^n \approx 1 + nx \quad \text{for } x \ll 1$$

where N is the number that you wish to raise to a power and x will be an error term in representing it. This question is analogous to asking what errors you might expect after ten multiplications using short reals. Remember that in matrix multiplications and inversions, hundreds or thousands of floating point operations may be required.

2

DOS, BASIC, Interpreters, Compilers, and Math Coprocessors

2.1 INTRODUCTION

IBM and PC clone computers come with a disk operating system (DOS) and sometimes Microsoft BASIC. The disk operating system is known as MS-DOS or IBM DOS; both are nearly the same. With DOS you can load and run programs from disk and manage your diskettes. Even your applications software interacts with the computer input/output devices and the disk drives through DOS. IBM computers might call the BASIC BASICA, while on generic MS-DOS machines it might be called BASIC, BASICA, or GWBASIC. Virtually all of these versions of BASIC were written by Microsoft and differ little. We call them BASIC.

In this chapter we describe some capabilities of DOS. We show you how to bring the system up and how to develop, edit, and run programs in BASIC. In addition, we compare compilers and interpreters, and examine the benefits of a math coprocessor.

Like other chapters, this one is a tutorial and should be worked through. Experiments and problems demonstrate key points. A brief description of each experiment is given in the text with the full experiment described in Appendix A Experiments.

Programming is an experimental science and merely reading the material is inadequate for learning and for developing computer instincts.

2.2 MICROSOFT DISK OPERATING SYSTEM (DOS)

The disk system that comes with IBM-style personal computers is written by Microsoft Corporation. It goes by a variety of names including IBM DOS, PCDOS, MS-DOS, or just DOS. There are substantial differences between different DOS releases (versions); at the time of this writing, DOS is up to version 4. However, with few exceptions, the same version for any machine will be very similar.

DOS is a descendant of the older eight-bit computer operating system CP/M from Digital Research Corporation. The much larger memories available for DOS make it more powerful, user-friendly, and forgiving; a typical maximum memory size for CP/M was 64K, while for DOS machines the minimum is 64K. Indeed, it is difficult to find an old 64K DOS machine. DOS still lacks many error messages and error checking before trying to execute functions.

The standardized DOS operating system is largely responsible for the great popularity of IBM-style PCs. DOS is divided into the Basic Disk Operating System (BDOS) and a supporting Basic Input/Output System (BIOS). These handle all input and output to disk drives and controller, all keyboard functions, all video display, all serial communications, and all printer output.

There are standardized entry points into the DOS that control all Input/Output (I/O) functions. These functions do all the basic operations required of a computer, such as outputting a character to the display, checking the keyboard for use, reading a character from the keyboard, and reading or writing a block of memory content to the disk in a specific drive. Other software that is written to run on the computer generally handles most or all I/O operations via DOS or BIOS routines.

The specific DOS depends on the computer and input and output details (e.g., the disk controllers, the video display controller, and the keyboard). Regardless of the hardware, however, every DOS has the same standardized set of entry points that are used in the same fashion. Thus, other programs do not have to know anything at all about the hardware details; any generic DOS machine runs any program that uses only the standard DOS entry points. While in the past different operating systems were the rule, software publishers now need only generate one software version for all PC computers. This yields inexpensive and plentiful software of high quality.

This standardized DOS concept is like a shell that insulates the user from the dirty machine details, much like the standardized operating system in automobiles. The steering wheel, clutch, brake pedal, gear shift, and accelerator pedal are the handles. It does not matter whether you have four, six, eight, or twelve cylinders, a diesel or a gas engine, or power accessories. The user interface is still the same, and if you can drive one automobile, you can pretty much drive any.

Since DOS depends on hardware, the DOS for one machine might not work properly or at all on a different machine. This is especially true if the software bypasses DOS and goes directly to the hardware for enhanced performance. Fortunately, the vast majority of general purpose software and generic PCs are compatible; however, always verify that your important software will work with a new machine before you buy it.

2.2.1 Booting the System (Running DOS)

Before you can run any other program, you must load DOS into the computer. For now we assume that you have a system disk (i.e., one with an installed operating system). Later we will show how to generate your own. The following description is for a floppy-based computer. To load and begin execution of the DOS:

(1) Insert the system disk into the A drive with the label side up. Close the drive door.
(2) Turn the computer on with the switch on the side or back.

After a pause, while the computer checks itself for proper operation and displays various messages on the screen, the light on the A drive will come on. The light indicates that the computer is accessing the drive. If you have the correct diskette in the drive, DOS will load, a message will be displayed, and the DOS prompt will be displayed. The prompt is a letter, usually A followed by ">" or "A>". The prompt indicates that DOS is in control and the A drive is currently logged on (i.e., active). If your system has a hard disk drive, you should not have to insert a disk; the hard disk, usually C, is automatically logged on if there is no disk in A. Even with a hard disk, you can always start from a system disk in A.

This act of initializing the system and bringing DOS into memory is called a boot or, more commonly, "booting the system." If you have a piece of software that has frozen the system, you can sometimes boot the system by simultaneously pressing the control (Ctrl), the alternate (Alt), and the Delete keys. This is a faster boot than turning on the computer or hitting the reset button (if available) because much of the system checking is omitted. On a boot, DOS is reloaded and the standard hardware is reinitialized. A boot must be performed at turn-on or following a software foul-up where some of the system information in RAM may be garbled.

Warning: There is a reason that the boot key combination is quite unlikely to be pressed accidentally—once you have initiated a boot sequence, everything that you have in computer memory is lost forever.

2.2.2 Running Programs and Resident Commands

Once DOS is loaded you can run programs that reside on the disk or execute one of the many commands that are inherent in DOS. Commands are executed by typing the command word and a carriage return, which is the hooked arrow key on the right hand side of the keyboard. We denote a carriage return by <CR>. Commands built directly into DOS are called internal commands. External DOS commands are ones that DOS must load from disk before it can execute them. Internal and external programs are both executed by typing the program name and <CR>. An example of internal function is the directory program DIR, which is executed by typing:

A> **DIR** **<CR>**   "A> is the prompt and is already there"

We use the convention of putting any DOS comments in regular text, boldfacing all user-supplied input, and putting comments in quotation marks to the right. Comments must not be included in actual use. DOS and BASIC are case insensitive. FORMAT, format, FoRmAt, and FORmat are the same to DOS. Generally, we indicate DOS and BASIC commands in all capital letters.

Try the DIR command and see what happens. You have just displayed a directory of the currently logged disk. Now execute the external program to check the disk by typing:

    A> **CHKDISK <CR>**   "Run check disk program"

This command causes DOS to look for the program CHKDISK on the currently logged disk. If the program is there, DOS loads the program into memory and executes it.

DOS has a number of internal and external utilities associated with it. We next describe a subset of these.

2.2.3   Changing the Logged Drive

Programs are frequently run from the currently logged disk (A and B on a dual floppy system). Remember the currently logged drive is indicated by the letter being prompted. Multiple drives are labelled A, B, C, D, and so forth; by default the C drive is assigned to a hard disk if present.

To change the logged drive, type the letter specification of the drive, a colon (:), and <CR>. For example, if you are logged on A, type:

    A>**B: <CR>**   "Change to the B drive"

In subsequent text, we frequently omit the prompt and the <CR>. In DOS the prompt is always there, and <CR> is required for any command to be processed.

There must be a disk in the new logged drive or there will be a system error. This is not a fatal error. DOS prompts you to retry (R), ignore (I) the error, or abort (A) the command. If you have left the disk out or failed to shut the door, correct the oversight and Retry. If you Abort, you are kicked back into the DOS. That is all right here but would be a disaster if you were saving a 50-page manuscript for the first time. Entering I rarely corrects the basic error.

You can also run a program on another disk drive. Suppose that you want to run the program PROG on the B drive. You can do this one of two ways. First, you could change the logged drive to B and then run PROG directly:

    A>**B:**   "Change to B drive"
    B>**PROG**   "Run PROG"

Alternatively, you could directly execute PROG without changing the logged drive with the following command:

A>**B:PROG**   "Run PROG on B drive from A drive"

In this case, DOS sees the B drive specification for PROG and goes to that drive to load the program. The logged drive remains unchanged.

2.2.4   File Names and Wild Cards

The contents of disks are organized as files. Each file has a unique file name. It is through the file name that DOS and the user keep track of, and access, what is on the disk. File names are made up of two parts. The first part, which must be present, is the name of the file and can be one to eight letters or numbers in length. The optional second part is the file extension and supplies information about the file type. Extensions may be omitted or be up to three characters long. When written out, the two portions are normally separated by a period. Valid file names include GWBASIC.EXE, BASICA.COM, DATA, DATA., and DATA.DTA. The complete name includes the name and the extension. Thus, DATA and DATA.DTA above are different files. Invalid characters in a name are *, ?, \, :, quotation marks, and multiple periods.

Before we go deeper into commands, we introduce the concept of wild cards. Wild cards in file names permit file handling programs to process multiple files without having to spell out each file explicitly. There are two wild card characters, * and ?. A wild card indicates that a match is acceptable for any character or combination of characters. The * stands for the complete file name, the complete extension, or whatever could be left in the name. The ? stands for any single character. For example, TEST????.DTA stands for all files with extension DTA and a file name that begins with TEST. TEST*.DAT has the same meaning since the * corresponds to all remaining characters in the name up to the period. The expression *.* corresponds to all files. *.COM means all .COM files. The following file names match TEST*.DAT: TEST.DAT, TEST1.DAT, and TEST1234.DAT, but not 1TEST.DAT. Again, *.* matches all files. This is very powerful and with great potential for mischief. Rather irritatingly, *xyz.*t is equivalent to *.*; once DOS sees the *, it ignores everything else in the file name or the extension.

2.2.5   Viewing the Disk Directory (DIR)

The internal directory command DIR is used for viewing the files on the disks. Type:

A>**DIR**   "Directory on logged (A) disk"

The currently logged drive comes on and the directory pops up on the screen. An abbreviated directory listing might look like:

```
Volume in drive A is ATANDT1
Directory of  A:\
COMMAND  COM    15957    6-05-85   12:00p
AUTOEXEC BAT      128    2-16-84   10:15p
```

```
GRAPHICS  COM      6481    6-05-85   12:00p
GWBASIC   EXE     70704    6-05-85   12:00p
FORMAT    COM      7166    6-05-85   12:00p
PRF85-2   BAK      1664    1-01-84    9:20p
PRF85-2           1664    1-01-84    9:21p
   ...  other files here...
WSOVLY1   OVR     41216    4-12-83   12:15a
DOUBLE    BAS       154    1-04-85    2:20p
DISKCOPY  COM      4665    6-05-85   12:00p
CHKDSK    COM      6468    6-05-85   12:00p
         46 File(s)      11264 bytes free
```

The first two lines are header information and give the label assigned to that particular disk and the drive from which the directory was taken. The first two words are the name of the file. In directory listings, spaces rather than periods separate the name and the extension. Next comes the file length in bytes, and the date and time the file was created or last modified. The last line of the listing is the number of files on the diskette and the number of bytes free: 11264 out of about 360,000 on this diskette.

There is a relatively small number of extension types on this diskette (COM, EXE, OVR, BAS, BAK, and none); this is typical as there is a relatively small number of different types of files that one usually uses.

The only executable files end with a COM or EXE extension. For example, the BASIC interpreter listed is labelled GWBASIC.EXE. The OVR extension in this case indicates overlay files for programs that will not fit into memory all at once. The blank extensions are word processor files and the BAK extensions indicate back up word processor files. The BAS extension indicates a BASIC program file. The BAT extension indicates a batch file that automatically executes a series of commands without the necessity of typing them in.

If you have many files and the information scrolls past too fast to read, you have several options. You can stop the scroll by pressing Ctrl and S simultaneously. Verbally this is called a "control S." A shorthand form that we adopt is ^S. Many pieces of software that display typed control characters display this combination. Pressing ^S again will cause scrolling to resume. The ^C combination aborts the directory listing completely. Alternatively, you can use two other forms of the directory command:

DIR/P
DIR/W

The /'s are frequently used to add parameters or modifiers to a command. The /P option (Pause) causes the display to stop after each screen is full and then permits resumption by pressing another key. The /W option (Wide) gives more file name listings per line, but omits the file length and creation date. Try the different methods. Both can be used at once (i.e., /P/W), but this is rarely necessary.

To run a program from DOS, type its file name and <CR>. Since only COM or EXE is an executable program, the extension is not needed and, in fact, cannot be used. To run the BASIC interpreter, GWBASIC.EXE, or the Turbo Pascal compiler, TURBO.EXE, type GWBASIC<CR> or TURBO<CR> only. Do not name anything but directly executable programs with the EXE or COM extensions. If you do, you run the risk of trying to execute a word processor file.

The DIR command has more power still. To see only a single file, type:

DIR filename   "Give directory information on filename"

where filename is the file name plus extension of the desired program. If it is on the logged disk, the information concerning it will be displayed. Also, wild cards are suitable in the filename. For example,

DIR *.COM   "Directory information on all .COM files"
DIR *.*   "Directory information on all files"

The first command displays all COM files, while the second one displays all files.

2.2.6   Preparing a Work Diskette (FORMAT)

New diskettes are not ready for storing data and programs. Every operating system expects data to be organized in a very specific way on the diskette in terms of the number of tracks, the number of sectors per track, the number of bytes per sector, the header and the trailer information after each sector, and so on. Each system will organize, or format, the disk to suit its own requirements. To format a diskette, you must run the external DOS format program. With the a: drive logged on and the system diskette in the A drive, type the format command as shown below (your input is in boldface, comments are in quotation marks, and the rest is displayed by the computer):

```
A> FORMAT B:
Insert new diskette for drive B:
and strike any key when ready        "Insert disk in B; press any key"
Formatting...Format complete

    362496 bytes total disk space
    362496 bytes available on disk

Format another (Y/N)?N
```

This command runs the FORMAT program and formats on the B drive. You can format a diskette in the A drive by issuing the command FORMAT, but this is dangerous as the A drive usually contains your system diskette. This brings us to a warning.

WARNING: Formatting a diskette destroys the diskette's contents. There is no way to recover it. Be absolutely sure that the diskette that you wish to format is in the correct drive before pressing any key. You can safeguard disks and protect them so that they will not be written onto by DOS. On a 5.25" disk, you will notice a rectangular notch on one edge. If this notch is covered by a protective tab or dark tape, the disk is protected and DOS will not write on, erase, or format the disk. Remember to remove it before you try to write to the disk. The 3.5" diskettes are protected by a little slip tab; in this case protection occurs when the hole is open.

2.2.7 Preparing a Bootable Disk

A freshly formatted disk cannot function as a system disk, since it lacks the boot routine and three important files. To make a bootable (system) disk, you will have to add these routines. We describe briefly the different routines.

The boot routine is a very primitive operating system that permits the computer to load the more sophisticated operating system. This boot routine is unnamed and kept on special system tracks. With DOS you cannot determine whether the boot is present except by trying to boot from the disk. When you turn on the computer or reboot, a low level permanently stored ROM routine loads the disk boot. If the boot routine is not there or there is an error, the boot process halts. Generally, you are given the option of putting a bootable disk into the computer and continuing. Because most of your disks are not system disks (the extra files take up a lot of space), you will try to boot from a non-bootable disk many times. When the error message comes up, put a system disk in the A drive and hit any key.

The three program files on the disk are named files. Two are the basic disk operating system (DOS) and the basic input output system (BIOS). These programs are hidden files and will not show with DIR. Files are hidden to prevent accidental erasure and directory clutter. A CHKDSK also reveals the presence of hidden files. The third necessary file is COMMAND.COM, which is the command processor that forms the DOS shell. COMMAND is what actually interprets and runs the internal commands such as DIR and COPY. It also handles all DOS keyboard and video input and output.

Since COMMAND need not be present during the running of most programs, many applications programs remove it to provide more memory, but they must then supply all the user interface. For DOS to regain control, COMMAND must be reloaded on exiting the application. In this case if you have removed the disk with COMMAND, DOS is unable to regain full control and will ask you to put a disk with COMMAND back in the A drive. This minor inconvenience does no harm.

On the IBM system disks these hidden files are the Basic Input/Output System (IBMBIOS.COM) and the Disk Operating System (IBMDOS.COM), which were written for IBM by Microsoft. Interestingly, on the AT&T 2.11 DOS diskettes, which were also written by Microsoft, these two hidden files are still called IBMBIOS.COM and IBMDOS.COM—showing their common heritage.

In order to set up a runnable disk, we must first install the system tracks and the system files. This can be done during FORMAT by using the /S option:

```
A>FORMAT B:/S        "Format disk in B drive with system tracks"
```

This automatically copies the system tracks after a format. Alternatively, you can first format the disk, then use the external SYS command that copies the system track. For example, with the receiving disk in B and the system disk in A type:

A>**SYS B:**   "Transfer system tracks from A to B drive"

This copies the system tracks onto your new disk in drive B. The SYS command can only be used on a formatted but empty diskette; if the disk has any other files, the system tracks are copied into the wrong place. The COMMAND file is not hidden and must be copied directly from an operating system disk or your DOS master with COPY. The COMMAND file is not copied automatically by either the SYS command or the /S format option and you must explicitly do this.

It is always a good idea to check your new bootable disk by inserting it into the A drive and rebooting the system. Having confirmed its suitable operation, you can then add any necessary program that you wish to run from the disk.

2.2.8   Transferring Files (COPY)

One of the most important disk functions is copying files from one disk to another or one file to another file on the same disk. An example of such an application is backing up an important disk by making a copy of it. The internal COPY command is used for copying. Using wild cards with copy enormously increases its power. Examples are:

COPY PROG B:PROG	"Copies file PROG on A into file PROG on B"
COPY PROG B:XYZ	"Copies file PROG on A into file XYZ on B"
COPY LETT LETT2	"Copies file LETT on A into file LETT2 on A"
COPY *.* B:	"Copies all files on A to same files on B"
COPY *.COM B:	"Copies all .COM files on A to the same files on B"
COPY LETT*. B:	"Copies all files whose file name begins with the four letters LETT and have no extension to the same files on B"
COPY BAS???IC. B:	"Copies all extensionless files on A having the first three letters BAS and the last two of IC to the same name files on B"

where the A drive is assumed to be the logged drive.

2.2.9   Erasing Files (ERASE)

Good file management necessitates regularly eliminating unwanted files. The ERASE command, which supports wild cards handles this. Examples include:

ERASE DATA	"Erase the file DATA"
ERASE DATA*	"Erase extensionless files begining with DATA preface"
ERASE *.COM	"Erase all COM files"
ERASE *.BAK	"Erase all BAK files"
ERASE *.*	"Erase ALL files!!!"

The ERASE command is very powerful, but dangerous. When using wildcards, carefully avoid accidental matches. The *.* command is particularly dangerous, but it does give you a chance to reconsider before it goes ahead. Misplaced spaces can spell disaster. Consider the following erase statement:

ERASE * .tst   "Erases all extensionless files"

You meant to erase all files with a TST extension, but you erased all files with NO extension. The space breaks the file name, so DOS wipes out all extensionless files.

2.2.10   Examining Files (TYPE)

In many cases you would like to examine the contents of text files quickly. TYPE performs this function. The format is:

TYPE drive:filename.ext   "Type specified file on drive"

The full file name including the extension must be used. If the file is a character oriented text file, it will be displayed line by line on the video display. ^S stops scrolling so that you can examine the screen. Any other key will resume scrolling. ^C aborts the display process completely.

2.2.11   Printing and Generating Files with COPY

Being able to type files to the screen is very useful, but you will invariably want to make hard copies on the printer. For text files, there are several ways. BASIC files, which are normally not in text format, involve a special problem that we will return to later. One can use the COPY command or a special external DOS command PRINT for making hard copy. Also, most word processors and many text editors permit directly printing text files while you are in the program. We will deal here only with the COPY method since it is an internal DOS command and is, therefore, always available from DOS.

The basic method of printing with the COPY command depends on the fact that you can copy information not only between files but also between files and other devices. DOS recognizes several devices besides disk files. These devices are listed below:

```
CON:                    Console. Keyboard for input; video display for output
LPT1: and LPT2:         Line printer communication port.
COM1: and COM2:         Serial communications ports.
```

Devices are differentiated from files with the trailing colon, which files cannot use. All computers will have the keyboard and display console devices, but line printer and serial communication ports are only options on many machines. Even those that have printer and serial communication ports are generally only configured with one of each, although others can be added. Most machines now will have one printer and one serial port with default names of LPT1: and COM1:.

One uses any of these devices as though they were another file in the copy command. For example, the following command:

```
COPY CON: B:SAVEDAT
```

takes data directly from the keyboard and copies it into the file SAVEDAT on the B drive. To terminate keyboard input, save your work to disk, and return to DOS, type a ^Z followed by a <CR>. Alternatively, in DOS the F6 special function key generates a ^Z. The ^Z is copied to the file and functions as an end-of-file (EOF) marker so that software that uses the file can tell where it ends. The inverse operation:

```
COPY filename CON:
```

copies the specified file from disk to the video display. This is equivalent to the TYPE command. More useful is to COPY a file to the line printer:

```
COPY B:EXPER1 LPT1:
```

which lists file EXPER1 (drive B) on line printer #1 (normally the default printer). This is a standard way to list a disk program. Non-text files do not list properly.

2.2.12 Getting Hard Copy from the Screen

There are many times when you would like to make a quick copy of a display screen (e.g., a displayed directory list, results of a computation, or a plot). You can print the screen directly to the printer by pressing the shift "PrtSc" key combination. This method works as long as the display is in the text mode, and there are no graphics characters displayed. Graphics characters are generally printed out as regular text characters.

You can print graphics displays if you first run the DOS program GRAPHICS.COM. GRAPHICS.COM installs itself in RAM, and the next time you do a Shift PrtSc you get a graphics dump to the printer. This is much slower than the text dump because every dot on the screen is transcribed to the printer. GRAPHICS.COM is a terminate and stay resident (TSR) program; we will explain later how it installs itself and stays there while other programs are running.

2.2.13 DOS Environmental Variables

DOS keeps space for variables and their current values. These variables can be accessed and used by any DOS function or by programs. Once set, these variables hold their values until you change them, an applications program changes them, or the system is rebooted. The primary use is for storage of global information that is used with other programs. The primary way of setting a variable is with the DOS *set* command:

```
SET variablename=string
```

where variablename is assigned the string value. For example, the following are valid:

```
>set no87=8087 used
>set testno=3
```

To read the environmental variables issue the set command without arguments:

```
>SET              "Display all environmental variables"
```

or clear it by using SET with the name and no assignment:

```
>SET no87=     "Clears variable no8087"
```

For the autoexec.bat and config.sys files shown in the next section we would see:

```
COMSPEC=C:\COMMAND.COM
PATH=C:\;C:\MSDOS;C:\PASCAL;C:\UNIX;C:\BIN;C:\NORTON
SPFLAG=-sSlc:\unix\lib
PROMPT=$T$H$H$H$H$H$H-$p$g
```

There are four variables specified COMSPEC, PATH, SPFLAG, and PROMPT. All of these were set by the user except COMSPEC, which is initialized by DOS to point at COMMAND.COM. After exiting programs that remove COMMAND from memory to get more space, this variable tells DOS to reload COMMAND. Redefining this variable to point at other programs allows users to install their own COMMAND functions.

There is one quirk of the environmental space. It is unlimited in size as long as you add no TSR program such as GRAPHICS. A TSR program caps the environment space. The default size is 128 bytes, and you can use more as long as you set them before you run a TSR program. Once you run a TSR, you are limited to 128 bytes or the size claimed by existing variables—whichever is bigger. Convince yourself of this by running GRAPHICS and then SET several large variables. When you fill up the space, you get an "Out of environmental space" message.

2.2.14 AUTOEXEC.BAT, CONFIG.SYS, and DEV Files

When you examine the disk directory of your boot disks, you frequently find a file AUTOEXEC.BAT. You may also find files labeled .DEV and CONFIG.SYS. These files set up and configure the system the way you want it. Without these you would be forced to run manually a number of set up routines.

The AUTOEXEC.BAT file is a batch file that runs automatically when the system boots. A batch file is a text file list of DOS commands that are automatically executed when the name of the batch file is invoked. AUTOEXEC.BAT is a batch file that is executed automatically during the boot process. Virtually anything that can be done from the keyboard or a batch file can run automatically from AUTOEXEC.BAT. A simple one line AUTOEXEC.BAT is:

```
GRAPHICS
```

On boot, this runs GRAPHICS to allow printing of graphics displays. A more complex hard disk file might look like:

```
echo off
path c:;c:\msdos;c:\pascal;c:\unix;c:\bin;c:\norton
banner2 -Z WORK HARDER
set SPFLAG=-sSlc:\unix\lib
echo on
prompt $D-$p$g
echo off
prompt $T$H$H$H$H$H$H-$p$g
graphics
```

These commands can be described briefly. The first line turns off the echoing or display of each command as it is read and executed. The "path" command sets up the hard disk so that it can find programs hidden at different corners of the disk. BANNER (not part of DOS) displays a sign on message. The "set" command initializes the variable SPFLAG for use by several UNIX utilities on our system. The first "prompt" displays the system date so that we can verify that the clock is correct. The last "prompt" changes the normal ">" prompt to one that has the time and shows where you are on the hard disk. Finally, we install graphics.

CONFIG.SYS is a text file with system configuration information. It sets up such things as how many memory based disks you will use (RAM disk), whether certain device driver software packages will be installed, and so on. Ours reads:

```
device=ramdisk.dev 200
buffers=30
```

The device statement loads a DOS 2 device driver called ramdisk.dev and sets the size of the disk to 200K. The file ramdisk.dev must be available on the main directory. The buffers statement sets the number of buffer or scratch pad locations used by DOS for file activity. There is a default value of 2 (PC) or 3 (AT), but good hard disk performance requires much more space. Experimentally, we found that our largest program loaded fastest with buffers equal to about 30.

The .DEV are actually device drivers. These are routines that, if installed by the config.sys file, add new or different functions to the system.

Experiments 2–1 – 2–5. In these experiments you start the computer, run simple programs, explore wildcards and various DOS functions, set up your own bootable disk, explore a simple batch file, and generate copies of the screen on the printer.

2.3 BASIC INTERPRETER

BASIC is a powerful, versatile and easily learned high level language. It is now taught in rudimentary forms in many elementary and middle schools. It has a number of weaknesses including slowness of execution. However, its greatest fault is that it teaches poor programming because the language lends itself so readily to writing unstructured spaghetti code with multiple intertwined GOTO statements. However, it is available as part of the operating system or for a small additional fee. While BASIC will be around for the forseeable future, it will become more structured and will more and more closely resemble structured languages like PASCAL.

2.3.1 Entering and Running a BASIC Program

Verify that you have a version of BASIC on your system disk using the directory command. BASICA is one IBM version and must be used on an old PC while GWBASIC is the generic BASIC. Assuming you have GWBASIC on the A drive, begin its execution in the normal fashion by typing GWBASIC <CR>. GWBASIC loads from disk, signs on, tells you how much memory is available for programs, and is ready to go.

Use the following example to learn about the workings of the BASIC interpreter and its interactions with the DOS. Perform the indicated steps. Programs are entered as sequentially numbered lines. Each line is entered beginning with a line number, a space, and the BASIC instruction. Regardless of the order in which you type the lines, they are sorted into ascending numerical order. Enter the following program:

```
10 A=12
20 PRINT RESULT
15 RESULT=A+B
14 B=3
```

Now list it with the BASIC LIST command (i.e., LIST <CR>):

```
10 A=12
14 B=3
15 RESULT=A+B
20 PRINT RESULT
```

GWBASIC accepts long, meaningful variable names (e.g., SUMX2, SUMXY, RESULT, NUMITERATIONS). Variables must begin with a letter and can be up to 40 characters long. Variables are unique up to the full length. Thus, ARRAYNUMBER1 and ARRAYNUMBER2 are different variables. Careful use of long names improves program documentation and readability.

To run a BASIC program that you have typed in or loaded from diskette, you must be in the BASIC interpreter. Type RUN followed by the obligatory <CR>. Try this on the current program. The above program responds with:

```
15
OK
```

No matter how carefully you program, you will write programs that get into infinite loops or that run longer than you want to wait. To stop a running GWBASIC program and return control to the interpreter, type a Ctrl Break.

2.3.2   Renumbering Programs (RENUM)

After a while you may find that you lack available space to insert a new line. You can renumber with the RENUM. Explanatory material will be listed in quotation marks to the right of the BASIC statement.

```
RENUM                    "Renumber starting with 10 in steps of 10"
RENUM start,step         "Renumber starting with start in increments of step"
RENUM 100                "Renumber starting at 100 in increments of 10"
RENUM 1000,2             "Renumber starting at 1000 in increments of 2"
```

2.3.3   Saving and Loading BASIC Programs

To save a program from BASIC use one of the following commands:

```
SAVE "drive:filename"        "Save file in compact format"
SAVE "drive:filename",a      "Save file in text format"
```

where the drive is the desired one to save on and may be A or B on a dual floppy system. The : is required if the drive is specified explicitly. The file name, filename, can be up to eight letters with no spaces or extensions. Do not use an extension since BASIC supplies its own extension BAS to identify BASIC programs. If you omit the drive: portion, the default drive (i.e., the currently logged one) is assumed. Without the ",a" option, the program is saved in a very compact but human-unreadable form (i.e., when displayed with TYPE, it is gibberish). The ",a" stores it in a human-readable text form code called ASCII (see Chapter 3). For example:

```
SAVE "A:bilge"       "Saves the current program on the A disk drive under
                      the name BILGE.BAS."
SAVE "bILge",a       "Saves the current program on the A drive as a text
                      file (assuming that BASIC was executed from the A
                      drive) under the name BILGE.BAS."
```

Since we supply the system disk for drive A and you supply the work disk for the B drive, always save your programs on the B drive using the B: preface. If you make a mistake and inadvertently save on the A disk, resave on the right one. Before going on, save the current example on your initialized work disk in the B drive.

Loading or reloading a program from disk is a similar operation, except that you use LOAD rather than SAVE:

```
LOAD "drive:filename"
```

This example loads the file filename.BAS from the specified drive. Do not include the extension BAS since it is assumed.

Modify the program that you just entered. Then LOAD the original version from disk. Verify that it was loaded properly by LISTing and RUNning.

When you are through with a program and want to do something different, you clear the work space by typing NEW<CR>. Try this, and verify that the program is gone by LISTing it. NEW is an irreversible command, so save first if you will need the material. LOAD clears the work space automatically.

2.3.4   Editing BASIC Programs

Your BASIC has a moderately sophisticated editor. To avoid confusion, we describe only a few features. You can delete characters as soon as you have typed them by using the delete key (back arrow). The character is erased on the screen. One way to change a line is to type the line number and retype the line with the correct contents. The old line is replaced with the latest version. To delete a line, type the line number and a <CR>. As BASIC will not save null lines (i.e., lines with nothing or only spaces), the indicated line is purged from the file.

It is much more convenient to modify an existing line. All of the cursor controls (the directional arrows on the numeric key pad on the right) move the cursor around on the video display. Once you have moved to a line and position, you can type over errors or delete them using the "Delete" key.

You can also insert more material. First move the cursor to the line you wish to expand, then put the editor into the insert mode by typing the Insert key. Any material added will be inserted where the cursor sits. Simply typing the change does not automatically update the program. All insertions and deletions must be registered by typing the return key. Moving to another line or striking the return key or the insert key again takes you out of the insert mode.

To delete an entire line from the screen, position the cursor on the line after the line number and type Ctrl End. This clears everything to the right of the cursor, but does not eliminate the line from the program. To finish deletion, type Return. To clear the screen, type CLS on a blank line followed by <CR>.

2.3.5   Printing BASIC Programs

BASIC programs can be listed on the line printer in one of two ways. First, you can save the file from BASIC in text format using the ",A" option. Then, after exiting BASIC you COPY it to the line printer. The other method permits printing programs or fragments directly from the BASIC interpreter with the LLIST commands:

```
LLIST
LLIST starting line number - ending line number
```

LLIST lists the entire program. The second command lists the inclusive line numbers.

2.3.6 Returning to DOS from BASIC

When you are through with BASIC, return to the DOS by the SYSTEM command.

2.4 INTEGRATED QuickBASIC 4.0 COMPILER

For demonstrating compilers, we use Microsoft QuickBASIC 4 (QB.EXE), which we call QB. QB is inexpensive ($100), relatively simple to use, compiles extraordinarily quickly, and generates efficient code. QuickBASIC 4 is radically different from previous versions. For our current application, these features are:

- An integrated editor-compiler that allows writing, editing, compiling, running, debugging, and correcting errors without ever exiting QB.
- Virtually instantaneous compilation of all but the largest programs.
- Support for the 8087 math coprocessor.
- The ability to exit QB, execute other programs such as standard DOS operations, and return to QB where you left off.
- Highly compatible with the GWBASIC interpreter, which allows a direct comparison of interpreted GWBASIC programs with compiled ones.

Actually, Microsoft supplies two compilers that generate quite different code. QB is the integrated editor, incremental compiler, operating system package. The second is a classic command line compiler (BC.EXE) that generates stand alone EXE files. BC can be executed transparently from QB and the user is almost unaware of the added complexities. We will actually bypass running BC from QB for pedagogical reasons. The command line version shows better the intimate working of a compiler and is the way that most other compilers must still be used. In this section we describe only QB, and defer BC to the next section.

We now show how to use QB and important differences between an interpeter, a compiler, and a compiler that supports the math coprocessor.

2.4.1 Running QB

We supply a bootable system disk with the QB compiler present. This disk has the following files:

COMMAND.COM	"COMMAND processor"
GRAPHICS.COM	"standard graphics printer program"
AUTOEXEC.BAT	"start up file that loads GRAPHICS"
QB.EXE	"QB compiler"
QB.INI	"QB initialization file"
QB.HLP	"QB help file"
RAMDISK.DEV	"RAM disk driver"
CONFIG.SYS	"Configuration disk"

QB 4 is very memory-hungry, and it will not run in a 256K computer or a 640K computer with a 360K RAM disk. The current bootable disk sets up a small 200K RAM disk.

To use QB, boot the computer with the QB disk in drive A. QB works best with a color monitor, but will work with a monochrome if configured for one. A blank central display comes up first, into which you can begin writing a program directly. While there are many similarities with GWBASIC, note the following:

- The cursor keys work as with GWBASIC, but you do not have to press ENTER to register a line. In fact if you press ENTER, it will break the line at the cursor with part of the original line on one line and the remainder on the next line.
- Moving off the line with a cursor key or an ENTER at the end causes all BASIC reserved words to be capitalized. Variable names will be kept with the combination of upper and lower case that you enter.
- Line numbers are not required and are used only as labels. They have no relationship to line positions in a file. QB will not reorder by line number if you enter them out of order; they are not line numbers but line labels. Typing in a line number with a blank field after it will not erase an existing line. However, QB will complain about two lines with the same label. To erase lines, you must delete them directly in the file with the editor.
- The delete key removes the character under the cursor. QB starts in the insert mode. To toggle it press the Insert key. The cursor for overwriting is large while the default insert cursor is the underline character. Unlike GWBASIC, moving off a line or deleting a character has no effect on the insert state of the editor.
- QB can only read text BASIC files from GWBASIC. That is, any BASIC program created with GWBASIC must be saved with the ",a" option or QB cannot read it.

Once QB is entered, the various accessible options are listed across the top. An option is selected by pressing ALT and the first letter of the command. We only discuss the File and Run options. To select an option press ALT and the highlighted letter of the command. A new submenu window is brought up. For example, simultaneously pressing the ALT and f keys brings up the menu of Figure 2–1.

Each option within a menu is selected by pressing the highlighted letter or by moving the highlight bar with up/down cursor keys to the appropriate item followed by RETURN. To escape a menu press ESC. In the File menu press the function of the various options (see Figure 2–1); the functions are described below. "New Program" starts a new and as yet unnamed program. "Open Program" loads an existing program. "Merge" inserts an existing file at the current cursor position. "Save" stores the current program under its existing name. "Save As" stores the current program under a new name. "Save All" stores all modules. "Create File" starts a new program under a specified name. "Load File" loads an existing program from disk. "Unload File" removes an existing program from memory; you should use this before writing a new program. "Print . . ." prints a program to the line printer. "DOS Shell" exits to DOS and allows you to execute any DOS program, but you can return to where you left off in QuickBASIC by typing EXIT in DOS. "Exit" exits QB irreversibly.

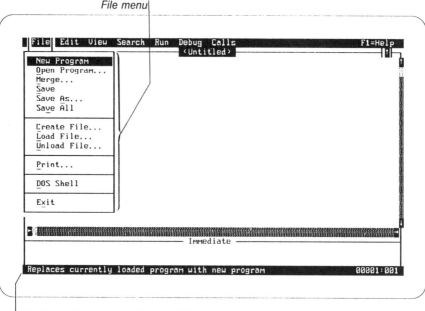

File menu

Help line tells you about the highlighted command.

Figure 2–1. QuickBASIC screen after initial loading and pressing the Alt F combination. The window in the center is added when the Alt F is pressed. From *Learning and Using Microsoft® QuickBASIC,* **© 1987 Microsoft Corporation. Reprinted with permission from Microsoft Corporation.**

The use of the various options is generally straightforward. However, some menus such as the Load File will bring up several windows. To move between windows, use the TAB or SHIFT TAB key, which moves forward or backward, respectively, through the menus. Once you are in the desired window, use the cursor keys to select the desired item, then the ENTER key to execute the function.

For example, with the Load File, you will have the File Name option highlighted with the *.bas. You can type in the name of the desired file; as soon as you start, the *.bas is deleted. Alternatively, you can advance to the directory window on the bottom by pressing TAB twice. You will pass through the Load As window, which is set as the default value. Then use the cursor keys to highlight the desired file. Finally, type RETURN to automatically load the specified file and return you to the editor. The editor is quite powerful (see Appendix B).

2.4.2 Running a Program

To run a program, select the Run function from the editing mode with ALT R. In the Run submenu, use the highlighted start with the ENTER key. The program will run; any output will appear on the screen window; and when the program terminates, QB displays "Press any key to continue" on the bottom of the screen. Pressing any key returns you to the editor. If you encounter an error during execution (this is called a "run time error"), QB stops execution and returns you to the editor with the cursor on the error and a window message that describes the error. For example, a statement z=1/0 will give a "Division by zero" error with the cursor on the z. Press RETURN to clear the error message and use the editor to correct the error.

2.4.3   Saving QuickBASIC Programs

There are several ways to save a program. You can save one at any time using the Save option of the File menu. If you created the program using New, it will be unnamed. You can name it at any time with Save or save it under any name with Save As. If you have not saved a program since the last editing, any attempt to exit will start a dialog in which you will be asked to give the program a file name under which to save it. If currently named, the program is saved under that name. To save it under some other name, use the Save As command; again you will be prompted for a name. Save As has no effect on the originally named file.

2.4.4   Loading a New Program in QuickBASIC

While QB can have several program modules present at once and there are commands for managing these modules, it is not our intent to get into QB intricacies. To avoid errors, we recommend that you unload each program module after you are finished with it, using the Unload command of the File menu. Only then load or start a new program with the Load or New command of the File menu. This combination is equivalent to using NEW followed by LOAD in GWBASIC.

2.4.5   QuickBASIC Support of the Math Coprocessor

QB automatically senses the presence of the math coprocessor. If the math coprocessor is absent, the 80X87 math functions are simulated in software with all mathematical calculations performed with full 80X87 precision. QB does not mimic GWBASIC's 32-bit single precision. Note that even in double precison, GWBASIC does all transcendental functions to single precision accuracy. Thus, QB can be quite slow without an 80X87—even slower sometimes than GWBASIC although the results are more accurate.

If the only machine available has a math coprocessor, you can disable the coprocessor by typing the following statement while still in DOS:

```
>set NO87=No 8087 is used
```

When QB is entered, the statement "No 8087 is used" (or whatever statement you typed after the =) appears. To restore use of the 8087, reenter DOS and type:

```
>set NO87=
```

There must be no blanks after the equal sign. If you put in blanks, QB will display these blanks when you run and still ignore the 8087. In this variable, to register any changes QB must be executed with the QB command from DOS. You cannot exit to the shell from QB, change the variable, and reenter QB with EXIT. QB only detects the status of this variable when it is first loaded.

Problems 2–2 to 2–7 demonstrate very strikingly the differences between a compiled and an interpreted language. However, even those quite familiar with software may find amusing and unexpected behavior.

2.5 QuickBASIC COMMAND LINE COMPILER (BC)

The compilation is divided into several distinct stages:

(1) Source code preparation.
(2) Compilation of the source code to an object code (.OBJ) module.
(3) Linking the object code module to the necessary library routines from the compiler to generate an EXE file.
(4) Running the EXE file.

We now outline in greater detail each step. The major advantages of BC versus QB are directly runnable EXE files, smaller memory requirements, and faster code.

2.5.1 Source Code Generation

The BASIC source code can be generated by using any standard editor that uses text (ASCII) encoding of the characters. We will return to ASCII later. However, not all editors or word processors generate ASCII source files. WordPerfect, XY Write, or WordStar in the normal word processor mode turn source code into gibberish for the compiler. We provide a Borland style editor ED to our students. You should terminate all BASIC programs written for compilation with an END statement. Interpreted BASIC programs will accept the END.

Alternatively, use GWBASIC to generate the source file. This has the advantage that you can run and debug the program directly from the interpreter. You must save the source file in ASCII (",A" option).

2.5.2 Compiling the Source File

There are two types of BASIC EXE files. One is a stand-alone EXE file that needs nothing further in order to run. The other is a compact partial program that must pick up the necessary library routines from a separate file at run time. We show how to generate both.

The following discussion assumes that you have 360K floppies. For compact EXE files, you need only one compiler disk. For stand-alone programs, you need two disks. One possible configuration for each is shown below:

| Compact EXE Files | | Stand-Alone EXE Files | |
A disk	B disk	A disk	B disk
COMMAND.COM	Program	COMMAND.COM	BCOM40.LIB
BC.EXE		BC.EXE	Program
BRUN40.LIB		LINK.EXE	
BRUN40.EXE			
LINK.EXE			

BCOM40.LIB and BRUN40.LIB are the libraries of routines that must be linked to your object (.OBJ) code to make, respectively, stand-alone and compact EXE files. LINK is the linker for tying program fragments together. BRUN40.EXE runs programs linked with BRUN40.LIB. The 40 refers to the version (4.0) and changes.

As the library portion is very large, several stand-alone EXE files can rapidly fill up a disk. In contrast, if you link your program to BRUN40.LIB, you generate a small module that picks up the necessary library routines when the program runs. Small program modules are very small until they are linked to the library at run time. Thus, many small modules can coexist on one disk and call up a single large library as they are run.

A sample session for generation of a compact EXE file with BC and LINK is shown below. The program, DRAW.BAS, is on B. Again your input is in boldface.

```
A>BC
Microsoft Quick BASIC Compiler
Version 1.00
(C) Copyright Microsoft Corp. 1982, 1983, 1984, 1985

Source filename [.BAS]: B:draw <CR> "give drive and filename"
Object filename [DRAW.OBJ]: B:draw  "tell it where and name"
Source listing  [NUL.LST]: <CR>     "You don't need a listing"

49160 Bytes Available
48077 Bytes Free

0 Warning Error(s)                  "No errors"
0 Severe  Error(s)
```

Values in [. . .] are default values. If you are satisfied with the item as listed, merely press the <CR>. "NUL" indicates that no file of the specified type will be generated. You can change part of the default value. For example, if you want to generate an OBJ file of the name DRAW.OBJ on the C drive, you could answer "C:"<CR> to the Object filename prompt; everything else is accepted as shown.

```
A>LINK

Microsoft 8086 Object Linker
Version 3.02 (C) Copyright Microsoft Corp 1983, 1984, 1985

Object Modules [.OBJ]: b:draw   "Where and name"
```

```
Run File [DRAW.EXE]: B:draw      "Where to and with what name"
List File [NUL.MAP]: <CR>        "No need for map"
Libraries [.LIB]: <CR>          "Library here is automatic"
```

The simplest way to run the program is from the A drive with the BC diskette still in A. Then, for this example, type:

```
A>B:DRAW
```

Both the A and the B drive will be accessed before the program executes. After compilation, the B diskette has the file with the .OBJ extension. After the LINK you have an analogous EXE file. When you run the EXE file, it goes first to the default drive and links in the run time library. Every time you run a program compiled this way, you need the BRUN40 LIB and EXE files.

A shorter way of invoking the compiler or linker has the file name in the command:

```
A>BC B:DRAW
A>LINK B:DRAW
```

Running a program while logged on the B drive is a little different. When the program goes to link with the run time library, it looks on the logged B drive and fails to find it. It then asks you the path to the BRUN40.LIB. If you still have the compiler disk in the A drive, then respond with A:<CR>. Linking is completed and the program runs as before. If the compiler disk is no longer in the A drive, the program asks you to switch to a disk that has the necessary files.

If you want to generate the stand-alone EXE files using the compiler, the procedure is nearly the same as before except that you set a switch (send a message) to the compiler when you first invoke it. This is done by issuing one of the following commands:

```
A>BC/O              "Compile to a stand-alone EXE file"
A>BC B:DRAW/O       "Compile DRAW to a stand-alone EXE file"
```

The /O tells the compiler to link to BCOM40.LIB and generate a stand-alone module. Compare the size of the EXE modules in each case. When you link, you specify the location of BCOM40.LIB and, since this will not fit on a 360K floppy with BC.EXE, you might need another disk.

2.6 RAM DISKS

As you have discovered, disk access, especially with floppies, greatly slows programs. This is certainly true of compilers, linkers, and systems that contain large libraries or data bases. Fortunately, a RAM disk greatly accelerates work that is slowed by a lot of disk accesses. A RAM disk is merely a block of computer W/R memory (RAM) that is set aside for use as a pseudo-disk coupled with software that allows DOS to treat this memory as if it were another physical disk drive. This RAM disk software intercepts any

DOS commands that would be directed to a physical disk and converts them into the necessary memory access instructions.

The advantages of RAM disks are enormous. Physical disks are limited in speed by how fast the heads move to new tracks or the disks rotate to new portions of a track. In contrast, a RAM disk has no moving parts. Access to any portion of the "disk" is made at electronic—not mechanical—speeds. Thus, while a floppy disk drive seeks a new track in hundreds of milliseconds, a RAM disk works in microseconds.

The actual improvement in speed is not this great. The applications software takes time to execute, as does the RAM disk software. The RAM disk does not even remotely resemble a floppy disk in layout and it is not addressed by the commands that would be issued to the disk controller. The disk emulator software takes all the disk drive commands and converts them into RAM-compatible commands; this takes time and degrades performance. In practice, one generally expects a minimum of twofold increase in performance with a RAM disk, and factors of 5–10 are not uncommon for disk intensive floppy disk based software.

A RAM disk is generally configured as part of the boot sequence. Depending on your DOS (2 and greater) you use either a RAMDISK.DEV driver or VDISK. Consult your DOS manual.

RAM disk software allows selecting the size of the RAM disk. Size is determined by machine memory and the software to be run. On our 640K machines we frequently configure a 200 RAM disk. This leaves 440K for DOS and applications software; QuickBASIC and Turbo Pascal can still run—barely. Machines with extended or expanded memory allow RAM disks to be placed above the 640K program memory.

The RAM disk is usually installed above the highest existing physical drive. Thus, a dual floppy system (A and B) will have the first RAM disk as drive C. A dual floppy (A and B), one hard disk (C) system has the first RAM disk as drive D.

To verify whether you have a RAM disk, take a directory or run a CHKDSK on the suspected drive. If it is not there, DOS tells you. You can do virtually everything on a RAM disk (e.g., copying, running, and erasing) that can be done on physical drive except formating. A RAM disk does not need to be formated.

WARNING: RAM disks, unless battery backed up, forget everything when the power even flickers. If you use a RAM disk for irreplaceable material, periodically copy data to a physical disk. Then, at worst, you only lose data since the last copy.

Experiment 2–6. In this experiment you compare the speed of several disk operations using a physical drive and a RAM disk.

2.7   BATCH FILES

There are many series of DOS commands that you repeat frequently. DOS permits you to stack series of operations in a batch file and execute them automatically. We will briefly describe the basics of batch files, including parameter passing and conditional branching.

In their simplest form batch files are nothing more than a list of DOS commands that are executed automatically by invoking the file name. Batch files must have the extension .BAT, and are invoked by typing the file name without the extension. This is similar to invoking a COM or EXE file, except in this case you are initiating execution of a series of commands or programs. For example, the following batch file:

```
ERASE *.OBJ
ERASE *.BAK
A:
GWBASIC
```

erases all OBJ files and all BAK files, logs onto the A drive, and then executes GWBASIC. If the file were called SWEEP.BAT, you could execute these commands by typing SWEEP<CR>. A BAT file should not have the same name as a COM or EXE file.

Parameters. A little thought indicates that it would be useful if we could pass specific information to the BAT file, such as which data files should be processed or which files should be compiled and linked. BAT files permit you to pass up to nine arguments (parameters) or names to the BAT file. The form is:

```
filename argument#1 argument#2 ... argument#9
```

in which the arguments are information that you pass to the BAT file. When you write the BAT file, you denote each parameter with "%" in front of the parameter number. For example, %1 in the BAT file corresponds to argument#1, %2 corresponds to argument#2, and so forth. Therefore, everywhere in the batch file that %2 is used, it is replaced by argument#2. This is more clearly seen in the following example, a BAT file called BCOM.BAT:

```
B:                  "Change to B:"
A:BC %1;            "Execute BC with specified file"
A:LINK %1;          "Link the specified file"
ERASE B:*.OBJ       "Erase the .OBJ file of specified file"
DIR B:%1.*          "Check to make sure compile OK"
B:                  "Log B drive where EXE file is"
%1                  "Execute compile EXE program"
```

Execution of the BAT file and passing an argument TEST1 to it would be done by typing:

```
C>BCOM TEST1
```

Using BC and LINK on the A drive, this BAT file compiles TEST1 on the B drive with BC, links TEST1.OBJ on the B drive, erases TEST1.OBJ on the B drive, does a directory of all files on the B with file name TEST1, and executes TEST1.EXE. The time savings in this simple example are substantial, and the advantage increases with more complicated examples. In this example, the compilation will not proceed flawlessly. The linker and the running program expect the BRUN10 files on the default B drive when they are probably on the A drive. The program queries you for the appropriate drives when it does not find them, so you can easily overcome the problem.

ECHO. The previous examples type out each command as it was processed. The ECHO command allows you to turn this feature on and off and to print out messages. The basic formats are:

```
ECHO [on/off]        "Turn echoing of commands on or off"
ECHO message         "Display message"
```

ECHO Off turns off display of the BAT file as it is executed. Once you have a BAT file debugged, it runs faster with less distracting output if ECHO is off. DOS prompts and information are still displayed. ECHO On (default) enables BAT file display. ECHO message displays message even if ECHO is off. If ECHO is on, the line with the ECHO command is printed first, followed by a separate line with the message.

PAUSE. Pause stops execution. This is useful for changing disks and setting environmental variables to determine subsequent branching in the program.

Conditional Operations and Branching. DOS has primitive testing and conditional branching capabilities. The branch command is the GOTO, analogous to the GOTO in BASIC:

```
GOTO label
```

where label is any alphanumeric word. The destination is specified by placing the label on a separate line that starts with a colon (:). For example:

```
ECHO off
ECHO branching to one
GOTO ONE
ECHO before one
:ONE
ECHO at one
```

Since the GOTO is unconditional, you never see the message "before one."

The conditional test statement is the IF, which has the basic forms:

```
IF condition DOSCommand
IF NOT condition  DOSCommand
```

In the first, if the condition is true, DOSCommand is executed. In the second, if the condition is false, DOSCommand is executed. There are three valid tests:

ERRORLEVEL value   "True if program error exit code ERRORLEVEL is greater than or equal to value"

EXIST file specification   "True if specified file exists"
string1==string2   "True if both strings are identical"

ERRORLEVEL is a DOS variable that can be set on exiting from programs. It is useful for determining what happened or for controlling subsequent execution of the BAT file. Consider an example:

```
ECHO OFF
IF EXIST c:HD  GOTO HARDDISK
ECHO  No hard Disk.  Installing Word Processor on C: RAM Disk
COPY a:wp C:
C:
GOTO END
:HARDDISK
ECHO Hard Disk Exists.  Installing WP on D: RAM disk.
COPY c:wp D:
D:
:END
WP
```

The purpose is to allow our word processor WP to run from a RAM disk regardless of the configuration of the machine. As we have dual floppy based machines (A and B) and hard disk systems (A, B, and C), the RAM disk could be either C or D. To allow the batch file to distinguish, we have a small file HD on the root directory of all of our hard disks. If HD exists on C:, then the RAM disk is D and WP is copied to D. Otherwise, the RAM disk is C, and the processor is copied to C. Our actual program uses subdirectories (Section 2.9), but the principle is the same.

The following Turbo Pascal program compiled to an EXE file allows you to set the DOS ERRORLEVEL:

```
PROGRAM Seterror;                {Sets dos ERRORLEVEL}

VAR
  ERRORLEVEL : Integer;

BEGIN
  REPEAT
    Write('Enter value for ERRORLEVEL set (0-5) :');
    ReadLn(ERRORLEVEL);
  UNTIL ERRORLEVEL IN [0..5];
  Halt(ERRORLEVEL);      {Set ERRORLEVEL, return to DOS}
END.
```

The following batch file displays the current value of ERRORLEVEL up to 2. It shows the awkwardness of the DOS control structures. UNIX is more powerful and friendly.

```
echo off
Rem Check and display current DOS ERRORLEVEL
if ErrorLevel 3 goto Greater2
if ERRORLEVEL 2 GOTO 2
IF Errorlevel 1 goto 1
echo  ERRORLEVEL = 0
goto end

:GREATER2
echo ERRORLEVEL greater than 2
goto end

:2
echo ERRORLEVEL = 2
goto end

:1
Echo ERRORLEVEL =1

:end
```

Upper and lower cases are mixed to remind you of the case insensitivity of DOS batch files.

We have only touched on the complexity of the BAT file. For example, it can process lists of files. The interested reader is referred to DOS books.

2.8 FORTRAN

FORTRAN (Formula Translation) is a compiled language widely used by scientists and engineers. Microsoft markets a reasonable PC implementation. Unfortunately, the compiler is slow and FORTRAN does not come in an interpreted version, which makes program development more difficult. A FORTRAN compilation disk might include:

```
FOR1.EXE    PAS3.EXE    FORTRAN.LIB    ALTMATH.LIB
PAS2.EXE    LINK.EXE    MATH.LIB       8087.LIB
```

These files are quite large and a hard disk is virtually essential. There is one main FORTRAN library, FORTRAN.LIB and three math libraries (MATH, ALTMATH, and 8087). There is also a BCD math library, which is of little use to scientists. The default library is MATH.LIB, which corresponds to number storage using the IEEE standard for floating point numbers (8087 format). The 8087.LIB uses the math coprocessor. The ALTMATH.LIB uses Microsoft's own faster number representation. Only one math library can be used at a time.

The FORTRAN compiler is a two or three pass compiler. One must run at least FOR1 and PAS2 to get executable code. If everything is on a hard disk, a sample FORTRAN compilation of a source DATTIM.FOR looks similar to a compilation in BASIC:

```
C>FOR1 DATTIM
C>PAS2 DATTIM
C>LINK DATTIM
C>DATTIM
```

If necessary files are not on the logged disk, you are given an opportunity to redirect the search or change diskettes. A hard disk greatly accelerates compiling and linking but, as with BC, the linker is still painfully slow.

2.9 HARD OR FIXED DISKS

While the floppy disk is an inexpensive media, its capacity is generally limited. The hard disk (or fixed disk in IBM's notation) provides much larger storage capacity. Not long ago the 10M hard disk was standard. Currently, no one would consider anything smaller than a 20M or 30M disk, and the 40M, 70M, and 140M capacity are rapidly coming into their own. Prices have fallen, and any general purpose computer should have at least a 20M hard disk.

The hard disk has special problems. A major one is the sheer size. It is impossible to have thousands of files on a single disk without some way to organize them. The major tool for hard disk management is the subdirectory. A related tool is the path command, which allows software to be used even if it is in some corner of the disk hidden from the user.

2.9.1 Subdirectories

Subdirectories partition a disk into small and logically integrated pieces. For example, a well organized office will have the most important items kept in different filing cabinets with different topics in different drawers. Hanging files containing manila folders would be used for further logical subdivisions. Subdirectories perform a similar organization on a hard disk or floppies.

Figure 2–2 shows how a disk for working on papers and a book might be partitioned. The root directory or topmost level has no name and is specified by a \. We have partitioned the root directory into three subdirectories: SOFTWARE, BOOK, and PAPERS. Within SOFTWARE, there are three further levels of partitioning: MSDOS, PASCAL, and WORDPR for the DOS utilities, Pascal, and the word processor. Within the PAPERS subdirectory, there are two separate paper subdirectories: LUM and LIFE-TIME. The BOOK has subdirectories for individual chapters CH1 and CH2.

When you boot, the active directory is the root directory. If you do a DIR, you might find something like this:

```
Volume in drive A has no label
Directory of A:\

COMMAND    COM        17792    10-20-83    12:00P
AUTOEXEC   BAT           15     8-17-87    12:11a
BOOK       <DIR>                1-01-80    12:32a
PAPERS     <DIR>                1-01-80    12:32a
```

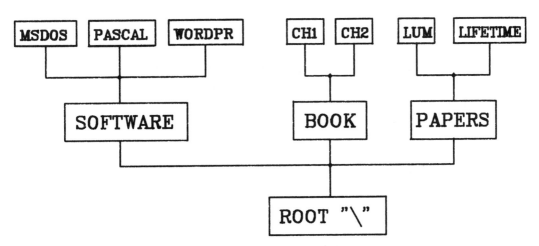

Figure 2–2. A simple tree-structured disk directory showing the root along with subdirectories containing subdirectories.

```
UN2ITAL    COM        11318      1-01-80    12:50a
SOFTWARE   <DIR>                 1-01-80    12:32a
          6 File(s)         12288 bytes free
```

Note that the listed directory is A:\ where the \ indicates that we are on the root directory. COMMAND.COM and AUTOEXEC.BAT must be in the root directory for a proper boot. The only anomalies here are BOOK, PAPERS, and SOFTWARE, which have no size or extension but are denoted as subdirectory entries by the <DIR> notation. Each of these subdirectories can contain files or further subdirectories as noted above.

2.9.2 Changing Subdirectories (CD)

The first problem is getting into these subdirectories. The change path (CD) command does this. It has the form:

CD path

where path specifies the path or route to the new location. Path may be nothing more complicated than the root. Alternatively, it may be a subdirectory of the current subdirectory or a subdirectory buried deeply in the directory hierarchy. Path is a complete description of where you want to go and how to get there (i.e., a road map). Examples are:

CD   "Change to the root directory"

CD papers	"Change to the currently visible papers subdirectory"
CD\papers	"Starting at the root change to the papers subdirectory of the root directory"
CD\papers\lum	"Starting at the root, change to the paper subdirectory, then to lum subdirectory of papers"

If we change to the paper's subdirectory and do a DIR, we might get:

```
Volume in drive A has no label
Directory of A:\papers

.               <DIR>      7-27-88    8:55a
..              <DIR>      7-27-88    8:55a
LUM             <DIR>      8-01-88   12:41a
LIFETIME        <DIR>      8-01-88   12:41a
DELBAK    BAT        55    8-1-88     3:42a
        5 File(s)                 9216 bytes free
```

Note that the listing shows that we are in the \papers subdirectory and that we have a batch file DELBAK.BAT and two subdirectories LUM and LIFETIME within the \PAPERS subdirectory. The only oddities are the . and . . entries. The . stands for the current subdirectory and the . . means the previous subdirectory. The . . allows you to move backward one level at a time toward the root; you do not need to know the name of the previous directory.

Assuming that you are in the LIFETIME subdirectory, the following command will have the indicated effect:

CD	"Return to the root directory"
CD ..	"Change to the PAPERS subdirectory. The space is essential in DOS 2, but not DOS 3"
CD\MSDOS	"From the root change to the MSDOS subdirectory"
CD lum	"From the current papers subdirectory change to the lum subdirectory"

Several points bear comment. To move several layers higher in the tree, use cd..\.. constructions or specify the complete path. It is possible to have more than one subdirectory or file with the same name on a disk. For example, we could have a LUM subdirectory in both the BOOK and the PAPERS subdirectories. Do not try to create both a file and a subdirectory with the same name in a directory or subdirectory; DOS balks.

2.9.3 Operating on Subdirectories

You can carry out operations on a subdirectory or execute a program in a subdirectory just as if you were running it or examining it on another disk. You must specify a complete path to the desired file or function. For example, assume that we are in the root directory and wish to TYPE VER1 in \PAPERS\LUM, type:

TYPE\papers\lum\ver1

or if you wish to take a directory listing of \book\ch1, type:

dir\book\ch1

Finally, to run the format program in \software\msdos\, type:

\software\msdos\format   "DOS 3 or later only"

DOS 2 does not let you run a program in another subdirectory. You must either change to that subdirectory or use the PATH command. To erase vers1 in lum, type:

erase\papers\lum\ver1

Warning. The erase command will actually work on a complete subdirectory. Thus:

erase\papers\lum

will, after asking you to confirm the action, erase all files in the lum subdirectory. This can be insidious. The following command:

erase\papers\lum ver1

will not just erase ver1, but it will erase the entire contents of the lum subdirectory. The break in the path terminates the path and the remainder of the line is ignored.
You can also copy the contents of one subdirectory into another. For example:

copy\papers\lum*.* \papers\lifetime

will copy all files in the \papers\lum subdirectory into the \papers\lifetime subdirectory.
Path can include a disk drive specification. For example, from the a: drive, you can view all exe files in the \MSDOS subdirectory of the c: drive with:

dir c:\msdos

2.9.4   Creating and Removing Subdirectories (MKDIR and RMDIR)
We now describe how to create new subdirectories and remove unwanted ones. The two commands are:

`MKDIR path name`	"Make directory name at specified location"
`RMDIR path name`	"Remove directory name at specified location"

If you are in the root directory, the following commands create subdirectories:

`MKDIR\papers\lum`	"Create lum subdirectory used above"
`MKDIR\paper\lum\ch1`	"Create ch1 subdirectory in lum subdirectory"
`RMDIR\papers\lum\ch1`	"Delete the ch 1 subdirectory"

If you were in the book subdirectory, the following would create a new CH7 subdirectory within the book subdirectory:

`MKDIR ch7`

Note that we do not have to specify the complete path if we are working only from the current location. Subdirectory uses the same conventions as DOS files. Thus, LUM.CH1 is a perfectly acceptable subdirectory.

DOS protects you from some lethal mistakes. If you try to delete a subdirectory with any files in it, DOS balks. You must first delete all files and subdirectories within a subdirectory before you can delete the subdirectory itself. This prevents you from accidentally destroying files or the paths to reach them.

2.9.5   Remote Program Execution (PATH)

With systems organized as above, you must specify explicitly the path to every executable file in the \MSDOS and \WORDPR subdirectory, which becomes tiresome for common functions. DOS provides the PATH command for automatically searching subdirectories for executable programs. PATH can be executed from DOS, but it is better to include it in the AUTOEXECT.BAT file. The PATH statement has the following format:

`PATH=path#1;path#2; etc`

where path#1, path#2, and so on are the complete subdirectory paths that DOS should search before giving up on a program. Entries are separated by semicolons with no embedded blanks. The search begins in the current subdirectory, then continues with path#1, then path#2, and so on until the program is found or the possibilities are exhausted. Consider:

`PATH=a:\software\msdos;a:\software\wordpr`

If you are in the \papers\lum subdirectory and try to execute a SORT command, DOS first looks for it in the current directory (i.e., \papers\lum). If it is not there, DOS then goes to the PATH statement and checks in the lum\software\msdos subdirectory. If it is not there, DOS looks in the \software\wordpr subdirectory. If not present in any of these places, DOS gives up and informs you that you have an invalid name.

An insidious problem can arise when using the path statement. Many pieces of software use overlays to fit more program into less memory. The main program (COM or EXE file) is entered in the normal way. Once in control, however, this supervisory program can load other pieces into memory over part of itself and run them. This is common in word processors in which less commonly used functions are called up as needed rather than occupying valuable memory. These overlays are not regular COM or EXE files that are run by DOS, but rather are programs run by your applications program. They frequently have the OVR extensions.

A problem arises when you PATH the main program. If you execute it from another subdirectory, the PATH finds this program, but when the application tries to load an overlay, it does not know where to look and will usually give up with a complaint about being unable to find the overlays.

The solution is generally simple, but highly software dependent. Go to the manual. Software designed to run on a hard disk usually has an installation routine that allows it to recognize where you have the overlays.

2.9.6 Setting the DOS Prompt

Unless you specifically set up the DOS prompt, it will always be the > regardless of where you are on the disk. There are inconvenient and nasty consequences if you think that you are in one subdirectory and are actually in another. To assist you in this problem, DOS allows you to change the prompt with the prompt statement. There are many variations on this. For example, you might indicate what subdirectory you are in, or you could display the current time. The following statement included in the AUTOEXEC.BAT file always displays where you are in the disk hierarchy:

```
PROMPT $p$g
```

You can also enter this from the DOS command line. After being executed, the prompt now tells you exactly where you are. For example, if you are in the \papers\lum subdirectory the prompt is:

```
C:\PAPERS\LUM>
```

If you are interested in more exotic prompts, check the DOS manual.

Experiment 2–7. In this experiment you use directory management commands.

2.10 REFERENCES

The best reference on QuickBASIC is the set of extensive Microsoft manuals. Inman and Albrecht have written a more basic manual. Your DOS manual is the standard DOS reference. Jamsa has a very readable account of DOS along with a detailed explanation of its workings.

Problems

2–1 [2.5.2]. Using a FOR NEXT loop, determine the execution time of different BASIC operations. For example, to find out how long it takes to do an addition, run the following two programs:
Program 1:

```
10 FOR J=1 to 10000
20 NEXT J
```

Program 2:

```
10 FOR J=1 to 10000
15 A=J+J
20 NEXT J
```

When the computation is complete, BASIC responds with OK. The time required between RUN <CR> and OK is the program execution time. The difference in execution times for Program 2 and Program 1 is the time for 1000 additions.

Repeat the calculation for multiplication (*), division (/), square root (SQR(variable)), natural log (LOG(variable)), and sine (SIN(variable)). Adjust the number of iterations to get accurate or reasonable times.

Some functions fail for large integer J arguments. For example, EXP(89) exceeds the range of the BASIC floating point math package. To circumvent this problem, use constructions like the following, which gives 10,000 iterations:

```
10 FOR J=0.001 TO 10 step 0.001
15 Y=EXP(J)
20 NEXT J
```

Automatic Timing: GWBASIC has a built in time function, TIME$, that reads the computer's clock. PRINT TIME$ displays the current time. If you include this statement immediately before and after your loop, the program times itself.

2–2 [2.4.5]. Repeat the calculations of Problem 2–1 using QB with and without the math coprocessor enabled.

2–3 [2.4.5]. Repeat the calculations of 2–1 for the empty loop (Program 1) using GWBASIC and one form of QB, but with "j" replaced by "LongLoopVariableJ".

2–4 [2.4.5]. Repeat the calculations of 2–1 for the empty loop using GWBASIC and one form of QB, but add nine lines (number 11 to 19), each with a single REM on it (e.g., 11 rem).

2–5 [2.4.5]. Time the empty loop of 2–1 using GWBASIC and one of the QB forms, but replace lines 10 and 20 with:

```
10                                    for j=1 to 10000
20                                    next j
```

The precise number of blanks is not critical but should be large.

2–6 [2.4.5]. Explain the differences in behavior between the versions of the software. In particular, comment on the very poor performance of the non-math coprocessor version of compiled QB code relative to interpreted GWBASIC code. If possible, compare QB and BC for the empty loop calculations where there are interesting differences.

2–7 [2.5.2]. Write a linear least squares program for fitting data (x_i, y_i) pairs to:

$$y = I + S*x$$

I is the intercept and S is the slope. I and S are given by:

$$I = \left[\sum x_i^2 \ \sum y_i - \sum x_i \ \sum x_i y_i \right] / \Delta$$

$$S = \left[N \sum x_i y_i - \sum x_i \ \sum y_i \right] / \Delta$$

$$\Delta = N \sum x_i^2 - \left(\sum x_i \right)^2$$

where N is the total number of points used in the fit (i.e., 500 for the current example) and the summations are over all points used. Store your data in X and Y arrays with a maximum size of 500 elements (i.e., DIM X[500], Y[500]). Load these arrays with data before doing the calculations. Print out the slope and the intercept with a label identifying the items printed out. Time the calculations with GWBASIC and QB with and without 8087 support. You need several iterations to time the 8087 version. To check your program, generate synthetic data with a known slope and intercept.

2–8 [2.5.2]. Write a BASIC program that generates a 500 point exponential decay using the formula:

$$D(t) = K*exp(-t/\tau)$$

where t has integer step values of 0 to 499 and K=10,000 and τ=100. Store the data in a 500 element array named DECAY. Fit the data by first linearizing the equation. The necessary relationships for generating the slope and intercept are the same as for the linear case except that:

$$y = \ln(D(t))$$
$$x = t$$
$$I = \ln(K)$$
$$S = -(1/\tau)$$

Then use linear least squares fitting of the previous problem to obtain K and τ. Time the calculation using GWBASIC and QB with and without the 8087 enabled.

2–9 [2.5.2]. The following calculation is a common floating point benchmark. It tests speed and round off errors, especially for transcendental functions. In this calculation, x is initialized to 1.0 and the following calculation is performed for a specific number of iterations:

$$x = \tan(\text{atn}(\exp(\log(\text{sqr}(x*x))))) + 1$$

In the absence of numeric round off errors, the result equals the number of iterations.

Carry out this calculation using GWBASIC and QB with and without the 8087. Set up the program so that you can vary the number of iterations in response to a question. Exit when you answer 0 for the number of iterations. In GWBASIC use double precision for all floating point variables except for your loop variable, which should be integers.

Determine the time per iteration for the three variations of BASIC and the error for a calculation involving a number of iterations large enough to give detectible error. You will find some interesting and unexpected results in terms of accuracy and time. In particular, these give insight into some of the short-cuts that were taken with GWBASIC.

2–10 [2.5.2]. Another benchmark is matrix multiplication. Generate two 30x30 real matrices A[30,30] and B[30,30] where the elements are given by:

$$B(i,j) = A(i,j) = 1/(i+j+1)$$

Matrix multiply A and B to give a third 30X30 matrix C using the following formula:

$$C(i,j) = \sum_{k=1}^{30} A(i,k)\,B(k,j)$$

This program tests the ability of the program to access and index through large arrays and perform multiplication and addition.

Time the operations using GWBASIC and QB with and without the 8087. You can always stop the program at any time with CTRL Break. Then, in the command mode, you can print out the current values of your i and j index to see how far the program progressed.

2–11 [2.5.2]. Take one of your previous programs and compare the speed of execution using the QB and BC compilers. In general, the BC EXE files are faster.

2–12 [2.7]. Write a BAT file that simplifies using the QuickBASIC compiler by utilizing a RAM disk. Your .BAS and .BAT programs should reside on the B drive, and the compiler should be in A. The program should be called up by:

```
QBAS filename
```

QBAS should automatically complete the following functions:

(1) Transfer all the compiler files and the linker from A to the RAM drive. Do not transfer the COMMAND file.
(2) Transfer your program filename.BAS to the RAM drive.
(3) Log onto the RAM drive. This avoids the need to specify which drive the files are on; the compiler and linker assume all files are on the logged drive unless instructed otherwise.
(4) Compile and link your program. Use the /O option to generate a stand alone EXE file on the RAM drive. Also, use the semicolon after the file name in the compile and link commands so that you do not have to supply any input as the BAT file runs.
(5) Erase the OBJ file generated by the compiler.
(6) Run the program by invoking its name.

Time your program. Measure the time between the initiation of the BAT file and the time that the program starts to run. Also, measure the time between when the compiler logs on and when your program begins execution.

Compare these times with a similar run that does not utilize the RAM disk. This program starts with a disk in the B drive that contains only your batch file, BCOM40.LIB, and your BASIC source code. Repeat the above operations, excluding step 2, which is no longer necessary.

2–13 [2.8]. Write a FORTRAN program that carries out the benchmark calculation described in Problem 2–8. Time the calculation using the default MATHLIB, 8087, and ALTMATH libraries. Note that it is not necessary to recompile the program each time. Just relink your original OBJ module with the appropriate math library.

2–14 [2.8]. Repeat problem 2–13 using the benchmark of Problem 2–9.

2–15 [2.8]. Repeat problem 2–13 using the benchmark of Problem 2–10.

3

Timing, Serial/Parallel I/O, and Pipes and Filters

3.1 INTRODUCTION

We now go into greater detail concerning the interactions of the computer with the outside world and your level of control. We introduce timing in Pascal, interactions with the keyboard, serial and parallel input/output (I/O), and the very useful UNIX-like concept of pipes and filters. Experiments clarify the concepts.

A parallel port presents multiple bits simultaneously on multiple lines; for example, a full byte is output at once on eight lines plus a signal return. In serial I/O, a multibit block of input or output is handled one bit at a time on a single signal line plus a return.

On most PCs, you find at least two plugs for external communications (besides the video and keyboard). One plug is a limited parallel printer port, which is only good for running printers. The other plug, which may be labeled an RS-232 or a communications port, is for serial data communication. The serial port is commonly used for communicating with a display terminal, another computer, and many instruments. General purpose parallel I/O is the standard method of high speed instrument or device control, but this requires additional interface cards.

We explain in detail how serial and parallel I/O work, and you experiment with both. You begin Pascal programming, which we assume you are familiar with or are learning from another text. We do not dwell on many features of the Turbo Pascal compiler, but do point out areas that you should review elsewhere as well as nonstandard or especially important features. Appendix B has a brief description of running the Turbo Pascal editor. To begin honing your Pascal skills, work out the demonstration problems.

3.2   TIMING AND UNITS

Standard Pascal has no direct provisions for timing, direct string manipulations, calls to the operating system, or graphics. Turbo Pascal overcomes many of these limitations by extensions to standard Pascal. While there is controversy over whether or not these extensions degrade the pristine elegance of the language, there is no doubt that they make the language far more valuable for interfacing and scientific applications, albeit at the expense of portability to other Pascals.

Directly running the Turbo Pascal 4/5 compiler, you have a high, but not perfect, degree of compatiblity with standard Pascal. Turbo's string variables, operations, and file handling are areas of differences. If you want any of Borland's extensions, you incorporate Units. These are partially precompiled libraries that the Turbo compiler links into your code as needed. Units are extensions to the basic language. As a bonus, Turbo allows you to write your own Units, thus allowing compiler customization. To include Units you add the following line after your program name:

```
USES unit1, unit2, unit3, and so on;
```

where unit1, unit2 are the names of the precompiled units. The principal Turbo units that you will use are Dos, Crt, and Graphics. Dos gives you access to the operating system. Crt gives you fast screen display plus a few other useful operations. Graphics gives you a library of basic graphics routines. Turbo's linker is smart, so even if you list unneeded units they do not get incorporated into, and increase the size of, your code.   We now demonstrate the construction and use of a set of timing routines. The Crt Unit timing procedure has the following format:

```
GetTime(hour, minute, second, sec100: integer);
```

where we use the notation of specifying the type in the procedure definition. Hour (0–23), minute (0–59), second (0–59), sec100 (0–99) are the current hour, time, minute, second, and 1/100th of a second using a 24-hour clock. The system clock is used for this timing and it ticks 18.2 times per second, so the real clock resolution is about 50 ms, not 10 ms. Clearly, from this information you could construct the number of 1/100ths of a second into the day and by subtracting the differences of these quantities, you can measure the interval between two calls to GetTime. Note that since GetTime is in the Crt Unit, your program must use the statement USES Crt;.

To make GetTime more useful, we have a Unit Timer that contains three independently running and readable clocks. Timer adds two additional procedures:

```
FUNCTION ReadTimer(TimerNumber : Integer) : LongInt;
PROCEDURE StartTimer(TimerNumber : Integer);
```

StartTimer starts one of three indicated timers, which saves the current clock value at the time of the call. ReadTimer reads the interval between when the specified clock was started and the call to ReadTimer. It does this by reading the current clock time and subtracting the start time for that timer from the current time. ReadTimer returns the time since the specified timer was started in 1/100ths of a second as a longint. Once you start a timer, you may read it as many times as you like without affecting the start value. To reinitialize or restart a timer, execute a StartTime call. Before we describe in detail the operation of timer, we use it to measure the speed of passing parameters to procedures by value or by reference in the following program:

```
PROGRAM ParPass;
USES Timer;

Type
  Data500=ARRAY[1..500] of Real;
Var
  j, N : integer;
  W, Z : Data500;

  PROCEDURE Dummy1(X, Y : data500);
  BEGIN    END;

  PROCEDURE Dummy2(VAR X, Y : data500);
  BEGIN    END;

BEGIN
  N := 1000;
  WriteLn('Beginning Dummy1');
  StartTimer(1);
  FOR j := 1 TO N DO Dummy1(W, Z);
  WriteLn('Time in Dummy1 ',(0.01*ReadTimer(1)): 8:2);
  StartTimer(2);
  FOR j := 1 TO N DO Dummy2(W, Z);
  WriteLn('Time in Dummy2 ',(0.01*ReadTimer(2)): 8:2);
END.
```

Note that even though Timer USES Dos, we do not need to define it in our USES statement.

Timer is given in Program Listing 3–1. It is not our intent to go into detail about the construction of Units; this information is available in the Borland reference manual or the books on Turbo such as Swan's. Several points bear comment. The first line declares that a Unit follows; the indicated name is the Unit name under which it will be incorporated in USES statements. The interface section describes any units that are required and the public portion of the routine; the public part is the only portion visible from the outside. Everything below the implementation is hidden from you, including all

---

Program Listing 3–1. Timer Unit

```
Unit Timer;

INTERFACE
USES dos;

FUNCTION ReadTimer(TimerNumber : Integer) : LongInt;
PROCEDURE StartTimer(TimerNumber : Integer);

IMPLEMENTATION

CONST
  StartTime : ARRAY[1..3] OF LongInt = (0, 0, 0);

  FUNCTION ReadTime : LongInt;
  VAR
    hour, minute, second, sec100 : Word;
  BEGIN
    GetTime(hour, minute, second, sec100);
    ReadTime := sec100+100*second+6000*minute+360000*hour;
  END;

  PROCEDURE StartTimer(TimerNumber : Integer);
  BEGIN
    StartTime[TimerNumber] := ReadTime;
  END;

  FUNCTION ReadTimer(TimerNumber : Integer) : LongInt;
  BEGIN
    ReadTimer := ReadTime-StartTime[TimerNumber];
  END;

BEGIN               { required only if initilization next}
    {initialization code would go here}
END.
```

---

data structures, constants, and variables. In short, you can use a variable j as a constant in one Unit, as an array in another, as a string in a third, and as a real in the main. They are all different and isolated, and they never interact.

The implementation is the actual Unit code along with any variables or constants that must be isolated. Any procedures and functions that should be public must be listed in the interface section.

We turn to typed constants, an important, but non-standard Turbo Pascal feature. True constants cannot be changed. Typed constants are declared in the const section, but are actually initialized variables that can be altered at any time. Typed constants are useful for: 1) variable initialization without an initialization section; and 2) long-term storage of numbers without the need to define global variables. A typed constant in a procedure holds its value from call to call, while a local variable does not.

Typed constants can have one subtle side effect. They are initialized only when a program is compiled, not when a program is run. Thus, if you compile a program to memory and run it several times without recompiling it, it might run one way the first time and differently thereafter if the typed constants were altered. If compiled to an EXE file program, the typed constants are effectively reinitialized every time you run the program.

In Timer, we have an array StartTime (array[1. .3] of longint) that is initialized to all zeros. StartTime holds the initial value of each timer after it is started.

3.3 ASCII CODES FOR CHARACTER REPRESENTATIONS

Central to any computer's operation is text and numeric input and display. However, computers cannot directly handle characters; they can only store and manipulate binary numbers. Therefore, some efficient method of character manipulation is essential.

The obvious solution is to assign a binary code to each character. On input, translate the characters into the corresponding binary code and carry out all manipulations and storage on the code. Output uses the inverse translation.

While there are numerous binary representations of the common characters, the most popular text coding scheme for the micro- and minicomputer world is ASCII (pronounced "as-kee two"). ASCII stands for American Standard for Character Information Interchange. ASCII is used by virtually all software in the microcomputer area, except for a few IBM items that use EBCIDIC.

ASCII is a 7-bit code that represents 128 different characters. Since computer memory is byte or 8-bit oriented, the standard way of storing and manipulating characters is one character per byte. The overhead of packing and unpacking parts of characters in different bytes is unacceptably cumbersome. In normal ASCII, the 8th bit is set to zero, but when the 8th bit is included 256 characters can be represented. This extra information is frequently used to represent other non-text characters such as graphics symbols or to assign special significance in word processors.

Table 3–1 shows the complete ASCII code. The numeric codes for each character (Char) are shown in decimal (dec) and hexadecimal (hex) for 7-bit ASCII (i.e., bit 7 set to 0). Also shown are older names for some of the special characters with special data communication meanings. However, you rarely encounter their original use, and they function mainly as labels. The commonly used definitions are given at the bottom. ASCII codes 0 through 26 also go by the names control @ (^@) through control Z (^Z); these widely correspond to the same key strokes on most keyboards. There is no separate ^a to ^z. Turbo accepts ^a to ^z as the corresponding ^A to ^Z.

Carriage return (CR) and line feed (LF) are different characters with different functions. Many printers only advance a line if you send them an LF or only return the print head to the first position for a CR. Thus, they may need both a CR and an LF to start a new line. A CR LF pair is called a carriage return line feed and is frequently written CRLF. The order can be significant, since some terminals erase the current line if they are reversed.

Table 3-1. Complete ASCII Table

Ch		Dec	Hex	Ch	Dec	Hex	Ch	Dec	Hex
NUL	(^@)	0	00	+	43	2B	V	86	56
SOH	(^A)	1	01	,	44	2C	W	87	57
STX	(^B)	2	02	-	45	2D	X	88	58
ETX	(^C)	3	03	.	46	2E	Y	89	59
EOT	(^D)	4	04	/	47	2F	Z	90	5A
ENQ	(^E)	5	05	0	48	30	[	91	5B
ACK	(^F)	6	06	1	49	31	\	92	5C
BEL	(^G)	7	07	2	50	32	]	93	5D
BS	(^H)	8	08	3	51	33	^	94	5E
HT	(^I)	9	09	4	52	34	_	95	5F
LF	(^J)	10	0A	5	53	35	`	96	60
VT	(^K)	11	0B	6	54	36	a	97	61
FF	(^L)	12	0C	7	55	37	b	98	62
CR	(^M)	13	0D	8	56	38	c	99	63
SO	(^N)	14	0E	9	57	39	d	100	64
SI	(^O)	15	0F	:	58	3A	e	101	65
DLE	(^P)	16	10	;	59	3B	f	102	66
DC1	(^Q)	17	11	<	60	3C	g	103	67
DC2	(^R)	18	12	=	61	3D	h	104	68
DC3	(^S)	19	13	>	62	3E	i	105	69
DC4	(^T)	20	14	?	63	3F	j	106	6A
NAK	(^U)	21	15	@	64	40	k	107	6B
SYN	(^V)	22	16	A	65	41	l	108	6C
ETB	(^W)	23	17	B	66	42	m	109	6D
CAN	(^X)	24	18	C	67	43	n	110	6E
EM	(^Y)	25	19	D	68	44	o	111	6F
SUB	(^Z)	26	1A	E	69	45	p	112	70
ESC		27	1B	F	70	46	q	113	71
FS		28	1C	G	71	47	r	114	72
GS		29	1D	H	72	48	s	115	73
RS		30	1E	I	73	49	t	116	74
US		31	1F	J	74	4A	u	117	75
SP		32	20	K	75	4B	v	118	76
!		33	21	L	76	4C	w	119	77
"		34	22	M	77	4D	x	120	78
#		35	23	N	78	4E	y	121	79
$		36	24	O	79	4F	z	122	7A
%		37	25	P	80	50	{	123	7B
&		38	26	Q	81	51	|	124	7C
'		39	27	R	82	52	}	125	7D
(		40	28	S	83	53	~	126	7E
)		41	29	T	84	54	DEL	127	7F
*		42	2A	U	85	55			

BEL = bell; BS = back space; HT = horizontal tab or tab; LF = linefeed; FF = form feed (start of new page); CR = carriage return; ESC = escape; SP = space; DEL = delete.

3.4 CHARACTER CONVERSIONS AND VIDEO OUTPUT

For binary characters sent to the PC's video display, all 256 characters are significant. Table 3–2 shows the displayed characters for all 256 values. This is the character set used in the PC's custom display character generator. We show a program that displays most of the characters after we describe several Pascal functions or procedures: Chr(), Ord(), and Delay().

Chr(argument:byte or integer) is a function that converts a byte or integer type to its equivalent character representation. This is equivalent to generating the character that corresponds to a specific ASCII code. With integers, Chr only uses the lower byte.

Ord(Ch:Char) is a function that returns the ordinal position of a character in a set. For a character, this is its ASCII code. Thus, for characters, Ord and Chr are inverses of each other.

Delay(Time:integer) is a Crt Unit procedure that sets a pause of approximately ($\pm 10\%$) Time milliseconds.

Table 3–2. Complete IBM style character set. To get the ASCII code for a character in decimal, sum the decimal value for the horizontal and vertical positions. For hexadecimal, append the vertical hex digital coordinate to the horizontal hex digit. Reprinted by permission from *Technical Reference from the Personal Computer Hardware Reference Library 6361453* © **1984 by International Business Machines Corporation.**

We now have the tools to display the 256 possible byte values on the video with the following program:

```
PROGRAM dspascii;
USES Crt;

CONST
  BEL = #7;
VAR
  Character : Char;
  j : Integer;

BEGIN                                   {main}
  FOR j := 0 TO 255 DO Write(Chr(j)); {display all characters}
  WriteLn;
  FOR j := 0 TO 255 DO WriteLn(j:3, ' ', Chr(j), 'X');
  WriteLn('String of CTRL Chars.:', BEL, ^G, #7, #1, #2, #3, #4);
END.                                    {main}
```

DspASCII converts and displays most of the 256 byte values as their corresponding characters, although not all print and some do strange things. Add Delay(100) after the first Write (carefully, watch BEGIN/END) so that you can see more clearly what is happening. A Delay after the WriteLn() is useful for sorting out what some of the Ctrl characters do. Note Turbo's flexible but non-standard way of defining or outputting special characters. The # before an ASCII code refers to the character corresponding to that code and is useful in constant declarations. For output, ^G and #7 are equivalent.

As another example of the use of character codes and their manipulations, we show a BCD to Hex character conversion function:

```
FUNCTION Hex2ASCII(m : Integer) : Char; {BCD hex to ASCII}
BEGIN
  IF m < 10 THEN Hex2ASCII := Chr(m+48)
  ELSE Hex2ASCII := Chr(m-10+Ord('A'));
END;
```

This routine accepts an integer [0. .15], and returns the hex character "0". ."9" or "A". ."F". Examine the different conversion modes; all are used.

3.5 KEYBOARD INPUT, VIDEO OUTPUT

Typically text I/O in Pascal are handled with the Read, Readln, Write, and Writeln statements. See your Pascal reference book. Turbo Pascal does not accept commas as variable delimiters. This is bothersome, since input of a comma rather than a space for a string of variables crashes the program.

The keyboard, your primary way of communicating with the computer, sits above a two dimensional X-Y grid of conductive lines that do not touch. If you press a key it connects the X and Y lines intersecting under the key. Information about key strokes is actually determined by applying a voltage sequentially to each of the lines on one coordinate and examining all of the lines on the other coordinate to see whether a voltage has appeared. This scanning of the X and Y lines is so quick that the computer keeps up with the fastest typist. This process generates scan codes with each key generating a unique code. Thus, the Shift or Alt keys actually generate scan codes. This is how QuickBASIC can detect a simultaneous Shift and F combination or a Shift followed by an F for generating menus. Also, left and right Shifts are recognizably different. Turbo does not allow this fine level of distinction, but it does allow detection of most important key strokes including the Ctrl, Alt combinations and special function keys. The operating system and Turbo translate these scan codes into ASCII information that your software can interpret.

To write software that can interpret keyboard information, you have to know something about how your operating system or applications software receives the information. You have already used some of the double strike combinations such as the control keys for editing. In addition to the Ctrl key, the PC keyboard also has a shift and an Alt key as well as the special function keys. With the 256 possible characters that can be represented by a byte, it would have been feasible to encode all possible key combinations as a single byte. In practice, the manufacturers use a two byte scan code to expand the available number of unique key strokes.

Suppose we wished to detect when a single s key was struck. Read and Readln, which must be terminated with a CR, will not work. The solution to detecting single key strokes or special keys is two functions in the Crt Unit:

KeyPressed "Boolean function that is true if a key was pressed, otherwise it is false."

ReadKey "Function that returns the current character in the keyboard. Once called, it waits until a character is ready."

KeyPressed does not tell you what the keyboard character is, only that a new one is waiting to be read. For all single ASCII code characters except ^@ (NUL), ReadKey returns the character itself. For a special function key combination or cursor control key, the keyboard routines return an extended code. For Turbo Pascal this consists of a NUL (0) for the first character, which tells your routine that there is additional information waiting. You then ReadKey the next character, which gives you a unique code for the key or combination. Thus, KeyPressed and ReadKey allow the determination of single keystrokes or a combination of key strokes (e.g., ^F5, Alt F10, or PgLn).

The following program ReadKeys determines the codes and/or character for the key or combination struck. Note that even though NUL should be a ^@, it is converted into the extended code of NUL followed by a ^C. A 'q' allows an escape from this program:

```
PROGRAM ReadKeys;                    {reads-displays scans code}
USES Crt;                            {exit with 'q'}
VAR
  Ch : Char;

BEGIN                                {begin main}
```

Table 3–3. Second Character Codes for Special Keys

Key	Normal	Alt	Ctrl	Shift
F1	; (59)	h (104)	^ (94)	T (84)
F2	< (60)	i (105)	– (95)	U (85)
F3	= (61)	j (106)	' (96)	V (86)
F4	> (62)	k (107)	a (97)	W (87)
F5	? (63)	l (108)	b (98)	X (88)
F6	@(64)	m (109)	c (99)	Y (89)
F7	A (65)	n (110)	d (100)	Z (90)
F8	B (66)	o (111)	e (101)	[(91)
F9	C (67)	p (112)	f (102)	\ (92)
F10	D (68)	q (113)	g (103)	] (93)

Home	G (71)	End	O (79)
Up Arrow	H (72)	Down Arrow	P (80)
Pg Up	I (73)	PgDn	Q (81)
Left Arrow	K (75)	Ins	R (82)
Right Arrow	M (77)	Del	S (83)

```
REPEAT
  REPEAT UNTIL keypressed;         {wait for a key stroke}
  Ch := ReadKey;                   {get first char}
  IF (Ord(Ch) = 0) THEN            {=0 specials only}
    BEGIN                          {begin if}
      Ch := ReadKey;               {if special, get 2nd ch}
      Write('Special key. Extra code: ');
    END;                           {end if}
    WriteLn(Ch, ' ', Ord(Ch):3);   {Display character}
  UNTIL Ch = 'q';                  {repeat until a 'q'}
END.                               {end main}
```

The second codes (character and ASCII) for the special function keys are shown in Table 3–3. Also shown are the second character codes for the cursor and page control keys and Insert and Delete. These keys only pass codes; your program is entirely responsible for what each key stroke does.

3.6 SERIAL DATA TRANSMISSION

In serial data transmission, one sends or receives the information one bit at a time. On reception, a complete data word is then built up by assembling the bits in the proper pattern. Serial transmission has the primary advantage of using only two lines (signal and ground return). The primary disadvantage is the slowness; it takes a minimum of eight transmissions per byte. Serial transmission also has some sticky problems of implementation. We demonstrate these by showing some attempted serial solutions and the reasons for their failure. This leads naturally to a workable solution.

You might first try sending the data out bit by bit and expect the receiver to pick it up. However, the receiver cannot differentiate between eight binary ones sent contiguously and rapidly from a single binary one sent one eighth as fast.

Next you might clock the sender and the receiver with two different clocks that have been adjusted to the same rate and synchronized. Thus, if we send out a new bit every 0.01 sec, the receiver will look for a new bit every 0.01 sec. Although this is better, no matter how closely we initially match the clocks, synchronization is lost with time. Suppose that they are perfectly synchronized initially with frequencies differing only by one part in 10^6. After 24 h, the two clocks are out of phase by 0.086 s or almost 9 digital bits. Also, how would we synchronize them initially, especially when the only connection between them might be data lines? Finally, how does the receiver know when data are being sent? There are only two line states, so the receiver cannot differentiate between no signal and a continuous string of bits that matches the line's idle state. What is needed is a synchronization of the clocks and an indication of when information is on the data line.

The above problems can be handled by using a common clock between the sender and the receiver. This works and belongs to the class of synchronous transfer methods. It requires an extra clock line between the sender and the receiver. It would not work well over a phone line, where we effectively have only one line. As synchronous transfer is uncommon in a PC laboratory environment, we do not explore it further.

Far and away the most common serial communications scheme is asynchronous and uses two similar clocks with one at the transmitter and the other at the receiver. Typically, the data are transmitted in words that are 5, 6, 7, or 8 bits long. To synchronize the transmitter and receiver, the transmitter appends header and trailer bits.

Figure 3–1 shows how this works. Consider transmission of a 7-bit word. The data line is initially in an idle state with no information. We show this as a logic level high. The transmitter now starts sending. Data transmission proceeds as follows:

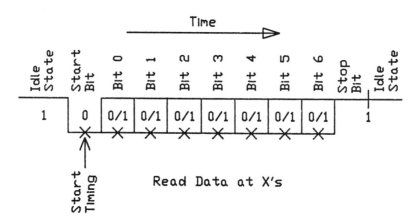

Figure 3–1. Bit patterns used in asynchronous serial data transmission. A 7-bit word with no parity and one stop bit is shown.

(1)   The transmitter tells the receiver to expect a data word by transmitting a low for one clock cycle. This is called a start bit.

(2)   The transmitter then sends out each data bit in order (low bit first), holding each bit for one clock cycle.

(3)   The receiver detects the high-to-low transition of the start bit and thinks a data word may be coming. To insure that this transition was not just line noise, the receiver waits one half of a clock cyle and checks again. If the line is still low, the receiver assumes a valid word is being sent, waits one more clock cycle and reads the first bit. The receiver waits another clock cycle and reads the second bit. This process of waiting and reading is repeated until all 7 bits have been read.

(4)   A safeguard is included at the end of a word transmission. The transmitter puts a high on the line for one, one and a half, or two clock cycles. These are called stop bits.

(5)   The receiver checks for the stop bits. If they are absent, then there is a transfer problem, and the receiver signals a problem to whoever is processing the information.

Notice that the stop bits and idle are the same, a high. Once the transmitter sends the stop bit(s), all it needs to do to send another character is insert a start bit and begin the next word just as before. If no other word is ready, the line remains idle until the transmitter is ready to transmit another word. If we had no stop bit and the last bit of the previous word was a low, we would lack the high-to-low transition needed to synchronize the receiver.

Note several points. First, the sender and receiver must agree in advance on the length of the data word. If the receiver expects 5 bits and gets 8, it loses the last 3 bits and gets confused about the start of the next word. Similarly, if the sender sends a 5-bit word and the receiver expects 8 bits, the transmitter could begin sending another word while the receiver is still collecting what it thinks is the first one.

Also, we ignored the asynchronous nature of the two clocks. How close must their frequencies be? The above sequence works as long as the receiver does not drift so far as to sample an adjacent clock cycle. By starting at the middle of the start bit up to one half a clock cycle of drift is acceptable. For an 8-bit word this is one half cycle in 9 or about 5%. The situation is actually a little worse, but clocks within 3% of each other give no errors. Since the clocks are usually crystal controlled and agree to better than 0.01%, clock timing errors are not a problem.

If the clock cycle is one bit wide, how did we manage to wait half a cycle before sampling the middle of the start bit? Actually, the master clock cycle is 16, 32, or 64 times shorter than the bit clock. One timing bit is obtained by counting 16, 32, or 64 master cycles. To get to the middle of a bit, half that number is counted. This means that we might not sample exactly at the middle of the cycle, which is one of the reasons the 5% figure above was a little optimistic.

Serial transmission and reception are complicated, and old serial communications systems might take up an entire computer board. The enormous need for such technology led semiconductor manufacturers to make single LSI chips that have both send and receive functions. These chips also include error checking and error detection. These features are either selectable by setting control inputs or, if tied into a computer bus, are software programmable. These chips are called USARTs (Universal Synchronous Asynchronous Receiver Transmitter) or, if they do not support synchronous transmission, UARTs. In spite of the complexity of thousands of transistors, they sell for a few dollars. IBM PC-type computers use a programmable USART.

We turn now to error detection. Serial data transmission is notoriously unreliable. In particular, bad phone lines and noise can corrupt data. Long wires in plants or even electrically noisy laboratories can invalidate data transmission. UARTs provide simple but powerful error detection utilizing **parity**. A digital word has even parity if it has an even number of 1s and odd parity if it has an odd number.

For error detection the UART adds an extra parity bit to every word transmitted. If even parity is set, the UART adjusts the extra bit so that the total number of bits in the word plus the parity bit is even. If odd parity is specified, the total number of ones is set odd. For example, the 5-bit word 01111 is expanded to the 6-bit 101111 for odd parity or to 001111 for even parity.

Again, the sender and receiver must agree in advance on the parity. A mismatch leads to accurate data being flagged as erroneous. Parity detects only odd numbers of errors; even bit errors are missed. A parity test detects but does not correct errors. More complex error correction schemes can correct one or multiple bit errors, but they are not widely used in a laboratory environment and are not discussed further. The common response to a parity error is for the receiver to request that the transmitter send the offending line until the error disappears.

We return now to transmission rate. Serial transmission rates are specified in **baud** where a baud is a bit per second. The rates are standardized so that different pieces of equipment can talk to each other. The most common rates are 110, 300, 1200, 2400, 4800, 9600, and 19200 baud.

A 110 baud Teletype drive with 1-start bit, 8-data bits, and 2-stop bits (11 total) sends 10 characters per second. Two stop bits here are necessitated by the Teletype's mechanical nature. Inherently faster electronic devices typically use 1 stop bit. Transmission rates to printers, terminals, and computers are usually higher (>1200), although printers must have provisions for stopping data flow when the printer gets behind in its printing.

DOS limits the PC to 9,600 baud maximum, which is >1000 characters per second. However, by directly addressing the hardware, PCs can run at >100,000 baud. All of the UART functions are programmable including baud rate, parity, word length, and number of stop bits. We describe briefly the external DOS MODE command that is used to program the UART. MODE command is actually much more versatile and can be used to vary the display, to reroute data from one device to another, and so on. GWBASIC permits even greater control than does DOS. See the manuals for details. The command form is:

```
MODE COMn:baud[,parity[,databits[,stopbits[,p]]]]
```

Items in square brackets are optional, but if a later option is selected, the earlier ones must be explicitly given. COMn is the number of the communications port, which is 1 or 2 on a standard PC or up to 4 on an AT class machine. Baud is the baud rate and can assume 110, 300, 600, 1200, 2400, 4800, and 9600; either the entire baud value or the one or two nonzero leading digits may be used. Parity is optional with e (even), o (odd), and n (none) where the parity bit is omitted completely; default is even parity. Databits is optional and can be 7 or 8 (default 7). Stopbits is optional (default 2 for 110 baud and 1 otherwise). The p option instructs the system to keep trying if the serial device does not respond. If p is omitted, the system gives a system error (time out) if the device does not respond after a fixed period. The following example:

```
MODE COM1:24,n,8
```

programs the #1 communications port, COM1, to 2400 baud, no parity, and 8-bit words. The default values of 1 stop bit and "do not retry after a time out" are used.

The above description has been purposefully vague about the electrical details of serial data transmission. UARTs are TTL compatible and use positive true logic. Thus, data directly out of the UART matches your ASCII table. UARTs have poor drive capabilities, cannot drive long lines, and the 1.2V minimum difference between TTL true and false makes TTL lines very susceptible to noise pick up and signal corruption.

To avoid the problems of TTL transmission, the RS-232 serial transmission standard uses special driver chips to convert the TTL levels to RS-232 levels. The boosted levels are increased and also inverted. Thus, a true is −3 to −20 while a false is +3 to +20 V. This is a negative true logic. RS-232 is much less susceptible to noise because of the 6 V difference between the true and false states. Negative true logic introduces no problems as long as the receiver circuitry shifts the levels back to TTL levels and inverts the logic so that the receiving UART sees positive true TTL logic. Again, special ICs make this conversion. The biggest problem is remembering that transmitted signal lines are negative true logic.

We now introduce several serial communications terms. Above we have discussed only a single transmitter and receiver. This arrangement is called **simplex** communications. For two-way communication there are two bidirectional forms. In a **full duplex** mode each device transmits to the other on its own separate line. This could take four lines if each transmitter-receiver circuit is separate or three if both circuits share a common ground or signal return. In **half duplex**, both transmitters and receivers share the same pair of lines and only one transmitter may talk at a time. Also, the receivers always listen to their own transmitters.

Full duplex is the most versatile and efficient method of serial communication. Both ends can, in principle, simultaneously transmit and receive, and there is never any conflict over who can speak.

Figure 3–2 shows a configuration that allows examination of the individual bits in serial data transmission. The odd wiring on the PC's COM port is a quirk of the communications standard. The RS-232 serial port has safeguards against sending data unless the receiver is ready. Handshake lines control information flow. Since the oscilloscope does not satisfy the PC's handshake protocol, the PC would never send unless you fooled it into thinking that the oscilloscope was ready. The wiring takes the PC line that says the PC is ready (DTR or Data Terminal Ready) and feeds it back into the PCs input lines that must be satisfied. In this way the PC thinks the oscilloscope is ready whenever the PC itself is ready. We return in a later chapter to details of RS-232 handshake lines.

Experiment 3–1. In this experiment, you explore serial data output.

3.7 PARALLEL I/O

Serial data transmission is very nice because it requires few lines and works over long distances. In the minimum implementation, two wires are required in half duplex (one ground and one signal line) and three in full duplex (one ground, one send, and one receive line). However, its serial nature makes it rather slow. Even the PC's maximum 9600 baud (about 1000 characters per second) is nowhere near CPU speeds, which can exceed 200,000 bytes per second.

To overcome the speed limitation of serial transmission, many devices receive and transmit data directly to the CPU in full 8-, 16-, or 32-bit wide parallel chunks. For example, the UART interface to the CPU is all byte wide. Clearly, for speed, parallel transmission is the interface method of choice.

PCs have a byte wide parallel printer I/O port with control lines to regulate printer-computer data flow. Its function is limited, and we do not consider it further.

In later chapters we show parallel interfacing with a Data Translation 2800 series interface board. For the moment we consider the general purpose Intel 8255A programmable parallel port. We first discuss the CPU ports on the 80X86 processors.

3.7.1 Ports

The 8088 and 80X86 CPUs have 2^{16} possible different byte or word wide parallel input and output ports. Only a few are used in any system. The CPU sends the necessary control signals to read/write to these ports, and suitable I/O circuitry decodes the address for each device and inputs or outputs the data.

The actual machine language instructions for port input and output are INPUT and OUTPUT, which we discuss later. In GWBASIC, you find two instructions:

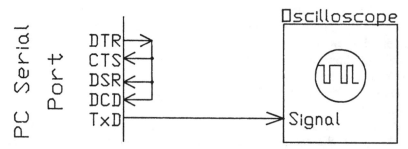

Figure 3–2. Serial connections for viewing characters on an oscilloscope.

```
OUT port, byte
INP port, byte
```

where port is a port number (0–65535) and byte is a byte. Functionally, BASIC's instructions are virtually identical to the machine language instruction.

Turbo Pascal deviates from this instruction style with predefined port arrays:

```
PORT [address]          "Byte port with word address [0. .65535]."
PORTW [address]         "Word port with word address [0. .65535]."
```

where PORT and PORTW are byte or 16-bit wide input and output ports, and address is a 16-bit address. To read from a port, assign a variable to the specific port address; to write to a port, assign a value to the specific array element. For example:

```
PORT[3333]:=5;          {output 5 decimal to port 3333}
UART_Status:=PORT[$75]; {Read port $75 into variable}
```

There are several important points. The 80X86 CPU permits reads and writes to memory locations that contain no memory or to ports that have no circuitry. Therefore, an erroneous read or write gives no warning. Second, to be able to talk to any device on the PC's bus, you must know its addresses and the protocol that it uses for communicating with the CPU. There are no device standards; you must extract this information from the manufacturer's literature.

3.7.2 Bit Level Operations

In interfacing, you frequently must isolate, test, or manipulate individual bits or portions of binary numbers. Turbo allows flexible operations on values of type shortint, byte, integer, word, and longint with the following:

```
NOT (var)           "Bitwise NOT the bits of variable or constant var."
var1 AND var2       "Bitwise AND variables or constants var1 and var2."
var1 OR var2        "Bitwise OR variables or constants var1 and var2."
var1 XOR var2       "Bitwise XOR variables or constants var1 and var2."
var SHR N           "Shift right by N bits variable or constant var. Shift a zero
                    into the leftmost bit with each shift."
var SHL N           "Shift left by N bits variable or constant var. Shift a zero into
                    the rightmost bit with each shift."
LO (var)            "Extract the low 8 bits (0 to 7) of word variable or constant
                    var."
HI (var)            "Extract the high 8 bits of word variable or constant var."
```

Suppose that word1 and word2 are word variables equal to $3f07 and $0113, respectively. The following operations yield:

```
X:= HI(word1);              {Assigns X the value $3F}
Y:= LO(word2);              {Assigns Y the value $13}
Z:= word1 AND word2;        {Assigns Z the value $0103}
Q:= word1 OR word2;         {Assigns Q the value $3F17}
R:= word2 SHR 4;            {Assigns R the value $0011}
T:= word1 SHL 1;            {Assigns T the value $7E0E}
```

In particular the AND operation is used for isolating individual bits. To examine bit 3 of a byte variable, byte1:

```
Mask:= $04;             {set up mask that isolates bit 3}
Z:= byte1 AND Mask;     {isolate bit}
```

The AND operation zeroes out all but bit 3, which is left unchanged. If Z is 0 then bit 3 of byte1 was 0. If Z is nonzero, then bit 3 is 1. Zeroing or hiding unwanted bits is called **masking**, and the template for selecting the bit or bits is a **mask**. Masking is extraordinarily important in interfacing. A more complex example is the conversion and display of integers or words as hex and binary:

```
PROGRAM HexBin;
TYPE
  str16 = STRING[16];
VAR
  w : Word;
  j : Integer;

  FUNCTION Hex2ASCII(m : Integer) : Char;
    {BCD hex to Ascii char  --    taken from above}

  FUNCTION binary(k : Integer) : str16; {integer to Ascii string}
    {intentionally left out--see problem}

  FUNCTION hex(n : Integer) : str16; {integer to hex character}
  VAR
    L, k : Integer;
    tmp : str16;
  BEGIN
    tmp := '';
    FOR L := 3 DOWNTO 0 DO
      tmp := tmp+(Hex2ASCII((n SHR (4*L)) AND $000F));
    hex := tmp;
  END;

BEGIN                               {main}
  w := $73fb;
  WriteLn('Decimal=', w:7, binary(w):18, hex(w):6);
  j := -32100;
  WriteLn('Decimal=', j:7, binary(j):18, hex(j):6);
END.                                {main}
```

HexBin uses the procedure Hex2ASCII given earlier. The hex integer to hexadecimal string display conversion routine uses shifting/masking to isolate each BCD nibble. The final hex string is built from left to right. For the first character, we shift the integer right twelve times to place the first BCD nibble in the 4 rightmost bits followed by an AND with $0F to mask all but these 4 bits. Hex2ASCII then generates the character. By setting up a loop and concatenating the hex digits, we build the four digit hex number.

Note the use of both integer and word types. Word types will not accept negative integers, and integers will not accept hex numbers greater than $7fff. Turbo's type checking does allow free interchange of words and integers.

3.7.3 8255A Programmable Parallel Chip
The Intel 8255A is a programmable 24-line parallel I/O chip. It is divided into three byte wide ports A, B, and C. Any port can be set as input or output. Further, the C port can be divided into nibbles and each can be set independently as input or output. The 8255A can also be configured in a variety of ways with automatic handshakes with devices, CPU interrupt when data are available, and bidirectional three state data transfer. PCs generally use several board level 8255As for interfacing to different devices. For simplicity's sake, we consider only the simple Mode 0 parallel I/O mode.

Figure 3–3 is a schematic representation of the 8255A. It has four write registers and three read registers as shown in Table 3–4. The read register reads data from ports configured for input. The write registers are used to write to output ports, and the control register sets the I/O configuration and handshake modes. 8255A interfaces generally use ports for addressing the registers. The interface has a base address to which the register addresses are added. Thus, if the base address is $3f0 then register 0 is at $3f0, register 1 at $3f1, register 2 at $3f2, and register 3 at $3f3. Read and write ports can have the same address since input and output are completely independent operations.

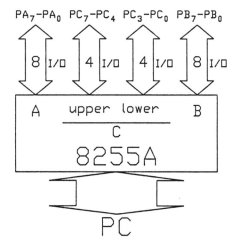

Figure 3–3. Configuration of 8255A programmable parallel I/O chip.

Table 3–4. Input/Output Register Functions in 8255A

Register Number	Read Function	Write Function
0	Read from A	Write to A
1	Read from B	Write to B
2	Read from C	Write to C
3	No function	Write to control register

The 8255A has three possible modes of operation. We only consider Mode 0, which basically uses the ports as simple parallel input and output ports. When used as outputs, the data are latched (i.e., held) until updated by another output.

Figure 3–4 shows the control register configuration. To set the ports to different values, bit 7 is set to 1 and the remaining bits are assigned to give the desired configuration. For example, using mode 0 to set Port A to input, port B to output, port C (lower nibble) to input, and port C (upper nibble) to output we build up the following word:

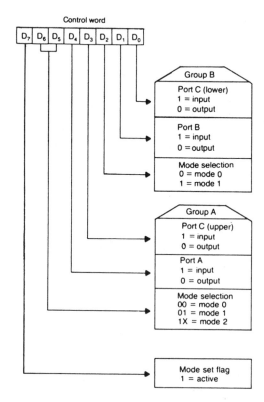

Figure 3–4. Bit definitions for the 8255A control register. Reprinted by permission of Intel Corporation, Copyright/Intel Corporation 1988.

```
Port Setting word = 1 00 10 001₂ =  10010001₂ = $91
```

Thus, for an 8255A base address (i.e., register 0) of Base8255, the 8255A is set to the above combination with:

```
Port [ Base8255+ 3 ] := $91;
```

The +3 comes from the control register being 3 above the base. Now to output 7 to Port B and read Port A, we would:

```
Port [ Base8255+ 1 ] := 7;  { output to B  }
Data := Port [ Base8255];   { input from A }
```

The following type definitions and procedure allow simple setting of the 8255A I/O configuration. Since Base8255A is a typed constant, it is initialized. However, if you have more than one 8255A at different addresses, you can change Base8255 on the fly and use the same procedures.

```
CONST
  Base8255: Word = $300;              {device and board dependent}
TYPE
  Flag8255IO = (Input, Output);
  bit = 0..1;
  addbit = 0..7;

  PROCEDURE Set8255IO(AIO, BIO, ClowerIO, CupperIO : Flag8255IO);
  VAR
    IOcontrol : Byte;
    Abit, Bbit, Clowerbit, Cupperbit : Integer;
  BEGIN                           {initializes using Mode 0 only}
    IOcontrol := $80;                 {set high bit for IO option}
    IF AIO = Input THEN Abit := 1 ELSE Abit := 0;
    IF BIO = Input THEN Bbit := 1 ELSE Bbit := 0;
    IF ClowerIO = Input THEN Clowerbit := 1 ELSE Clowerbit : = 0;
    IF CupperIO = Input THEN Cupperbit := 1 ELSE Cupperbit : = 0;
    IOcontrol := IOcontrol OR (Abit SHL 4) OR (Bbit SHL 1) OR
    (Cupperbit SHL 3) OR (Clowerbit);
  END;
```

With this procedure, the following statement configures the 8255A with A, B, Clower as input and Cupper as output:

```
Set8255IO(Input, Input, Input, Output);
```

An important function of output ports is setting single control line bits. If one of these bits is part of an entire nibble or word that also uses other bits for independent functions, there is a problem since a port or nibble output changes all bits. You could avoid this problem by keeping a copy of the current output. Then to change one bit, alter that bit in the copy, and output the revised copy. The 8255A simplifies this task with another control instruction that allows setting or resetting a single bit in Port C. Use the following control word:

Bits	Significance and Value
0	Value to set output bit to (0=0 and 1=1)
3, 2, 1	Bit address number to set or reset (000=bit0. .111=bit7)
6, 5, 4	Don't Care
7	Control bit for bit instruction (must be 0)

Thus, writing the binary pattern 00000110 to the control register resets (zeroes) bit 3 of Port C. The 8255A has no error reporting when you carry out completely meaningless instructions. For example, you could "set" a bit in Port C, which is configured for input. However, no bit is actually set. The following procedure simplifies altering C bits:

```
PROCEDURE Set8255C(bitadd : addbit; data : bit);
{Change bitadd of port C to data}
BEGIN
  Port[Base8255+3] := (bitadd SHL 1) OR data;
END;
```

With this procedure, the following code sets to 1 bit 7 of Port C:

```
Set8255C(7, 1);
```

The types give some error checking to prevent inadvertently passing illegal arguments. Also the use of input and output as parameters improves readability and reduces the chances of errors over numeric arguments. However, for error checking to work, Range Checking must be on, either in the compiler options or with a {$R+} at the beginning of the program.

3.7.4 Examples of Parallel Input and Output

We now demonstrate several examples of the use of parallel I/O. Figure 3–5 shows a simple parallel interface for driving a light emitting diode display (LED) with one LED per output line. An open collector inverter drives each LED. When the input is high the transistor is on, and current flows from the +5V supply through a current limiting resistor to the LED. Thus, an on LED indicates a high input.

Figure 3–6 shows a parallel interface for a quad two-input NAND logic gate checker. One byte wide port sets the eight inputs and another port is used to read the NAND ouputs.

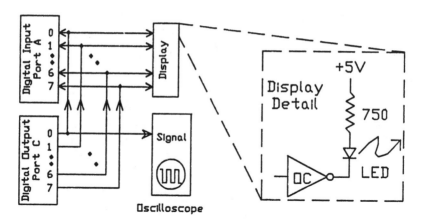

Figure 3–5. Simple test of parallel I/O ports with one output port connected to an input port. The scope shows the speed of output.

A more interesting parallel interface problem is presented by the GE/RCA/Intersil 7226 Universal counter/timer/period meter demonstrator kit. This has an eight-digit display and measures: total counts, frequency (to 10 MHz with 0.01, 0.1, 1, or 10 s counting periods), periods (0.1 μs resolution), and ratios of two input frequencies. Features are set manually, but acquisition can be triggered externally (maximum rate ≈2 Hz).

The board uses a multiplexed display in which each digit is on only for a small fraction of the time. Each digit is enabled or turned on sequentially for ≈200–300 μs. All eight digits are turned on 500 times per second leaving the eye with the impression of a continuous display. Multiplexing greatly simplifies display wiring, but not interfacing.

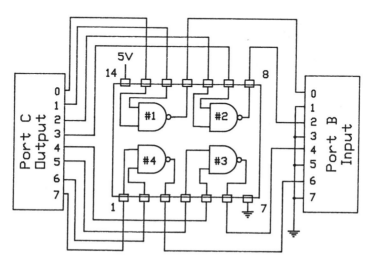

Figure 3–6. Parallel port based logic gate tester for a 7400 quad NAND gate. The view of the IC is from the top.

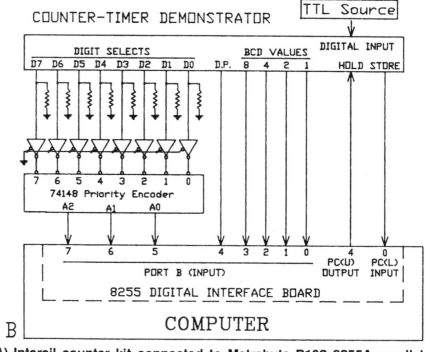

Figure 3–7. (A) Intersil counter kit connected to Metrabyte P102 8255A parallel card via a prototype bread boarded interface and a Metrabyte patch board. (B) Schematic of PC to counter interface. Pull down resistors (1K) insure reliable operation of the display and digital interface. A 74LS240 hex inverter buffers and inverts the digit lines for the encoder. From Xu, Demas, and Grubb (1989). Adapted with permission from the *Journal of Chemical Education.*

For interfacing, the board outputs the multiplexed display lines (eight active high lines for enabling each seven segment display and the decimal point indicator) plus the BCD code of the currently enabled LED. Thus, as each digit is turned on, the line for that digit goes high, the BCD code for the digit is placed on the BCD outputs, and—if the decimal point directly to the right of the digit is enabled—the decimal point line is set high. Reading these lines as the counter sweeps the display, allows the current digit to be read.

The interface seems simple. Use a byte wide input port to monitor the eight digit-enable lines. When the digit to be read is enabled, read the BCD code and the decimal point through a second port. In fast assembly language this is a viable configuration. In a slower high-level language, there is a problem. Since each digit is enabled only 200–300 μs at a time, the digit might change to another digit by the time you read the BCD code; this causes you to read the wrong digit. A word wide input port would solve the problem by allowing the reading in of the eight digit enables, the decimal point, and the BCD code simultaneously, but we must make do with an 8-bit port. We adopted the solution shown in Figure 3–7 where all necessary information is encoded into a single byte.

The encoding is done with a 74148 priority encoder, which has eight input lines (0. .7) and gives a digit code for the line pulled low that has the highest priority (the highest priority is 7, the lowest 0). We do not use the priority encoding feature, since only one digit enable line is active at a time. However, what the 74148 does is output the 3-bit inverse of the address of any single line pulled low. This 3-bit code, the decimal point bit, and the 4-bit BCD code fit exactly into a byte input port. Now when you read the port, if the proper digit is enabled, you have the decimal and BCD information for that digit. However, your software must extract all the information from a single byte. Since the priority encoder requires a low on the active input line and the counter gives a high, all digit enable lines are inverted before the priority encoder. Figure 3–7 shows the counter kit and a rat's nest (but fully functional) prototype breadboarded interface.

We now show how to synchronize the counter. On its own, it more or less begins a new counting or conversion on finishing the last one. If your reading of the counter is asynchronous with the conversion, you risk reading some of the digits from the old conversion and some from the new, which for a changing signal is a disaster. To overcome this problem, the counter allows external control of conversions and monitoring of the state of the conversions with HOLD and STORE.

If HOLD is high, no new conversions are made on frequency and period measurements. If HOLD is dropped (1→0), the counter triggers and begins making conversions. If HOLD is left at 0, then the counter runs continuously. When a complete counting period is finished, the counter latches its output, updates the display, and drops STORE to 0 for 40 ms to indicate that a new reading is available. To block further conversions, raise HOLD to 1. HOLDing the counter blocks further conversions, but the display continues to show the last reading, which you read at your leisure. To initiate another acquisition, drop HOLD to 0, and repeat the monitoring process.

Experiment 3–2 – 3–4. Here you input and output data on a parallel interface and demonstrate the speed of parallel I/O using Pascal.

Experiment 3–5. You wire and test a logic gate tester.

Experiment 3–6. You wire and test a parallel interface to a digital counter. You write software to control the counter and read the display.

3.8 FILTERS, PIPES, AND STANDARD INPUT AND OUTPUT

You have used a number of DOS commands and other programs that display output. Typically, output has been routed to the default output device, the video. However, frequently it would be useful to send this information directly to disk files. For example, creating a master directory of all your files by writing them directly to a disk file is much more convenient than printing and retyping them with an editor.

DOS 2.0 and later allows rerouting of input and output. The "standard" output of a program or command can be sent to other devices or to files. Also, the standard output of one program can be used as the standard input of another, which allows chaining programs to do quite delightful things. The linking or connecting of programs in this fashion is called **piping**. A program that modifies a stream of data as it passes through the program is a **filter**. We use the DOS external filter programs FIND, MORE, and SORT to explore pipes and filters. More importantly, we show you how to build your own filters in Turbo Pascal.

There are four special symbols that are used with filters and pipes. These symbols and a brief description of the function of each is given below:

|	Pipe output of the program on the left into the program on the right.
>	Take standard output from the left and feed it into the file on the right. This user-entered character has nothing to do with the DOS prompt.
<	Take standard output from the right and input it into the program or file on the left.
>>	Append standard output from the left into the file on the right.

We first show the use of simple standard I/O redirection. To create a disk file, SYSDIR, on B that contained the system disk directory, merely direct the output of the DIR command into SYSDIR with:

```
A> DIR > B:SYSDIR
```

While on A, execute this command with a disk in B. Both disks whirr, but no directory appears on the screen. However, there is a new file SYSDIR on B. TYPE it. It looks exactly like the display that you would have gotten on the screen with DIR alone. The output of DIR was redirected to the new destination, the file SYSDIR. If SYSDIR did not exist on B, it was created. If SYSDIR existed, any material in it was erased before the current data was added.

To add material to a file, use the append redirection command >>. Replace the disk in A, and execute the following command:

```
A> DIR >> B:SYSDIR
```

The >> indicates that the standard output from DIR on drive A is appended to SYS-DIR in B. After executing this command, SYSDIR contains the full listing of both directories, with the second appended to the first.

The output of many programs is standard output and can be redirected. The earlier shown dialogue between the compiler and linker was actually recorded by redirecting their outputs into a file that was then read into our word processor. We merely typed "BC > BCOMDIALOG". The compiler executed and all output was put in COMPDIA-LOG. Since no compiler output was displayed, we had to note beforehand the compiler messages so that we could respond correctly.

3.8.1   MORE Filter

The simple MORE filter displays a single screen full of material at a time, stops, asks for "MORE?", and lists the next full screen after you strike a key. The standard output of other commands and programs can be redirected into MORE. For example, to type an ASCII program file WORDCONT.PAS to the video and pause after every screen, use:

```
A> TYPE WORDCONT | MORE
```

The | stands for pipe. The output of TYPE is piped or run into the input of the program MORE. Since MOREs output is not directed into a new file, its output is to the default device, the video. MORE fills the screen and waits for a key strike. The special pipe symbol is required in place of > or >>. If we had used >, DOS would have written the data into the file MORE.

Use MORE to list a long directory. It is functionally similar to DIR/P. MORE works with almost any kind of program that writes like a typewriter to the screen. For example, BASIC and FORTRAN compiler output can be stopped by MORE so that long error message listings do not scroll off the screen too fast to read.

MORE will not work with everything. Turbo Pascal 4 and 5 do not give output to MORE if you use the Crt Unit. With Crt, the display completely bypasses the DOS routines that generate standard output, and MORE never sees it.

3.8.2   SORT Filter

SORT is the DOS filter for sorting ("alphabetizing") files or input. While not very flexible, it is still useful for simple applications. To sort the SYSDIR file above by file name use:

```
B> SORT < SYSDIR > SRTDIR
```

This command says take SYSDIR as standard input for the program SORT and output it to the file SRTDIR. The odd organization of this command is used to prevent confusion; we could not have the file name SYSDIR first, or DOS would try to interpret it as a command. After this SORT, SRTDIR might look like:

```
              17 File(s)       226304 bytes free
       Directory of   C:\
       Volume in drive C has no label
       1                      835    2-06-86    4:22p
       ASSIGN   COM           896    1-07-84   12:52p
       C        BAT             7    2-17-84    6:10a
       COMMAND  COM         15957    6-05-85   12:00p
       CONFIG   SYS           128    2-16-84   10:07p
       DIRECT                 753    2-06-86    4:25p
       FILTERS              5504    2-05-86   11:13p
       FILTERS  BAK         5248    2-05-86   11:11p
       SDL      DOC         2048   10-09-84    9:41a
       SORT     EXE         1632    6-05-85   12:00p
       ST       DOC         1152    1-14-87   12:05a
       SYSDIR                  0    2-06-86    4:40p
       WS       COM        21376    6-30-85    7:17p
       WSMSGS   OVR        29056    4-12-83   12:14a
       WSOVLY1  OVR        41216    4-12-83   12:15a
       WSRAM    BAT          384    1-07-84   12:50p
```

Without modifiers, sorting starts in the first column. Files are sorted "alphabetically" by ASCII code, which yields some funny-looking sorts. DIRs last line becomes the first line after the sort since the ASCII code for a blank is numerically smaller than any other printable character. Also, numbers occur before letters and capital letters before lowercase ones.

SORT has two modifiers (switches) that increase its usefulness. Their format is:

```
SORT/+n     Sort starting on the nth column.
SORT/B      Sort in inverse order.
```

In the first, sorting starts at the nth column and ignores earlier columns. The "/+" must both be present. In the second, the sort is done backward or in reverse "alphabetic" order. To sort SYSDIR by file extension rather than by file name, use:

```
B> A:SORT/+10 < SYSDIR > SRT10DIR
```

because the extension starts on the tenth column of each line. The result is:

```
       SYSDIR                  0    2-06-86    4:40p
       DIRECT                753    2-06-86    4:25p
       1                     835    2-06-86    4:22p
       FILTERS              5504    2-05-86   11:13p
              17 File(s)     226304 bytes free
       WSRAM    BAK          384    1-07-84   12:48p
       FILTERS  BAK         5248    2-05-86   11:11p
```

```
C          BAT          7     2-17-84    6:10a
WSRAM      BAT        384     1-07-84   12:50p
ASSIGN     COM        896     1-07-84   12:52p
COMMAND    COM      15957     6-05-85   12:00p
WS         COM      21376     6-30-85    7:17p
ST         DOC       1152     1-14-87   12:05a
SDL        DOC       2048    10-09-84    9:41a
SORT       EXE       1632     6-05-85   12:00p
  Volume in drive C has no label
WSMSGS     OVR      29056     4-12-83   12:14a
WSOVLY1    OVR      41216     4-12-83   12:15a
CONFIG     SYS        128     2-16-84   10:07p
  Directory of  C:\
```

All files with the same extensions are grouped together. " Directory of C:\" is last because y comes after S. There is no order in the first field and, with DOS SORT, no way to do a secondary ordering. The UNIX SORT and its PC implementations are much more powerful but not as easy to use.

Another way in which we could do this would be as follows:

B> **A:SORT < SYSDIR | MORE**

which reads: use SYSDIR as standard input for SORT then take the standard output of this and pass it through the MORE filter for viewing. Again, | indicates that the ouput of SORT is a piped program, not a file. Other applications could sort files by size. Unfortunately, SORT is not powerful enough to sort by date. Why?

After using pipes, you may see some leftover garbage:

```
%PIPE1     $$$          0     2-06-86    4:42p
%PIPE2     $$$          0     2-06-86    4:42p
```

These are temporary filter files. Since they now have zero size, they do not waste disk space. However, they have size during the filtering. Thus, piping or filtering can fail if the necessary space for the temporary files is unavailable.

3.8.3   FIND Filter

FIND is a primitive search routine. It searches for exact string matches, but lacks provisions for wild cards. The forms are:

```
FIND "string" filename1 filename2 ..
FIND/V "string" filename1 filename2 ..
FIND/C "string" filename1 filename2 ..
FIND/N "string" filename1 filename2 ..
```

The first form lists all the lines in filename1, filename2, and so on, that contain an exact match to the quoted string. To search several files, separate each file name by one or more spaces. Thus,

```
B>  A:FIND " COM " SYSDIR SYSDIR2
```

lists all lines in SYSDIR and SYSDIR2 that contain " COM " (i.e., all COM files). The blanks both before and after COM insure that we only match COM files. If we leave out the blanks, we also find lines with COMMAND and DATACOM, that have COM in them. A search for "com" gives no matches in SYSDIR; there are no lower case "com"s.

The /V switch displays only those lines that do not contain the string. Thus, if you wanted to exclude all the COM files from your listing, type:

```
B>  A:FIND/V " COM " SYSDIR
```

The /C option gives only a count of the number of lines that match. You could, for example, count the number of COM files in SYSDIR with:

```
B>  A:FIND/C " COM " SYSDIR
```

The /N assigns line numbers to each line and lists them along with the output. This is useful in finding lines in the file later.

Multiple switches can be set in one command. Thus:

```
B>  A:FIND/V/N " COM " SYSDIR
```

lists all lines that do not have a " COM " in them with line numbers.

Remember two things. First, if you do not specify an output file, the video is used. Second, you can pipe filters together to accomplish more complex processes. For example, to sort SYSDIR without the descriptive information about drive, volume, name, and so on, use the following command to remove the lines with "Dir", " Vol", and "File(s)":

```
FIND/V "Dir" SYSDIR|FIND/V " Vol"|FIND/V "File(s)"|SORT>CLEAN
```

The result is put into a file CLEAN. This simply says: 1) find all lines in SYSDIR that do not contain "Dir"; 2) use the output of this filter as input for FIND that removes all lines containing "Vol"; 3) use the output of this filter as input for FIND, which removes all lines containing "File(s)"; and 4) sort alphabetically this output and place it in a file CLEAN. Clearly, such complex pipes and filters demand the use of batch files with dummy arguments.

3.8.4 Filters and Redirection in Turbo Pascal

Turbo Pascal 3.0 and later provide for writing programs that read or write standard input and output. In short, you can write your own filters, which gives you enormous power. We show how you can write and use a Turbo Pascal program that accepts standard input and output. One of these filters converts the ubiquitous WordStar word processor files into ASCII files. Another determines the distribution of letters in a file and plots the character frequency distribution as a simple bar graph.

As long as you are not using the Crt Unit, Turbo Pascal 4/5 programs accept standard input and output directly, and I/O redirection could not be simpler. One merely compiles the program to an .EXE file and uses the standard I/O redirection with the EXE file.

The following program reads one text file and writes it to another without any change:

```
PROGRAM CopyFile;   {Copies one file to another with I/O
                    redirection.  Program must be EXE file}
VAR
  CH : Char;
BEGIN
  WHILE NOT EoF DO
    BEGIN
       Read(CH);            {Read character from input stream}
       Write(CH);           {Write that character back out}
    END;
  Write(^Z);                {Terminate file with EoF marker}
END.
```

The WHILE statement checks a Boolean EoF before each character read. EoF is a test for the end of file marker in the file that tells the operating system when the end of file is about to be reached. The EoF is a ^Z, and you should terminate your output file similarly with a ^Z.

All we have done is redirect the normal Input and Output routines so that they handle standard input and output. The complex disk file reading/writing is reduced to simple reads and writes.

Character filters work only with ASCII text files that contain the ^Z EoF marker. Binary program and data files can have a ^Z as part of the data stream, which would be erroneously interpreted as an end of file.

There is a potential minefield in filters. Sometimes you want to replace a file with its filtered form. It is tempting to filter a file onto itself.

>**WFILTER < inputfile > inputfile**

This might work—for a while. What happens is that the filter is working on both the input and output simultaneously. If the writing advances faster than the reading through the file, you overwrite data before it is read and can trash an entire file. It is essential to filter into a temporary file and then copy it back to the original after verifying that the copy is correct. Do not do it automatically in a batch file. If something goes wrong, the filtered file may be created with a zero length, and when you copy back to the original, you lose the original.

CopyFile is rather uninteresting, but slight modifications make it quite useful. We turn to a WordStar-to-ASCII conversion filter. While the standard ASCII codes are all less than 128, WordStar and many other word processors embed funny control codes and odd character sequences or otherwise modify the characters. Attempts to TYPE or print these files from DOS give very strange output. WordStar sets the high bit of the last character of each word and the end of line carriage returns (end of paragraph CRs do not have the high bit set). By a simple modification of CopyFile, we can do a WordStar-to-ASCII conversion. Merely define several new constants:

```
CONST
  MaskHighBit = $7F;
  CR = #13;
  LF = #10;
  TAB = #9;
```

and replace the Write(CH) with:

```
      CH := Chr(Ord(CH) AND MaskHighBit);
      IF (Ord(CH) > 31) OR (CH IN [CR, LF, TAB])
      THEN Write(CH);
```

The first line masks the unwanted bit with the familiar AND. The conditional IF discards all remaining non-printable characters except CR, LF and TAB. Clearly, by changing the tests and the character's output, you could easily modify the program to eliminate other codes or to translate them into any desired character or character string. This could prove useful as a printer driver in which you intercept certain combinations and generate printer control code sequences for fonts, characters, or attributes. Thus, this simple program is a prototype text file conversion routine or print formatter.

Program Listing 3–2 is a character counter and histogram frequency distribution plotter for word processor files. Portions of the program © 1985, Borland International, Inc. Used by permission. The format for using it is:

```
>CHARCNT < TEXT.DOC > TEXT.PRN     "Generate file for printing"
```

where TEXT.DOC is the source file to be analyzed, and TEXT.PRN receives the histogram plot. Hard copy output can be obtained from using different DOS commands:

```
>COPY filename LPT1:
>TYPE filename > LPT1:
>CHARCNT < TEXT.DOC > LPT1:          "Print directly"
```

Program Listing 3–2.
CharCnt for finding and plotting distribution of characters in a text file

---

```
PROGRAM CharCnt;
CONST
  Bar = '*';                    {#223 give a solid video bar}
VAR
  Count : ARRAY[65..90] OF longint;
  Ch : Char;
  I, Graph : Integer;
  NumChars, Total : Real;
CONST
  MaskHighBit = $7F;

BEGIN                           {main}
  NumChars := 0;                {Intialize variables}
  Total := 0;
  FOR I := 65 TO 90 DO Count[I] := 0;
  WHILE NOT EoF DO
    BEGIN
      Read(Ch);
      Ch := Chr(Ord(Ch) AND MaskHighBit); {Hide bit 7}
      Ch := UpCase(Ch);         {everyting upper case for counting}
      IF Ch IN ['A'..'Z'] THEN
        BEGIN
          Count[Ord(Ch)] := Count[(Ord(Ch))]+1;
          IF Count[Ord(Ch)]>NumChars THEN
              NumChars:=Count[Ord(Ch)];
          Total := Total+1;
        END;
    END;
  WriteLn('      Count      %');
  FOR I := 65 TO 90 DO
    BEGIN
      Write(Chr(I), ':  ', Count[I]:5,
      Count[I]*100.0/Total:5:0, ' ');
      FOR Graph:=1 TO Round(Count[I]*63/NumChars) DO Write(Bar);
      WriteLn;
    END;
  WriteLn('Total', (Round(Total)):6);
END.                            {main}
```

Note the use of the mask for hiding bit 7. The maximum finder avoids the need to examine the entire array after all characters are read. The use of a counting array indexed directly to the ASCII value of each character and of UpCase to convert all characters to upper case before counting simplifies program design and enhances performance.

Passing Parameters to Pascal Programs. When you execute a Pascal EXE program you frequently want to pass command line parameters to it. In filters you can use these parameters to affectfilter operation or to give it numeric values to alter data. To permit passing command line arguments, Turbo has two predefined variables:

```
ParamCount=integer;
ParamStr= array of strings;
```

ParamCount is the number of parameters (separated by spaces) passed to the program, and ParamStr is the string array of these parameters. For example, if you entered the program DSPPARAM with:

> **DSPPARAM 1 3 5.5 A string**

then the following program extracts and displays five character strings:

```
PROGRAM dspparam;   {extract, display command line parameters}
VAR
  j : Integer;
BEGIN
  WriteLn('Number of parameter passed: ', ParamCount);
  FOR j := 1 TO ParamCount DO
    WriteLn('Parameter[', j, ']= ', ParamStr(j));
END.
```

Note that these are string, not numeric, parameters. If you need numeric values you must use a string conversion routine.

Two problems arise in writing filters. First, how do you display video output or input keyboard information while sending data to a file, and how do you switch the redirection? Second, if you use the Crt Unit, output no longer goes through the DOS standard output routine and I/O redirection is lost. We address only the first, most common, problem. See the Borland Reference manuals for details on the other problem.

3.8.5 Text Files

In Pascal all input and output are sent to "files," a carryover from the mainframe days when all I/O came from disk or tape files. In a micro or mini computer environment, the user directly interacts with the program through the display/keyboard, but the term "files" is still used. This is, in part, so that these devices can be treated like actual files in programs. This makes for more program regularity and simplifies changing I/O devices.

Turbo allows the interchange of devices and files for reads and writes.

Indeed, the Read and Write statements are special cases of the general statements:

```
Read(filvar, var1, var2,...varN);
Readln(filvar, var1, var2,...varN);
Write(filvar, var1, var2,...varN);
Writeln(filvar, var1, var2,...varN);
```

where filvar specifies the input or output file that input or output is directed to. Filvar can be an actual tape or disk file or it can correspond to an actual physical device. Pascal has two standard predefined input and output files labelled "Input" and "Output". Input and Output are nominally the display and the keyboard. Thus, when we are reading or writing to these devices we should actually be using:

```
Read(input, var1, ...varN);
Readln(input, var1,...varN);
Write(output, var1, ...varN);
Writeln(output, var1,...varN);
```

For common operations, this would be needlessly cumbersome. Therefore, if no filvar is specified, the default Input and Output are assumed.

The following short program shows how to read and write to a file. For purposes of demonstration, we use only Text files, but similar principles apply to any other file types:

```
PROGRAM files;                  {writes and reads to files}
VAR
  First : Text;
  j, k, l : Integer;
  dummy : STRING[9];

BEGIN                           {make 'file1' of 1st 10 squares}
  Assign(First, 'file1');       {associate with text file handle}
  Rewrite(First);               {clear and open file for writing}
  FOR j:=1 TO 10 DO WriteLn(First, 'Square of ', j:3, j*j:6);
  Close(First);                  {ALWAYS close file when done}

  Assign(First, 'file1');       {associate with text file handle}
  Reset(First);                 {move pointer to file beginning}

  WHILE NOT eof(First) DO       {do not read past end of file}
    BEGIN                       {read and display each square}
      ReadLn(First, dummy, k, l); {dummy skips string part}
      WriteLn(k:3, l:6);
    END;

  Close(First);
END.
```

We have defined First as of type Text, which means that it can handle anything that normal keyboard reads and video writes handle. The Assign gives a value to First (i.e., 'file1'). Until another Assign, First is associated with 'file1'. The name assigned can include disk and path information and can be a string variable rather than an explicit string.

Rewrite opens First (currently associated with 'file1') for writing and positions the file write pointer at the beginning of the file. If file1 existed, any contents are erased. If file1, did not exist, it is created.

All subsequent writes to the text file variable First append the printed material to file1 in the same fashion that text is appended to the screen with writes.

After writing to the file, you must Close it with the appropriate Text file variable. If you do not do this, you leave off the Eof marker ^Z, and the file is trashed.

Reading from a file is similar. First, assign a text file variable with the appropriate name. Then position the file read pointer at the beginning of the file with Reset, which is a nondestructive operation because it merely points at the first item in the file. Now read from the file just as from the keyboard, except that the text file variable is used in all read statements. However, we must determine when we reach the file end. The Boolean Eof is used here before each read, although it must be a test for the end of file for the currently open file (i.e., EoF(first)). We find that the EoF test without a file specifier is one of the most common bugs in file read programs.

We have explicitly included string information in the input file to demonstrate a complication. If we attempt to read a nonnumeric string into a numeric variable, the program crashes. We must read past the string information to get to the data. The temporary string variable dummy accepts exactly nine characters from the beginning of each input line (i.e., the exact length of the unneeded string) and is then discarded.

3.8.6 Special Predefined Pascal Devices

Turbo has several predetermined text device file names. These include:

CON	"Console (output) and keyboard (input).
LPT1, LPT2, LP2	"Line printers 1, 2, and 3 (output only)."
NUL	"Bit bucket (output). Anything directed here is discarded."
COM1, COM2, COM3	"Serial communications ports (input and output)."

CON is especially useful in redirection programs. If we have redirected I/O to files, we cannot do video display for messages or use the keyboard for prompts. CON allows keyboard/video I/O in redirected programs. Consider the following program fragment that cues the operator to input a message. Every line read from standard input has this message inserted at the beginning, and the augmented line is written to standard output. The f is of type Text, and s and Message are of type string.

```
Assign(f, 'con');              {assign video, keyboard to f}
Rewrite(f);                    {must rewrite before a write}
Write(f, 'Input message on ');
```

```
WriteLn(f, 'next line');            {can stack writes }
Reset(f);                           {reset to start new reads}
ReadLn(f, Message);
Rewrite(f);                         {rewrite to start new writes}
WriteLn(f, 'Message to insert : ', Message);
Close(f);
WHILE NOT EoF DO                    {standard input/output}
  BEGIN
    ReadLn(s);                      {uses standard input}
    WriteLn(Message, ':', s);       {uses standard output}
  END;
```

We assign the file variable f to the console devices. Then whenever we want video output or keyboard input we write or read with this variable. However, since CON is both an input and an output, we have to Rewrite before every series of writes and Reset before every series of reads. A single read breaks a series of writes and vice versa.

The above discussion assumes that you are not using the Crt Unit. Inclusion of Crt greatly complicates standard console I/O; see the Borland manuals.

3.9 REFERENCES

The authoritative reference on Turbo Pascal is the latest Borland reference manual. An excellent overall discussion of the Turbo Pascal 5 language, ASCII, and I/O redirection is given by Swan, although he does not cover such details as configuring the compiler, using the editor, or other nuts and bolts details. For basic hardware details, Sargent, III and Shoemaker, Liebson, and Eggebrecht all have excellent discussions of programmable I/O devices and their interactions with the PC. Sargent and Shoemaker give many examples of assembly language programming using these devices.

Problems

3–1 [3.1]. Turbo can get some very strange and perplexing errors. This problem and the next one demonstrate some of the more insidious errors. Run the following:

```
PROGRAM Funny;
VAR
  Sum : Real;
  j : Integer;
  Data : ARRAY [1..10] of Integer;
BEGIN
  Sum := 0;
  FOR j := 1 TO 300 DO Sum := Sum+j*j;
  WriteLn(Sum:10:0);
END.
```

This deceptively simple program is the heart of many least squares programs, and the answer is wrong. Why? Try printing out the partial sums and j*j in the loop for a hint. When you see where it is going wrong, review Table 1–2. How can you get around the problem? Think of making a variable type change; look closely at what Turbo has to offer.

3–2 [3.1]. Replace the body of the previous problem with the following code:

```
j := 0;
REPEAT
  Data[j] := -5;
  WriteLn(j:5, Data[j]:5);
  j := j+1;
UNTIL j = 10;
```

Also, place as the first line of your program, "{$R−}". This is a compiler directive that tells the compiler not to bother to check that subscripts are within the range specified in the variable declaration. Many people turn it off in order to make programs run a little faster. Our student compiler is set with range checking on in the options.

Run the program that was intended to initialize every array element to −5. It does not properly initialize; in fact, it never gets out of the loop. You must terminate it with Ctrl Break. Why does it fail? The hint comes in the variable declaration section. Note the order of declaration of variables and the fact that we are addressing an array element that does not exist.

Now run the program with range checking on. Delete the {$R−} or change it to {$R+}. The program now warns you of the problem. Always use range checking unless turning it off is absolutely critical to program performance; then only do it after the program is completely debugged.

3–3 [3.1]. Rewrite the BASIC least squares of Problem 2–8 in Pascal.

3–4 [3.1]. Convert your least squares routine to a procedure of the format:

```
Procedure LogLeastSquares(X,Y        : data500;
                          Start, End  : integer;
                          var slope   : real;
                          var intercept : real);
```

where data500 is a type of array[1. .500] of real, and start and end are the first and last points to be used in the fit. The slope and intercept are returned as variable parameters. To avoid side effects, do not use any global variables in this procedure.

3–5 [3.1]. This classic and apparently easy problem causes great trouble for the unwary. We want to move contiguous blocks of data from one portion of an array of twenty integers to another portion. The difficulty arises when the source and destination range overlap. Consider an array of only eleven elements:

```
Index        1   2   3   4   5    6    7    8    9   10   11
Data[Index]  2   3   4   5   6    7    8    9   10   11   12
```

Suppose we move five elements starting at Data[1] to the section starting at Data[3]. If we start at Data[1] and move data on a one-to-one basis to the final elements (starting at Data[3]), we get the incorrect:

```
Data[Index]  2   3   2   3   2    3    2    9   10   11   12
```

During the move we overwrote Data[3], Data[4], and Data[5] before we moved them. To avoid this problem, make the move from the end and work backward. That is, move Data[5] to Data[7], then Data[4] to Data[6], and so on. Your program must be able to: 1) make begin-to-begin moves; 2) make end-to-end moves; 3) decide when to do which; and 4) trap any errors. An error is an attempt to move data outside the array or a move that does nothing (i.e., the start and final addresses are the same).

3–6 [3.2]. Time several variations of Problem 3–3. Try each version with and without the math coprocessor enabled. To enable compilation of 80X87 code, you can use either the Options menu of the compiler (we set this to coprocessor enabled on our machines) or you can do it with a compiler directive in your program. To turn the numeric coprocessor on, insert the following compiler directive at the very beginning of your program {$n+}; to turn it off use {$n−}. While these look like comments, they are actually compiler directives.

Time your original version with all floating point variables declared as REAL, as SINGLE, as DOUBLE, and as EXTENDED. Comment on the differences in speed, precision, and the memory usage.

3–7 [3.2]. Use ParPass to demonstrate the difference in speed between passing arguments as variables and as value parameters. Comment on the difference in timing and the hazards of passing parameters by reference when you do not intend to change them in the procedure.

3–8 [3.2]. The Timer Unit as shown in Listing 3–1 has a major shortcoming: it returns an incorrect interval if the day changes. Rewrite Timer to return a correct interval as long as the maximum is less than twenty-four hours.

3–9 [3.5]. Rewrite ReadKeys so that the termination character (q) is not printed out.

3–10 [3.5]. Write a program that reads the keyboard and terminates on a 'q', but prints nothing unless a special function key is pressed, when it prints out:

```
Special Function Key # (number) Pressed
```

3–11 [3.7.2]. Write the function Binary in HexBin. It should return a sixteen character string of 1s and 0s, which is the binary representation of the integer passed.

3–12 [3.7.2]. Write a one-line statement that takes a byte variable, Status, and inverts bits 3, 4, and 5 while not affecting any other bits. Write a one line statement that inverts bits 3, 4, and 5 and zeros all remaining bits.

3–13 [3.7.2]. Two ways of isolating the high byte of a 16-bit word are the function Hi and a right shift eight times. Set up loops that time both methods. Comment on the relative speeds.

3–14 [3.8.4]. Run CHARCNT.PAS on a WordStar file provided and view the output. CHARCNT.PAS has inefficiencies. The ORD value of a character is called repeatedly. Remove all uses of ORD except for initial conversion to the ASCII code. How much does this speed up the program? At what cost in clarity?

3–15 [3.8.4]. Write a batch file that uses DOS I/O redirection to extract all lines in a Pascal program that have a write or writeln on them, append line numbers, and generate a file that lists these lines in increasing order of line number. Your program must handle the cases in which write and writeln appear as write, writeln, Write, Writeln, WriteLn, WRITE, and WRITELN; remember that FIND is case sensitive. Assume that you will not encounter pathological cases such as WrItE and that there are no more than nine lines. Why?

3–16 [3.8.4]. Write a filter that converts a single-spaced ASCII file into a double-spaced one. That is, every time you find a CRLF sequence, send two CRLFs.

3–17 [3.8.4]. Write a filter that prints an ASCII file in a neat multisheet format. Do this by assuming that the print head starts at the top of the page. Space down four lines before beginning printing. Skip four lines at the bottom of every page. Begin and end each subsequent page with four blank lines. There are 66 lines on a full standard page. Make the number of lines on a page and the top and bottom margins constants. This makes the program more general and allows easy modification should you decide to change the page format.

3–18 [3.8.4]. Write a filter that removes all blank spaces and punctuation from an ASCII file. Leave CRLF sequences intact.

3–19 [3.8.4]. Write a filter, CAPALL, that takes an ASCII file and capitalizes every letter.

3–20 [3.8.4]. Write a filter that takes an ASCII file and capitalizes the first letter of every word. A new word is defined as one that occurs after a space, punctuation, or CR. This is a more interesting problem than the earlier ones.

3–21 [3.8.4]. Write a filter, DELPUN, that replaces all characters that are not A. .Z or CR with a space.

3–22 [3.8.4]. Write a filter, WORDPLIN, that places each word on a separate line and deletes all blanks.

3–23 [3.8.4]. Combine CAPALL, DELPUN, WORDPLIN, and SORT in a single command stack filter that gives an alphabetical listing of all words in the file.

3–24 [3.8.4]. The output of 3–23 has the same word repeated on as many lines as the word occurred in the original file. Write a filter REMCOMM that removes all multiple occurrences from the output of 3–23.

Hint: ReadLn each word into a string variable (NewWord), compare it with the word from the previous line (LastWord). Only if NewWord does not match LastWord, write NewWord to the output file and update LastWord with NewWord. Repeat until the file ends, and watch the initialization.

3–25 [3.8.4]. Filters work perfectly well with any Readln statement, and we frequently write filters for processing numeric data. Our graphics program uses ASCII files and has one (x,y) data pair per line separated by at least one space. The graphics routine lacks two important abilities: you cannot vertically offset the data on the existing y axis or scale the y magnitude. Write a filter ADDXY that scales each y by a multiplicative constant and adds another specified constant to all y values. The format for entry should be:

```
ADDXY Yoffset Scale < inputfile > output file
```

where you must specify a Yoffset or the program terminates. If you have only one parameter passed, offset all y points. If two are passed, both offset and scale the data.

3–26 [3.8.6]. Rewrite 3–25 so that it prompts the user for Yoffset and Scale.

3–27 [3.8.6]. This is more difficult. Delay of the Crt Unit is nice, but if I/O redirection is required it imposes an extra complexity. Write a Unit CrtEmul that has procedure CrtDelay that mimics Delay. The delay can be set with a counting loop using a Longint variable. Have your program set the range of the loop to give the correct delay.

(A) Initially, calibrate the loop counter range to time conversion factor manually with the Timer Unit. However, your empirically determined calibration will depend on the computer clock and CPU.

(B) Now the challenging part. Make the Unit self-calibrating. During the Unit initialization (between the BEGIN and END at the end of the Unit), have the Unit determine the conversion factor, save it in a type constant, and then on all subsequent calls to CrtDelay use the correct conversion factor for that system. Since the Crt Delay works reasonably accurately on all systems, it is carrying out a similar calibration.

4

Video Graphics and Digitizers

4.1 INTRODUCTION

We have shown the PC's substantial computational capabilities. However, I/O has been limited to printed tabular results or as primitive printer graphics. In this chapter we show how Turbo Pascal adds graphics capabilities with the Graph Unit. We greatly enhance these capabilities with our own Unit VIDGR4. Our procedures are fine for rough plots and for data monitoring, but hard copies are not always publication-quality. In the experiments, we obtain publication-quality plots with printers or digital plotters.

We also demonstrate how the much overlooked digitization tablet can interface a variety of uninterfaced or uninterfaceable instruments. The digitizing tablet is particularly useful for taking data from strip chart recorders, photographs, or printed material and transforming it into computer-readable form.

4.2 VIDEO GRAPHICS

PCs equipped with a suitable standard color graphics adapter (CGA) permit crude scientific graphics. In the medium resolution mode, the resolution is 320x200 (horizontal by vertical) with three colors plus the background. In the high resolution mode, monochrome graphics with 640x200 resolution provides one color plus a background. Some Olivetti, AT&T, and Xerox machines provide 640x400 in monochrome. The widely available enhanced graphics adaptor (EGA) provides up to 640x350 with four colors and the Hercules monochrome cards (720x348) provide excellent resolution. The newer video graphics adaptor (VGA) standard has 640x480 resolution with sixteen colors, and enhanced VGAs have higher resolution with more colors. Many graphics cards support several different standards and Turbo 4 and 5 support all of these modes.

"Color" graphics can be displayed on monochrome displays with different colors being shaded differently. This avoids the need for an expensive color display; however,

Table 4–1. Graphics Drivers and Modes Supported by the Graphics Unit

Graphics Drivers

Detect	=0;	EGAMono	=5;
CGA	=1;	Reserved	=6;
MCGA	=2;	HercMono	=7;
EGA	=3;	ATT400	=8;
EGA64	=4;	VGA	=9;

Graphics modes for each driver

CGAC0	=0;	320x200 palette 0: LightGreen, LightRed, Yellow
CGAC1	=1;	320x200 palette 1: LightCyan, LightMagenta, White
CGAC2	=2;	320x200 palette 2: Green, Red, Brown
CGAC3	=3;	320x200 palette 3: Cyan, Magenta, LightGray
CGAHi	=4;	640x200
MCGAC0	=0;	320x200 palette 0: LightGreen, LightRed, Yellow
MCGAC1	=1;	320x200 palette 1: LightCyan, LightMagenta, White
MCGAC2	=2;	320x200 palette 2: Green, Red, Brown
MCGAC3	=3;	320x200 palette 3: Cyan, Magenta, LightGray
MCGMed	=4;	640x200
MCGAHi	=5;	640x480
EGALo	=0;	640x200 16 color
EGAHi	=1;	640x350 4 color
EGA64Lo	=0;	640x200 16 color
EGA64HI	=1;	640x350 4 color
EGAMonoHi	=3;	640x350
HercMonoHi	=0;	720x348
ATT400C0	=0;	320x200 palette 0: LightGreen, LightRed, Yellow
ATT400C1	=1;	320x200 palette 1: LightCyan, LightMagenta, White
ATT400C2	=2;	320x200 palette 2: Green, Red, Brown
ATT400C3	=3;	320x200 palette 3: Cyan, Magenta, LightGray
ATT400Med	=4;	320x200 palette 3: Cyan, Magenta, LightGray
ATT400Hi	=5;	640x400
VGALo	=0;	640x200 16 color
VGAMed	=1;	640x350 16 color
VGAHi	=2;	640x480 16 color

true color is much better and should be used if money is available.

Graphics are not in the Pascal standard since they are system-dependent, but for scientific machines graphics are essential. Turbo Pascal adds many non-standard graphics procedures that can greatly enhance system utility. We describe below some of the Turbo graphics primitives and show how more useful routines can be built from them.

4.2.1   Initializing the Graphics Mode (InitGraph)

All of the graphics routines of Turbo Pascal are included in the Graph Unit. To do any graphics, your program must include an appropriate "USES Graph,.." statement.

To use graphics you must initialize the graphics system and set the mode. This means supplying the compiler with information on the current graphics system, the desired mode, and the location of the necessary graphics file. The initialization command is performed with InitGraph:

```
InitGraph(var GrDriver,GrMode:integer;DrivePath:
STRING);
```

GrDriver is the code for the appropriate graphics systems (i.e., CGA, EGA, VGA, AT&T 6300, and so on). GrMode is the specific graphics mode (e.g., 320x200 CGA or 640x200 monochrome CGA) for the system. If the default graphics mode is not used, then a drive and a path to the graphics information must be provided. The graphics information file will normally be a .BGI file. Some specific graphics drivers, modes, and their properties are shown in Table 4–1.

To set up an AT&T computer in the high resolution 640x400 monochrome mode, for example, use:

```
InitGraph(ATT400, ATT400Hi, 'c:\tp5');
```

where the graphics interface ATT400.BGI is available in the c:\tp5 subdirectory.

The process can be more complicated. Graphics initialization can fail for many reasons (e.g., the .BGI or font files are not available, no graphics system was detected, or there is inadequate memory). Turbo provides a function, GraphResults, which returns an error code after InitGraph. If the code is 0, the system is initialized. If initialization fails, the value provides the reasons for the failure. The codes are listed in the Turbo Pascal manuals.

In addition, Turbo has an autodetect mode function that can frequently tell which graphics system is present. An example of both auto detection and error checking is shown below:

```
PROGRAM autodet;
  uses graph;
VAR
  GrDriver, GrMode, GrErrorCode : Integer;
```

```
BEGIN
  GrDriver := Detect;
  WriteLn('Code for auto detected system is ', GrDriver);
  GrMode := cgac0;
  initgraph(GrDriver, GrMode, 'c:\tp');
  GrErrorCode := GraphResult;
  IF GrErrorCode <> 0 THEN
    BEGIN
      WriteLn('Intialize Failure.  Code = ', GrErrorCode);
      Halt;
    END
END.
```

This program automatically detects the graphics system and tells you whether or not the system was satisfactorily initialized.

Detect does not always correctly characterize the system. For example, Detect thinks that an AT&T 6300 is an IBM CGA and will not exploit the higher resolution. Thus, while Detect is convenient and works with virtually all systems, it does not always provide optimum performance.

To install a different graphics mode after initialization, use SetGraphMode rather than a second call to InitGraph:

```
SetGraphMode(GrMode: integer);
```

where GrMode is an appropriate code or identifier taken from the Table 4–1 for the current graphics interface. For example, to change the ATT400 high resolution graphics mode installed above to a CGA 320x200 four color mode with palette 1, use:

```
SetGraphMode(1);
```

or more clearly:

```
SetGraphMode(ATT400C1);
```

Note that the different graphics mode identifiers (e.g., ATT400C0, CGAC0, VGALo) are the constants in the Graph Unit with the indicated integer values of Table 4–1.

Switching between Graphics and Text Screens. The computer defaults to the text mode. Both the InitGraph and SetGraphMode switch it to the graphics mode. To return to the text mode, RestoreCrtMode returns the screen to the Crt mode prior to graphic initialization. To return to the graphics mode use SetGraphMode again. The following program switches back and forth between the text and graphics mode:

```
PROGRAM graptext;              {switches between text-graph modes}
USES Graph;

  PROCEDURE InitVideo( GrDriver : Integer;
```

```
                         GrMode : Integer;
                         DriverPath : STRING);
   VAR
     GrErrorCode : Integer;
   BEGIN
     InitGraph(GrDriver, GrMode, DriverPath);
     GrErrorCode := GraphResult;
     IF GrErrorCode <> 0 THEN
        BEGIN
           WriteLn('Graphics Initialization Failure: Code=',
                   GrErrorCode);
           Halt
        END;
   END;

BEGIN
   InitVideo(att400, att400c3, 'c:\tp');
   OutText('In Low Resolution Graphics Mode');
   ReadLn;
   RestoreCrtMode;                    {return to text mode}
   WriteLn('In Normal Text Mode');
   ReadLn;
   SetGraphMode(ATT400Hi);            {back in graphics mode}
   WriteLn('In High Resolution Graphics Mode');
   ReadLn;
END.
```

Here we show a procedure InitVideo to simplify graphics initialization and testing for error conditions. Incidentally, autodetect works if GrDriver is set to Detect in the call to InitVideo.

Note that all the information on the text or graphics display is lost when you change the graphics modes. We return to OutText and OutTextXY, which are analogous to writing in the text mode while in graphics.

Erasing the Screen. ClearDevice clears the graphics display when you are in the Graphics mode:

```
ClearDevice; {clear graphic display; stay in graphics
mode}
```

4.2.2 Turbo Pascal Graphics Routine

We turn now to a subset of Turbo's graphics routines of the Graph Unit. Beyond initializing the graphics system, operations permit drawing and text display.

Pen Colors. The pen can be set to a variety of colors that depend on the graphics card and mode currently in effect. The procedure for setting pen color is:

```
SetColor(N)
```

where N is a valid color code that can include the following predefined constants in the Graph Unit. Similarly, the background color can be set with:

```
SetBkColor(N);
```

Suitable color constants are:

Black	=	0;	DarkGrey	=	8;
Blue	=	1;	LightBlue	=	9;
Green	=	2;	LightGreen	=	10;
Cyan	=	3;	LightCyan	=	11;
Red	=	4;	LightRed	=	12;
Magenta	=	5;	LightMagneta	=	13;
Brown	=	6;	Yellow	=	14;
LightGrey	=	7;	White	=	15;

While each color code generally yields a recognizable difference, the actual colors do not always match the table. Different systems use codes in different ways and alternative color palettes might have been selected. A color palette is just another way of mapping the color codes onto the actual colors. For example, palette 0 (ATT400C0 for an AT&T and CGA0 for a CGA adaptor) uses light green for code 1, light red for code 2, and yellow for code 3 while palette 1 (ATT400C1 and CGA1) for the same codes yields light cyan, light magenta, and white (Table 4–1). Thus, depending on the palette specified in GrMode, you might select blue but end up with green, light cyan, or cyan.

Also, do not use a color code that is larger than the maximum for a specific adaptor and graphics mode. This can be checked with the function **GetMaxColor**, which returns the largest possible numeric code. In many cases something will be shown if you use an unrecognized number, while in other cases the background color will be plotted with no visible effect on the screen.

The background color can be changed using the SetBkColor procedure:

```
SetBkColor(N);
```

where N is 0 to 15 on most color systems. Its maximum value can be interrogated with the GetBkColor function. Generally, a 0 is a black background. Again the precise color and the correlation with the palettes is system-dependent and should be checked by the user.

4.2.3 Plotting and Moving the Pen

We first turn to the screen graphics units used by Turbo Pascal. Screen units are based on pixels, which is the smallest dot that can be turned on or off for a given mode. The upper left hand corner of the screen is (0,0) while the lower right is (MaxX−1, MaxY) where MaxX and MaxY are the X and Y resolution of the graphics mode. During graphics operations, think of an imaginary pen that moves over the screen much like a plotter pen. With many operations, Turbo keeps track of the pen position with a current position pointer (CP) and maintains the position of the pen until the next operation. Thus, you do not have to keep track of where you left the pen while calculating the new pen position.

Turbo 4/5 provide functions **GetMaxX** and **GetMaxY** to give the maximum X and Y coordinates respectively for the current graphics mode. This is useful for automatically adjusting plots to the current mode.

We turn now to the graphics primitives pen movement and plotting. These are Put-Pixel for point plotting and Line, Lineto, and LineRel for line plotting. Pen movement is accomplished with Moveto. All forms use absolute screen coordinates for the current graphics mode.

PutPixel(X, Y, Color:integer);

Plot a point (pixel) at screen coordinate (X,Y) in the specified color. The color code uses the integer constants of Table 4–1. Thus, the following program fragment will color every other pixel on a horizontal line positioned halfway up the screen:

```
J:=0
repeat
  PutPixel(j,GetMaxY div 2, blue);
  j:=J+2;
until J > GetMaxX
```

Line(X1, Y1, X2, Y2 : integer);

Draw a line in the current color between points (X1,Y1) and (X2,Y2). The CP is not updated. The following statement draws a horizontal line halfway up the screen:

```
line(0,GetMaxY div 2, GetMaxX, GetMaxY div 2);
```

Lineto(X2, Y2:integer);

Draw a line in the current color from the current pen position to (X2,Y2). The CP is updated. If the current CP is (0,0), which is the initial value, the following code frames the plotting area:

```
Lineto (0, GetMaxY);
Lineto (GetMaxX,GetMaxY);
Lineto (GetMax,0);
Lineto (0,0) ;
```

LineRel(DeltaX, DeltaY : integer);

Draw a line relative to the current CP. If the CP coordinates are (X,Y), a line is drawn from (X,Y) to (X+DeltaX, Y+DeltaY). The CP is updated. Thus, the following draws a right triangle starting at any point on the screen:

```
LineRel(0,10);
LineRel(10,0);
LineRel(-10,-10);
```

Moveto(X, Y : integer);
   Move the pen to position (X,Y) without drawing. The CP is updated. If in the above framing example, the CP were not initially at (0,0), Moveto(0,0) would place it there.

   Remember these procedures all use absolute screen coordinates (e.g., 320x200 in medium resolution and 640x200 in high resolution on a CGA) with (0,0) at the upper left hand corner). Thus, you must translate user units into absolute screen coordinates. Before we worry about this translation process, we give a graphics example by plotting:

$$y = 100 + 100 * \exp(-x/100) * \cos(x/(2*pi))$$

using the program:

```
PROGRAM expcos;
USES graph, Crt;

VAR
   j, x, y, HalfY : Integer;

BEGIN
   InitVideo(ATT400, ATT400C0, 'c:\tp');
   HalfY := GetMaxY DIV 2;
   SetColor(1);
   line(0, 0, 0, GetMaxY);                {draw Y axis}
   SetColor(2);
   line(0, GetMaxY DIV 2, GetMaxX, GetMaxY DIV 2); {X axis}
   SetColor(3);
   Moveto(0, GetMaxY);                    {move pen to start of plot}
   FOR j := 0 TO GetMaxX DO
     BEGIN
       y := Round(HalfY+HalfY*Exp(-j/100)*Cos(j/(2.0*pi)));
{
replace lineto(j,y) with following to get a colored point plot
       putpixel(j, y, 1+(j MOD (GetMaxColor)));
}
       lineto(j, y);
     END;
   SetTextJustify(CenterText, TopText);
   OutTextXY(GetMaxX DIV 2, 0, 'y =100exp(-x/100)cos(x/2 pi)');
   ReadLn;
END.
```

We use, but do not list, the Procedure InitVideo given earlier.

The plot is shown in Figure 4–1. This plot was made on the printer using the PrtSc key. There are several noteworthy points. First, since the expression on the right hand side evaluates as a real and the plotting coordinates must be integers, we must convert the reals into integers. Second, note the differences in densities of the different lines in the printer plot; the graphics dump converts different screen colors into differently shaded lines on the printer. We use OutTextXY to locate the text material that was printed as a heading. The large character size is due to the use of medium resolution but can be adjusted. Finally, because the upper left hand corner of the screen is (0,0), the plot is upside down.

The function is plotted as a continuous curve using Lineto. Replacing the "Lineto(X,Y)" as indicated in the program yields a multi-colored point plot.

Line Types. Turbo 4/5 allows several different line styles (types). These types and their numeric codes are SolidLn (0), DottedLn (1), CenterLn (2), DashedLn (3), NormWidth (1), and ThickWidth (2). Different line types are invoked with:

```
SetLineStyle(Linestyle: word; pattern: word;
Thickness:word);
```

where Linestyle can be any of the above listed line types and the thickness is Normal or Wide. Pattern applies only to custom lines (see the Turbo manual for details).

SetLineStyle is useful for highlighting different curves. However, after a line style is turned on, everything except text is plotted in that style. Remember to return to the default normal width solid line style when finished with special effects.

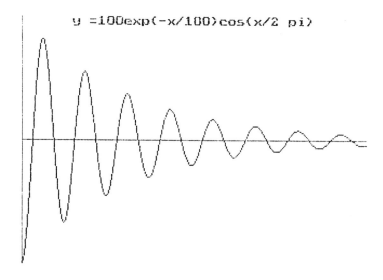

Figure 4–1. Medium resolution (320x200) plot of damped cosine wave using the program expcos. The different density gradations of lines are different colors.

There are weaknesses for line styles other than solid. The pattern's repeat length differs for horizontal and vertical lines and depends on the graphics mode; line appearance depends on steepness. Furthermore, the pattern restarts with each new line drawn; this can cause a broken pattern to become solid or lose its character if line segments are too short. Nevertheless, SetLineStyle is a welcome addition.

Text Display. Text can be placed on a graphics screen. The font, size and direction are adjustable within limits by SetTextMode. The default text font is loaded at all times while other fonts must be loaded as needed:

```
SetTextStyle(Font; Direction; CharSize: integer);
```

where the following Font and direction constants are predefined in the Graph Unit:

```
type
DefaultFont      =    0;    {8x8 pixel font}
TriplexFont      =    1;    {quality stroked (drawn) fonts}
Smallfont        =    2;
SanserifFont     =    3;
Gothic           =    4;

HorizDir         =    0;    {left to right text display]
VertDir          =    1;    {bottom to top text direction]
```

CharSize is an integer. The actual character size varies significantly depending on the font and graphics mode. The default font is bit mapped and looks reasonable for smaller sizes, but degrades as the size increases. The remaining fonts are stroked, which means that they are drawn as a series of lines. Quality remains good for larger sizes.

There is one significant quirk to using the default font. If so much as one pixel of a character would be printed off the screen, no character is displayed at all. If you are having trouble getting default font characters to display, there is a good chance that the text is too big for the screen. Try a smaller size or justification.

Additionally, you can set the text relative to the current pen position with:

```
SetTextJustify(Horiz, Vert: integer);
```

For horizontal justification, text can be justified to the left of the current pen (Right-Text=2), centered around the pen (CenterText=1), or just to the right of the pen (Left-Text=0). Similarly, there is vertical justification around the current position. These positions justify text below the pen (TopText=0), centered vertically around the pen (Center-Text=1), or above the pen (BottomText=2). For example, the following places text just above and to the left of the current pen position:

```
SetTextJustify(RightText,BottomText);
```

String Output. To output text strings in the graphics mode use OutText or OutTextXY:

```
OutText(Mess : STRING);                {output Mess at CP}
OutTextXY(X,Y : word; Mess : STRING); {output Mess at
(X,Y)}
```

where X and Y are integer values in screen coordinates. OutText and OutTextXY work fine with different justifications in the horizontal mode, but are inconsistent for the vertical string directions (i.e., vertical writing).

We turn now to developing a set of procedures that makes graphics more natural. We have modeled our graphics procedure calls after those used in Hewlett-Packard computers. These machines are widely used and the calling sequence is natural and convenient. Further, Hewlett-Packard's digital plotter high level graphics language lends itself in a very natural way to our model.

We explain some of the fundamentals of our graphics procedures and provide details of the use of the full set. There are several additional features that would be useful, but it is reasonably powerful and compact. The routines provide automatic redefinition of the plotting area into user units, primitive axes drawing, framing the plotting area, labeling control, centered symbols, and pen control.

Table 4–2. VIDGR4 Unit Procedures

InitVideo	Sets up graphics system and mode
Scale	Redefines plotting area in user units
Pen	Picks up or puts down pen
Color	Changes the pen color
Cls	Erases the screen
Frame	Draws a frame around full plotting area
MovePen	Picks pen and moves it
Plot	Moves pen to new location and puts it down
Rplot	Relative pen move to new position, then puts down
Point	Plots a point
SetTicLength	Sets tic size and direction on Xaxis and Yaxis
Xaxis	Draws and tics the X-axis
Yaxis	Draws and tics the Y-axis
SymbolSize	Sets centered symbol size
Symbol	Plots a centered □, diamond, + or *.
LabelOrg	Sets label origin
LabelDir	Sets label direction
LabelFont	Sets label text font
LabelSize	Sets label size
GLabel	Plots a text label on graphics screen
WaitForKey	Pauses and waits for any key strike
PrintScreen	Prints the video screen on the printer

A full list of our procedures is given in Table 4–2. We now describe in detail the function and calling sequence for each procedure. The coordinates X, Y, X0, Y0, X1, X2, Y1, and Y2 are in user units (type real) rather than screen coordinates.

InitVideo(GrDriver, GrMode : Integer; DriverPath : STRING);

This initializes the system to a specific graphics driver and mode (Table 4–1) and checks for intialization errors. The necessary binary graphics interface (.BGI) and any required font (.CHR) files must be available on the specified DrivePath.

Scale(X1, X2, Y1, Y2 : real);

This redefines the display area to user units for use by our other graphics routines. The point (X1,Y1) is the lower left hand corner of the screen and (X2,Y2) is the upper right hand corner in user units. Scale does not affect the standard Pascal graphics commands.

Pen(state : penstate);

Take the imaginary pen that you use on the screen and pick it up or put it down. PenState is either "up" or "down". For example, if the pen is up, then Pen(down) puts it down.

Color(color: integer);

Set pen color to specified color code (Table 4–1). Remember the actual color depends on the palette in use.

Cls;

This clears the screen while leaving the screen in the current graphics mode.

Frame

This draws a box in the current pen color around the screen plotting area.

MovePen(X, Y : Real);

This picks the pen up and moves it to the specified location without putting it down.

Plot(X, Y : real);

With the pen in its current state, this moves it from its current position to (X,Y) and then puts the pen down.

Rplot(DeltaX, DeltaY : real);

With the pen in its current state and position (X1,Y1), this moves it to (X1+DeltaX,Y1+DeltaY) in user units. Then the pen is put down if necessary. It uses the current pen color. The procedure CenteredBox draws a box of width Width and height Height centered at the current pen position:

```
PROCEDURE CenteredBox(width,height:real);
{Draw a box centered around pen position of width and height}
BEGIN
```

```
    Pen(up);
    RPlot(-width/2,-height/2);
    RPlot(width,0);
    RPlot(0,height);
    Rplot(-width,0);
    Rplot(0,-height);
    Pen(up);
  END;
```

Point(X, Y : real);

This plots a point in the current pen color at the point (X,Y) in user units.

SetTicLength(TicLenPlus, TicLenMinus : real);

This sets the size of the tics to be drawn on X and Y axes by the Xaxis and Yaxis routines. Lengths are given in percentage of the width of the screen in the X direction. X tics (vertical lines) are adjusted to compensate for screen resolution to maintain approximately the same appearance on both axes. TicLenMinus and TicLenPlus times the appropriate factor are the length of the tic below and above the X axis respectively and left and right of the Y axis. Only magnitude is used.

Xaxis(X0, X1, DeltX, Ycross: real; Majortics: integer);

This draws an X axis in the current pen color. The line starts at X0, runs to X1, and crosses the Y axis at Ycross. There is a tic spacing DeltX between tics. The leftmost tic and every Majortic tic after that are major tics while the remainder are minor tics. Minor tics are half the size of major tics.

Yaxis(Y0, Y1, DeltY, Xcross: real; Majortics: Integer);

This draws a Y axis in the current pen color. The line starts at Y0 and runs to Y1 and crosses the X axis at Xcross. There is a tic spacing DeltY between tic. The bottom tic and every Majortic tic after that are major tics while the remainder are minor tics. Minor tics are half the size of major tics.

SymbolSize(CharSize : integer);

This sets the size of the symbol used in ChrPlt. The size of the character is affected by the global variable VidCharSize. VidCharSize is an integer value that must be at least 1. The size defaults to 2. Actual size and shapes depend on the graphics mode in effect. A 2 for 320x200 resolution is reasonable, but for 620x400 resolution it is small.

Symbol(SymbolCode : integer);

This plots the specified symbol centered around the current pen position. Allowed codes are 1 (□), 2(diamond), 3(+), and 4(*). The pen state and position are unchanged and the current color is used. Size is set by SymbolSize.

LabelOrg (i : integer);

This sets the orientation, relative to the current pen position, in which a text label will be placed. Relative to the initial point, labels can be horizontally centered, or placed

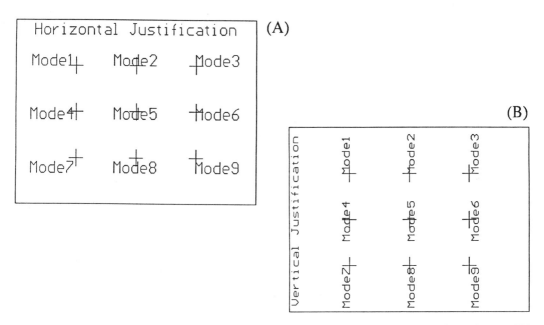

Figure 4–2. Orientation of labels printed using different justification. (A) Horizontal justification. (B) Vertical justification. The justification mode number is shown on each label relative to the pen position, which is centered on the +. Resolution is 640x400 with the Small font.

to the left or right. They can also be placed above or below or centered vertically on the pen position. Allowable values are 1 to 9. Any other value defaults to 5. Figure 4–2 shows the orientation of a text label plotted relative to the pen position, which is marked by a +. We define a set of constants in VIDGR4 that simplify remembering the numeric codes. These are:

```
CONST
    LeftUpper       = 1;        RightCenter     = 6;
    CenterUpper     = 2;        LeftLower       = 7;
    RightUpper      = 3;        CenterLower     = 8;
    LeftCenter      = 4;        RightLower      = 9;
    CenterCenter    = 5;
```

One can invoke any of the orientations merely by calling LabelOrg with one named constant as the parameter. Thus, LabelOrg(RightLower) places a string plotted by GLabel completely to the right and below the pen position.

LabelDir(X : integer);
This sets the direction that labels are written. Only 0 (left to right) and 90 (bottom to top) are currently allowed.

LabelFont(font : fontstyles);

This sets the graphics text mode to one of the allowable fonts. Currently, Borland supports Default, Triplex, Small, Sanserif, and Gothic. Except for the Default, the fonts must exist as the appropriate .CHR file on the directory pointed at in InitVideo. If you are running on a floppy based system and must limit the fonts, Small is the most versatile scientific set.

LabelSize(X : integer);

The text sizes are not matched to the different graphics modes and font styles. For example, a size 5 in Default is different than a size 5 in Small. Therefore, you will have to play with these in order to judge size. In the ATT ATT400Hi mode with the small font, 5 yields a reasonable starting point.

GLabel(s : STRING);

Without changing the current pen position, this outputs the specified string at the current pen position using the current size, font, label direction, and character size. The following procedure LabeledBox outputs a box of width Width and height Height centered around the current pen position and places a label s in the center of the the box. LabeledBox uses the procedure CenteredBox listed above:

```
PROCEDURE LabeledBox( xcenter, ycenter,
                      width, height : real ;
                      Mess:string);
{generate box centered around pen of width and height with
a centered labeled Mess}
BEGIN
  movePen(xcenter,ycenter);
  LabelOrg(centercenter);
  GLabel(Mess);
  CenteredBox(width,height);
END;
```

WaitForKey

This stops continuation and waits for any key to be struck before resuming program execution. The keyboard buffer is cleared. WaitForKey is useful for pausing to view the screen.

PrintScreen

This immediately prints the screen to the graphics printer followed by NumCR carriage returns. NumCr is a typed constant that can be set by your program to force spacing between plots, such as advancing to the next page for a plot. If there is no printer or the printer is off, the program hangs. PrintScreen works fine with CGA systems, but at least at this writing most EGA and VGA systems do not have a suitable GRAPHICS program that allows dumping higher resolution modes to printers. In place of GRAPHICS, we use the very versatile program Pizzaz. To name only some of the features, Pizzaz handles all the different graphics modes, dumps to most printers including laser jet printers, and allows customization of the way color displays will appear on single color printers. Many of the high resolution plots shown here were saved from the screen and printed to a laser jet printer with Pizzaz.

We will not discuss the details of our Unit VIDGR4. A complete listing is available from the authors. We supply one for our students.

We do discuss two features: Mapping user units onto absolute screen coordinates, and implementing penlike movements. The first problem is transforming user units onto absolute screen coordinates. We do this with Scale, which defines the plotting area on the screen in user units. The Scale procedure sets Unit variables Vidxmin, Vidymin, Vidxmax, and Vidymax where (Vidxmin,Vidymin) and (Vidxmax, Vidymax) correspond to the lower left and upper right hand corners of the user's plotting area. These are initialized to (0,0) and (100,100) to prevent crashes in the plotting routines if Scale was not called. Typed constants are used so that every procedure has access to information such as the pen state and position. If the point to be plotted is (x,y) in user units, then the point plotted on the screen at (xplt,yplt) is given by:

```
xplt:=round(VidMaxX*(x-Vidxmin)/(Vidxmax-Vidxmin));
yplt:=round(VidMaxY*(y-Vidymax)/(Vidymin-Vidymax));
```

where VidMaxX and VidMaxY are the maximum screen coordinates for the current mode and are determined from GetMaxX and GetMaxY.

The next issue is implementation of penlike controls. Pens move from the last position while Line draws between two specified points. Thus, for continuous plots the routines must remember the previous pen position every time we call a pen movement command. This feature was accomplished by defining global variables Xold and Yold, which correspond to the last pen position. Any Line statements are then initiated from this last point.

VIDGR4 keeps track explicitly of the pen position and draws all lines with Line statements. Use of Moveto and Lineto might have simplified bookkeeping. However, VIDGR4 directly descends from a Turbo 3 version that did not keep track of the CP.

VIDGR4 declares several visible types and constants. You cannot declare these in your program. If you inadvertently do so, the compiler flags the error as a duplication and you can use the editor to globally change the offending identifier in your program.

We give an example of a program that used VIDGR4 in Program Listing 4–1. The results of running the first half of this program are shown in Figure 4–3. The program uses the procedures CenteredBox and LabeledBox listed earlier. With rather little effort, we plotted a reasonably complex figure.

Drawing continuous curves with Plot(X,Y) is straightforward. First pick the pen up (pen(up)) and plot to the first point on the curve with Plot(X0,Y0). This moves the pen to the first point without leaving a mark and puts the pen down. Subsequent Plot(X,Y) statements move the pen while marking the screen until the pen is lifted.

Rplot was used to generate the rectangle. Rplot is useful for generating shapes placed at different starting positions. A subroutine using only Rplot statements can be used to draw the same figure around any initial position merely by moving the pen and calling the routine.

Program Listing 4–1. Demonstration of VIDGR4 Unit

```
PROGRAM demovid4;
USES graph, VIDGR4;

VAR        j : Integer;

BEGIN                                {main program}
  InitVideo(ATT400, ATT400hi, 'c:\tp');

  scale(-0.5, 11, -110, 110);        {scale plotting area}
  LabelFont(small); LabelOrg(5);  LabelSize(6);

  Color(blue);                       {change pen Color}
  LabeledBox(5.5,80,5,10,'Centered Label');

  xaxis(0, 10, 1, 0, 2);             {draw X and Y axes}
  yaxis(-100, 100, 5, 0, 2);

  SetTicLength(5, 2);                {adjust axis tics}
  xaxis(0, 10, 1, -100, 5);

  Color(Red); frame;                 {frame screen in red}

  Color(cyan); pen(up);     {set brown pen color, pen up}
  SymbolSize(3);            {set character size}
  plot(5, 50); Symbol(1);  {move to (5,50), draw square}
  plot(6, 60); Symbol(2);  {line to a diamond}
  plot(7, 50); Symbol(3);  {line to a +}
  plot(8, 30); Symbol(4);  {line to a *}
  pen(up);                  {pick pen up}

  {plot exponentially damped cosine wave then a square function}
  FOR j := 0 TO 200 DO plot(j/20, 100*Exp(-j/40)*Cos(pi*j/20));

  pen(up); Color(Green);
  FOR j := 0 TO 200 DO plot(j/20, Sqr(j/20));
  waitforkey;

  cls; frame;                        {plot a pretty figure}
  scale(-15, 15, -10, 10);           {new scale}
  LabelSize(8);      LabelDir(90);
  movepen(-14, 0); Glabel('x=t*Cos(2*pi*t)');
  movepen(14, 0);  Glabel('y=t*Sin(4*pi*t)');

  pen(up); Color(3);      {change color, plot pretty function}
  FOR j := 1 TO 1000 DO
        plot((j/100)*Cos(pi*j/50), (j/100)*Sin(pi*j/25));
  waitforkey;
END.                                 {main}
```

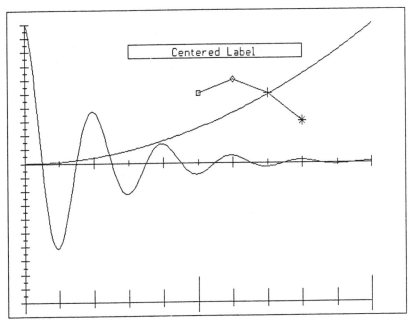

Figure 4–3. Demonstration of the use of VIDGR4 to produce a complex figure. The program is given in Listing 4–1. Resolution is 640x400 with the Small font.

The axis routines can also be used to generate grids. For example, if we make the positive tic lengths 100, we generate a grid rather than an axis with tics. Alternatively, we could generate axes that went completely around a plot with the tics all pointing inward.

4.3 DIGITIZERS

Many instruments and data sources are not directly interfaceable. This includes many older analog instruments with built-in strip chart recorders and oscilloscopes in which the data must be extracted from strip chart records or photographs. In order to extract data from figures in reports or journal articles, it is frequently necessary to hand-digitize the data with ruler or calipers and then transcribe it into a computer for further processing.

Digitizers are powerful tools for attacking such problems and, as we show in a later chapter, digital plotters can be used as versatile digitizers. The most common digitizer uses a platen with an embedded crosshatch of wires and a loop coil attached to a stylus or cross-haired cursor. By transmitting a signal from one of these elements and picking it up with the other, the position of the cursor or stylus can be determined with remarkable accuracy. The digitized position of the cursor can be sent directly to a computer, and the worker can completely avoid tedious manual digitization. Modern low-cost digitizing tablets typically provide resolutions of 0.001 inch, and accuracies of better than 0.015 inch over a 12-inch square grid. Larger digitizers can have a square meter or more of digitizing area.

Figure 4–4 shows typical digitizers. The HiPad and Summagraphics both have a stylus and cursors. The HiPad shows a one-button cursor and the Summapad a four-button cursor; two- and three-button cursors are common. The cursor has fine, built-in cross hairs and a magnifying glass to permit precise alignment of the cursor over the point to be digitized. The coil in the Summapad cursor is barely visible. The plotter uses an optical sight that sits in the pen holder. Since the plotter positions the pen, it knows its digital coordinates.

Several digitization modes are possible. In the Point mode, the coordinates of a single point are transmitted to the computer by depressing the stylus or pressing a cursor button. Stream and Switch Stream modes digitize and transmit continuously. In stream, continuous digitization is switched on by depressing a cursor button and stopped by releasing it. Some digitizers can be interrogated to return the current coordinates of the cursor to the computer.

On a multi-button cursor, information about the specific button or combination of buttons is usually also transmitted. This extra information can be used to control what the computer does. For example, a specific button might begin digitizing, instruct the computer that the last point was sent, integrate a curve, redefine zero, and so on. Many digitizers have a specially marked area on the platen that can be digitized to transmit software-defined commands.

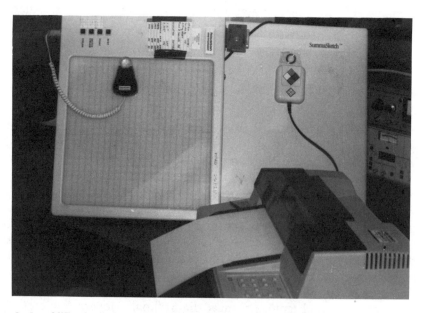

Figure 4–4. HiPad (left) and Summagraphics (right) digitizers and Hewlett-Packard digital plotter (foreground) that can function as a digitizer.

Interfacing of digitizers to computers is generally done via a serial RS-232 or an IEEE-488 parallel interface bus. We will deal only with the RS-232 in this chapter. Depending on size and accuracy, prices can range from about five-hundred dollars to tens-of-thousands of dollars.

To demonstrate the features of modern digitizers, we describe the Houston Instruments HiPad and the Summagraphics MM1201. The more modern Summagraphics has more features. We describe only their serial interfaces here.

4.3.1 Buffered Hardware Serial Interrupts

While sending data serially from the computer with Async was simple, serial character reception has a subtle but important complication. How does the computer avoid missing characters if they come in while the CPU is off doing something else? The answer involves the important concept of hardware interrupts. There are two ways to determine whether a character has been received: software polling and interrupts.

A polled scheme repeatedly tests the appropriate UART port to determine when a character has been received. Once the software detects the presence of a character, it reads it from the proper UART port. Unfortunately, if the software is not polling the UART fast enough, another character can overwrite the last character before it is read. To avoid data loss, polled software tends to spend most of the time monitoring the UART and doing little else.

A hardware interrupt works quite differently. The UART is programmed to work with an interrupt controller and a piece of installed software called an interrupt service routine (ISR); Async_Open installs the ISR. A hardware interrupt actually interrupts or diverts the program from whatever it is doing and forces execution of the ISR. The ISR reads the character from the UART and stores it in a buffer for later processing. After saving the character and updating the necessary variables to tell your program how many characters are available in the buffer, the ISR returns control to the place where it interrupted the main program. As new characters are received they are added to the buffer and the buffer fills. A hardware interrupt can be considered a special kind of subroutine call in which the call statement is inserted into the code at the time the interrupt occurs.

As the interrupts are asynchronous and can occur anywhere in the main program's execution, the ISR and interrupt controller must keep track of exactly how to get back to the main program and must restore any CPU information that is altered in the ISR. We explain in a later chapter exactly what transpires during an interrupt.

At any time your program can check to see whether the buffer has characters available and fetch them. Buffer reads are not synchronized with data reception. Each time you fetch a character, the buffer empties by one character. Thus, receiving a character adds a character to the buffer and each buffer read removes one. If too many characters come in too fast, the buffer can overflow and information is lost. If overflow occurs, a flag or variable is set to warn the main program of this loss.

In the Async Unit the buffer size is set to 4096 characters. Even at a maximum data input rate of 9600 baud, your program can leave an initially empty buffer for about four seconds without fear of overflow.

Async uses a circular buffer, and we describe briefly how this useful technique works. Async maintains two pointers, Async_Head and Async_Tail, which we abbreviate

HEAD and TAIL. HEAD and TAIL initially point at the start of the buffer area. When a character is received, the ISR stores it at the location pointed to by HEAD, and HEAD is incremented by one to point at the next free location. If HEAD points past the end of the buffer area, it is reset to point to the first location in the buffer.

When Async_Buffer_Check(var c:char) is called to get a character, it checks to see if HEAD=TAIL. If the two are equal, all characters have been read from the buffer, and Async_Buffer_Check returns a false. If characters are present, TAIL points at the earliest received character in the buffer. The character is read from the buffer, assigned the variable parameter C, and TAIL is incremented. If incrementation of TAIL causes it to point past the buffer, TAIL is reset to point at the beginning of the buffer.

Thus, as characters arrive they are stored at HEAD and HEAD is incremented to point at the next free buffer location. TAIL points at the earliest unread character received. As characters are read from the buffer, TAIL advances towards HEAD. When TAIL catches up with HEAD, the buffer is empty. The buffer is called circular since the pointers revolve around it. If HEAD catches up with TAIL when it is incremented, the buffer is filled and any further additions overflow the buffer.

While Microsoft and Borland BASICs have buffered interrupt serial inputs, Turbo Pascal lacks serial buffering. For serial input in Pascal, you could use Read or ReadLn(COM1, variable list), but if the program is not reading the port as data comes in, characters are lost. Therefore, the maximum transmission rate with Turbo Pascal can be quite low if you try to do anything other than input the data (e.g., print out the points on the video as they come in). This is another reason why we use the buffered Async routines for serial communications.

In actuality, you have been using hardware interrupts extensively. You can type several characters ahead of what the processor is doing since the keyboard interrupts the CPU. An 8-byte circular buffer is used, which is why it is still easy to overtype the buffer. Also, the PC's clock interrupts your programs about twenty times per second to tick the system clock.

4.3.2 Houston Instruments HiPad Digitizer

The Houston Instruments HiPad digitizer shown in Figure 4–4 has Digitize, Stream, and Switch Stream modes. Each mode is selected by depressing the appropriate push button on the left side of the pad.

The rates of digitization and transmission in the Stream and Switch Stream modes are limited by the digitization and transmission times. A new point is digitized only after the last one is transmitted. At high baud rates, digitization and transmission times both contribute to the maximum rate. At lower baud rates, transmission time limits the digitization rate. The HiPad digitizes data at about seventeen points per second at 4800 baud and about two points per second at 300 baud. In order to prevent a data glut in Stream and Switch Stream, data transmission is suspended if the cursor is not moved to a new point. Transmission resumes when the cursor is moved. Due to bobbles in the digitization circuit and susceptibility to vibration, there is generally a low transmission rate when the cursor is held stationary.

Point and Switch Stream modes are most useful for digitization. Point is best for fine work and Switch Stream for sweeping rapidly through and digitizing entire curves.

Table 4–3. Transmitted Numeric Codes on HiPad	
Code	Meaning
0	First point in a switch stream mode
1	All subsequent in switch stream mode
2	Point Mode
3	Stream Mode (all points)
4	Button depressed during Stream Mode

Data Format. The format for the transmitted digitized data varies for different digitizers. For the HiPad series, the data format for each digitized point is always a 13 character string of the form:

```
C±XXXXX±YYYYY<CR>
```

where C is a code digit that depends on the digitization mode. XXXXX and YYYYY are the X and Y coordinates of the digitized points in 0.001 inch. A sign (+ or −) is always present. The HiPad is switch-programmable as to origin. In one mode the lower left corner of the pad is always (0,0). In the other mode, depressing the reset button defines the current cursor position as (0,0).

The HiPad digitizer codes are listed in Table 4–3. The code depends on mode and, in the stream mode, whether it is the first point.

4.3.3 Summagraphics MM 1201 Digitization Tablet

The MM1201 digitization tablet has many additional enhancements. Its functions are largely serially software-programmable. It has stream, switch stream, variable rate stream mode, point mode, request mode, a relative mode, and several modes that report data only on specific grid sizes or if the cursor is moved more than a specified amount. It has an autobaud mode that allows the digitizer to set itself automatically to the baud rate of the controlling computer. The data report format is a compact binary format or an expanded ASCII format similar to that of the HiPad.

The MM1201 can use a stylus and three- or four-button cursors. The stylus is activated by pressing it to the tablet or by pushing the button on its side. The cursor is activated by pressing any button.

A weakness of the 1201 is the absence of an external switch to set or reset pad parameters. Most functions must be set by software. If it becomes locked, the only way to reset it is to unplug the power supply.

For our experiments we set the internal dip switch settings to ASCII BCD format, autobaud, and no parity. If you do not set the autobaud rate, the baud rate can only be 9600.

Programming the Baud Rate. To set the baud rate, the first character you send the digitizer after power up must be a single space character. Do not send any character immediately afterward; we use a 500 ms delay. The digitizer uses this delay to calculate

Table 4–4. 1201 Modes, Resolutions and Programming Codes

Mode	Programming Character
Baud Rate	Space
Stream	@
Switch Stream	A
Point	B
Remote Request	
Mode Command	D
Trigger	P

Resolution	
10 lpmm (254 lpi)	f
20 lpmm (508 lpi)	i
40 lpmm (1016 lpi)	q
100 lpi	d
200 lpi	e
400 lpi	g
500 lpi	h
1000 lpi	j

the baud rate from the appearance of the space character and then to initialize itself. If any other character is received first after a power up, the digitizer becomes very confused and must be turned off and then on again to recover.

Mode Selection. The digitizer powers up in the switch stream mode. It also has a stream and a point mode. Each can be selected by sending the single character shown in Table 4–4. This table is not exhaustive. In the switch stream mode, if the cursor is moved out of range of the tablet (about a half an inch) or off the sensing area while a button is pressed, the last valid point is sent continuously. If the cursor is out of range and a button is pressed, the last valid point is sent continuously.

In the stream mode, if the cursor is moved out of range of the tablet, the last point is sent three times and the digitizer stops transmitting. Then, pressing any key on the cursor causes the last point to be sent continuously. In the point mode, if the cursor is out of range, the last valid point is sent once.

In the remote request mode, the digitizer only transmits the current position when the computer issues a request for data. To enable the remote request mode, send a single D character. Then any requests for points are made by sending a P character and reading the digitized information.

Programming the Resolution. The digitizer is set to different resolutions by sending the appropriate ASCII programming characters (Table 4–4). The resolution is the smallest movement that the digitizer resolves. The different resolutions are given in lines per mm (lpmm) or lines per inch (lpi).

Data Format. In the BCD mode, the digitized data format except for the 100 lpi resolution is:

Table 4–5. Button Flag Digit for Different Button Combinations

Stylus	3-Button Cursor	4-Button Cursor	Flag Character
none	none	none	0
Tip	1	1	1
Barrel switch	2	2	2
	3	3	3
		4	4
	1+3 or 2+3	1+2,1+3, 2+3, 2+4, or 1+2+3	3
	1+3	1+4	5
	1+2+3	1+2+4 or 2+3+4 or 1+2+3+4	7

```
XXXX,YYYY,F<CRLF>
```

while for the 1000 lpi resolution mode the format is:

```
XXXXX,YYYYY,F<CRLF>
```

where XXXX or XXXXX and YYYY or YYYYY are the four- or five-digit X and Y coordinates respectively for the cursor position. The coordinates are given in units of the digitizer resolution. Thus, at a resolution of 500 lpi, the basic unit is 0.002 inch and 1000 is actually 2.000 inches (1000x0.002). F is the button flag and has the ASCII value for the different buttons being pushed as given in Table 4–5.

The MM1201 also has a 5-byte binary format, which is the factory setting supplying more information than the BCD mode; it can identify two different tablets and indicates when the sensor is within operating range of the tablet. The binary mode is, however, harder to decode. The binary and BCD modes can be changed only by reconfiguring motherboard jumpers, which requires disassembling the digitizer.

Experiments 4–1 – 4–11. These experiments familiarize you with the use of a digitizer and graphics. An oscilloscope photograph of a laser luminescence decay is supplied and you digitize the data, correct for the baseline, and fit the data by least squares to obtain the lifetime. Graphics are used to select the fitting regions and to judge the quality of the fit.

Experiments 4–12 and 4–13. In these experiments you familiarize yourself with a commercial graphics package that allows making publication quality fits on a dot matrix printer or a digital plotter.

4.4 REFERENCES

The expensive, indexless Summagraphics Corp. manual is essential for additional work with the Summapad. The Turbo Pascal manuals give much more extensive descriptions of the rich set of graphics procedures and functions in the Graph Unit. Swan's book on Turbo Pascal has an excellent discussion of Pascal graphics.

Problems

4–1 [4.2]. Write a program to plot the exponential decay of the least squares problem. Use the whole plotting field of the screen. Put X and Y axes on the plot.

4–2 [4.2]. Write a program to plot the LN of the exponential decay of Problem 4–1 on the same plot as the decay. It will be necessary to rescale between plots. Scale the plot so that the decay spans the entire screen. This is feasible as changing the scale does not affect what is already on the screen.

4–3 [4.2]. Rewrite Problem 4–1 so that you have a user-supplied label centered on the top of the display. Scale the axis and plotting area so that the label does not fall in the plotting area.

4–4 [4.2]. Extend Problem 4–3 so that you can also put a user-defined X-axis label under the lower X axis.

4–5 [4.2]. Rewrite Problem 4–4 so that you can also put a vertical Y-axis label, which is outside the data plotting area.

5

Analog Considerations

5.1 INTRODUCTION

Having previously discussed digital logic, we turn to analog or continuous signal processing. In this chapter we discuss the primary analog building block, the operational amplifier, and several important applications. Next we cover digital-to-analog conversion and some of the more important analog-to-digital conversion schemes with their relative strengths and weaknesses. Finally, we consider several important points concerning analog signal processing. An understanding of some basic direct current (dc) circuit theory is assumed.

5.2 OPERATIONAL AMPLIFIERS

The single most important analog building block is the operational amplifier commonly known as the op amp. The subject of op amps is extensive; we merely present some basic theory and terminology to prepare you for subsequent circuitry.

Op amps are very high gain dc difference amplifiers. They amplify the difference between two dc input signals by a large amount. Figure 5–1 shows the symbol for an op amp that has a noninverting (+) and an inverting (−) input. The output voltage, V_{out}, is given by:

$$V_{out} = (V_+ - V_-) A \qquad (5-1)$$

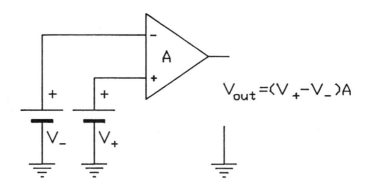

$$V_{out} = (V_+ - V_-)A$$

Figure 5–1. Representation and characteristics of an operational amplifier. Power supply connections (typically ±15 V) and zeroing connections are omitted for clarity.

where the Vs are the input voltages with respect to ground. The + and − respectively denote the noninverting and the inverting input voltages. A is the open loop gain of the amplifier, or the gain without any feedback. By tailoring the feedback between the inputs and the outputs, you can make an op amp do almost anything in analog signal processing. Our subsequent analysis is based on two simplifying assumptions:

(1)   The open loop gain (A) is infinite and the circuit has a finite output. Thus, from Equation 5–1, the difference between the inverting and the noninverting inputs is zero. This means that $V_+ - V_- = 0$.

(2)   The input resistance of both op amp inputs is infinite. Thus, no current flows into them.

While these assumptions are not rigorously correct, deviations will not be significant for our understanding of basic circuit theory and applications. The deviations can generally be easily accounted for and must be explicitly encountered in design work. We now describe in detail several important op amp circuits.

5.2.1 Operational Feedback

A widely used configuration is operational feedback, which is shown in Figure 5–2A. The noninverting input is connected to ground potential (0 V). Based on Rule 1, $V_+ = V_- = 0$. Thus, V_- is at ground potential. This point is known as a virtual ground since it is virtually at ground potential but is not a circuit ground. It is shown in the figure by a ground symbol in parenthesis. This point is also called a summing point. Thus, the input current flow, i_{in}, in R_i is:

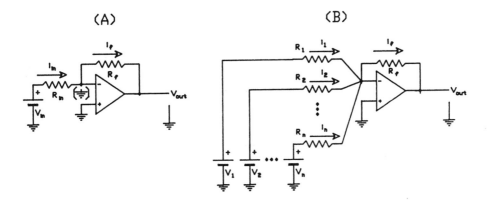

Figure 5–2. (A) Operational feedback configuration. (B) Summing amplifier.

$$i_{in} = \frac{V_{in} - V_-}{R_{in}} = \frac{V_{in}}{R_{in}} \tag{5-2}$$

By rule 2, all of i_{in} must exit through R_f and $i_f = i_{in}$. V_{out} is given by:

$$V_{out} = -i_f R_f = -(V_{in}/R_i) R_f \tag{5-3}$$

The minus sign results since the current flow in the resistor causes the end connected to the output to be more negative than the V_- end. The critical characteristic of an amplifier is its effective gain, A_{eff}, which is the ratio of the output voltage to the input voltage:

$$A_{eff} = V_{out}/V_{in} = -(R_f/R_{in}) \tag{5-4}$$

Thus, the effective gain of an operations feedback circuit is determined solely by the ratio of two resistors. One can easily tailor the circuit to give any desired inverting gain.

5.2.2 Summing Amplifier

A slight but useful variation of operational feedback is the summing amplifier of Figure 5–2B. This allows two or more inputs to be summed and scaled by different relative amounts. The summing amplifier has two or more inputs with each connected to the summing point through a different resistor. Since the virtual ground is at zero potential, the total current in the feedback resistor equals the sum of all the currents entering the summing point from the different sources:

$$i_f = \sum_{j=1}^{N} i_j \tag{5-5}$$

and V_{out} is given by:

$$V_{out} = -i_f R_f = -R_f \sum_{j=1}^{N} \left[\frac{V_j}{R_j} \right] \tag{5-6}$$

Thus, the output is the sum of the input voltages with each weighted by the factor (R_f/R_j).

If all resistors are equal, the output is the simple scaled sum of all inputs. By making the R_js different, the output can be made any weighted linear sum of several inputs. A music mixer for combining signals from different instrumental and vocal tracks is readily built using a summer with variable R_js.

5.2.3 Voltage Follower

Operational feedback has one limitation. It is current-activated and draws current from, or loads, your signal source. Many sources are incapable of supplying the current or loading makes the measured voltage incorrect.

The follower configuration of Figure 5–3 has a very high input resistance and draws no current from the source. The operation is straightforward. The output stabilizes when $V_+=V_-$. Since $V_+=V_{out}$ and $V_-=V_{in}$, then $V_{out}=V_{in}$ or the output follows the input. As the input voltage is connected only to the op amp input, which draws no current, there is no loading of the source. Current drawn at the output is supplied by the operational amplifier and not the signal source. A follower is also known as a buffer since it buffers or isolates the input from the output.

Followers are widely used to isolate high resistance sources such as pH electrodes. The input of most commercial analog-to-digital converter (ADC) modules contains a follower to prevent perturbation of the measurement by the ADC.

5.2.4 Difference Amplifiers

Frequently it is necessary to measure the voltage difference between two points, neither of which is at ground potential. A suitable one-amplifier circuit is shown in Figure 5–4. The effective gain, A_{eff}, can be determined by the following analysis. V_+ and V_- are given by:

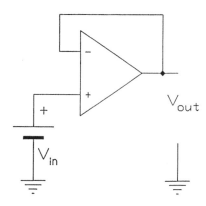

Figure 5–3. Voltage follower configuration.

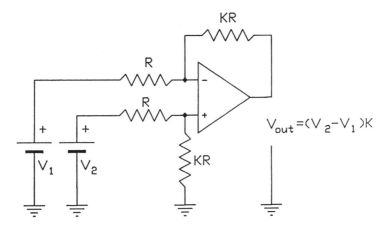

Figure 5–4. Difference amplifier.

$$V_+ = \frac{V_2 KR}{R + KR} \tag{5–7a}$$

$$V_- = V_1 + (V_{out} - V_1)\left[\frac{R}{R + KR}\right] = V_1 + \left[\frac{V_{out} - V_1}{1 + K}\right] \tag{5–7b}$$

By rule 1, $V_+ = V_-$ and suitable rearrangement yields:

$$\frac{V_{out}}{1 + K} = V_2\left[\frac{K}{1 + K}\right] + \left[-\frac{V_1(1 + K) + V_1}{1 + K}\right] \tag{5–7c}$$

which simplifies to:

$$V_{out} = K(V_2 - V_1) \tag{5–7d}$$

Thus, we have a circuit that directly and precisely amplifies the difference between two grounded input voltages. This design suffers from being current-activated, requires careful resistor matching, and requires that the ratios of two pairs of resistors be changed simultaneously in order to vary the gain. To solve the loading problem, a buffer can be placed before each input, which yields a high input resistance. There are multiamplifier schemes that have both high input resistance and a gain that can be varied by changing one resistor.

A high input resistance, variable gain difference amplifier is frequently called an instrumentation amplifier. These find wide use as transducer input stages and work well with bridge circuits due to their differential inputs. Several semiconductor manufacturers make inexpensive single IC instrumentation amplifiers whose gain can be set by changing one or two resistors.

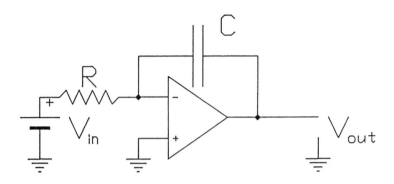

Figure 5–5. Operational amplifier integrator.

5.2.5 Integrator

Signal integration is a critical component of many ADC schemes. An analog integrator (Figure 5–5) can be made from a variation on operational feedback. The feedback resistor is replaced with a capacitor, which prevents the current flowing into the summing point from continuing to the op amp's ouput, and the charge accumulates on the capacitor. The voltage on a capacitor is given by:

$$V_C = Q / C \qquad (5\text{--}8)$$

where the V_C is in volts if the capacitance (C) is in Farads, and the accumulated charge Q is in coulombs. If at t=0 the capacitor is discharged, Q is related to current flow by:

$$Q = \int_{t=0}^{t} I(t)\,dt = \int_{t=0}^{t} V(t)/R\,dt \qquad (5\text{--}9)$$

where I(t) in amperes and $V_{in}(t)$ are the time dependence of the summing point current and input voltage, respectively. Combining Equations 5–8 and 5–9 yields:

$$V_{out} = -\left[\frac{1}{RC}\right] \int_{t=0}^{t} V(t)dt \qquad (5\text{--}10)$$

The minus or inversion comes from the fact that the output voltage is derived from the capacitor, one end of which is effectively connected to ground (the virtual ground). Thus, if a positive voltage is developed on the virtual ground side of the capacitor, the output is negative with respect to the virtual ground or real ground.

5.2.6 Analog Comparator

An analog comparator compares two analog signals and provides an output that indicates which of the two is larger. It is the analog of a digital comparator. The symbol for a comparator is the same as that of an operational amplifier; however, the internal circuitry is quite different and they cannot be used in feedback configurations as can op amps. Frequently, the output of the comparator is open collector and the user provides the pull up resistor and necessary voltage. This has the advantage that one comparator can work with different logic families by merely changing the pull up resistor and voltage.

The analog comparator can be thought of as a 1-bit ADC. Its output tells you whether an unknown voltage is above or below some reference voltage. As we will see, the comparator is the critical element of all ADC schemes.

5.2.7 Voltage-to-Frequency Converter (VFC)

An important method of analog-to-digital conversions is the VFC. A simple VFC can be made from an integrator, a comparator, and a precision pulsed charge source. This is shown in Figure 5–6. The input voltage is integrated. When the integrator crosses zero, the comparator senses this and fires the unit charge generator, which delivers a unit charge Q_u to the integrator. The charge is of opposite sign to that from V_{in}. As charge is delivered by V_{in}, the unit charge generator is fired to counterbalance this charge. The larger V_{in} is, the more often the generator fires. During a period of one second, the charge delivered by V_{in} is V_{in}/R. To counterbalance this, the unit charge generator delivers an equal opposite charge of:

$$Q = f Q_u \tag{5-11}$$

where f is the frequency of unit charge generation. By equating the charges delivered by the two sources we obtain f:

$$f = \left[\frac{1}{Q_u R} \right] V_{in} \tag{5-12}$$

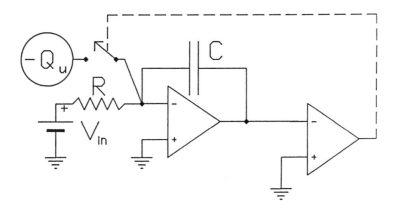

Figure 5–6. Voltage-to-frequency converter using a comparator triggered unit charge generator.

Thus, the frequency is directly proportional to known or readily determined quantities and V_{in}. By adjusting Q_u and R, specific calibration factors can be set. Generally, the response is given in kilohertz or megahertz per volt of input.

5.2.8   Sample and Hold (S/H) or Track and Hold (T/H)

A track and hold is a device with an output that will follow or track an input signal until a hold command is issued. The output will then be held equal to the input at the instant that the hold command was issued. The hold state persists until the control returns to the track level, at which time the output catches up to the input and follows it until another hold command is issued. One of the most important uses of a T/H from our standpoint is holding a signal stable during analog-to-digital conversion.

A simple S/H is shown in Figure 5–7. When the T/H is in the track mode the analog switch is closed; the output of the follower charges the memory capacitor through the switch resistance, R. If the RC time constant is short compared to the changes in the signal, the capacitor voltages follow the signal. The output of the T/H is the buffer capacitor voltage.

In the hold mode the switch is open, and the capacitor is not charged or discharged by the input. The second follower prevents the capacitor from discharging into the output circuits. Thus, once the switch is opened, the capacitor holds at its value at the instant the switch was opened, which also equals the input voltage at that time.

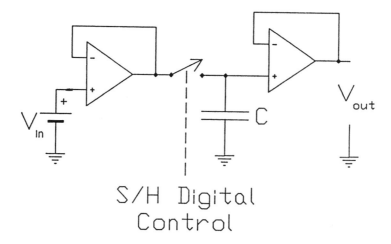

Figure 5–7. Simple sample-and-hold or track-and-hold circuit. Hold is with the switch open.

5.2.9 Digital-to-Analog Converters (DAC)

A DAC converts a digital code into a corresponding voltage. Most DACs give out-puts that are directly proportional to the binary code, but logarithmic DACs are used for signal compression. Most commonly DACs use binary or offset binary coding. A few accept BCD inputs.

The general DAC strategy uses a series of digitally controlled switches. When each switch is on, it injects a controlled current into the summing point of a summing amplif-ier. By weighting each current by the significance of each digital bit, the output of the summing amplifier is made directly proportional to the binary code.

Figure 5–8 shows a primitive binary DAC. For n bit binary value, $b_{n-1} . . b_1 b_0$, the current in the summing point is given by:

$$i = b_{n-1}\left[\frac{V}{2R}\right] + \cdots + b_1\left[\frac{V}{2^{n-1}R}\right] + b_0\left[\frac{V}{2^n R}\right] \tag{5-13}$$

and the output voltage is given by:

$$V_{out} = -i\,R_f \tag{5-14}$$

Since each resistor current is weighted by the relative significance of each bit, the output voltage is directly proportional to the binary value of the code.

In practice the indicated $2^n R$ resistances are not used. The large resistors necessary for large numbers of bits produce large RC time constants and slow responses. Further, accurate generation of such a wide range of resistors is difficult and the necessary resis-tances exceed that which can be fabricated accurately on a single chip. A clever scheme

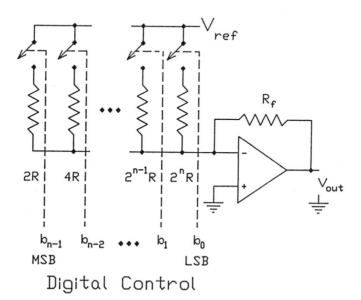

Figure 5–8. Simple digital-to-analog converter using binary weighted currents controlled by analog switches.

called an R–2R ladder network solves both problems. A ladder network using R and 2R resistors performs the same functions as Figure 5–8. The two resistors can be made small and fast; precise matching of only two values can be performed easily.

5.3 ANALOG-TO-DIGITAL CONVERSIONS

There are many analog-to-digital conversion schemes. We focus on the most widely used ones and compare their merits.

5.3.1 Voltage-to-Frequency Conversion (VFC)

A particularly simple conversion method uses a VFC and a frequency counter. The output of the VFC is fed directly into the counter and the counter totals the number of counts during a fixed period, typically 0.01, 0.1, 1 or 10 s. If the voltage-to-frequency conversion factor is 100 KHz/V with a 0–10 V range, then a 1 s counting time gives a resolution of $1/10^5$ of full scale or 0.1 mV. This is a dynamic range of five orders of magnitude. Higher frequency conversion factors or longer counting periods provide even finer resolution.

One very nice feature of VFCs is the ease of using them with isolated sources. Sometimes a signal source sits at a different potential than where we wish to process it. For example, many mass spectrometer detectors sit thousands of volts above ground, and it is very awkward to place a computer and other processing equipment at that potential.

A VFC coupled with an **optical isolator** solves the problem. An optical isolator has a light emitting diode (LED), an insulating transparent separator, and an optical detector (e.g., photodiode or phototransistor). A logic high can turn the LED on, which in turn shines light on the phototransistor and turns it on. The phototransistor can then be used as a switch to turn on other logic. Since the only connection between the LED and phototransistor is optical, it does not matter whether one is at 5 KV above ground and the other at ground potential. Now, by sensing the detector output with a VFC and driving the LED with its output, the frequency and thus the voltage of the source can be determined with the counter sitting at ground potential.

5.3.2 Servo Converters

Servo converters all use the basic system of Figure 5–9. The input voltage is compared with the voltage derived from a DAC. The comparator senses the magnitude of V_{DAC} versus V_{in}. This information is passed back to the logic block, which readjusts V_{DAC} until V_{DAC} equals V_{in}. The strategy for adjusting V_{DAC} determines the ADC method. There are three common strategies which we will discuss in greater detail below:

(1) Linear Ramp.
(2) Tracking.
(3) Successive Approximation.

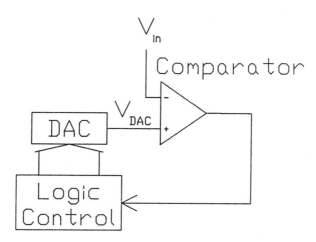

Figure 5–9.   Block diagram for DAC based servo analog-to-digital conversion schemes.

Linear Ramp. The simplest method is linear ramp. The first test digital word is the most negative voltage DAC value. This is tested with the comparator. If the voltage is too low, the digital output word is incremented by one and the test repeated. This process of incrementing and testing is repeated until $V_{DAC} > V_{in}$. The digital output word that causes the change at the time is the digitized value. The term linear ramp arises from the shape of V_{DAC} versus time. V_{DAC} ramps up until it crosses V_{in}. A new conversion is then started by resetting the digital test word to its most negative value and starting over. In practice, a linear ramp is implemented by using a binary counter to drive the DAC directly. A master clock determines each increment (counter up) compare cycle.

Linear ramp ADC is simple and inexpensive. It suffers from generally slow conversion times, and the digitization rate depends on the signal amplitude. An n-bit conversion takes from 1 to 2^n comparison-test cycles (e.g., 1–4095 for a 12-bit converter).

Tracking ADC. A slight variation of the linear ramp makes a more powerful converter. Instead of resetting the counter to zero after each conversion, the digital word is continuously adjusted to make it match the input signal. This is done by incrementing the test word if V_{DAC} is too small and decrementing it if V_{DAC} is large. For a slowly changing signal, V_{DAC} tracks V_{in} after V_{DAC} initially catches up with V_{in}.

While it is an improvement over the linear ramp, the tracking ADC still suffers response time problems for signals that change more rapidly than V_{DAC} can ramp up or down. In addition, some tracking ADCs can suffer from a very perplexing problem. Consider the case where V_{in} is greater than the maximum V_{DAC}. When the digital counter gets to its maximum value, it rolls over and resets to zero. For example, an 8-bit converter goes from 255_{10} to zero. Since V_{DAC} is still less than V_{in}, the counter continues to ramp up until it reaches 255 where it resets to zero. This resetting and ramping is continuous. If the counter is read at random times, the digitized value assumes random values between 0 and 255. A similar effect is observed for V_{in} below the most negative DAC output. These problems can be, but are not always, compensated for in hardware.

Successive Approximation ADC. Successive approximation is the most popular intermediate speed ADC technique. It is based on the well-known strategy of binary division and comparison. Suppose that we had an 8-bit DAC. We would begin by trying half of full scale of 128_{10} (10000000_2); this is done by setting the most significant bit (MSB). If this digital word generates a V_{DAC} that is above V_{in}, then the MSB must be set in the final digitized value and we keep the test bit set. If $V_{DAC} > V_{in}$, then the MSB must be reset to zero in the final result. We now have a digitized value $(0/1)0000000$ where the $(0/1)$ indicates that the correct 0 or a 1 have been determined for a bit.

Next we test the MSB by setting the DAC with $(0/1)1000000_2$. If this new test word yields $V_{DAC} < V_{in}$, then this bit is kept in the final result; otherwise it is cleared. We now have $(0/1)(0/1)000000$. The process of setting and testing each bit in turn continues by working from the MSB to the least significant bit (LSB). For an n-bit conversion, only n tests are required for a complete conversion.

Experiment 5–1. Servo linear ramp, tracking, and successive approximation ADCs are implemented using a software-driven DAC. They are compared with respect to speed and the ability to reproduce input waveforms.

Dual Slope Integrating ADCs. Dual slope conversion uses an integrator, a precision current source, a comparator, and a timing circuit. Figure 5–10 shows a simplified dual slope converter. In operation, the digital counter is reset to zero and the integrating capacitor is shorted out to discharge C to zero. Conversion is divided into two cycles, an

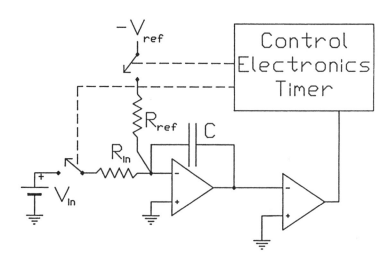

Figure 5–10. Simplified dual slope analog-to-digital converter.

integrate and a deintegrate cycle. For a period Δt_{int} the input signal is integrated. This charges the integrating capacitor with charge Q_{int} given by:

$$Q_{int} = (V_{in} / R_{in}) \, \Delta t_{int} \tag{5-15}$$

The input source is disconnected from the integrator and connected to the precision voltage source-reference resistor, which forms a precision current source for the integrator. The time necessary for the reference source to discharge the integrating capacitor to zero is measured. The comparator senses the zero crossing and halts the timing. The charge delivered to the integrator is given by:

$$Q_{ref} = (V_{ref} / R_{ref}) \, t_{deint} \tag{5-16}$$

Since $Q_{ref}=Q_{int}$, the necessary deintegration time is:

$$t_{deint} = V_{in} \left[\frac{1}{R_{in}} \right] \left[\frac{R_{ref}}{V_{ref}} \right] \Delta t_{int} \tag{5-17}$$

Thus, t_{deint} is directly proportional to V_{in} and known or measureable quantities. Now if we can time t_{deint} digitally, we have a digital quantity that is proportional to V_{in}. Timing is done by gating an oscillator into a counter string when the deintegrate cycle starts and stopping it when the comparator reports that the integrator output crosses zero. By adjusting the two resistances and V_{ref}, we can cause the number of counts to come out as a digital representation of the input voltage (e.g., 10 V gives 10,000 counts). This would give a digital voltmeter with one part in 10^4 resolution.

We have overlooked many complexities. Useful dual slope ADCs can handle bipolar signals by sensing their polarity and inverting either the signal or the reference voltage. Also, the scheme has problems with low amplitude signals, which require special attention. Consult the references for details.

The laboratory environment is rich with 60 Hz noise that frequently gets into your signal. However, an integrating converter can largely eliminate errors from alternating current (ac) pickup. The integrate cycle is set to an integer number of power line cycles (typically 6 or 60, which corresponds to 0.1 or 1 s integrations). Since power line noise is largely the 60 Hz fundamental that integrates to zero for any integer number of periods, power line pickup has little or no effect on the digitized values.

Flash Converters. Flash, parallel, or video converters make a conversion by simultaneously comparing the input voltage with all possible digitization levels. Figure 5–11 shows a block diagram. The resistive voltage divider establishes a set of reference levels for the comparator that are each separated by a single quantization step. For 8 bits, about 255 comparators are required. Under and overrange detection can increase this by one or two. For example, if the input voltage digitizes to 5_{10} or 101_2, the first five comparators find V_{in} less than their reference levels while the remaining comparators see reference voltages that are above V_{in}. The output of the approximately 2^n comparators is then decoded to an n-bit word.

The advantage of flash converters is speed. Low cost IC converters give more than 25 million conversions per second with 8-bit conversion, and 500 MHz systems are available. Their main disadvantage is limited resolution (typically 6–8 bits).

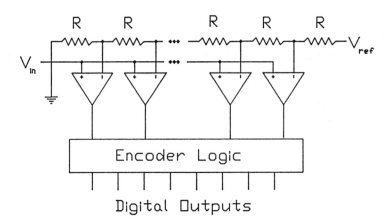

Figure 5–11. An n-bit flash converter based on 2^n comparators.

A very popular application is the digital oscilloscope, which is now made by a number of manufacturers. These scopes will store several waveforms, signal average, and transfer digitized data to a computer for further processing. Video frame graphers that digitize an entire video image from a single video camera sweep also use them.

Where more resolution is required, flash converters can be series-connected to increase their resolution. The signal is first digitized at a coarse level. The coarse component is subtracted off, and the difference, which contains the finer resolution information, is digitized with a second flash converter. Combining the coarse and fine digitized values gives a higher resolution conversion. For example, a 0–8 V full scale 6-bit converter can be made with two 3-bit 7 V full-scale converters, a 3-bit DAC, and a difference amplifier. We demonstrate this by carrying out a conversion on 5.375 V.

The first converter digitizes V_{in} at the volt level (i.e., 0, 1, 2,. .7). Our example yields 5_{10} or 101_2. This 3-bit digitization is converted to the corresponding voltage with a 3-bit 7 V range DAC. Our example gives 5.000V. A difference amplifier with a gain of 8 subtracts the DAC output from the input. This is equivalent to removing the integer component of the input voltage from V_{in} and amplifying the difference by 8 to yield a 0–8 V signal that contains the remaining undigitized information. Our 0.375 V difference is amplified to 3.0V. A second 3-bit ADC then digitizes the remaining three bits of V_{in}. In our case, the 3 V gives 011_2. Concatenating the high and low three bits gives a 6-bit conversion. Our example gives 101011_2. More realistic 6-bit converters might be used to form a 12-bit converter.

IC flash converters with 10- and 12-bit resolution are not yet available. ADCs with this resolution and 1 μs or less conversion times generally use this serial flash method.

Comparison of ADC Schemes. Table 5–1 summarizes the salient features of different ADC methods. Dual slope is most widely used where speed is not critical but freedom from ac pickup is, as in digital voltmeters. Successive approximation is the mainstay of intermediate speed and resolution measurements (25 KHz-1 MHz at 12 bits).

Table 5–1. Comparison of Different ADC Schemes

	Speed (Conversions per second)	Resolution (Bits)	AC Rejection
VFC	1–1000	12–17	high[1]
Dual Slope	1–100	12–17	high[1]
Linear Ramp	100–1000	8–12	poor
Tracking	100–10000[2]	8–12	poor
Successive Approximation	2000–10M	8–16	poor
Flash	20M–>500M	6–8	poor

[1] High if integration time is integer number of ac cycles.
[2] Initial rate is same as linear ramp, then effectively higher.

Flash conversion finds its place in digital scopes, video converters for video cameras or digital home VCRs, and in many fast transient recorders. In many places, more than one type of converter works, and the choice rests on availability and convenience.

5.4 ANALOG SWITCHES AND MULTIPLEXERS

Analog signal switching is critical in many applications (e.g., ADC schemes described above). In terms of ideal switching characteristics, relays have nearly perfect off and on resistances, but are slow (typically 200 μs for good reed relays). Relays are still found in very low current or voltage applications. More common is the use of field effect transistors (FETs). FETs are much better analog switches than standard transistors, and can have on resistances in the 10–100 Ω and off resistances in the $100–10^4$ MΩ range. Analog switches are used in the signal routing in many ADC schemes and in multiplexers.

A multiplexer selects one of several inputs and routes it to a single output. The input is selected with a digital code. Because ADCs tend to be rather expensive, it is common to place an analog multiplexer in front of a single ADC. By properly selecting the input channel, any one of several inputs can be digitized. This has two advantages. If the ADC conversion speed and multiplexer are fast with respect to the rate of change of the input signals, then even though the points are digitized sequentially, they appear to have been taken simultaneously. The second advantage is convenience. Many times a single acquisition system is used with several instruments. If only a few channels were available, every time you changed instruments you would have to reconfigure all the inputs; this takes time and increases the chances of error. With multiple channels, all can be connected at once and software can, in effect, do the reconfigurations by selecting the appropriate channels for different instrumentation.

Multiplexers are either single-ended or differential. Figure 5–12 shows a sixteen-channel ADC multiplexer wired as both single-ended and differential. In single-ended all inputs have a common ground return. In differential, a difference amplifier looks at

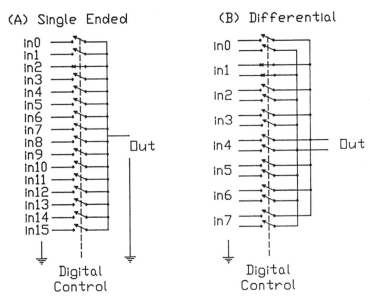

Figure 5–12. Single-ended (A) and differential (B) multiplexer. The digital control (dashed line) selects the single or pair of switches.

the difference between two points. Each switching of the differential multiplexer shifts both switches to a new signal. Generally, a sixteen-channel multiplexer can be used as a sixteen-channel single-ended or eight-channel differential.

We note two places where differential measurements are useful: floating signal source and elimination of ground noise. Many sources float off ground and thus have two ungrounded signal lines, which a single-ended measurement cannot handle. The common bridge circuit used for many transducers (e.g., thermistors and strain gauges) is an example; it uses a grounded power supply with two ungrounded signal lines. In the other case, noise pickup can arise from noise signals in the ground system since no two ground

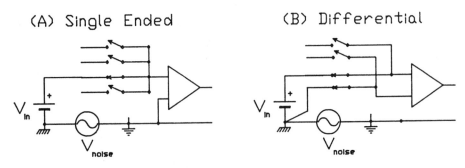

Figure 5–13. Single (A) and differential (B) multiplexer with a difference amplifier showing the effect of ground noise.

points in a system are at the same potential. This is shown schematically in Figure 5–13A. We show the multiplexer connected to a distant signal via a signal wire and a ground return. V_{noise} is noise in the finite resistance ground return line. Circulating power line ground currents flow in these return lines and produce voltages. V_{noise} is in series with and is indistinguishable from the desired signal; unless accounted for, V_{noise} can decrease the accuracy of measurement of V_{in} or even hide it completely.

The noise problem is most severe with low-to-submillivolt level signals or very high resolutions, and you may not notice the problem with large (1–10 V) medium resolution (12-bit) measurements. It is also more prevalent where long connections are made between several different instruments.

The solution is shown in Figure 5–13B. While we still have the ground return, a differential multiplexer and an instrumentation amplifier look at the signal directly at its source. Clearly, this configuration is virtually immune to V_{noise} since V_{noise} is common to both inputs and the difference amplifier eliminates it.

We successfully exploited the benefits of differential measurements in a 48-channel data acquisition system that we helped install on a lake environment monitoring system. The sensors and the preamplifiers were placed on a raft in the middle of the lake. A single ADC was mounted with the computer in a shed about 150 m from the raft. Without differential measurements, the interactions between signal channels made the system largely unusable; the long ground return introduced severe ground noise and ac pickup. Because we used a full differential configuration with a separate pair of wires run to each preamplifier (one to the amplifier and one to the amplifier's local ground point) and an integrating ADC with an integration period of ten power line cycles, there was no detectible interaction or ac pickup.

Track and Hold for ADCs.   As we can easily appreciate, all of the nonintegrating ADC schemes depend on a signal that is stable during conversion. It would not do for a successive approximation converter to initially set the MSB only to have the signal fall below this value during the rest of the conversion. However, the ease with which errors can arise from this source is not so obvious.

To consider the magnitude of the problem, consider a 12-bit ADC with a 25 μs conversion time and ±10 V full scale range. Each bit then corresponds to 4.9 mV. Now, without a T/H, how fast a full scale sine wave can we digitize and not incur more than a 1-bit error? Another way of putting this is: How fast a sine wave can we have that will not change by more than one bit during the conversion time of 25 μs? A sine wave and its rate of change are given by:

$$V(t) = 10 \, V \; \sin(2 \pi f t) \qquad (5\text{–}18)$$

$$\frac{d \, V(t)}{dt} = 10 \, V \; (2 \pi f) \cos(2 \pi f t) \qquad (5\text{–}19)$$

The worst case occurs at the maximum rate of change or at t=0:

$$\left[\frac{d \, V(t)}{dt} \right]_{max} = 10 \, V \; (2 \pi f) \qquad (5\text{–}20)$$

The signal change, ΔV_{dig}, during the conversion time, Δt_{dig}, is approximated by:

$$\Delta V_{dig} = \left[\frac{d\,V(t)}{dt} \right]_{max} \Delta t_{dig} = 10\,V\ (2\,\pi\,f)\,\Delta t_{dig} \qquad (5\text{--}21)$$

For our 40 KHz conversion rate, the maximum frequency that we can use without a 1-bit error is 3 Hz! This is subaudio and does not begin to approach the ranges that frequently interest us.

Placing a track and hold in front of the ADC largely solves the problem. The T/H grabs the signal at the initiation of the digitization period, and after the T/H is stable the ADC makes the conversions. Even though the signal is changing, the voltage being digitized remains fixed and there is no error from an input.

5.5 NYQUIST SAMPLING THEOREM

An insidious problem in digital signal processing has to do with information theory. You must sample each frequency present in your waveform at least twice per cycle to obtain information about that component. It is intuitively obvious that if we do not sample at least that often, we lack any information about a waveform. For example, a single point on a single cycle of a sine wave gives virtually no information. The Nyquist frequency is the minimum frequency of sampling that will preserve the frequency content of the original waveform and equals twice the highest frequency present.

Less obvious, however, is that if we fail to digitize fast enough, higher frequency components actually distort low frequency measurements. Consider the digitized signals of Figure 5–14. All three signals appear to be clean sinusoidal waveforms of different frequencies with one each at 2, 3 and 4 Hz. Yet they are actually the same 25 Hz

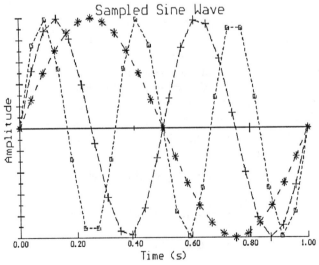

Figure 5–14. A sine wave digitized at 22 Hz (□ – – –□), 23 Hz (+ —— +), and 24 Hz (*— — *).

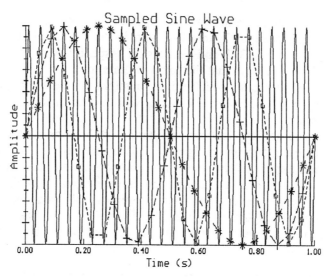

Figure 5–15. The waveforms of Figure 5–14 replotted and superimposed on the original digitized 25 Hz waveform. Digitization rates: 22 Hz (□ – – –□), 23 Hz (+ —— +), and 24 Hz (*— — *).

waveform digitized at three different rates. Figure 5–15 shows the explanation of the apparent paradox. Clearly what happens is that you are digitizing no more than a single point on each occurrence of the waveform, and each succeeding sampling is occurring at progressively later and later points in the cycle. Different sampling rates change the delay time into each succeeding cycle and, thus, the apparent frequency.

This appearance of lower frequency when you sample is exactly analogous to the stroboscopic slowing of motion or the appearance of moving objects in movies. If a strobe lamp fires at a rate that exactly equals one rotation period of an object or a multiple of this period, the object appears to be stationary. If the firing rate is a little longer or shorter, the object will appear to rotate slowly forward or backward. The slowed or reverse movement of wheels in movies arises from the same effect except that the camera shutter replaces the sampling of the strobe lamp.

The appearance of high frequency signals at lower frequencies is called **aliasing**. If the sampling rate is f_{sample} and the digitized waveform is of frequency f, then the frequency of the alias signal depends on the signal frequency.

Consider an f_{sample} of 1000 Hz. For an input f up to 500 Hz, the sampling rate meets the Nyquist criteria and the digitized signal will faithfully match the input. That is, the apparent frequency in the digitized signal increases and matches the input signal. There will be no false signals or aliases. As the f rises above $f_{Nyquist}/2$, however, the apparent frequency of the digitized signal starts to decrease. A 600 Hz sine wave appears to be a 400 Hz signal, a 700 Hz appears at 300 Hz, and a 1000 Hz signal gives zero output frequency. Still higher input signals then appear to rise again with an 1100 Hz input appearing as 100 Hz. With a 1500 Hz input, the output signal peaks at 500 Hz and begins to decrease, falling again to zero with a 2000 Hz input.

Aliasing is clearly seen in Figures 5–14 and 5–15. The 25 Hz input sampled at 22, 23, and 24 Hz appears to be a 3, 2, and 1 Hz signal, respectively.

The Nyquist Theorem says that the sampling rate must be at least twice the highest frequency present in the signal, which might or might not be the highest frequency of interest. High frequency undersampled signals will be aliased to a lower frequency and appear as distortions.

Some people feel that applications of filtering methods on the digitized signal will eliminate undesirable undersampled signals. This is incorrect. If the digitization is too slow, aliased signals appear as low frequency components and are completely indistinguishable from low frequencies actually present in the original waveform. Analog filtering must be done before digitization so as to remove all frequencies that would be aliased. For example, in Figure 5–14, the 22 Hz sampled signal has an irreducible 3 Hz component. From this undersampled signal, the original waveform can never be reconstructed.

Experiments 5–2 and 5–3. With an ADC, DAC, and speaker you demonstrate the Nyquist sampling theorem. Alternatively, a computer program can be used to demonstrate the Nyquist theorem.

5.6 REFERENCES

Horowitz and Hill; Vassos and Ewing; and Malmstadt, Enke, and Crouch are good overall introductions to electronics, op amps, and DACs and ADCs. Rutkowski has numerous details and applications of operational amplifiers. Foster gives an excellent discussion of aliasing.

Problems

5–1 [5.2]. For the summing amplifier of Figure 5–2B with only two input resistors (R_1=1K, R_2=5K, and R_f=100K), calculate the output voltage if V_1=0.1 V and V_2=–0.03 V.

5–2 [5.2]. Many signal sources are intrinsically current rather than voltage actuated (e.g., ionization detectors and photomultipliers). While it is possible to allow the current to pass through a resistor and then process the resultant voltage, this approach slows circuit response and increases the chances of loading. A better way is the current-to-voltage converter, which is a variation of operational feedback (Figure 5–2A). R_{in} is deleted and the current is allowed to flow directly into the summing point. Since the summing point is at essentially zero volts, the current source in effect works directly into ground and no opposing voltage is developed that will distort the input signal. For a current-to-voltage converter, what is the output voltage in terms of the input current, i_{in}, and R_f? If the current source supplies electrons to the summing point, is the output voltage positive or negative?

5–3 [5.2]. For the integrator of Figure 5–5, C=1.0 μF and R=1 M. For an input voltage of 0.1 V, what is the time dependence of the output voltage?

5–4 [5.2]. For the VFC of Figure 5–6, the system is calibrated to give a VFC factor of 10 KHz/V. When the system is unused for three weeks, the only change in the circuit is that C changes from 100 pF to 110 pF. When you now use the VFC, what is the VFC factor? Justify your answer.

5–5 [5.2]. (A) For the DAC of Figure 5–8 with V_{ref}=1 V and R_f=10K, design a 3-bit DAC that will give 0 to 7 V in 1 V steps. Give the values of each resistor. (B) Alter your design so that the DAC gives –4 V for 000_2 and +3 V for 111_2.

5–6 [5.2]. Design a two digit BCD coded DAC that supplies 0 V for 00 (BCD) up to 9.9 V for 99 (BCD). Remember in BCD each decimal digit is replaced by its corresponding 4-bit binary code.

5–7 [5.2]. For a 4-bit successive approximation ADC with a range of 0 to 15 V (i.e., 1 V steps), sketch the DAC waveform for conversion of a static 7 V input, for a 12.58 V input, and for a 2.5 V input.

5–8 [5.2]. For the dual slope ADC of Figure 5–10, what effect does a slow (i.e., multi-hour) 0.1% change in R_{in} have on the accuracy? Of R_{ref}? Of V_{ref}? Of C?

6

Data Translation
Analog-Digital I/O System

6.1 INTRODUCTION

There are many sophisticated and versatile general purpose analog-digital I/O boards available commercially for PCs. In our course, we use the Data Translation DT2801 series data acquisition system. This series of cards has a variety of performance characteristics for different applications.

The DT2801 series interface cards, which we reference, are the DT2801, DT2801-A, DT2801/5716, DT2805, and DT2805/5716. All are complete analog-digital I/O systems. They provide a multiplexed ADC, DACs, programmable instrumentation amplifiers, a real time clock, and provisions for synchronizing the board to the outside world or using external clocks. Table 6–1 summarizes the salient features, and Figure 6–1 shows a block diagram.

The A option gives a higher conversion rate and a faster system clock. The 2801 and 2805 have low and high gain preamplifiers respectively. The 5716 option improves resolution from 12- to 16-bits. Higher resolution dramatically slows conversion rate. The high gain 2805 also slows conversion rate, but this is due to on-board filters used to reduce noise at the higher gains. Reducing these filter capacitors increases speed to the same as the 2801. The preamplifier gain, the multiplexer channel, trigger mode, and the clock rate are all software programmable. The different ADC ranges are set by on-board jumpers and require disassembling the PC.

Table 6–1. Characteristics of DT2801 Series Interface Boards

Digital Input and Output:
Two 8-bit parallel TTL I/O ports   Programmable as inputs or outputs

Digital-to-Analog Outputs:
Two 12-bit DACs
Jumper selected ranges   0 to 10 V, 0 to 5 V, ±10 V, ±2.5 V
Settling time   50 μs to 1/2-bit for 20 V step

Analog-to-Digital Converter:
Preamplifier Gains   1, 2, 4, 8 (2801, 2801-A, 2801/5716)
                                  1, 10, 100, 500 (2805, 2805/5716)
Basic ADC Ranges (jumper selected) 0 to 10 V, 0 to 5 V, ±10 V
Input Channels   16 single-ended (2801, 2801-A)
                                  8 differential (all models)
Resolution   12-bit (2801, 2801-A, 2805)
                                  16-bit (2801/5716, 2805/5716)
Data Codes   Binary (unipolar ranges)
                                  Offset binary for bipolar (2801/A, 2805)
                                  2s complement binary
Conversion Rate (Maximum)   13.7 KHz (2801)
                                  27.5 KHz (2801-A)
                                  6 KHz (2805) faster with small C
                                  2.5 KHz (2801/5716)
                                  0.1 KHz (2805/5716) faster with small C

Clock:
Base frequency   800 KHz (2801-A)
                                  400 KHz (all other models)

Trigger and Clock Inputs:
Triggering   TTL on high to low (minimum 200 ns pulse)

We use our ADCs on the ±10 V ranges as this matches the outputs of most op amp circuits. The programmable instrumentation preamplifier can be used to boost smaller signals. Our DACs are jumpered to ±10 V ranges, but the ±2.5 V range is useful for electrochemical measurements.

The two 8-bit programmable digital I/O ports are neither as fast nor as flexible as the 8255A (Chapter 3). Thus, if you do not need ADC or DAC functions, the 8255 is a less expensive, better choice.

Input and output can be handled in several different ways: software triggered, triggered by an external signal, triggered off an internal or external clock, or free running. In addition, I/O can be handled by software controlled input and output or by direct memory access (DMA) without direct software intervention. We describe these different modes in greater detail.

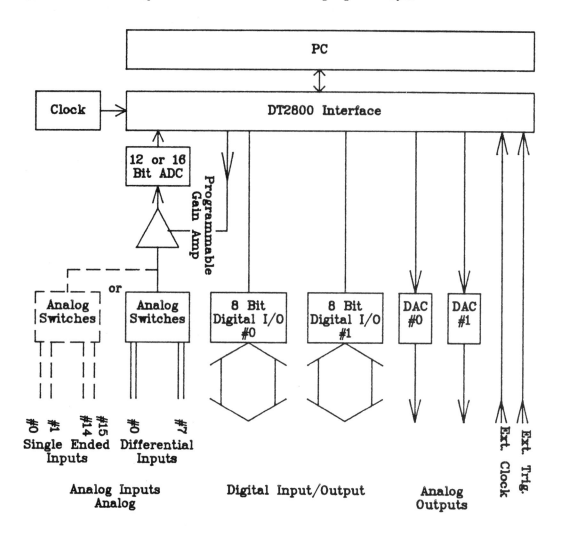

Figure 6–1. Schematic representation of DT2801 data acquisition boards.

Software Triggering. The function is triggered by a command write. As soon as the complete software command is issued and the DT2801's on-board microprocessor is ready, the function is executed.

External Triggering. An external trigger initiates a single event or a block of actions. This mode is similar to the external triggering on an oscilloscope. It is useful for synchronizing the board to an external event that is asynchronous with the computer's operation. Virtually any external event that was not initiated by the computer falls into this category.

Clock Triggering. Once programmed, the function is triggered by the tick of a clock, either the internal DT2801 clock or an external clock. With an internal clock, the user programs the number of clock cycles between triggers. This is 5 μs to 0.1638 s in 5 μs increments (2801 and 2805) or 2.5 μs to 81.9 ms in 2.5 μs increments (2801-A). The limited clock range is a shortcoming of the DT2800s.

The clock provides a rhythmic pacemaker for data acquisition or output. For example, clock triggering would be used to record data at even time intervals.

Continuous. In the continuous mode, data input or output runs without stopping.

DMA. Most high-level languages are incapable of driving the 2801 at its maximum rate; assembly language is an exception. DMA is a hardware way to circumvent the speed limitations of a high-level language. In DMA, data are transferred directly between the 2801s and memory without CPU or software intervention. A DMA controller chip performs most of the work.

The DMA controller must be initialized with the location or destination of the data, and how many bytes to transfer. Then, all the DMA controller requires is a trigger, and it takes off like a gazelle and carries out its function independent of the CPU. Indeed, DMA usually occurs while the CPU is doing something else, yet neither interferes with the other. Since the DMA controller is much faster than the 2801, it spends most of its time waiting for the 2801.

Other Features. The DT2801s have **immediate** and **block** modes. For the immediate modes, a single operation is accomplished per command. In block operations, multiple events are initiated per software command. The only block commands are READ A/D and WRITE D/A.

The DT2801, which actually runs from an onboard computer, requires significant programming. Setting up the DT board only tells the onboard micro what to do; getting or sending information is reading data from or writing data to the micro. The micro approach reduces cost and increases power, but is appreciably slower than a hardware implementation.

As with graphics, it is incredibly wasteful for you to write your own specialized routines for every application. We provide Pascal utilities in a unit DTUtil to do much of the dog work. The code runs to over 500 lines, so we only show some major features and how the programming is implemented. A complete listing is supplied to our students.

6.2 DT 2801 ORGANIZATION

All CPU interactions with the DT2801 are via two input and two output ports. Their nominal address and functions are shown in Table 6–2. Read and write are referenced from the CPU's viewpoint, but Data In and Data Out are from the DT2801's viewpoint.

Commands are issued to the command register. The status register supplies information on the status or state of current operations (e.g., availability of new data, readiness to accept new data or commands, and the existence of an error). Results are read

Table 6–2. Port Assignments for DT2801 Data Acquisition Boards[1]

Port[1]	Write output port	Read input port
$02ED	Command	Status
$02EC	Data In	Data Out

[1] Nominal factory-set port assignments. Switch selectable.

from the Data Out register. Command modifiers or data are written to the Data In register.

The DT2801 accepts fifteen legal 1-byte commands. First, we describe a generic procedure for issuing a command. To issue a command, the command byte is written to the command register. However, synchronization is needed to prevent overwriting or losing data and garbling commands. The Status Register is used for regulating this flow. The status bits are shown below followed by a more detailed description:

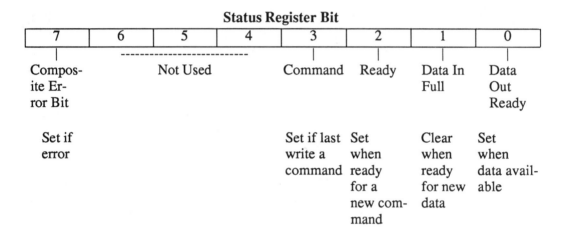

Status Register Bit

7	6	5	4	3	2	1	0
Compos-ite Er-ror Bit		Not Used		Command	Ready	Data In Full	Data Out Ready
Set if error				Set if last write a command	Set when ready for a new command	Clear when ready for new data	Set when data available

Bit 0: Data Out Ready

When set, Data Out Ready indicates that unread A/D data, digital input, or error information are available in the Data Out register. Reading the Data Out register resets this bit.

Bit 1: Data In Full

When set, Data In Full indicates that D/A datum (digital output datum), or a command parameter is still in the Data In register or a command is still in the Command register. If new data are written to Data In before the old information is processed, the previous data or command is overwritten and lost.

Bit 2: Ready

When set, the Ready bit indicates the board has completed the previous command and is ready to execute a new command. When Ready is clear, a command is in progress, and writing to the command register will generate a command overwrite error.

Bit 3: Command

When set, this bit indicates that the last byte written to the DT2801 was to the command register; otherwise it was written to the Data In Register.

Bits 4, 5, and 6: Unused

These bits are unused and always read as 0s.

Bit 7: Composite Error

When set, Composite Error indicates that an error has occurred on the DT2801. The particular error(s) can be determined by the Read Error command. Once set, this bit is only cleared by a Reset or Clear Error.

We now describe the basic operation in reading and writing and show suitable Pascal code. Then we describe the individual operations. We use four constants as the masks for selecting the desired bits:

```
CONST   {Masks }
  DataOut = $1;        {00000001B Select DataOut bit}
  DataIn = $2;         {00000010B Select DataIn bit}
  Ready = $4;          {00000100B Select Ready bit}
  Error = $80;         {10000000B Select Error bit}
```

Write Command Sequence. Usually a new command cannot be written to the DT2801 until it is ready to accept data. Readiness is signaled when the Ready bit is clear and the DataIn bit is set. From a pedagogical standpoint, we first write a function, DTReady, that determines when the DT2801 is ready:

```
FUNCTION DTReady : Boolean;      {True if clear for command}
BEGIN
  IF ((Port[Status] AND DataIn) <> 0) OR
  ((Port[Status] AND Ready) = 0) THEN
    DTReady := False
  ELSE
    DTReady := True;
END;
```

A command write sequence waits for the DT2801 to be ready. When it is ready, the command is written to the command register. A suitable Pascal procedure for issuing a "Command" is:

```
PROCEDURE DTCommand(Command : Byte);
BEGIN
  REPEAT UNTIL DTReady;
  Port[CommandReg] := Command;
END;
```

The DT2801 can become hung and never be Ready, especially if you failed to read or write the prescribed number of bytes or if an external or internal clock or trigger fails to occur. Always write or read all necessary information and provide any necessary external triggers.

The exception to the rule that a command can only be issued when the board is Ready is the Stop command. The Stop command unsticks a hung board without rebooting the entire system and is issued by:

```
Port[CommandReg]:= Stop;   { Stop DT2801 }
```

where Stop is the byte code for a Stop. Errors can be read after a stop.

Writing Data Bytes. Execute the following steps to write data:

(1)   Issue a command that requires reading data.
(2)   Check the DataIn bit until it shows that the board is ready to accept data (clear).
(3)   Write the datum byte.
(4)   Repeat steps 2 and 3 until all command data are issued.

Again we code steps 2–3 as a procedure DTDataWrite where DataByte is a datum byte to be written:

```
PROCEDURE DTDataWrite(databyte : Byte); {Write byte to DT2801}
BEGIN
  WHILE ((Port[Status] AND DataIn) <> 0) DO ;
  Port[DataReg] := databyte;
END;
```

Read Datum Byte Sequence. The datum byte read sequence is:

(1)   Issue command that requires data.
(2)   Check the DataOut register until it shows the DT2801 is ready to accept data (DataOut set) or that an error has occurred (Ready set).
(3)   Read the data from the data register.

As before, the coding of the byte read is straightforward. The following procedure returns the variable parameter ReadByte:

```
PROCEDURE DTDataRead(VAR ReadByte : Byte); {Read 2801 byte}
BEGIN
  REPEAT UNTIL
    ((Port[Status] AND DataOut) = 1) OR
    ((Port[Status] AND Ready) <> 0);
  ReadByte := Port[DataReg];
END;
```

The Ready bit test is necessary since certain errors can cause DataOut to never become true (e.g., any error that aborts the current command). If this happens, the

DataOut test never responds and the program sticks in an infinite loop. The Ready bit test prevents hangup.

Reading and Writing Datum Words. The writing of a 16-bit word is straightforward. Since the DT2801 only accepts bytes, the word is torn down and output as two bytes. The convention, which matches CPU usage of memory, is that first the low byte is output and then the high byte. The following sends out a 16-bit DataWord with the low byte first:

```
DTDataWrite( Lo (DataWord) );
DTDataWrite( Hi (DataWord) );
```

Note the use of the Hi and Lo functions (Chapter 3) for dissecting DataWord.

The word read sequence is similar. The low byte is read first followed by the high byte:

```
DTDataRead (LowByte);
DTDataRead (HighByte);
Result := ( HighByte shl 8) + LowByte;
```

LowByte and HighByte are the low and high byte of the input data respectively. Result is the 16-bit result. Shl 8 is roughly four times faster than integer multiplication by 256.

6.2.1 DT2801 Commands and Modifiers

All DT2801 commands are one byte and have the following format:

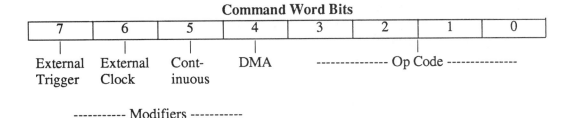

Command Word Bits

7	6	5	4	3	2	1	0
External Trigger	External Clock	Cont- inuous	DMA	---------------- Op Code ----------------			

----------- Modifiers -----------

The low nibble is the command (op code) and the upper nibble any modifiers. Modifier bits alter the basic commands. Not all op codes-modifier combinations are valid. Table 6–3 shows all op codes, their mnemonics, and valid modifiers.

Before we get into the basic commands, we discuss the role of each modifier bit. The instructions are convoluted; as you learn more about the Op Codes, you will want to refer back to this section. The modifier bits are DMA, Continuous, External Clock, and External Trigger. When a bit is set, the specified mode is enabled.

DMA (bit 4). When set, the Read A/D and Write D/A commands operate in the DMA mode. This permits higher maximum transfer rates than are possible under a high level language. Programming the DMA controller is discussed later.

Table 6–3. DT2801 Command Codes (Op Codes) and Allowed Modifiers

Command Name	Data Byte	Mnemonic	Ext. Trig.	Ext. Clk.	Cont	DMA
Reset	$00	Reset				
Clear Error	$01	ClearError				
Read Error Register	$02	ReadError				
Set Internal Clock Period	$03	SetIntClock				
Set Digital Port for Input	$04	SetDigPortIn	X			
Set Digital Port for Output	$05	SetDigPortOut	X			
Read Digital In Immediate	$06	ReadDigIm	X			
Write Digital Out Immediate	$07	WriteDigIm	X			
Write D/A Immediate	$08	WriteDACIm	X			
Set D/A Parameters	$09	SetDACPar				
Write D/A	$10	WriteDAC	X	X	X	X
Test	$11	Test	X			
Read A/D Immediate	$12	ReadADCIm	X			
Set A/D immediate	$13	SetADCIm				
Read A/D	$14	ReadADC	X	X	X	X
Stop	$15	Stop				

Allowed Modifiers[1]

[1] "X" indicates an allowed functional modifier.

Continuous (bit 5). When bit 5 is set, the Read A/D and Write D/A commands operate continuously until halted by a Stop command or an error. The Continuous mode ignores the number-of-bytes parameter specified in the block command.

External Clock (bit 6). When set, the clocked Read A/D and Write D/A commands use the external rather than the internal clock. If there is no external clock, the system locks up until one is provided.

External Trigger (bit 7). When set, affected commands are only initiated after a high-to-low external trigger.

In clocked Read A/D or Write D/A, the first clock pulse after the trigger synchronizes the internal DT2801 circuitry. Data conversion starts on the second clock pulse.

6.2.2 Basic Commands

Stop. Stop, the only command that does not require the DT2801 to be ready, halts any mode including Continuous or hung systems. Follow Stop by a Status register read to clear it.

If the board is running in the continuous mode, no error flag is set. Stopping any other mode sets the Error bit (Command Overwrite error), since you overwrote a running command.

Reset. To issue a Reset to the power up state, first issue a Stop command to insure that it will accept a command. The power up state is:

- The Composite Error bit (bit 7) of the status register is cleared.
- The Data Out Register is loaded with dummy data that must be cleared.
- The ADC channel, the gain setting, and the number of conversions are all set to illegal values. The DACs are set to their most negative voltages.
- Both digital ports are set for input.
- The on-board clock is set to 1 (2801) or 0.5 ms (2805).

The use of illegal initial ADC states is good defensive programming. You get error messages if you use functions without initialization. A Reset procedure is:

```
PROCEDURE DTReset;                   {Reset DT2801 and check state}
VAR
  Dummy : Integer;
BEGIN
  Port[CommandReg] := Stop;
  Dummy := Port[DataReg];
  DTCommand(Reset);
END;
```

Clear Error. The Clear Error command resets the board after an error. It clears the error bit on the Status register and resets all error register bits. Because the DT2801 may lock up due to an error condition, always Stop the board and read the Data Out register before issuing a Clear Error command. Clear Error does not affect ADC or DAC parameters, digital ports, the clock, or the Data Out register. A suitable procedure is:

```
PROCEDURE DTClearError;    {Clear error flag}
VAR
  Dummy : Byte;
BEGIN
  DTCommand(ClearError);
  REPEAT UNTIL DTReady;
  Dummy := Port[DataReg];
END;
```

A useful procedure that stops the board and clears any errors is:

```
PROCEDURE StopClear;    { Stops-Clears 2801 & Error Register}
VAR
  Dummy : Integer;
BEGIN                                  { stopclear Procedure }
  Port[CommandReg] := Stop;       { Stop board }
  Dummy := Port[DataReg]; {Clear bit 0 p2-15 manual}
  DTClearError;
END;                                   { stopclear Procedure }
```

Test. Test verifies a low level of DT2801 functionality. After issuing a Test command, read datum bytes. The first read gives 1 and each succeeding read returns a byte value incremented by 1.

In the external mode, the board waits for an external trigger before outputting the first byte. Subsequent reads require no other triggers. To halt Test, use StopClear.

Read Error Register. The DT2801 can give rise to possible errors when incompatible or illegal commands are issued or too much or too little data are written or read. The DT2801 identifies many errors.

After issuing a ReadError command, read the 16-bit Error Register with two DTDataReads. The low order byte is first. Table 6–4 shows the significance of the error bits.

Table 6–4. Read Error Register Bits

Error	Meaning	Interpretation
Low Byte		
ERR0	Reserved	
ERR1	Command Overwrite Error	Command issued before last done
ERR2	Clock Set Error	Illegal clock argument (0 or 1)
ERR3	Digital Port Select Error	Illegal digital port ($\neq$0,1,2)
ERR4	Digital Port Set Error	Illegal operation for port (e.g., read from output port)
ERR5	DAC Select Error	Illegal DAC selected ($\neq$0, 1, 2)
ERR6	DAC Clock Error	Clock before DAC ready. Clock too fast
ERR7	DAC # Conversions Error	Illegal number of conversions ($\neq$0, 1 or 2)
High Byte		
ERR8	ADC Channel Error	Illegal channel ($\neq$0–5 single ended or $\neq$0–7 differential)
ERR9	ADC Gain Error	Illegal gain set ($\neq$0-3)
ERR10	ADC Clock Error	Clock before ADC ready. Clock too fast or data read too slow
ERR11	ADC Multiplexer (MUX) Error	ADC conversion before MUX settled. Clock too fast
ERR12	ADC # Conversion Error	Illegal number of conversions ($\neq$0–2)
ERR13	Data where command expected	Data written before command or improper sequence
ERR14	Reserved	
ERR15	Reserved	

6.3 IMMEDIATE COMMANDS

The ADC and DAC functions have both simple immediate modes and block mode instructions. The immediate modes are simple instructions that do a single operation or set of operations with one command. All require modifiers. Parallel digital I/O as well as DAC and ADC operations support immediate modes.

6.3.1 Parallel I/O

The 2-byte wide digital ports are numbered 0 and 1 and only support byte operations. Each port can be set independently for input or output.

Set Digital Port for Input and Set Digital Port for Output. SetDigPortIn and SetDigPortOut set the ports' input-output states. Each command is followed by a parameter byte of 0, 1, or 2, which determines affected port(s). The parameter significance is shown in Table 6–5. To program the digital ports for input or output, issue a SetDigPortIn or SetDigPortOut command followed by the appropriate datum byte from Table 6–5. Typical program sequences:

```
DTCommand(SetDigPortInput);
DTDataWrite(1);            {Set port 1 for input}
```

or:

```
DTCommand(SetDigPortOutput);
DTDataWrite(2);            {Set both port 0 and 1 to output}
```

Read and Write Digital Data Immediate. ReadDigPortIn and WriteDigPortOut read or write bytes to a digital port. A SetDigPortIn command is followed by a parameter byte that specifies the code for the port or ports to be read. The first datum byte is immediately read. If a second port was specified, the next datum byte read is the second port data.

To write data, issue a SetDigPortOut command, write out the parameter byte for the port or ports, and then write out the datum byte. If two ports were specified, write the second port datum byte.

Table 6–5. Effect of Data Byte on Digital I/O, DAC, and ADC Gain

Data Byte	Port Selected for Input or Output	DAC Selected for Output	ADC Gain 2801	2805
0	0 only	0 only	1	1
1	1 only	1 only	2	10
2	0 and 1	0 and 1	4	100
3	Illegal	Illegal	8	500

Legal port codes are 0, 1, and 2 with the meaning shown in Table 6–5. If only one port is read, only one output byte is read. If both ports are specified, the DT2801 inputs two data bytes with port 0 first followed by port 1. Output is similar.

If Ext. Trig. is set, the DT2801 outputs or inputs no data until the External Trigger line is strobed (high to low). If two bytes are to be read, both are read on one strobe pulse. For output, the DT2801 outputs no digital data until External Trigger is strobed (high to low). If two bytes are to be output, both are output on one strobe pulse.

The following sets port 1 to output and port 0 to input. $FF is output to port 1 and port 0 is read:

```
DTCommand   ( SetDigPortIn );
DTDataWrite( 0 );                { Set ports 0 for input }

DTCommand   ( SetDigPortOut );
DTDataWrite( 1 );                { Set ports 1 for output }

DTCommand ( ReadDigIm );     { Prepare to read port 0}
DTDataWrite( 0 );
DTDataRead ( DigIn1 );       { Read port 1 byte into DigIn1}

DTCommand( WriteDigIm);      {Prepare to write port 1}
DTDataWrite(1);              {select port 1 for output}
DTDataWrite($FF);           { Write $FF to port 1}
```

If both ports had started as inputs, programming port 0 for input is redundant. Unless explicitly changed, ports hold their I/O states.

6.3.2 Digital-to-Analog Converter Functions

The two DACs are suitable for driving recorders, oscilloscopes, potentiostats, optical scanners, and so on. The immediate modes are simple and digital output data are immediately converted into analog outputs.

Write D/A Immediate. WriteDACIm is used to immediately output one or two digital words as analog signals on one or both DACs. The command is followed by a parameter byte that specifies the DAC(s) to be used. The parameter byte has codes of 0, 1 or 2 with the meanings specified in Table 6–5. One or two digital data words then follow. Writing data to the DAC requires writing four to six bytes to the DT2801:

(1)   Output the WriteDACIm op code.
(2)   Output the DACSelect byte, which selects the DAC or DACs used.
(3)   Output the low byte of the first word followed by its high byte.
(4)   If dual DAC operation was specified, output the low byte of the second word followed by its high byte.

The dual DAC mode is double buffered. Neither DAC changes state until after both DAC words are output, and then both change simultaneously. Thus, if one is driving an

X-Y plotter with the two outputs, the pen will not jump along one axis and then the other to get to a new point.

The following code first outputs 0 to DAC 0 then 4095 to DAC1. Then both DACs are simultaneously set with DAC0 to digital 0 and DAC1 to 4095 (i.e., the most negative and positive voltages, respectively):

```
DTCommand(WriteDACIm);    {output 4095 to DAC0}
DTDataWrite(0);
DTDataWrite(lo(4095));    DTDataWrite(hi(4095));

DTCommand(WriteDACIm);    {Simultaneously set DAC0 to 0}
DTDataWrite(2);          {and DAC1 to 4095}
DTDataWrite(lo(0));       DTDataWrite(hi(0));
DTDataWrite(lo(4095));    DTDataWrite(hi(4095));
```

6.3.3 Analog-to-Digital Conversion

The immediate ADC modes are similar to the DAC modes. There are more parameters, because there are channels and a selectable amplifier gain.

Read A/D Immediate. To read the ADC, you specify the gain setting and the channel, and then read the digitized data. The gain codes are shown in Table 6–5. The channel values can be 0 to 15 (single-ended) and 0 to 7 (differential). The instruction sequence is:

(1) Issue ReadADCIm command.
(2) Write the gain code data.
(3) Write the channel number.
(4) Read the low byte of the digitized number followed by the high byte.

The following sequence digitizes channel with a gain of 8 and stores the result in Result:

```
DTCommand(ReadADCIm);
DTDataWrite(3);                 {select gain x8}
DTDataWrite(7);                 {select channel 7}
DTDataRead(lowbyte);            {get digitized result-low byte}
DTDataRead(hibyte);            {get digitized result-high byte}
Result:=lowbyte+hibyte shl 8; {combine high-low to form word}
```

6.4 BLOCK COMMANDS

Block modes are software or hardware (DMA) driven. The op code is the same for either block mode, but the DMA modifier bit determines whether DMA transfer is used. The DMA mode is significantly different and is discussed separately. Block commands allow faster I/O than the immediate modes. The principle of block operations is the elimination of the redundancy that can arise in outputting a series of points. One frequently inputs a series of points from the same ADC channel(s) or outputs a series of points to the same DAC(s). Eliminating the information common to every set of points reduces overhead and increases throughput.

Block commands allow specifying basic conditions for the next series of points and the number of points in the block (no more than 2^{16}). You first output header information then the specified number of bytes. Data transfer rates are roughly double the immediate modes.

The clock only works in the block modes. We consider setting the clock and then the block DAC and ADC modes.

6.4.1 Setting the Clock

Set Clock Period. To set the clock, issue the SetIntClock followed by the number of master clock cycles (1.25 or 2.50 µs; see Table 6–1) between ticks. The desired number of master clock cycles is then output with the low byte first. Allowed values are 2 to 65,535. The following sets the clock to 1000 master clock cycles:

```
DTCommand (SetIntClock);
DTWriteData( Lo(1000) );
DTWriteData( Hi(1000) );
```

6.4.2 DAC Block Modes

The clock must first be set. Then using the SetDACPar, you tell the DT2801 which DAC(s) to use and how many bytes to expect in the block. Then to transfer the block, you use repeated calls to WriteDAC. The structure of the command is:

(1) Issue the SetDACPar command.
(2) Send the DAC select byte.
(3) Write the low byte of the number of words to be output followed by the high byte.
(4) Issue the WriteDAC command to initiate block transfer.
(5) Write the data byte.
(6) Repeat step 5 until the specified number of bytes have been transferred.

6.4.3 ADC Block Modes

The ADC block modes are similar to the DAC modes. One sets up the ADC and then issues the block commands. The set up procedure requires the following format:

(1)   Issue the SetADCPar command.
(2)   Output the gain code.
(3)   Output the ADC start channel.
(4)   Output the ADC end channel.
(5)   Output the number of words to be read with the low byte being first followed by the high byte.
(6)   Output the ReadADC command.
(7)   Read a datum byte.
(8)   Repeat step 7 until the specified number of bytes have been input. The low byte of each input word is read first.

The start and end channels require comment. The ADC automatically sequences through the specified multiplexer channels. It takes one point in turn from each of the channels in the specified range and then repeats. If start and end are 3 and 5 respectively, the first point is acquired from input 3, the next from 4, and then 5. Additional points start over at 3. Wraparound occurs if start is larger than end. For example, if the start and end were 7 and 3 on a board set for differential input, then the order of inputs would be 7, 0, 1, 2, 3, 7, . . .

Clock Synchronization. The ADC takes one point and only one point on each clock tick. Thus, if we have the clock set for 1 ms (start=1, end=3) and six bytes to be read, then the timing for all reads is:

```
Time (ms)        0     1     2     3     4     5     6
Channel Read   None    1     2     3     1     2     3
```

The first clock cycle sets up the DT2801. Data collection begins with the second one. It is not possible to take several points on a single clock tick.

Actually, the situation is more complicated. The DT2801 synchronization is poor, which we regard as a design flaw. The master board clock is free-running and not synchronized to software or hardware triggering. Thus, the 0 ms clock tick might occur immediately after you issue the block read command or it might just have occurred (i.e., you just missed it). The 0 ms tick in the latter case could be delayed for almost a full millisecond. This jitter means that if you recorded two identical waveforms, they could be out of synchronization by a one clock cycle (i.e., 1 ms). This one clock cycle bobble or jitter makes alignment of sharp features uncertain and rounds them in signal averaging. The solution is to take points closer together in time so that the one cycle bobble is insignificant, but this can only be done for slower data acquisitions. Point separation on a single transient is accurate.

6.5   DMA BLOCK MODES

Setup of the DMA modes is the most complicated on the DT2801s. You must first program the PC's 8237–5 DMA controller chip. This chip has sixteen read/write registers. Eggebrecht spends an entire chapter on programming the 8237–5 in a PC. We give you the flavor of this DMA chip without too many details.

Port Address (HEX)	Read Port Function	Write Port Function
Table 6–6. 8237–5 DMA Chip Port List		
Channel 0		
0000	Current Address	Base-Current Address
0001	Base-Current Word Count	Current Word Count
Channel 1		
0002	Current Address	Base-Current Address
0003	Base-Current Word Count	Current Word Count
Channel 2		
0004	Current Address	Base-Current Address
0005	Base-Current Word Count	Current Word Count
Channel 3		
0006	Current Address	Base-Current Address
0007	Base-Current Word Count	Current Word Count
0008	Status	Command
0009	Not used	Write Request
000A	Not used	Single-mask bit
000B	Not used	Mode Register
000C	Not used	Clear Byte Pointer
000D	Temporary	Master Clear
000E	Not used	Clear Mask
000F	Not used	Write All Mask

The 8237–5 has four DMA channels 0–3. In the PC, channel 0 is used for dynamic RAM refresh, and channel 2 is used by the diskette drive. Channels 1 and 3 are free for the DT2801, which can be board-level jumpered for either (default 1). If other hardware conflicts with this address, you must readdress one. Many 8237–5 features cannot be used because of the hardware configuration of the PC. Each channel is used independently and must be programmed with the memory address of the source or destination, the number of bytes to transfer, and several other pieces of information.

Table 6–6 summarizes the registers. The Mode Register (address $0B) is one of the most important. The significance of the bits is shown in Figure 6–2.

Bits 0 and 1 must be set for the channel that you are going to use. Bits 2 and 3 determine whether the DMA chip writes to memory (01) or reads from memory (10).

Bit 4 determines whether the DMA cycles through the transfers repeatedly and automatically. At the end of each block of data transfer, the DMA reloads its starting address and byte counter with the initial value and starts the transfer over again. This feature is used with the DT2801 in the Continuous mode.

Bit 5 determines whether the initial address is incremented (0) with each transfer or decremented (1). Bits 6 and 7 are hardware constrained in the PC to the single byte transfers (01).

Thus, to set up a DMA transfer to the DAC board using channel 1 with increasing memory and auto repeat, write 01011001_2 or $59 to the DMA mode register.

Mode Register

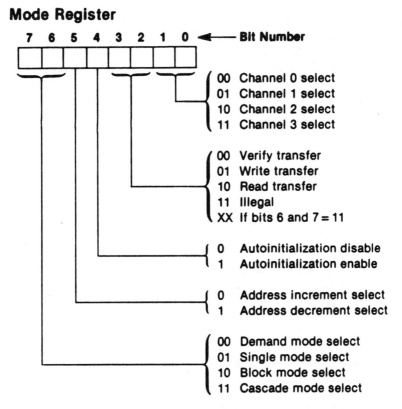

Figure 6–2. Mode register definitions for 8237–5 DMA controller. Adapted with permission of Intel Corporation, Copyright/Intel Corporation 1988.

Before transfer, the specific DMA channel must be loaded with the source/destination address and the number of bytes to transfer. For DMA channel 1 the base address register is $02 and the byte counter register is $03. Both take 16-bit values so each word is entered as two bytes with the low byte first followed by the high byte. The byte count is easy, but unfortunately the address is not.

Probably the most unfortunate aspect of the 8237–5 is the way IBM set it up for handling the PC memory. The 8237–5 was developed for an 8-bit system with only 64K. Transfers are limited to 2^{16} bytes, and some method was necessary to expand the 16-bit address to the 8086's 20-bit address. IBM did this by setting up a 4-bit register that is loaded. The full 20-bit address is formed by augmenting the 16 base address with these four bits. The four bits form the four most significant bits of the 20-bit address. Thus, the 4-bit register determines the 64K page that the DMA controller can work in, while the DMA controller handles addresses within the page.

The problem is that you cannot make a single transfer that occurs across a 64K page boundary. If only part of the transfer occurs on one page, the page register would have to be changed to the new page to complete the remainder of the transfer. This requires reprogramming the 8237, which cannot be done during a DT2801 DMA operation. Thus, all DT2801 DMA transfers must be complete on a single 64K page.

Each DMA channel has a specific port register that is used for its current page. DMA channel 1 uses port $83 and channel 3 uses $82. These are hardware registers built into the PC and are not indigenous to the 8237.

The clear register ($0C) keeps track of whether we are transferring the low or high datum byte. This must be cleared before starting transfer by writing any value to the register.

Suitable code for initializing the DMA controller to transfer DMACount bytes from page 0, offset $F000 is:

```
CONST
    DMAChannel = 1;
    EnableReg  = $000A ;
    ModeReg    = $000B ;
    ClearReg   = $000C ;
    DMApage    = $0 ;       {64K page of DMA transfer region}
    DMAOffset  = $f000;     {Offset Address of transfer region}


             (... earlier portion of code goes here)
    DMAmode := $59;         {autoinitialize read from memory}
    BaseReg  := $0002 ;     (***************************)
    CountReg := $0003 ;     (*      For DMA channel 1     *)
    PageReg  := $0083 ;     (***************************)

    Port[ModeReg]    := DMAmode ;       {Set mode}
    Port[ClearReg]   := 0 ;             {any value clears register }
    Port[BaseReg]    := Lo(DMAOffset);  {Load data offset}
    Port[BaseReg]    := Hi(DMAOffset);

    Port[CountReg]   := Lo(DMACounts);  {Load # byte in transfer
    Port[CountReg]   := Hi(DMACounts);

    Port[PageReg]    := DMApage ;       {Set DMA Page}
    Port[EnableReg]  := DMAchannel ;    {Enable Channel}
             ( ... Later portion of code goes here)
```

To carry out a transfer you then issue a suitable SetDACPar or SetADCPar command to the DT2801 with the DMA modifier set. Then to initiate transfer issue a WriteDAC or WriteADC command. You do not send any data to the DT2801. The DMA and DT2801 handle all the data transfer in the background. While transfer is taking place, the DT2801 indicates it is busy with a DTReady function. As soon as transfer is complete, DTReady is true.

6.6 DTUtil UNIT

The Unit DTUtil contains a number of routines that make using the DT2801s relatively straightforward. It is actually two units DTDef and DTUtil. DTDef is listed below:

```
Unit DTDef;
INTERFACE

CONST
  DMABufferSize = 2000;
  DMAchannel = $1;          {Channels 1 and 3 allowed on standard PC}

  BaseAddress = $02EC;                {Factory settings}
  CommandReg = BaseAddress+1 { $02ED } ; {Factory settings}
  Status = CommandReg;
  DataReg = BaseAddress;

  ClockPeriod = 1.2500; {usec for 2801-A.  Use 2.5 for other DTs}

  DMABufferInitialized :BOOLEAN = FALSE;

TYPE
  adcarray = ARRAY[0..(DMABufferSize-1)] OF Integer;
VAR
  DTDMABuffer : ^adcarray;

IMPLEMENTATION
END.
```

Important constants defined here are the Address of the DT2801 BaseAddress, the DMAChannel used, the internal master clock period, and the size of the DMA buffer. The name of the DMA buffer, DTDMABuffer, is also defined. DTUtil USES DTDef. Thus, all definitions here are available to DTUtil. If you need to change the DMA channel, the DMA buffer size or the BaseAddress of the DT2801, you need only edit and build DTUtil. Any programs that require these constants must include DTDef in the uses statement.

DTDMABuffer is a typed constant initialized to FALSE. When the DMA transfer region is initialized, it is changed to TRUE to prevent attempts to initialize the DMA buffer more than once. Initialization is done automatically when you use a command that requires a DMA buffer.

Program Listing 6–1 shows the complete interface of DTUtil. Note the defined constants such as DAC0, DAC1, DAC0and1, Gain1, Gain2, and so on. These can be used in place of the numeric codes listed earlier for improved readability. We now summarize the use of the different commands.

Most of the routines are straightforward implementations of the basic DT2801 routines described earlier. The DMA modes, however, require special comments.

The problem is in the placement of the DMA data transfer region, which must fall entirely in a 64K page. This is not easily done in Turbo Pascal with the normal static variables that we have been using. Variables may fall anywhere within a 64K page, and the location changes as you alter the program or compile it to an EXE file. For example, if you set up a 1000-element integer array for DMA data, only 500 elements might be available for a single DMA transfer if half the array fell below a 64K page boundary. If the array started ten words before the boundary, you would only be able to transfer ten

---

Program Listing 6–1. DTUtil Unit Interface Listing

```
Unit DTUtil;

INTERFACE
USES Crt, DTDef;
CONST
  ModDate : STRING = '3-12-89 for Turbo Pascal 5.';
  { Copyright 1986-89 by J. N. Demas.
  Routines for Data Translation DT2801 acquisition boards.
  Earlier verions by M. Saunders and N. P. Ayala}

TYPE
  flags = 0..1;
  FlagDTIO = (Input, Output);
  DigPortCode = 0..2;

CONST
  Port0    : integer = 0;      DAC0      : Integer = 0;
  Port1    : integer = 1;      DAC1      : Integer = 1;
  Port0and1: integer = 2;      DAC0and1  : Integer = 2;

  Gain1 : Integer = 0;
  Gain2 : Integer = 1;         Gain10   : Integer = 1;
  Gain4 : Integer = 2;         Gain100  : Integer = 2;
  Gain8 : Integer = 3;         Gain500  : Integer = 3;

PROCEDURE DTInitialize;
FUNCTION DTGetVersion : STRING;
PROCEDURE DTReset;
FUNCTION DTCheckErrors : Boolean;
PROCEDURE DTTest;
PROCEDURE DTStopClear;              { Stop/Clear Error Register}

FUNCTION DTReady : Boolean;
PROCEDURE DTSetModifiers(ExtTrig, ExtClock, Continuous : flags);

PROCEDURE DTSetDigitalIO(SetPort0, SetPort1 : FlagDTIO);
PROCEDURE DTDigitalOut(PortSelect : DigPortCode;
                       FirstPort, SecondPort : Byte);
PROCEDURE DTDigitalIn(PortSelect : DigPortCode;
                      VAR FirstPort, SecondPort : Byte);

FUNCTION DTSetClock(VAR Period : Real) : Boolean;

PROCEDURE DTWriteDACIm(VAR DAC, FirstDig, SecondDig : Integer);
PROCEDURE DTSetDACPar(VAR DACSelect, NumConv : Integer);
PROCEDURE DTWriteDAC(FirstPt, SecondPt: Integer);
PROCEDURE DTWriteDACDMA(VAR DACs, NumConv : Integer);

PROCEDURE DTReadADCIm(VAR ADCGain, Channel, Signal : Integer);
PROCEDURE DTSetADCPar(VAR ADCGain, ChanStart, ChanEnd,
                      NumConv : Integer);
PROCEDURE DTReadADC(VAR ADCResult : Integer);
PROCEDURE DTReadADCDMA(VAR ADCGain, ChanStart, ChanEnd,
                       NumConv : Integer);
```

---

words starting at the beginning of the array, although you could still transfer 990 words if you started the transfer at the page boundary.

To circumvent this problem, we use pointer variables on the heap. The heap is the remaining memory after Pascal's program and static variable requirements and all the other system memory requirements are satisfied. The heap is like a large scratchpad on which you can place all kinds of things.

We describe briefly how we forced an array in a 64K page. The following discussion uses some heap terminology. Refer to Swan or other Turbo reference books for details. In DTDef, we declare a pointer variable DTDMABuffer of type ^adcarray where adcarray is an array[0. .1999] of real. Until we place the variable on the heap, it has no address.

We determine the absolute address of the first free locations on the heap using Seg and Ofs. If the 4000 byte DTDMABuffer will fit entirely in the 64K page when placed at this address, we put DTDMABuffer there with a New(DTDMABuffer) and we are done.

If DTDMABuffer is too big, then we fill the balance of the 64K page by creating a dummy variable that exactly fills the space using GetMem(temp, NumBytesNeeded). Once the page is filled, we put DTDMABuffer on the heap with New, and it automatically starts at the beginning of the 64K page. To reclaim the space used by tmp, use FreeMem(temp, NumBytesNeeded). This frees the memory, but leaves DTDMABuffer where we need it for DMA transfer.

DTDMABuffer is treated like any other array except that we use the caret before the index to show that it is a pointer array. The following fills DTDMABuffer with $100:

```
for i:= 0 to 1999 do DTDMABuffer^[i]:=$100;
```

Note we have only one DMA buffer, DTDMABuffer. All DT2801 DMA goes through this buffer and always starts at the beginning of the array. If you input ADC data to the buffer and want to output DAC data, you must process or move the ADC data before refilling the buffer with the new data.

PROCEDURE DTInitialize;
This routine must be called to initialize the DT2801 boards.

FUNCTION DTGetVersion : STRING;
This returns a string that has the version that is being used.

PROCEDURE DTReset;
This performs a near power up reset.

FUNCTION DTCheckErrors : Boolean;
This checks for errors. It returns false if no errors. If TRUE, it lists all the error bits set. Since it slows program execution considerably, use it mainly for debugging and after you exit a section of code to insure that everything went well.

PROCEDURE DTTest;

Performs a board level test. Can use external triggering.

PROCEDURE DTStopClear;

This stops the board and clears any errors.

FUNCTION DTReady : Boolean;

This returns a true if the board is ready for new commands.

PROCEDURE DTSetModifiers(ExtTrig, ExtClock, Continuous : flags);

This sets the modifier bits in the global variables in the DTUtil Unit. All subsequent commands that require modifiers use these settings. Once altered, their state remains fixed until altered by another DTSetModifiers command. The default is off for each. A 1 sets a bit and a 0 clears it. The call:

```
DTSetModifiers(1,1,0);
```

turns on the external trigger and external clock bits in any instructions that allow these modifiers. Continuous is turned off.

PROCEDURE DTSetDigitalIO(SetPort0, SetPort1 : FlagDTIO);

This sets the I/O state for digital I/O. FlagDTIO can be either "input" or "output." The following sets port 1 to output and port 0 to input:

```
DTSetDigitalIO(input, output);
```

PROCEDURE DTDigitalOut(PortSelect : DigPortCode; FirstPort, SecondPort : Byte);

This outputs one or two bytes to the digital ports depending on PortSelect, which can be port0, port1, port1and2, or the corresponding digital codes. The first output argument is always output. The second is needed for two byte outputs, but must always be present.

PROCEDURE DTDigitalIn(PortSelect : DigPortCode; VAR FirstPort, SecondPort : Byte);

This inputs digital data from the selected port(s). The first input argument is always input. The second is only used if there is a second input byte.

If port 0 is connected bit-for-bit to port 1, then the following outputs every possible digital byte on port 1, inputs it on port 0, and confirms that the correct value was input:

```
USES DTUtil
VAR
  i : Integer;
  inputdata, dummy : Byte;
BEGIN
```

```
DTSetDigitalIO(Input, Output);
dummy := $00;
  FOR i := 0 TO 255 DO
    BEGIN
      DTSetModifiers(0, 0, 0);
      DTDigitalOut(Port1, i, dummy);
      DTDigitalIn(Port0, inputdata, dummy);
      IF inputdata<>i THEN WriteLn('Error ', inputdata,' ',i);
    END;
  IF DTCheckErrors THEN ;
  WriteLn;
END.
```

Figure 6–3 shows the DT2801 used as a digital transient recorder for automatically recording the waveforms for a 7490 decade counter. A master oscillator from a breadboarding station is divided down by a factor of 16 with a 7493 4-bit binary counter. The input clock for the 7490 and its 4 output bits are run into the low 5-bits of Port 1. The problem is still one of synchronization of the acquisition. Rather than use software to try to match the acquisition rate to the master TTL clock, we exploit the External Trigger mode of the DT2801. By connecting the master clock to the External Trigger we can initiate one acquisition point per master clock tick. Assuming Port 0 is set for input, we can record 200 points with the following program fragment:

```
DTSetModifier(1, 0, 0);
for k:=0 to 199 do DTDigitalIn(Port0,Count[k],dummy);
```

With External Trigger enabled, DTDigitalIn waits for a trigger before taking each point. Since the master oscillator is sixteen times faster than the clock driving the decade counter, we acquire sixteen points for each clock transition that triggers the 7490.

FUNCTION DTSetClock(VAR Period : Real) : Boolean;

This sets the DT2801 clock. Period is the desired period in microseconds (µs). DTSetClock returns TRUE for legal clock settings and FALSE otherwise. For an illegal clock setting, a default value of 1.000 ms is set.

The use of Period as a variable parameter rather than a value parameter demonstrates a design trade off. Allowable periods are integral multiples of the master clock period. Thus, for a master clock period of 1.25 µs, you cannot set a 36 µs period exactly. DTSetClock sets the clock to the nearest allowed period. To prevent you from using an incorrect period in calculations, DTSetClock changes Period to the actual clock value. Since Period is a variable parameter, it is changed in the calling routine. Then as long as you use this altered Period in subsequent calculations, no errors occur. The following routine sets the clock to 250 µs:

```
Per := 250;   {Set clock to 250 microsec per tick}
If NOT DTSetClock(Per) then WriteLn('Clock Error Setting');
```

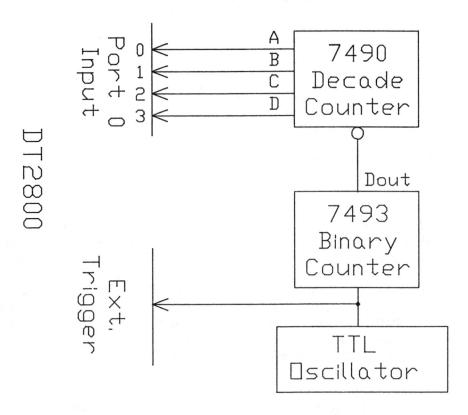

Figure 6-3. Digital transient recorder for recording outputs of 7490 decade counter.

PROCEDURE DTWriteDACIm(VAR DAC, FirstDig, SecondDig : Integer);
    This uses the one or two DAC codes with one or two data words; this outputs one of two DAC words. The following outputs a linear increasing ramp on DAC0 and a decreasing ramp on DAC1:

```
FOR  i := 0 to 4095 do
   BEGIN
     data1 :=4095-i;
     DTWriteDACIm(DAC0and1, i, data1);
   END;
```

PROCEDURE DTReadADCIm(VAR ADCGain, Channel, Signal : Integer);
    This inputs one point from the specified ADC channel using the specified gain. The following program continuously reads ADC channel 0 with a gain of 4 and outputs the data to DAC1:

```
PROGRAM DACADCIm;
```

```
USES Crt, DTUtil;
VAR
  i, datain, channel : Integer;
BEGIN
  DTInitialize;
  channel := 1;
  REPEAT
    DTReadADCIm(gain4, channel, datain);
    DTWriteDACIm(DAC1, datain, datain);
  UNTIL False;
END.
```

PROCEDURE DTSetDACPar(VAR DACSelect, NumConv : Integer);
PROCEDURE DTWriteDAC(FirstPt, SecondPt: Integer);
These set up the DAC parameters for the block mode. DACSelect specifies the DACs and NumConv, the number of data words to be output. The data are then output with repeated calls to DTWriteDAC. The first clock tick is ignored. The major quirk is that in the dual DAC mode, the points for both DACs are output on a single clock cycle. Thus, the fastest legal clock depends on whether we are using one or two DACs.

PROCEDURE DTSetADCPar(VAR ADCGain, ChanStart, ChanEnd, NumConv : Integer);
PROCEDURE DTReadADC(VAR ADCResult : Integer);
These set up and read in data from the ADC using the block modes. The channel gain, start and end channels, and the number of integers to be input (NumConv) are specified. The first clock tick is ignored. One point is taken per clock tick.

The following program uses both block ADC and block DAC modes to output DAC data on DAC0 and input data from ADC channel 1:

```
PROGRAM DACblk;
USES Crt, DTUtil;
VAR
  time : Real;
  i, numpts, channel : Integer;
  data : ARRAY[0..100] OF Integer;
BEGIN
  DTInitialize;
    time:=450;                    {450 microseconds per point}
    data[0]:= 0;    data[1]:=4095;      data[2]:=2048;
    data[3]:=1024;  data[4]:=512;       numpts := 100;
  REPEAT
    DTSetDACPar(dac0,numpts);
    for i:=0 to numpts-1 do dtwritedac(data[i],data[i]);
  UNTIL KeyPressed;
  IF DTCheckErrors then WriteLn('clock error');
```

```
DTSetModifiers(1, 0, 0);        {set external trigger}
numpts := 15;                   {input 15 pts from channel 1}
channel := 1;
dtsetadcpar(Gain1, channel, channel, numpts);
FOR i := 0 TO numpts-1 DO dtreadadc(data[i]);

FOR i := 0 TO numpts-1 DO WriteLn(i:5, data[i]:5);
IF NOT DTCheckErrors THEN WriteLn('no errror in ADC');
END.
```

We highlight the pairs of block commands to show them more clearly.

PROCEDURE DTWriteDACDMA(VAR DACs, NumConv : Integer);

Outputs NumConv points with the DMA mode using the current clock settings and modifiers. Data must be placed in the DTDMA buffer, DTDMABuffer, before output.

The following DAC and ADC DMA programs are designed to run with hardware configuration shown in Figure 6–4. The program DACDMA demonstrates how to fill the buffer for a dual DAC display; an exponential decay is placed in one half of the

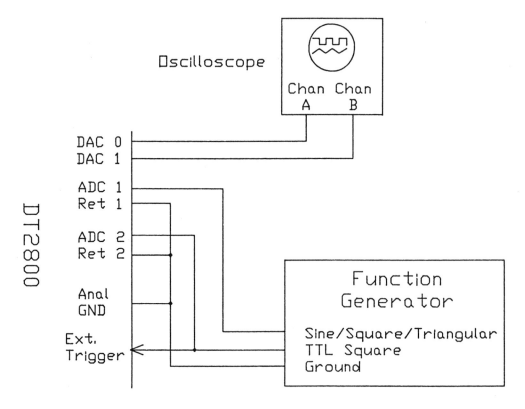

Figure 6–4. Connection of DAC and ADC channels to demonstrate DMA acquisition.

buffer and a sine wave in the other. It also clearly demonstrates several important aspects of DMA transfer. Note that the display begins before the buffer is filled. The program fills the buffer after DMA display begins. After displaying both waveforms, the program goes back and slowly zeroes out the exponent, regenerates it, and repeats the process until a key is pressed. By displaying the DAC outputs on a dual trace oscilloscope, we can watch this dynamic process. Even after the program is stopped and you are back in Pascal editing, the display continues on the scope. This demonstrates most convincingly that continuous DMA, once started, involves no CPU intervention:

```
PROGRAM DACDMA;
USES Crt, DTDef, DTUtil;
VAR
  time : Real;
  k, NumConversions : Integer;

BEGIN
  DTInitialize;
  DTSetModifiers(0, 0, 1);        {need continuous mode}
  time := 60;
  IF DTSetClock(time) THEN WriteLn('time ', time:10:2);

  DTDMABuffer^[0] := 4095;  {big spikes to trigger scope}
  DTDMABuffer^[1] := 4095;
  NumConversions := 400;        {start displaying DMA buffer}
  DTWriteDACDMA(DAC0and1,NumConversions);

  REPEAT                  {fill buffers with sine and exponential}
    FOR k := 1 TO 199 DO
      begin
        DTDMABuffer^[2*k]   := Round(4095.0*exp(-2*k/100));
        DTDMABuffer^[2*k+1] := Round(2048+2047*sin(k*PI/199));
      end;
    FOR k := 1 TO 199 DO        {slowly zero exponential buffer}
      BEGIN
        DTDMABuffer^[2*k] := 0;        delay(10);
      END;
  UNTIL keypressed;
END.
```

The DACs can also be used to drive a mechanical X-Y plotter (Figure 6–5). Many plotters have a pen lift control that can be used to raise and lower the pen. The digital output port can be used to control the pen. Many early so-called "digital plotters" were actually electrical X-Y plotters with an electrical pen lift. Modern digital plotters do not use such an electrical drive scheme.

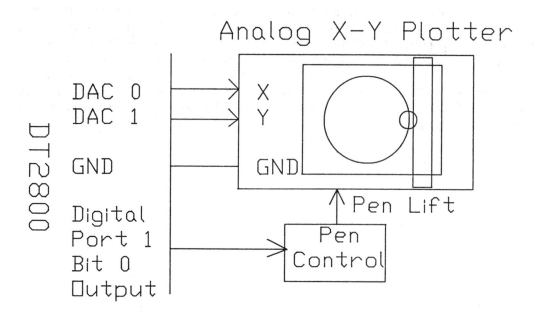

Figure 6–5. Arrangement for simulating a digital plotter using an X-Y electrical plotter.

PROCEDURE   DTReadADCDMA(VAR   ADCGain,   ChanStart,   ChanEnd, NumConv : Integer);

This reads in NumConv words with DMA into the DTDMABuffer using the current clock settings and modifiers. The program ADCDMA exercises both ADC and DAC functions. It records two channels of input data and displays it on the DAC first using a single DAC channel; this shows directly how the data are kept in memory, and the scope display is similar to that seen on a dual trace scope in the chopped mode. The second DAC display uses both DACs and sends each of the two waveforms to a separate DAC:

```
PROGRAM ADCDMA;
USES Crt, Dos, DTDef, DTUtil;
{  Records two channel ADC and outputs on DAC(s) with DMA  }

VAR
  StartChannel, EndChannel, datapoints : Integer;
BEGIN
  DTInitialize;
  DTperiod := 36;                         {fastest DT2801-A speed}
  IF DTSetClock(DTPeriod) THEN
                     WriteLn('time period ', DTPeriod:10:2);
  StartChannel := 0;            EndChannel := 1;
  datapoints := 200;

  DTSetModifiers(1, 0, 0);        {External Triggering}
  DTReadADCDMA(gain1, StartChannel, EndChannel, datapoints);
```

```
REPEAT UNTIL DTReady;            {wait until acquisition done}
IF DTcheckerrors THEN ;

DTDMAbuffer^[0] := 4095;         {big spikes to trigger scope}
DTDMAbuffer^[1] := 4095;

DTPeriod := 60;  {dac slower than ADC}
IF DTSetClock(DTPeriod) THEN WriteLn('time ok');

WriteLn('Displaying DTDMABuffer on single DAC to scope');
DTSetModifiers(0, 0, 1);         {set continuous mode}
DTWriteDACDMA(dac1, datapoints);
WriteLn('Return for Next Display');   ReadLn;

IF DTcheckerrors THEN ;  {must stop current DMA before next}
WriteLn('Displaying DTDMABuffer to both DACs on scope');
DTWriteDACDMA(dac0and1, datapoints);
END.
```

Again we highlight the DMA instructions. The use of the DTReady requires special comment. If we leave it out and go directly on to the DTCheckErrors, the program fails to execute properly. DTCheckErrors interrupts any currently executing DT commands. In this case it would be the DMA transfer. We must wait until transfer is complete. The only way to do that is to monitor the board status with DTReady until it is finished. Then we can go on with impunity.

Figure 6–6 shows the use of a data acquisition system to record the charging and discharging of an RC network. To initiate data acquisition, channel 2 can be monitored with an immediate mode. If the capacitor is charged, then closing the switch to ground causes the voltage to drop abruptly below 5 V. Similarly, in the discharge position switching to the charge position causes channel 1 to abruptly rise to the battery voltage.

Figure 6–6B shows typical charging and discharging transients. The linearized forms of the data are $\log[D(t)]$ versus t and $\log[D(\inf)-D(t)]$ versus t where $D(\inf)$ is the fully charged voltage. Linearized plots are shown in Figure 6–6B. The extraordinary linearity of the data is evident; the plots are linear over almost three decades and are limited by the 5 mV ADC resolution. The odd little staircase at the bottom is a result of the finite ADC resolution. This is called quantization noise and we return to it in the next chapter. The RC time constant evaluated from the charging data is 4.26 s and from the discharging data is 4.22 s. The discrepancy can be attributed to the inaccuracy in measuring $D(\inf)$ due to the finite ADC resolution or, possibly, to the small capacitor nonidealities, which are hard to eliminate even with the best film capacitors.

Experiment 6–1 – 6–2. Here you program and use the DT2801 parallel I/O ports including showing the effect of the External Triggering.

Experiment 6–3. Build a simple digital transient recorder to record the multiple outputs of a counter as it cycles through its counting sequence.

Experiment 6–4. Determine how fast a linear ramp can be output with the DAC.

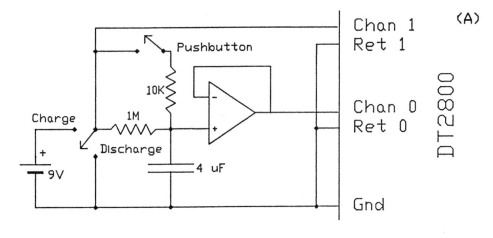

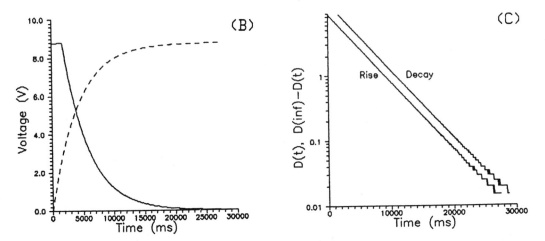

Figure 6–6. (A) System for measuring the charging and discharging time of an RC network. The pushbutton is used to accelerate full charging or discharging. (B) Typical charging (– – – –) and discharging (———) transients. (C) Linearized transients using the equations given in Appendix A.

Experiment 6–5 – 6–7. Output a user-generated waveform to the DAC for display on an oscilloscope using immediate and DMA modes.

Experiment 6–8. On an X-Y plotter, draw circles or roses with the DACs.

Experiment 6–9. A ramp is generated with the DAC and digitized with the ADC. The differences are examined.

Experiment 6–10 – 6–11. Charging and discharging characteristics of an RC network are recorded and the RC time constant is computed.

6.7 REFERENCES

The DT2801 Series User Manual is essential for program development with the 2801s. In contrast to so many technical reference manuals, it is rather clearly written. Eggebrecht clearly discusses programming the 8237 DMA controller.

Problems

6-1. If all of the ADC values are 12-bit 2s complement, write a real function ConvertVolts(Data, Gain) that returns the voltage when passed the digitized ADC value (Data) and the amplifier gain (Gain). If you were using a 16-bit ADC, would there be any special problems with this routine?

7

Signal-to-Noise (S/N) Enhancement

7.1 INTRODUCTION

A pervasive problem in all experimental disciplines is the extraction of quality data from noisy data. We demonstrate the nature of the problem and show several methods of enhancing the signal-to-noise ratio (S/N). These include:

(1) RC low pass filtering.
(2) Ensemble averaging.
(3) Lock-in amplifiers.
(4) Boxcar integrators.
(5) Mathematical methods.

We demonstrate and discuss the behavior of these different data acquisition and reduction methods as well as their strengths and weaknesses. We show quantization noise, which can be improved by actually making the signal noisier.

To give some idea of the nature of the problem we show a schematic representation of noise power as a function of frequency in Figure 7–1. There are several distinctive features. At very low frequencies the noise increases rapidly towards infinity, and there

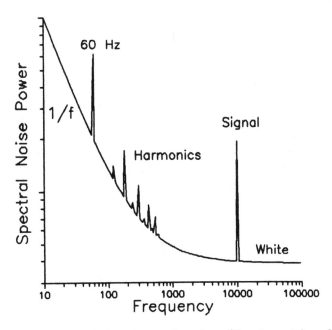

Figure 7–1. A typical power spectrum showing 1/f noise at low frequency, power line spikes, and high frequency white noise. At still higher frequencies, radio signals and instruments would start to appear. The peak at 10 KHz is a desired signal.

are characteristic noise spikes at certain frequencies. At very high frequency the noise distribution becomes flat with frequency.

The increasing noise with decreasing frequency is called 1/f (spoken "one over f") noise. One over f noise is also called flicker noise; some devices have outputs that flicker between a few different states. A large number of signal sources follow rather accurately this equation over a wide range of conditions. It is not immediately obvious why the noise might be expected to curve upwards for low frequencies (i.e., long periods). The reason, however, is easily visualized if you consider what happens to the output of virtually all instruments if your measurements take too long—they drift and have to be readjusted. This drift is low frequency noise in which the time scale of the drift is comparable to the inverse of the noise frequency. Such long term drift can arise from temperature cycling, drafts, component aging, and, ultimately, component failure.

The spikes are specific noise sources that arise from local noise sources. The most pronounced of these are the ubiquitous peaks at 60, 120, 180, 240 Hz, and so on. These arise from the power line fundamental and the higher harmonics that are radiated by the power lines, the lights, and any other ac-powered equipment. These can easily be seen by merely taking an oscilloscope probe, connecting several feet of wire to it and moving the wire around the room. Significant signals are clearly seen. Glitches frequently arise from fluorescent lamps; when the discharge turns on and off every half cycle the lamps radiate large amounts of electrical interference. You can also locate noisy hot spots such as ac-powered equipment. Particularly severe sources are transformers, and you can generally locate them with the probe without even opening the case.

The flat region of the spectral distribution is known as white noise. At high enough frequencies most sources will follow this dependence.

The noise power is given in units of power per unit bandwidth (e.g., microwatts/Hz). Alternatively, the noise voltage is frequently given by the square root of the noise power (e.g., volts/Hz$^{1/2}$).

Figure 7–2 shows typical room noise and its associated relative power spectrum. Computer, 60 Hz pickup, and fluorescent lamp noise are the dominant components. The 1/f, white noise and power line noise are all clearly evident in the power spectrum. The even harmonics, while barely detectable, are invariably much weaker than the odd harmonics. All the harmonics up through the eleventh are easily discernible in the unaveraged waveform. Note that this spectrum was generated by recording or averaging transients and performing a fast Fourier transform on the data to extract the power spectrum.

To quantitate signal quality, the signal-to-noise ratio, S/N, is used. S/N is frequently defined as:

$$S/N = \frac{\text{signal amplitude}}{\text{standard deviation in signal}} \qquad (7\text{–}1)$$

This is effectively the inverse fractional standard deviation in the signal. Alternatively, ratios of signal-to-noise powers are used. We will use Equation 7–1. An S/N=1 is considered about the limits of direct detection. An S/N below 1 is considered undetectible without further enhancement. In many analytical measurements, the detection limit is defined when the signal is two or three times the standard deviation from the noise.

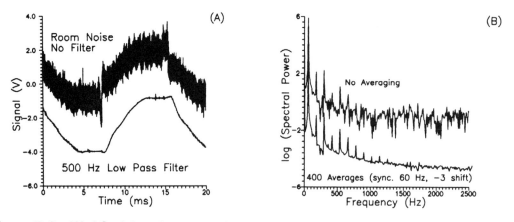

Figure 7–2. (A) AC pickup from a 15-foot wire strung near a computer and near a bank of fluorescent lights. The broad band of high frequency noise is largely from the computer and the lower waveform appears after passing through an active 500 Hz low pass filter. Absolute voltages cannot be compared. (B) The power spectrum of the low pass filter transient of (A). The upper trace is for a single transient while the lower is 400 averages synchronized with the 60 Hz power line frequency. Since the two traces would overlap, the lower was shifted down by 3 units.

There are many point noise sources. These include computers, calculators, pulsed lasers, and nuclear magnetic resonance and electron spin resonance spectrometers. To convince yourself of this, place your hand-held calculator near an AM radio. The pronounced interference changes as the calculator carries out different operations and as the display changes. Computers are a severe noise source, especially older machines that do not meet the FCC standards for radio frequency interference. These frequencies are related to the computer clocks and are generally in the megahertz range.

For classified work a computer must be certified by the Tempest program to be free of radiation leaks that can be used to detect its contents even at a distance of several yards. In particular, the displays must be very carefully shielded.

Experiment 7-1. In this experiment you examine various environmental noise sources including measuring the power spectrum of room noise using the program GET-POWER.

We turn now to the signal. Every signal has a characteristic frequency distribution. What is detected is the sum of all noise sources plus your signal. If your processing signal is sensitive to the noise present and your signal is weak compared to the noise, the signal disappears into the noise. Some devices are inherently immune to certain noise sources. For example, a mechanical recorder is largely immune to frequencies above a few hundred Hertz since the pen cannot keep up. However, in general you will have to do something to eliminate the noise.

Schematically, we show a nearly pure 10 KHz signal source superimposed on the noise spectrum of Figure 7-1. The goal is to extract the sine wave from the noise. Sources at different frequencies would, of course, be displaced to higher or lower frequencies.

Several points bear comment. First, because of 1/f noise, dc is one of the worst places to make a measurement. Second, signal sources should not be placed around 60 Hz and the power line harmonics. Clearly, to minimize the noise contributions, the signal should be a relatively high frequency and well clear of power line or other specific interference frequency. Finally, we note that if we had a way of restricting the detection to just the frequency of interest, we could reduce the total noise power without affecting the signal and, thus, increase S/N.

For ac signal processing, the signal must be forced to appear around a new nonzero frequency. This is usually done by modulating the source. For example, the light is measured with a photodetector and the signal is modulated by passing the light through a chopper (e.g., a motor driven slotted wheel through which the light passes).

A fast ac waveform is not useful directly for digitization or driving a recorder; some form of rectification or ac-to-dc conversion is necessary. However, simple half- or full-wave rectification of noise produces a spurious output. In the lock-in section, we show how to rectify only the signal and eliminate the noise.

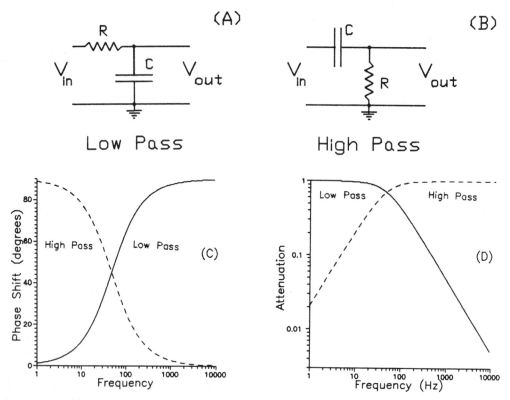

Figure 7–3. (A) Low pass RC filter. (B) High pass RC filter. (C) Phase shift and (D) attenuation versus frequency for the low (———) and high (- - - -) pass filters. The output lags behind the input for the low pass filter and leads it for the high pass filter. The RC time constant is 0.0033 s, which corresponds to a half power transmission frequency of 50 Hz.

7.2 RC FILTERS

Electrical filters can be used to reduce the transmission to the detector of frequencies outside the signal bandwidth. For measurements made near dc, the simplest filter is a low pass filter that cuts off frequencies above the signal frequency. The simple resistance capacitance network of Figure 7–3A serves nicely. We assume that the input source has negligible resistance and the output has a high input resistance or is buffered with a follower. Both low pass and high pass filters are shown. The attenuation factor and phase shift for a low pass filter is given below:

$$\text{Attenuation} = A = \frac{1}{\sqrt{1 + (\omega R C)^2}} \tag{7–2a}$$

$$\text{Phase Shift} = \arctan(\omega R C) \tag{7–2b}$$

$$\omega = 2 \pi f \tag{7–2c}$$

where A is the voltage gain and f is the frequency. The one-half power transmission frequency is $1/(2\pi RC)$, which corresponds to an attenuation of 0.707 of the voltage. The phase shift is defined for a single frequency input and is the phase shift or the angular differences between the input and output sine waves. Figure 7–3C and 7–3D show phase and attenuation factors for both high and low pass filters for a specific RC. For a low pass filter, the output lags or occurs later than the input and for a high pass filter the output leads the input.

A way of defining a filter is the noise bandwidth, Δf_{noise}. If the noise entering the filter was white with a power of N (watts/Hz), then the total noise power passing through the filter is $N\Delta f_{noise}$. For an RC low pass filter:

$$\Delta f = \frac{1}{4RC} \tag{7–3}$$

For RC=1, the half power point is at 0.16 Hz while the noise bandwidth is 0.25 Hz. The noise bandwidth is wider because of the long drawn out attenuation versus frequency.

Neither filter is particularly sharp, but what they lack in sharpness they make up for in simplicity. Sharpness of cutoff can be increased by stacking one filter after another with operational amplifier followers between each to prevent them from interacting with each other. Indeed, the filter in the Nyquist experiment (Figure A–2) is composed of two buffered series-connected low pass filters.

For low frequency signals (i.e., f→0), the low pass filter is very effective for removing higher frequency noise including 60 Hz ac pickup for a low enough cutoff. For signals that are intrinsically ac, a high pass filter can remove much of the 1/f noise.

The manner in which a low pass filter attenuates noise can be seen by considering its response to a square wave input of duration Δt. For a pulse of peak V_0 and width Δt starting at t=0, the output is:

$$V(t) = V_0 (1 - e^{-t/RC}), \quad 0 \le t \le \Delta t \tag{7–4a}$$

$$V(t) = V(\Delta t) \exp(-t/RC) \quad \Delta t \le t \tag{7–4b}$$

where $V(\Delta t)$ is the output voltage at the termination of the input pulse. It is clear that the greater $RC/\Delta t$, the smaller $V(\Delta t)$ will be and the more the short pulses will be attenuated and rounded. This rounding effectively attenuates high frequency (i.e., fast) signals while passing unattenuated signals, which change more slowly than RC. This rounding effect prevents abrupt excursions in the input from appearing unattenuated in the output. The higher the frequency (i.e., the more abrupt the noise changes), the more effective is RC filtering.

Figure 7–2A dramatically demonstrates low pass filtering to remove high frequency noise. A 500 Hz low pass filter virtually eliminates all the high frequency computer noise coming in on the antenna while letting through the 60 Hz and a few of the harmonics.

Figure 7–4 shows the effect of a low pass filter on a noisy repetitive waveform for different RC time constants. The noise-free signal is on the top, followed by the noisy one, and then the filtered signals. The improvement can be quite dramatic. However, if the cutoff frequency is made too low, the desired signal as well as the noise will be distorted or attenuated. For the 3.2-ms filter, it is clear that the noise level is lower than for

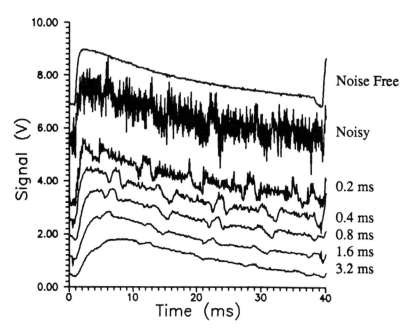

Figure 7–4. The effect of different RC time constants on the S/N of a periodic waveform. Slightly more than one cycle of the waveform is shown at the top followed by the noisy signal and signal passed through RC low pass filters with different RC time constants. The squarish features arise from 60 Hz interference in the noise generator.

the noise-free signal, although there is great loss of spectral details. However, if our waveforms were slower than the one shown, distortion could be reduced to an insignificant level while eliminating virtually all the high frequency noise.

For the signal source of Figure 7–1, a further S/N improvement would be to add a low frequency cutoff or high pass filter that attenuates lower frequency noise. The combination of a high and low pass filter yields a **bandpass filter.** If the transmission frequencies are made very narrow, a **narrow bandpass** filter results. In principle, by narrowing the bandpass enough the noise can be totally eliminated. A tunable narrow bandpass filter is known as a **tuned** amplifier. In practice, however, there are limits to how narrow the bandpass can be made. In most cases, the desired signal frequency and the center frequency of the narrow pass filter can only be made so accurate and kept so stable. As the filter gets too narrow, small drifts in either the signal frequency or the bandpass cause the desired signal to be totally attenuated; in other words, the filter cannot tell the signal from the noise. Digital filters can be made free of drift.

A notch filter strongly attenuates frequencies at and near a specific center frequency. Notch filters are good for eliminating specific known noise sources such as 60 Hz pickup.

For the moment we delay the questions of how to move intrinsically dc signals to higher frequency and how to process these signals and convert them into a form useful for processing on recorders or other output devices.

RC filtering is simple, cheap, and frequently very effective. It works best for low frequency signals contaminated by well-separated higher frequency noise. It should generally be considered one of the first signal-to-noise enhancement methods.

Experiment 7–2. You examine the characteristics of RC S/N enhancement.

7.3 GATED FILTERS

Another way of improving S/N is to integrate the signal over different windows. When the gate width is increased, more signal is integrated and the S/N ratio improves. A VFC interfaced to a frequency counter and computer can yield very dramatic S/N enhancement. Figure 7–5 shows how to interface the computer-interfaced Intersil counter of Chapter 3.

Operation is quite simple: the computer initiates data acquisition by triggering the signal source—an instrument simulator in this case—then at regularly timed intervals the computer triggers the counter and reads the number of counts for the switch set gate period. Longer gate periods collect more counts and average out more of the noise. Gate periods that are too long begin to average changes in the actual signal.

Figure 7–6A shows a test waveform. The actual signal that is combined with the noise is the "Small" signal. After adding noise, the signal is invisible with S/N=0.1. The recovered waveforms in Figure 7–6B are excellent. Even the 0.01 s period gives excellent recovery while the 0.1 s result is indistinguishable from the original. A 1 s gate begins to seriously distort the signal since the waveform changes in less than 1 s.

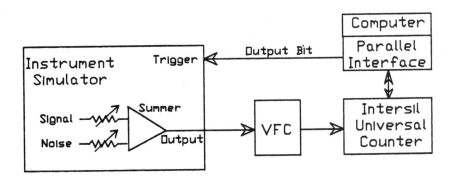

Figure 7–5. Computer interfaced ADC averager based on Intersil counter kit. The signals were derived from an instrument simulator that could be triggered from a parallel port bit. Details are given by Xu, Demas, and Grubb (1989).

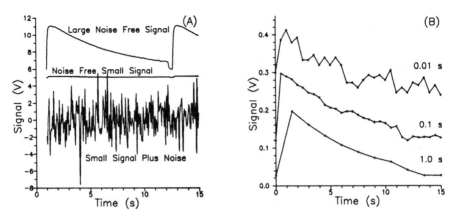

Figure 7–6. (A) From top to bottom, the amplifier noise free signal, the actual 0.2 V peak signal used in recovery, and the noise plus signal (S/N=0.1). (B) The recovered signals using different gate widths from 0.01 to 1 s. Xu, Demas, Grubb (1989). Adapted with permission of the *Journal of Chemical Education*.

Experiment 7–3. You examine the S/N enhancement using a digital integrator with a variable gate width.

7.4 LOCK-IN AMPLIFIERS

A special filter that drifts with, or is locked to, the signal and averages noise out to zero is the solution to both the drift problem of a tuned amplifier and to the issue of converting ac into dc. This instrument is a **lock-in amplifier** or **synchronous rectifier**. A lock-in requires a relatively noise-free signal that is locked to the noisy signal in both frequency and phase. This noise-free signal is used to lock the filter frequency to the signal. It also converts the high frequency signal into a dc signal that can be used to drive all the common readouts.

To understand how synchronous rectification works, consider the following experiment. You are making an optical measurement and the desired signal is a weak one riding on a large varying baseline. To compensate for the background you alternately take readings with the light on and the light off. A complete measurement cycle consists of one light-on reading and one light-off reading. The output is the difference between the two. If this is done often enough, the fluctuations in the background are compensated for automatically. This procedure works because you are synchronizing your data acquisition to the modulation of the signal source in both phase and frequency. A lock-in works in much the same way. It is critical that there be a clean reference waveform that is locked in both phase and frequency to the signal of interest to control the detection.

The operation of a lock-in is simple. A block diagram of a simple lock-in is shown in Figure 7–7. It has a signal and a reference channel. The signal is amplified and

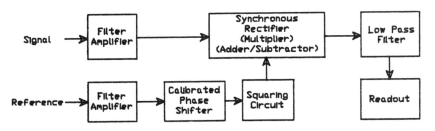

Figure 7–7. Schematic representation of a lock-in amplifier.

sometimes filtered to reduce the bandwidth. The reference signal must be at the same frequency and have a fixed phase relationship to the signal. The reference signal is filtered to remove all but the fundamental of the input signal and then squared to give a 50% duty cycle square wave. This square wave drives the synchronous rectifier. The low pass filter is where most of the noise rejection occurs. Since in many cases the phase of the reference does not exactly match the signal, a variable phase shifter is added to allow adjusting the relationship between the two.

In this system we will assume that the rectifier is controlled by the square wave. The rectifier passes (adds) the signal directly if the square wave is high and inverts (subtracts) the signal (i.e., just changes its sign) if the square wave is low. In other words it is just an amplifier with a controllable gain of 1 or −1. An alternative way of realizing this behavior is to make the square wave a precise value of +1 and −1 and multiply the input waveform by this signal. In practice, the switching amplifier is simpler to implement and more stable.

The effect of this is shown in Figure 7–8. For the square wave in phase with the signal, we have full wave signal rectification. This pulsating wave is passed through a low pass filter to obtain the average dc value.

However, the phase of the square wave need not match the phase of the ac signal. We can phase shift (lead or lag in time) the multiplier square wave with respect to the input waveform. The effect of delaying the multiplier waveform by 45° and 90° respectively is shown in Figure 7–8. In particular, for a 90° phase shift, there is as much positive portion as there is negative portion of the waveform; the average is zero so that after filtering there is no dc signal. For a 180° shift the signal is full-wave rectified but inverted over the 0° phase shift. The filter output is then the negative of the average voltage. If the phase shift between the reference square wave and the signal is ϕ_{li}, the average dc output, I_{av}:

$$I_{av}(\phi_{li}) = 0.707\, I_{peak} \cos(\phi_{li}) \qquad (7\text{--}5)$$

where I_{peak} is the peak voltage of the sine wave. When the waveform and reference are in phase this is referred to as the **in phase** signal, and when they are 90° out of phase, the lock-in is set in **quadrature** to the signal.

This phase dependence means that you must adjust the lock-in to match the signals. Commercial lock-in amplifiers have calibrated phase shifters with a switch that will set 0, 90, 270 and 360° of shift and a continuous dial that can be used to set the 0–100°.

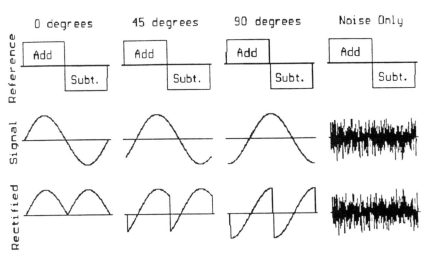

Figure 7–8. Operation of a synchronous rectifier with sine waves and noise having different phases with respect to the reference signal.

Although it is possible to adjust the phase to give the maximum output, this is not very precise because you are working on the peak of the cosine curve where the slope is smallest and changes in ϕ_{li} have a minimum effect. It is more common to adjust the phase to give zero output. Since the reference is now 90° out of phase with the signal, switching in a ±90° of phase shift gives the maximum signal.

What about the noise? It does not help if the noise is rectified along with the signal. The effect of the synchronous rectification process is shown in Figure 7–8. Since the noise is random around zero in each half cycle of the multiplier, the average value on smoothing tends towards zero. This is in marked contrast to the signal waveform, which is consistently reinforced by the rectification process. The lock-in not only discriminates against noise outside its bandpass, but it also rejects noise inside the bandpass by taking advantage of the fact that the phase of the noise is random with respect to the signal.

Actually, the low pass filter on the output of the rectifier gives the S/N enhancement. If all the output of the synchronous rectifier were passed to the detection system, we would still have the same S/N as we had at the input. The output filter is generally a simple RC low pass filter with a variable time constant (frequently specified as 6 decibel (db) per octave filter) or two RC filters connected in series (a 12 db per octave filter). The 6 and 12 db figures merely tell how sharp the cutoff frequency is. For normal signal processing, the 12 db filter gives excellent S/N with the fastest response. The 12 db filter will, however, produce unstable behavior and oscillations if the lock-in is used in a feedback control circuit.

If only the RC filter improves the S/N, why not just use an RC filter at the beginning? The answer is that many signals are low level, must be amplified, and are frequently contaminated with static dc levels. Modulations move the signal away from 1/f noise in the amplifiers that would corrupt dc measurements. High pass filtering removes static dc levels.

The selection of the final low pass filter time constant is critical. The rise and fall time of the filter output is exponential with a time constant of RC. Thus, for rapidly changing waveforms, the RC time can limit the rate at which the output signal can follow the input. Counterbalancing this is the fact that the longer the RC time constant, the smaller the Δf_{noise} and the greater the S/N.

Figure 7–9 shows the input and output of a lock-in amplifier for noisy and noise-free signals. Figure 7–9A shows the modulated noise-free signal amplified 100 times and the signal plus noise combined; the signal is invisible in the noise since S/N=0.03. The noisy signal is obtained by adding the noise and the signal.

Figure 7–9B shows the lock-in output for different RC time constants from 3 ms to 300 ms. To simulate a measurement, the signal source was turned on and then off during the measurement to simulate a rectangular waveform. Since this was done manually, the start and end points for the pulse are variable. For RC=3 ms, S/N=1.6 and as such the signal is barely discernible to the eye. For RC=10 ms, S/N=2.7. For 100 ms, S/N=10. For 300 ms, S/N=22. Although not shown, S/N for 1 s and 3 s time constants rise to 31 and 87, respectively. Of course, the response time is greatly slowed. Even the modest 100 ms time constant has improved the S/N by 320 times.

What happens if the signal drifts from the center frequency? Since the reference and signal are locked to each other, the multiplier waveform shifts along with the signal. The result is that even though the frequency might change, the rectification circuit stays locked to the signal frequency.

The dual channel lock-in amplifier is a powerful variation. It is not quite the two independent lock-ins in the same box that the name suggests. It is two lock-ins with the same reference, but the reference for the second lock-in is shifted by 90° from the first. This is shown schematically in Figure 7–10.

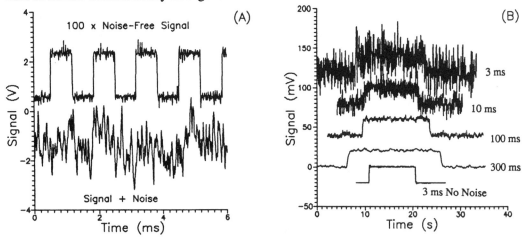

Figure 7–9. (A) Noise-free signal for lock-in amplifier and signal plus noise used in the recovery experiments. Note the 100-fold amplification of the noise-free signal to improve its viewing. (B) Recovery of a square wave pulse from the data of part A for different time constants. RC values are indicated by each waveform. All data are for the noisy data of A except for the lowest trace.

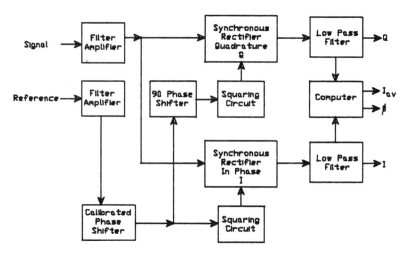

Figure 7–10. Schematic representation of a dual channel lock-in amplifier. Older lock-ins only supply I and Q while modern ones include the computer.

Either channel can be used as a single channel lock-in. However, by simple numerical calculation the in phase, I, and quadrature, Q, outputs can be combined as follows:

$$I_{av} = (I^2 + Q^2)^{1/2} \tag{7–6a}$$

$$\phi = Q/I \tag{7–6b}$$

where I_{av} is the average signal amplitude independent of noise and ϕ is the phase shift between the signal and the reference (assuming the variable phase shifter is set to zero shift).

Thus, a dual lock-in provides the capabilities of measuring the amplitude and the phase shift of an input signal in real time. Modern lock-ins supply I, Q, I_{av}, and ϕ outputs. Most of these are also directly computer interfaceable with RS-232 or IEEE-488 interfaces.

Figure 7–11 shows the Stanford Research Systems' dual channel lock-in set up to measure the phase and attenuation factor for its internal notch filter. The SR530 has built in DACs, an ADC, a voltage controlled oscillator (VCO) with a frequency that depends on applied voltage, and a frequency counter. All of these are computer controllable or can be read via the computer. Stanford Research Systems has a powerful menu-driven software package that allows making time scans, collecting data as a function of frequency, plotting and saving data, and doing simple arithmetic operations on data. In the experiment shown, the DAC output is varied with time to alter the frequency of the VCO, which is applied to lock-in input and the reference. The frequency meter determines the actual frequency of the oscillator. With the notch filter in and the lock-in set to yield I_{av} and ϕ, the I_{av} data are shown in Figure 7–11B. The large attenuation factors as the filter sweeps through the notch are quite evident. The data shown are not completely accurate representations since the amplitude of the VCO output varies with frequency. Thus, a

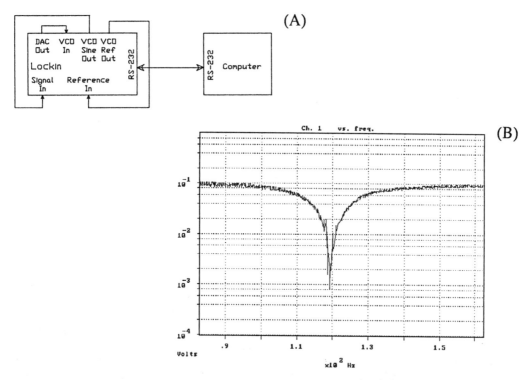

Figure 7–11. (A) Configuration of Stanford Research Systems SR530 to measure the phase and attenuation of the 120 Hz notch filter in the lock-in. (B) Attenuation factors for the filter. Data are not corrected for the frequency dependence of VCO output voltage. Data were obtained and plotted using Stanford's program.

full experiment would require repeating the experiment with the notch filter out, ratioing the amplitudes, and taking the differences of the phase shifts. Since the VCO gives different frequencies for each experiment, considerable software juggling would be required.

7.4.1 Applications of Lock-in Amplifiers

Lock-ins are ubiquitous signal processors. Virtually any physical measurement that can be modulated has been carried out using a lock-in. Applications include laser spectroscopy, electrochemistry, radar, cell physiology, and astronomy. We describe a few examples from our own work.

Drawing on the analogy we gave earlier for detecting light on a large unstable background, we developed a low frequency lock-in amplifier based on a digital voltmeter. A block diagram of the system is shown in Figure 7–12. The computer controlled whether the light emitting diode was on or off and synchronized data acquisition to it. For demonstration of S/N enhancement, room lights and our standard noise generator gave noise levels that were orders of magnitude above the signal level, but the integrating ADC averaged out all this higher frequency noise and no noise was detectable. The

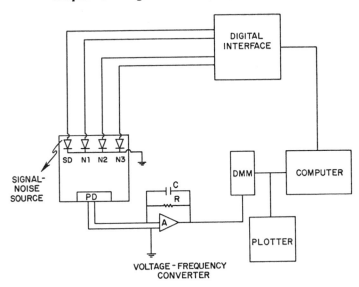

Figure 7–12. Low frequency computerized lock-in amplifier designed to detect low level light and test system. SD-Signal LED; N1, N3-Noise LEDs; PD-Silicon photodiode A-operational amplifier current-to-voltage converter; R-10 M; C-500 pF. DMM-Keithley 177 digital multimeter with IEEE bus adaptor; COMPUTER-Hewlett-Packard 9825A; PLOTTER-Hewlett-Packard 9872A. The computer controls the state of the light source and synchronizes data acquisition with the voltmeter. The computer controlled optical noise generator was required to give measureable noise levels. J. Toney and Demas, adapted with permission of the American Institute of Physics.

"noise" LEDs were necessary to generate adequate noise. These were turned on and off at random at a low frequency by the computer to give low frequency noise.

This system brings out one of the advantages of computer interfaced instruments: the ability to determine easily when the desired S/N is reached. Data points are taken in pairs with both a background point and a signal plus background point. With the signal source off, the DMM is read to give a background reading, B_i, with i = 1 for the first point. The signal source is turned on, and the voltage is read to give the composite background plus signal reading, x_i. For each pair a background corrected signal value, z_i, is calculated by:

$$z_i = x_i - B_i \qquad (7-7)$$

Since the noise level is not fixed but is fluctuating, the z_is are a noisy representation of the desired signal. For a noisy signal one z_i supplies negligible information, so signal averaging of a number of z_is is performed. Signal averaging and statistical computation on the accumulated information are carried out as follows. Running sums of z_is and z_i^2s are calculated and stored:

$$P_n = \sum_i z_i \qquad (7-8a)$$

$$Q_n = \sum z_i^2 \qquad (7\text{-}8b)$$

The mean, μ_n, the standard deviation of the mean, σ_{mn}, and S/N at each point are calculated by:

$$\mu_n = P_n/n \qquad (7\text{-}9a)$$

$$\sigma_{nm} = \sigma_n/n^{1/2} \qquad (7\text{-}9b)$$

$$\sigma_n = \frac{n\,Q_n - P_n^2}{[\,n\,(n-1\,)\,]^{1/2}} \qquad (7\text{-}9c)$$

$$(S/N)_n = \mu_n / \sigma_{nm} \qquad (7\text{-}9d)$$

where μ_n and σ_n are the mean and standard deviations of the samples calculated for points i = 1 to n of the z_is. $(S/N)_n$ is the S/N calculated using the first n points. The summations run from i = 1 to n. The σ_{mn} and σ_n are only calculated for n > 4 because with a smaller n the statistics are unreliable. S/N computations can be carried out very quickly since P_{n+1} and Q_{n+1} are derived from P_n and Q_n merely by adding another term. It is thus possible to calculate the S/N while the DMM is acquiring the next data point (400 ms with the slow ADC used). The process of collecting B_i and z_i and calculating the statistics is repeated until the maximum number of samples or the desired σ_{nm} or S/N has been reached.

Figure 7–13 shows the results of a typical experiment. The initial S/N is about 0.3 or undetectible. The mean and two times σ_{mn} are shown. After 250 averages, S/N has risen to 4.8 or an enhancement of about 16, which is close to that expected.

The beauty of such a computer interfaced system is that data acquisition can be done automatically and interactively. Since S/N is being calculated on the fly, the experiment can be stopped once the desired S/N is reached or after it becomes clear that it cannot be done in a reasonable time. During a spectral measurement, the system would race through those regions of good S/N and spend most of its time bringing the noisy regions up to acceptable levels. Extensive averaging of data in noisy regions would not be done. The instrument also has excellent rejection of static background such as room lights.

Another application of lock-ins is in luminescence. A luminescence sample of lifetime τ excited by a sinusoidal excitation gives a sinusoidal emission that is phase-shifted and attenuated from the excitation. The low pass filter equations are identical except that τ replaces RC:

$$A = \text{Attenuation} = \frac{1}{\sqrt{1 + (\omega\tau)^2}} \qquad (7\text{-}10a)$$

$$\text{Phase Shift} = \arctan(\omega\tau) \qquad (7\text{-}10b)$$

$$\omega = 2\,\pi\,f \qquad (7\text{-}10c)$$

Luminescence lifetime measurements down to the low picosecond range are routinely made by measuring the phase shift or reduction in the ac modulation caused by the samples.

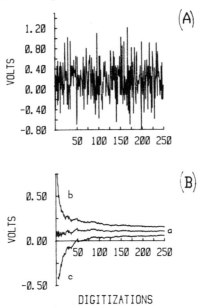

Figure 7–13. Typical performance of the computerized lock-in amplifier. (A) Baseline subtracted signal (z_i) versus digitization number. Original S/N = 0.3. (B) Calculated mean value of signal μ_n (a) and error bounds ($\mu_n + 2\sigma_{mn}$) (b,c) versus digitization. Final S/N = 4.8. Toney and Demas, adapted with permission of The American Institute of Physics.

A more interesting example has two samples emitting simultaneously with different lifetimes. Each sample will then have a different phase shift and ac attenuation factor. The composite signal is then the sum of the two emitting sine waves. Phase resolved spectroscopy allows one to completely remove one component and see only the other. To see how this works, we examine the equation for the total luminescence. If the sample is excited with a 100% sine wave modulated excitation given by 1-cos(ωt), then the emission is given by:

$$I(t) = K_1 A_1 \cos(\omega t - \phi_1) + K_2 A_2 \cos(\omega t - \phi_2) \qquad (7\text{–}11a)$$

$$A_i = \frac{1}{\sqrt{1 + (\omega \tau)^2}}, \quad i=1,2 \qquad (7\text{–}11b)$$

$$\phi_i = \arctan(\omega \tau_i), \quad i=1,2 \qquad (7\text{–}11c)$$

After processing this signal with a lock-in amplifier the rectified signal is given by:

$$I_{av} = 0.707\,[\,K_1 A_1 \cos(\phi_1 - \phi_{li}) + K_2 A_2 \cos(\phi_2 - \phi_{li})\,] \qquad (7\text{–}12)$$

where ϕ_{li} is the phase shift on the lock-in phase shifter. If $\phi_1 - \phi_{li}$ is set to $\pm 90^0$, the cosine term for component 1 is suppressed or nulled. However, if $\tau_1 \neq \tau_2$, component 2 is reduced but not totally eliminated. Thus, by adjusting ϕ_{li} correctly one can effectively make measurements on component 2 just as though component 1 was not present.

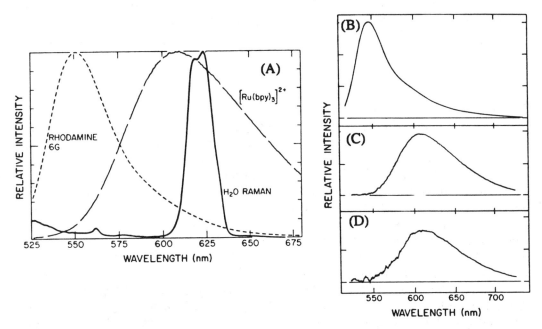

Figure 7–14. Phase resolution of overlapping emission spectra. (A) Emission spectra of pure rhodamine 6G, Ru(bpy)$_3^{2+}$ (bpy=2,2'-bipyridine) and the Raman spectrum of water. **(B)** Steady state (i.e., unresolved emission of a mixture of rhodamine 6G and Ru(bpy)$_3^{2+}$); the Ru(bpy)$_3^{2+}$ emission is barely visible as the bulge on the rhodamine emission. **(C)** Resolved Ru(bpy)$_3^{2+}$ emission after suppression of the rhodamine. **(D)** Resolved Ru(bpy)$_3^{2+}$ emission in which the rhodamine concentration has been increased eight times over that of B and the Ru(bpy)$_3^{2+}$ emission is invisible. Reprinted with permission from J. N. Demas and R. A. Keller, *Analytical Chemistry* **57**, p. 538. Copyright (1985) American Chemical Society.

Similarly, by nulling out component 2, we can measure component 1 as though it were free of component 2.

Figure 7–14 shows a phase resolved emission spectrum of a weak ruthenium metal complex emission (τ=350 ns) in the presence of a much stronger dye emission (τ=3.5 ns). The mixture emission is shown in Figure 7–14B while the beautifully resolved metal complex spectrum is shown in C. Even when the dye emission is eight times stronger still, D shows that excellent resolution can still be achieved. In such systems, it is possible to extract a component that is at about 1% of the total emission level. Other examples are shown in the reference.

Experiment 7–4. You examine the characteristics of a commercial lock-in amplifier.

Experiment 7–5. You measure the phase and attenuation factors for an RC filter by implementing a dual channel lock-in amplifier in software.

7.5 ENSEMBLE AVERAGING

One of the most powerful ways of signal averaging is **ensemble averaging.** Ensemble averaging is based on the well known fact that if you collect and average several datum points, the average is a better estimate of the signal than any single point. This works because in a typical noisy signal we can consider the total signal as being made up of a fixed signal component and a noisy one. The noise is random with respect to amplitude and sign. Thus, if we add noisy representations of waveforms together, the signal component will add coherently each time while the noise adds sometimes and subtracts sometimes. The signal component will then increase linearly with the number of summations while the noise component will increase, but less rapidly. The net effect is an S/N ratio that improves with the number of averages.

An ensemble averager is a transient recorder with memory and an arithmetic logic unit and controller. Instead of recording each point into a digit memory, however, each point is digitized and added to the memory element that corresponds to the specific time on the transient. Each new waveform is digitized and added in the same fashion. Thus, if we have a 1024 channel averager, we are in effect simultaneously processing 1024 channels as described above. As with most signal enhancement methods, ensemble averaging requires that waveforms be repetitive and synchronized to the averager by a noise-free signal.

We now consider the details of enhancement. From elementary error propagation, if we add p signals together, each with standard deviations of N_i, then the total noise, N_{total} is given by:

$$N_{total} = \left[\sum_{i=1}^{p} N_i^2 \right]^{1/2} \tag{7–13}$$

If the noise components are the same (i.e., $N_1 = N_2 \ldots = N$) then:

$$N_{total} = \left[\sum_{i=1}^{n} N^2 \right]^{1/2} = \left(nN^2 \right)^{1/2} = n^{1/2} N \tag{7–14}$$

Consider starting with a total signal made up of the signal component, S, and a noise component having a standard deviation N. We now show how the standard deviation changes with the number of averages. The original signal-to-noise ratio $(S/N)_{orig}$ is:

$$(S/N)_{orig} = S / N \tag{7–15}$$

After adding together n points, the signal component is nS and the noise component is $n^{1/2}N$. The final S/N is given by:

$$(S/N)_{final} = \frac{\text{Final Signal}}{\text{Final Noise}} = n S / (n^{1/2}N) = n^{1/2} (S/N)_{orig} \tag{7–16}$$

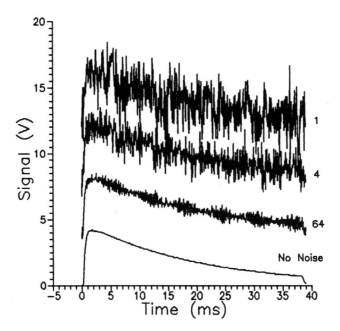

Figure 7–15. Enhancement of a noisy signal by ensemble averaging. The original noise-free signal is at the bottom. The number of averages for each signal is shown next to each plot.

Thus, the S/N improves with $n^{1/2}$. For 4 averages the improvement is 2, for 10 about 3, for 100 it is 10, and for 10,000 it is 100. The biggest improvement is at the beginning and further improvement becomes increasingly more time-consuming. Figure 7–15 shows a noise signal that has been averaged 4 and 64 times. In this case even a factor of 2 is a significant improvement in data quality and the factor of 8 enormously enhances the ability to extract information. In this case the undulations on the 64 average transient are caused by synchronous noise on our noise generator, which no amount of ensemble averaging will eliminate.

The effect of S/N enhancement can be seen very clearly with our room noise data. The noise in Figure 7–2B is made up of two components: power line related noise plus true random noise. Treating the power line noise as a desired signal, we ensemble averaged the room noise while synchronizing the averaging to the 60 Hz line. The effect in Figure 7–2B shows a dramatic reduction in the background with much greater definition of the power line related frequencies. The even harmonics are much more clearly defined and clearly visible at least up to the twenty-first harmonic—remember this is through a 500 Hz low pass filter.

The reasons for S/N enhancement by ensemble averaging are clearly seen by examining the power spectrum of the room after 400 averages taken asynchronously with the power line; that is, the trigger of the averager was done from an oscillator with no relationship to the power line frequency. The result is shown in Figure 7–16 along with the raw room spectrum. Unlike Figure 7–2B where a data shift was required for viewing, these data are plotted directly. There is a tremendous reduction in the detected power spectrum over the entire range; only the 60 Hz fundamental is visible and that is greatly

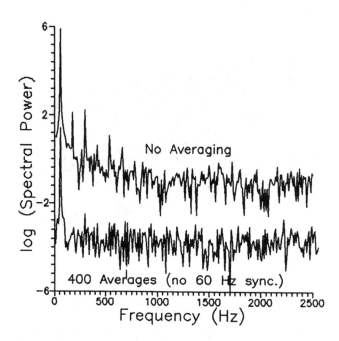

Figure 7–16. Reduction of background noise by asynchronous ensemble averaging. The top trace is the room noise while the bottom one is 400 averages of the room noise. There is no shift between the two data sets.

reduced. Clearly, the major benefit of ensemble averaging is reduction of noise power from all frequencies not locked to the signal.

A signal averaging program is extremely easy to implement from our transient recording ADCDMA program of Chapter 6. The critical portion of the code is shown below:

```
PROGRAM SigAv                    {Signal Averages Channel 2 }
USES Dos, DTDef, DTUtil;

CONST
  MaxDataPts = 1026;             {maximum # of points to average}
VAR
  NumAver, k, j, StartChannel, EndChannel, datapts : Integer;
  Average : ARRAY[0..MaxDataPts] OF Real;
  FilVar : Text;
  FileName : STRING;
  WaveFormPeriod : Real;         {Full period to record}

BEGIN                            {main}

   (... Initialization, set up file name, clock goes here)
```

```
WriteLn('number of averages ');
ReadLn(NumAver);
StartChannel := 2; EndChannel := 2;
FOR j := 0 TO datapts-1 DO
   Average[j] := 0;                {clear average array}

DTSetModifiers(1, 0, 0);          {External Triggering}
REPEAT UNTIL dtready;
FOR k := 1 TO NumAver DO
   BEGIN
     DTReadADCDMA(gain1, StartChannel, EndChannel, datapts);
     REPEAT UNTIL dtready;      {wait until acquisition done}
{ Update Average array by summing in new data }
     FOR j := 0 TO datapts-1 DO
        Average[j] := Average[j]+dtdmabuffer^[j];
        Write(k:4);                {Indicate # averages complete}
   END;
IF DTcheckerrors THEN WriteLn('Error');

FOR j := 0 TO datapts-1 DO    {GRAPHER format file output}
  BEGIN
    Average[j] := Average[j]/numaver;   {normalize data
    WriteLn(filvar, 0.001*j*DTperiod : 0 : 3, ' ',
                (Average[j] - 2048) : 8 : 4);
  END;
Close(filvar);

                 (... DAC output routine )

END.                          {main}
```

The major changes are establishing a new array, Average, to hold the running sum of the data, clearing it at the beginning, and adding each transient to the array after each acquisition. The DAC output routine requires rescaling of the sums to 12-bit data in DMA buffer for proper output.

Experiment 7–6. You examine S/N enhancement using ensemble averaging.

7.6   QUANTIZATION NOISE

A subtle and interesting form of noise inherent in digital acquisition is **quantization noise**. This noise is associated with finite resolution of the ADC. Consider digitization of the indicated low amplitude sine wave of Figure 7–17. The quantization levels of the waveform are indicated by the vertical tics. Any point at or above a level and below the next higher level digitizes at the lower level. Plot 7–17A shows the effect of digitizing 100 points without averaging; the systematic differences between the true and digitized values are shown. Quantization noise is observed for very low amplitude signals and poor resolution converters.

If we signal averaged many of the noise-free sine waves of Figure 7–17A, we get exactly the same staircase waveform because it digitizes the same each time. However, as we now show, a small amount of noise in the waveform actually improves the resolution. This is one of the few cases where noise is actually advantageous.

Figure 7–17B shows the digitization of the same sine wave to which Gaussian noise had been added; the noise had a standard deviation of 0.5 times the quantization step size. While at first glance the digitized signal of Figure 7–17B looks far worse than for

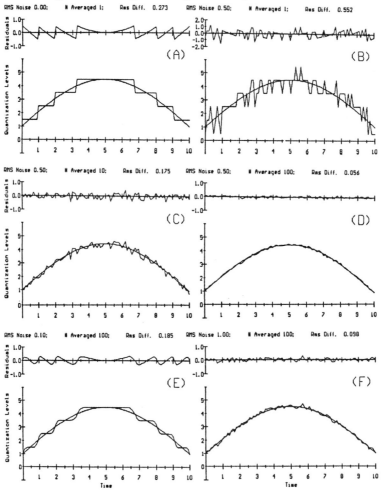

Figure 7–17. Effect of low ADC resolution on digitizing a sine wave and the reduction of quantization errors by adding noise and signal averaging. The quantization steps are the tics on the Y axis. The standard deviation of the added noise (in units of the quantization step size) and the standard deviations between the averaged and original signal are shown above the residuals plot. All data are generated by the program QUANT.

7–17A, inspection of the digitized transient reveals an interesting result. The closer the waveform approaches a quantization level, the more often the signal is digitized at the next higher level. If we now consider signal averaging this noisy signal, we average many values that cross levels. The closer a signal is to a higher level, the more often it crosses on the average and the higher the average. The further below the level, the lower the average. Thus, added noise serves as an interpolator. Figures 7–17C are for 10 averages and 7–17D are for 100 averages with noise of 0.5 times the quantization levels. The improvement is dramatic; 100 averages provide a signal that matches the original with a standard deviation that is about 16 times smaller than the quantization steps and shows no systematic bias.

A little thought suggests there is an optimum amount of noise—too little noise and we cannot span the quantization steps; too much noise and we add excess noise to our digitized signal. Intuition suggests that the optimum amount is a standard deviation about equal to half the step size. This would allow satisfactory interpolation across the entire step size. Figures 7–17E and 7–17F show the effect of 100 averages of noise with standard deviations of 0.1 and 1.0, respectively. Clearly, 0.1 is too little and 1.0 adds excess noise above that for the 0.5 level. Simulations demonstrate that the optimal range is 0.4–0.6 and that degradation is especially severe if the noise is too small ($<\approx 0.25$). However, it is clearly better to err on the side of a little too much rather than too little noise. In fact it has been shown that if the standard deviation for the noise is greater than or equal to q/2, where q is the quantization step size, the effective quantization noise has a variance of $q^2/12$ (Butterworth, et al.).

Consider the optimized noise level of q/2. The effective total noise has contributions from both the quantization and the random noise and is given by:

$$\left[(q/2)^2 + (q/12^{1/2})^2\right] \approx 0.6\,q \tag{7–17}$$

If we now average 100 transients, the effective noise is $\approx 0.06q$ or about 4 bits of improvement over q; this is confirmed by the simulations of Figure 7–17D. Thus, a lowly 3-bit converter is effectively a 7-bit converter. It is effectively a 9-bit converter after 1600 averages and a 10-bit one after 6400 averages. Thus, it is possible to obtain one part in a thousand resolution with a converter with only 8 quantization levels. Some very fast low resolution commercial averagers have included a noise switch to add noise to the signal if the signal was too clean.

One point is worth making. This technique increases converter resolution, but the accuracy is still limited by absolute converter accuracy. To realize 10-bit accuracy, the 3-bit converter must have levels that are accurate to 10 bits or one part in 1024.

Note that adding noise and averaging actually offsets the digitized results by −0.5 bit. This is easily seen by considering a value that exactly equals a quantization level. Without noise the answer is correct. With random noise, however, the signal digitizes half the time at the correct value and half the time at the next lower level. The average is then one-half bit too low. For looking at the relative shapes of waveforms, this shift has no effect since it is common to every point, but it should be kept in mind for absolute accuracy of low level signal or for comparing a noisy and a very clean signal at the highest resolution. The calculated values in Figure 7–17 have been corrected for the half-bit offset.

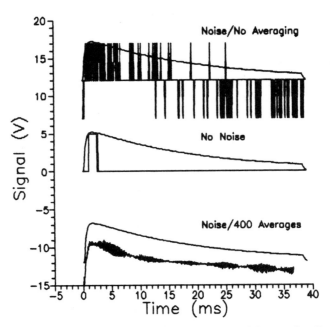

Figure 7–18. Effect of severe quantization noise and its reduction by ensemble averaging. The quantization levels are 5 V. Each group of pairs shows the original noise-free waveform and the results of different noise levels and averaging. The center pair shows no noise and no averaging, the top pair noise with no averaging, and the bottom pair noise plus averaging. The top pair is offset by +6 V and the bottom pair by –6 V.

Figure 7–18 shows an example of severe quantization noise on a real signal. The ADC has been effectively reduced to 2 bits with a level step size of 5 V! The recorded waveform shows only a rectangular pulse while the actual decay is decaying exponentially. The pulse occurs because of the poor ADC resolution. Also shown is a single average of a noisy waveform and 400 averages of the noisy waveform. Clearly, the averaging has converted the 2-bit converter into a useful 5- or 6-bit one. Note the half-bit shift in the averaged data. Synchronous noise in our noise generator causes the ripple in the averaged waveform.

Figure 7–19 shows data taken from a luminescence decay time instrument. The decays are single exponentials and are plotted on semilogarithmic plots versus time. A single decay and one with 5 averages are shown. The enhancement is about as expected by theory. The quantization noise near the end of the unaveraged decay is quite severe, and yet using only 5 averages greatly reduces the quantization noise as well as improves the overall S/N.

Experiment 7–7. You examine the effect of quantization noise using a computer program QUANT.

Experiment 7–8. You examine quantization noise and its reduction by adding noise using the instrument simulator.

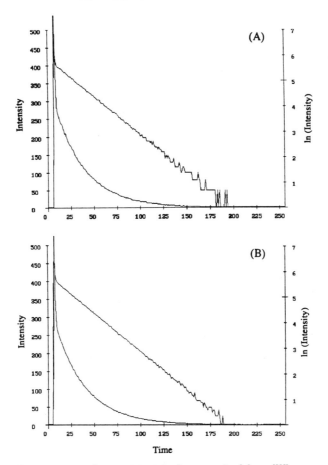

Figure 7–19. Luminescence decay curves from a terbium(III) complex. The lower curves are the observed decay and the upper are the semilogarithmic plot versus time. Each X-axis point is 36.25 μs. (A) Unaveraged single transient. (B) Five averages. Details are given by Ballew, Demas, and Grubb (1990).

Experiment 7–9. You examine S/N enhancement by ensemble averaging and reduction of quantization in a fast kinetic experiment.

7.7 BOXCAR INTEGRATOR

Boxcar integration is another method of averaging transient phenomena. Unlike ensemble averaging, which records and averages many points from each transient, **boxcar integration** collects only a single point or range of points on a single transient. By repeating the waveform many times and taking points at different times, we can obtain a complete representation of the waveform. To average, multiple points are collected and added at each time; the averager then increases the delay time, which moves the sampling point to a later time. By slowly scanning through the entire waveform, a complete reconstruction of the waveform can be obtained.

Figure 7–20A is a schematic representation of a boxcar. The key elements are the noise-free trigger pulse, a precision delay, and an analog switch/gate that allows the input signal to pass to an integrator. The integerator performs the averaging.

For scanning a waveform the delay can be varied linearly at different rates to sweep out the complete waveform (B). Frequently, the gate width is variable. The wider the gate, the more signal that is accumulated in the integrator for each transient, and the better the noise improvement. However, the wider the gate, the more distortion of narrow width or other rapidly changing features.

Besides averaging fast waveforms, another use of boxcars is as a gated detector to eliminate noise outside the range of interest (C). For example, a laser spectroscopist might only have information from his sample during the 10 ns laser pulse, which occurs 10 times per second. If a photomultiplier tube views the sample, the tube's dark current is being detected even when the laser is off; the tube is detecting signals only 10^{-7} fraction of the time (10 ns*10 pps/1 s) and monitoring dark noise the rest of the time. By gating the detection electronics on only during the 10 ns laser pulses, the background from the tube is decreased by seven orders of magnitude and no signal is lost. This function is easily performed by delaying the gate window to coincide with the laser pulse and the width to match that of the pulse.

Single photon detection is easily carried out with such an arrangement. An uncooled phototube may have a dark current of 10^4 counts per second. With gating, this is reduced to 0.001/s for the system described above. Thus, average photon count rates

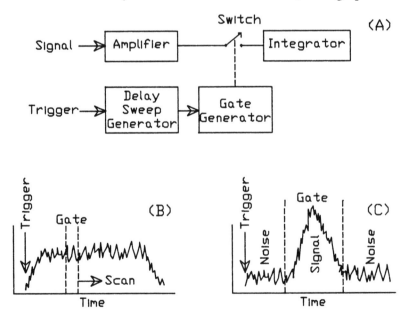

Figure 7–20. (A) Schematic representation of a boxcar integrator. (B) Scanning mode of operation for recording fast transients. (C) Fixed delay mode for eliminating noise outside the signal period.

well below 1/s can easily be detected above background, although a reasonable number of counts must be detected to give an acceptable S/N.

The primary disadvantage of the boxcar is the slow acquisition of information relative to an ensemble averager. If 100 averages are taken for a 512 point transient, then an ensemble averager requires only 100 transients while a boxcar requires 51,200 (100x512). Traditionally, boxcars could be made much faster than ensemble averagers, and found their primary use in high speed averaging. With the advent of increasingly rapid ADCs, ensemble averaging is progressively replacing boxcar integration for all but the most rapid transients or for gated detectors for suppressing noise.

Boxcar integration is likely to maintain its position for the forseeable future with subnanosecond averaging using a sampling oscilloscope. Sampling oscilloscopes can be made with risetimes as short as 10 ps. Figure 7–21 shows a block diagram of a sampling oscilloscope.

Sampling Methods. Before ultrahigh-speed oscilloscopes were available, sampling techniques were widely used for viewing fast repetitive transients. Rather than trying to

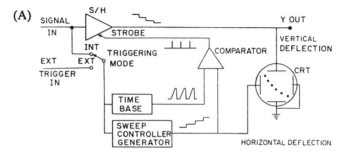

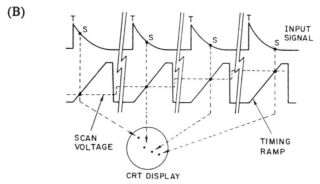

Figure 7–21. Schematic representation of a sampling oscilloscope (A) and relevant waveforms (B). (A) The time base is triggered on each occurrence of a waveform. The sweep controller output is increased by a fixed amount after each sweep. A CRT display is used as an X-Y point plotter. S/H is triggered once per waveform. (B) T indicates the trigger point at which the linear time base sweep is actuated. The S/H is strobed at the sampling points that occur when the scan voltage (– – – –) and linear timing ramp (——) are equal. Demas (1983). Adapted with permission of Academic Press.

view the entire transient on each occurrence, one acquires and views only a single point from the transient each time it occurs. By systematically varying the sampling time, one can build up a complete transient representation.

The standard sampling device for many years has been the sampling oscilloscope (Figure 7–21). The critical elements are a triggered fast linear time base similar to that of a conventional oscilloscope, a slow-sweep generator, an ultra-fast analog comparator, and an ultra-fast sample and hold. First, the slow-sweep generator is set at its lowest value. On triggering, the fast-sweep generator starts a linear rise. At the instant this fast signal crosses the value of the slow one, the comparator senses this and strobes the S/H to capture a data point. Until a new triggering, the output of the S/H equals the amplitude of the last acquired input signal. Each sampled point is plotted on the CRT, which functions as an X-Y plotter. The amplitude of the slow sweep is the X input. Since the delay between triggering and the crossing of the two sweeps is directly proportional to the amplitude of the slow sweep, the X coordinate of the display is proportional to the time of point sampling. After acquiring a point, the slow-sweep amplitude is incremented, which causes a longer delay between triggering and sampling. Thus, the complete transient is reconstructed by sequentially building it up by sampling at progressively longer times. In a sampling oscilloscope, point density (i.e., the interval between samples) can be set, and after the acquisition of one transient the entire process is started from the beginning.

Slow sampling oscilloscopes have rise times of 0.3–1.0 ns, and fast ones have 10–100 ps rise times. They are the devices of choice for repetitive subnanosecond signals. Since each (x,y) point is held on the screen for an extended period, the viewing problems of conventional scopes with fast low-repetition-rate signals is avoided. Finally, sampling lends itself to S/N enhancement in a boxcar-like mode.

In a conventional sampling scope there is a rapid sweep across the entire waveform; in the boxcar integrator the slow sweep is ramped up much more slowly so that many points are collected at each time delay. Then, merely by low pass filtering the output of the S/H, a signal-averaged waveform is obtained. The sweep is usually done slowly enough to display on a mechanical recorder. The sampling oscilloscope forms the basis of many ultrahigh-speed boxcar integrators; one need only disconnect the internal sweep generator and replace it with an external one, as well as connect the S/H output signal to a filter and a computer ADC. Computer driven DACs are used to generate the ramps. Details of such circuits are given in our papers (Taylor, et al. and Pearson, et al.) among others.

Figure 7–22 was obtained using an old 8-bit microcomputer and an ADC with an SO. The entire data acquisition, averaging, and display program was written in assembly language and contained in 512 bytes of PROM. Figure 7–22 shows averaged transients. Although only a slow 1 μs waveform is displayed, the circuit had an SO limited risetime of 0.35 ns.

The best commercial boxcar integrators have both conventional gated analog integrators and sampling capabilities, generally by changing plug-ins. They also provide direct computer interfacing via RS-232 or IEEE-488.

There are several nice variations on averaging that can be employed with an SO based averager. A common problem of boxcars is their sensitivity to changes in the scaled intensity. For example, in a laser excited signal, suppose the intensity decreased

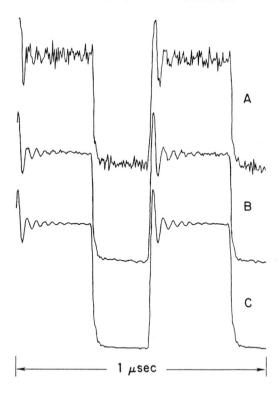

Figure 7–22. Signal averaged transient from a microcomputer interfaced sampling oscilloscope boxcar averager. Taylor, et al. (1980). Adapted with permission from the American Institute of Physics.

during the experiments. The last points then appear too weak in the averaged signal. However, this distortion can be minimized by taking the data in a different sequence. A complete waveform is recorded by taking a single point at each time. The process of scanning through the entire waveform and adding it to the accumulated waveform is repeated. Each point is averaged over the entire period of the transient collection so that all points feel the reduction or fluctuation in the waveform equally.

Many modern intermediate-speed digital storage oscilloscopes combine transient recording, ensemble averaging, and sampling into a single package. The transition from transient recorder to sampling mode is done in a very interesting way. For example, suppose the memory is 1000 words long and the maximum digitization rate is 10 MHz (actually longer memory and faster ADCs are common). For a 10 division-wide trace, 10 point/μs corresponds to 100 μs full sweep or 10 μs/division for the maximum rate without sampling. Now suppose the sweep speed is increased to 1 μs/division or 10 μs full scale. Now each point should be taken at a rate of 100 MHz or ten times faster than the ADC. On the first occurrence of the waveform, data are recorded at 10 MHz, filling only 10% of the available memory location. On the next transient, 10% more of the points are filled, and so on until all time points have been digitized. Averaging proceeds as before. Thus, we have the equivalent of a sampling scope that digitizes many points per transient. Scopes of this style have 50–100 MHz bandwidth. For truly fast phenomena, a real sampling scope or boxcar integrator with a sampling head is still required.

7.8 DIGITAL FILTERS

The RC filter is an example of a system that evolves in only one direction in time. This is, of course, a consequence of the nature of analog circuits. A circuit can only yield a result based on what it has already observed; a circuit cannot anticipate what the waveform will look like later. This time evolution feature of the RC filter causes symmetrical waveforms to be distorted asymmetrically. That is, they are dragged out to longer times. This asymmetric distortion is especially objectionable if data fitting with symmetrical functions is to be used later.

It would be nice to be able to filter waveforms in a way that preserved certain features such as symmetry. Fortunately, this is very easy if we first digitize the complete waveform and then do the filtering with a digital algorithm rather than with an electronic circuit. Such filters are called **digital filters**.

Digital filtering allows post- and real-time improvement S/N enhancement. At one time the computational requirements of digital filtering were too great to use on anything but previously acquired data. The development of very high speed digital signal processors (DSPs) now allows complex digital filtering in the tens of kilohertz range, and megahertz processing should be possible in the future.

It is a simple matter to implement virtually any digital filter on a DSP. This includes any analog filter scheme as well as virtually any filter function that can be described, even physically impossible ones.

There is a wide variety of possible filter functions. Some, such as the RC filter, are continuous. Others are intrinsically discrete. Discrete filters are most common in digital filters because the phenomena to be filtered are inherently discrete. The subject of digital filtering is extremely complex, and the texts are written in a condensed form that draws heavily on mathematics not used by many scientists. We limit ourselves to the common Savitzky-Golay filter.

The selection of filter function is largely based on several criteria. The filter should eliminate undesirable noise with minimal effect on the desired signal. It should be computationally fast. The RC filter is a popular filter in the analog domain because of its ease of implementation and reasonable noise rejection properties. In the digital domain, however, it is computationally slow and superior digital filters are generally used.

One of the beauties of post filtering of a stored digitized signal is that you can try a number of filter schemes until you find the one that is best for the current system. If you make a mistake and filter too aggressively in the analog domain, the distortions irrevocably degrade the information. If you are too aggressive on a post real-time filter, go back to the original data set and start over.

The most primitive and simplest digital filter is a simple boxcar or sliding window filter. Starting at the beginning of the waveform, an odd number (the window) of consecutive data points are averaged and the middle point is replaced with the average. The window is moved over by one point, a new average computed, and the central point is replaced again. To understand how this works, we perform a three-point window average on five points in Table 7–1. The three values to be averaged are asterisked.

Point #	Initial Value	After First Average	After Second Average	After Third Average
1	3*	3.00	3.00	3.00
2	6*	5.67*	5.67	5.67
3	8*	8.00*	6.22*	6.22
4	5	5.00*	5.00*	5.74
5	6	6.00	6.00*	6.00

Table 7–1. Digital Boxcar Averaging a Simple Signal

There are several important aspects of this filter. The end points do not get filtered at all. Further, this is not a very good filter since it weights all three points equally, even though common sense tells us that the central point should be given the highest weight. It is particularly damaging to signal fidelity when the filter passes through peaks that are narrow compared to the window; the peaks are severely broadened. Nevertheless, when computing power was scarce it represented a viable S/N enhancement technique that could be applied after the data was collected. For longer data sets, repetitive application of the same filter was used to further enhance the S/N. Alternatively, a wider window could be used to average more points.

A little thought reveals that we could use unequal coefficients; in particular, we could weight the center point the most with decreasing emphasis on points well removed from the center. Clearly, we could write down an infinite number of different sets of filter coefficients. Equally obvious, however, is that some logic should go into the selection of the filter function. We turn now to the basis for the popular Savitzky-Golay digital filters.

Basically what Savitzky and Golay did was take a group of an odd number of points, as was done with the window filter. They then fit a least squares polynomial through the selected points. The center point of the collection of points was replaced by the value of the polynomial at the center. The group of points was then moved over one, and the process was repeated. The entire process was repeated until the filter function had swept across the entire curve.

While this process sounds computationally horrendous, it turns out that the center value can be computed very simply from a tabular function. The function for calculating the smooth curve is given by:

$$y_j^* = \sum_{i=-m}^{i=m} C_i \, y_{j+i} / N \qquad (7\text{–}18)$$

where the y's are the original data points, the y^*'s are the smoothed points, and N is a normalization factor that preserves the same area under the smoothed curve. The index j runs over the range of the original data. The most common polynomial is the cubic or quadratic, which both give the same results. The number of points that are fit (2m+1) is varied to control the amount of signal averaging. Table 7–2 gives a few sets of Cs and Ns for different numbers of points.

Extensive tables of Cs are available, but in most applications it is more convenient to compute them directly. The appropriate formula is:

	Number of points in average			
m	11	9	7	5
−5	−36			
−4	9	−21		
−3	44	14	−2	
−2	69	39	3	−3
−1	84	54	6	12
0	89	59	7	17
1	84	54	6	12
2	69	39	3	−3
3	44	14	−2	
4	9	−21		
5	−36			
N=	429	231	21	35

Table 7–2. Savitzky-Golay Filter Coefficients

$$\frac{C_i}{N} = \frac{3\,(3\,m^2 + 3\,m - 1 - 5\,i^2)}{(2\,m - 1)\,(2\,m + 1)\,(2\,m + 3)} \tag{7-19}$$

The S/N is approximately proportional to the square root of the number of points used in the smooth. While repeated smoothing is possible, the best rule is probably to calculate the requisite number of points for the desired S/N enhancement and smooth only once.

However, one must also be careful not to smooth too aggressively as excessive signal distortion will result. The rule of thumb is that the ratio of the number of points in the smooth to the full width at half maximum of the curve to be smoothed should be about 1.83. A ratio appreciably larger than this will result in significant distortion.

Digital Signal Processors (DSPs). There are commercial hardware-software packages that allow you to specify the filter (low pass, high pass, bandpass) and the narrowness of the cutoff. The program then generates the necessary filter coefficients, calculates the precise filter characteristics that will be achieved, and generates the assembly language code for driving the DSP. This code can then be directly loaded into the DSP board in the same computer that calculated the filter and the filter can then be used experimentally.

To Smooth or Not to Smooth? We turn now to the real question. What is gained by smoothing? The answer is usually only a cosmetic improvement in the data. If visual evaluation of peak intensities, positions, or areas is used, this enhancement is beneficial. It is very easy to filter a signal, note the improved S/N, and forget that filtering may be removing both unwanted noise and desired signal information. Many commercial instruments are very offensive in this regard. They provide filtering algorithms, sometimes without even telling you they are used, but give little or no insight into the damage to data integrity.

If least squares data fitting to a model is used, most digital smoothing is not only not advantageous, it degrades the data quality and results in systematic errors in calculated parameters. Thus, when using mathematical fitting, it is generally better to fit the raw noisy data directly rather than introduce distortion by filtering and then fitting the "improved" distorted data.

If S/N enhancement is to truly improve the data, it must be done during the acquisition process by techniques that average multiple transients. These would include ensemble and boxcar averaging or lock-in detection.

The only time when filters (analog or digital) are truly beneficial is when the noise and signal spectra are significantly different in a known way; you can then design a filter that selectively attenuates the noise while emphasizing the signal frequencies. Examples include 60 Hz pickup or high frequency computer noise that is well outside the signal bandwidth; selective filters can then effectively suppress the noise. Under these conditions, filters can truly improve data quality.

Thus, our final recommendations: Understand your signal and the noise. Use selective analog or digital filtering to remove specific noise components. Fit the data mathematically with minimal additional filtering. Never blindly apply a filter algorithm, especially a black box one supplied by a manufacturer, without carefully examining its impact on your signal.

Experiment 7–10. You use the program SMOOTH to demonstrate the S/N enhancement and signal distortion with Savitzky-Golay filters of different lengths.

7.9   MONTE CARLO SIMULATIONS

A common and very powerful use of random number generators is in numerical simulation of phenomena too complicated to carry out in closed form. What one does is simulate an experiment using statistically and/or physically reasonable variations of the data going into a calculation. The variations are chosen with a suitable random number generator. The calculations are repeated a number of times until good statistics for the "experimental" results are obtained.

The computer's random number generator is distributed uniformly over the range zero to one and is actually a pseudo-random number generator. The number is derived from a mathematical algorithm and is reproducibly random if initialized the same each time. Since real data do not usually have a uniform distribution, we show how to generate the more useful Gaussian distribution and to simulate Poisson noise. We give applications.

Generation of Normally Distributed Noise. A simple, reliable method for transforming uniformly distributed zero-to-one random numbers, Us, to normal ones is from the Box, Muller, Marsaglia algorithm: Generate two Us, U_1 and U_2, calculate V_1 and V_2:

$$V_1 = 2U_1 - 1 \tag{7–20a}$$

$$V_2 = 2U_2 - 1 \tag{7–20b}$$

V_1 and V_2 are uniformly distributed over the interval −1 to +1. Now calculate:

$$S = V_1^2 + V_2^2 \tag{7-21}$$

If $S>1$, good random numbers will not be generated, and the calculation must be restarted with a new pair of Us. If $S \leq 1$, then compute G_1 and G_2 from:

$$M = (-2 \ln (S)/S)^{1/2} \tag{7-22a}$$

$$G_1 = V_1 M \tag{7-22b}$$

$$G_2 = V_2 M \tag{7-22c}$$

G_1 and G_2 are normally distributed with a mean of zero and standard deviation of one. Two normal deviates are computed per calculation. The following Unit Gaussian allows generation of a normally distributed deviate with a mean of zero and standard deviation of one using the function call Gauss that returns a real:

```
Unit Gaussian;
{Provides function Gauss; returns normally distributed
random number with mean=0 and standard deviation=1
using Box, Muller, Marsaglia algorithm--Demas (1983)
Use:  G:= Gauss;              }

INTERFACE
FUNCTION Gauss : Real;

IMPLEMENTATION
CONST
  FirstGaus : Boolean = True;   {need to start calc. again?}
  Gaus2 : Real = 1e38;          {save deviate from last call}

  FUNCTION Gauss : Real;
  VAR
    M, V, V1, V2 : Real;
  BEGIN
    IF FirstGaus THEN           {if first generate two deviates}
      BEGIN
        REPEAT
          V1 := 2.0*Random-1.0;
          V2 := 2.0*Random-1.0;
          V := Sqr(V1)+Sqr(V2);
        UNTIL V < 1;
        M := Sqrt(-2.0*ln(V)/V);
        Gauss := V1*M;
        Gaus2 := V2*M;
      END
    ELSE
      Gauss := Gaus2;           {otherwise use 2nd from last calc}

    FirstGaus := NOT(FirstGaus);  {reset state}
  END;
END.
```

Note the use of a typed constant to keep the second deviate until the next call to the function and the flag FirstGaus to indicate whether the second deviate has been used and a new cycle must be initiated.

Usually, one needs normally distributed data with a mean of μ and a standard deviation of σ. This is done by scaling and shifting the Gs:

$$W = \mu + \sigma G \tag{7-23}$$

where Ws will be normally distributed with a mean of μ and standard deviation of σ.

We use Gaussian in the programs QUANT and SMOOTH for showing quantization noise and Savitzky-Golay filtering, respectively. It is much easier and cheaper to implement these experiments in software rather than hardware.

Poisson noise is associated with many counting experiments such as nuclear statistics and single photon counting. The standard deviation is given by the square root of the number of counts. For counts greater than about 20, the distribution is very nearly normal and the Gaussian generator can be be used to add Poisson noise by:

$$D_P = D + D^{1/2} G \tag{7-24}$$

where D is a noise-free datum point, G is a normally distributed random number given above, and D_p is a point that will conform to Poisson statistics. For generating true Poisson statistics, see Press, et al. and Demas (1983).

We first consider a trivial application of Monte Carlo methods, error propagation. Suppose that you were measuring N x,y pairs (x_i, y_i) and evaluating the sum. For given statistical uncertainties on x and y of σ_x and σ_y respectively, what is the mean and standard deviation, σ_{x+y}, for the sum x+y? The average, $\overline{x+y}$, and the standard deviation are given in closed form by:

$$\overline{x+y} = \sum_{i=1}^{N} \frac{x_i + y_i}{N} \tag{7-25a}$$

$$\sigma_{x+y} = \left[\sigma_x{}^2 + \sigma_y{}^2 \right]^{1/2} \tag{7-25b}$$

However, we could also simulate a large number of experiments numerically. A suitable program is:

```
PROGRAM DistSum;
{generates distribution function for sum of normally
distributed data.  Uses unit wide windows
Use:  DistSum > sumxy.dat where sumxy.dat is grapher file}

USES Gaussian;
CONST
  CenterX = 35;                {mean of x}
  CenterY = 55;                {mean of y}
  SigmaX = 7.5;                {standard deviation of x}
  SigmaY = 15;                 {standard deviation of y}
  N = 100000;                  {number Monte Carlo simulations}
  MaxArray = 150;
```

```
TYPE
  Dist = ARRAY[0..MaxArray] OF LongInt;

VAR
  x, y, sumxy : Real;
  j : LongInt;
  distx, disty, distsumxy : Dist;

BEGIN
  {randomize; }
  {required to make each set of simulations different}
  FOR j := 0 TO MaxArray DO
    BEGIN
      distx[j] := 0;
      disty[j] := 0;
      distsumxy[j] := 0;
    END;
  FOR j := 0 TO N DO
    BEGIN
      x := CenterX+SigmaX*Gauss;
      y := CenterY+SigmaY*Gauss;
      sumxy := x+y;
      x := x-0.5;                  {set unit wide windows and center}
      y := y-0.5;
      sumxy := sumxy-0.5;
      IF (x >= 0) AND (x <= MaxArray) THEN
        Inc(distx[Round(x)]);
      IF (y >= 0) AND (y <= MaxArray) THEN
        Inc(disty[Round(y)]);
      IF (sumxy >= 0) AND (sumxy <= MaxArray) THEN
        Inc(distsumxy[Round(sumxy)]);
    END;
  FOR j := 0 TO MaxArray DO
    WriteLn(j:5, distx[j]:6, disty[j]:6, distsumxy[j]:6);
END.
```

The output is suitable for piping into a GRAPHER file. Changing the constants at the beginning permits altering the number of simulations as well as the mean and the standard deviations of each component.

Suppose that x=35 and σ_x=7.5 and y=55 and σ_y=7.5. Figure 7–23A shows a distribution for 100,000 random x's and y's and the distribution for the pairwise calculated sums. As expected, the width of the sum distribution is larger than that for either x or y. These results show clearly the effect of noise in x and y and its propagation into the final result. Also, the fact that Gaussian noise on x and y propagate to a Gaussian distribution in x+y is clearly shown.

Repeating the calculation with σ_y=15 gives the results of Figure 7–23B. The calculated mean and standard deviation for x, y and x+y are 34.994±7.494, 55.014±15.033, and 90.007±16.861, respectively. These agree well with the expected values; the standard deviation for x+y calculated from Equation 7–25b is 16.77. It is clear that the

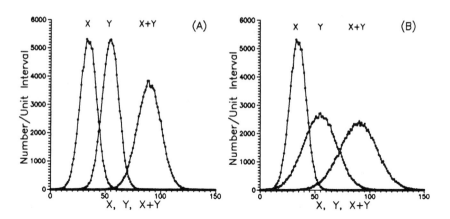

Figure 7–23.   Monte Carlo calculations on error propagation.   Both x and y are normally distributed with x̄=35 and ȳ=55.   The histogram distribution of x, y, and x+y are shown in windows of width 1.   (A) $\sigma_x = \sigma_y = 7.5$. **(B)** $\sigma_x = 7.5$ **and** $\sigma_y = 15$.

dominant, but not only, contribution to the final noise level comes from y noise. This arises from the properties of Equation 7–25b where an error more than twice the size of another will control the overall error.

Since the above example has a simple closed form solution, consider the more interesting problem of error propagation in the following equation:

$$F = (t+u^{1/2})^2 \cos(t/u)\exp(t/10) \qquad (7\text{–}26)$$

What is the uncertainty in F, if t=2 and with a standard deviaton of 0.2 and u=5 with a standard deviation of 1.2? While standard error propagation methods could be used, the algebra is messy and a Monte Carlo calculation is simpler for a few points. In the next chapter we use the Monte Carlo approach to demonstrate different least squares methods.

7.10   REFERENCES

Horowitz and Hill as well as Malmstadt, et al. have excellent discussions of S/N enhancement. Ott gives a very readable account of noise and its suppression. Press, et al. is the standard reference book on numerical and filtering methods; programs of all methods in Turbo Pascal 5 are provided. They also lucidly discuss digital filtering. The Savitzky-Golay paper is a classic; also see the papers by Madden and by Enke and Nieman.

Problems

7–1 [7.2]. Calculate and plot the phase and attenuation factor of the dual RC filter of Figure A–2. What is the 0.707 voltage transmission frequency? Remember that the filters are isolated from each other so the attenuation is the product of the two attenuations and the phase shift is the sum of the two.

7–2 [7.4]. Prove Equation 7–5.

7–3 [7.4]. Prove Equation 7–6.

7–4 [7.4]. For a 20 V peak-to-peak sine wave (i.e., $V_p=10V$), what is the output of the filter for $\phi_{li}=0°$? For $\phi_{li}=90°$? If ϕ_{li} changes by $1°$ what is the change in voltage for each case? This result clearly shows the advantage of setting a signal at the null point and then changing the phase shifter by $90°$ rather than trying to peak it up for the in phase signal.

7–5. [7.9]. Write a filter that adds Poisson noise to the y data in a data file of x,y pairs. Usage of filter should be:

```
Poisson < input.data > output.data
```

7–6. [7.9]. Write a filter, CONNOISE, that adds a constant level of noise to y data in a file of x,y pairs. The usage should be:

```
CONNOISE noise <input.dat>output.dat
```

where noise is the standard deviation of the noise to be added.

7–7. [7.9]. Write a filter, CONPERNO, that adds noise that is a percentage of the y size in an x,y data file. The usage is:

```
CONPERNO percentnoise < infile.dat > outfile.dat
```

where percentnoise is the standard deviation as a percentage of each y.

7–8 [7.9]. Using Monte Carlo methods, carry out an error propagation experiment on xy where x=2 and y=1 with $\sigma_x=\sigma_y=0.1$. Provide plots of the distribution of x, of y, and of xy. What is the "measured" mean and σ for each? From error propagation, what is the expected σ for the product? Use 10,000 simulations.

7–9 [7.9]. (A) Using Monte Carlo methods, carry out an error propagation experiment on x^2 where $x=1$ with $\sigma_x=0.1$. Provide plots of the distribution of x^2. What is the "measured" mean and σ for each? From error propagation, what is the expected σ for the product? Use 10,000 simulations.

(B) Repeat the calculations for x^3.

7–10 [7.9]. For Equation 7–26, what is the standard deviation for F with the values given in the text? Use 10,000 simulations.

8

Least Squares Data Reduction

8.1 INTRODUCTION TO LEAST SQUARES

Getting the data is only part of the task. The key element is fitting the data to some model and determining whether or not our model adequately describes the data. Generally, given specific parameters, it is simple to calculate an expected curve, but often we have the much more difficult task of extracting the parameter values from experimental data. A number of the systems can be handled easily by graphical methods with visual fitting; the linear fit to the semilogarithmic plot versus time of an exponential decay is an example. Linear fitting is not the most accurate method for complex defining equations and might not even be possible (e.g., a sum of two exponentials).

The method of least squares is a relatively simple, general curve fitting method where the defining equations for the data set are known and the values of the parameters giving the best fit are desired. In this chapter we first develop the method of linear least squares and discuss some pitfalls. The linearization of functions and the weighting factor problem are discussed. The least squares approach is then extended to the fitting of nonlinear and nonlinearizable equations such as the sum of exponentials. Several different nonlinear fitting methods and the estimation of statistical error in the final parameter estimates will be covered.

We assume that we are fitting data pairs (x_i, y_i) with the function $y = F(x)$. The least squares method seeks the parameter values in $F(x)$ that minimize the chi-square, χ^2:

$$\chi^2 = \sum_{i=1}^{N} w_i R_i^2 \qquad (8\text{--}1a)$$

$$R_i = y_i - F(x_i) \qquad (8\text{--}1b)$$

$$w_i = 1 / \sigma_i^2 \qquad (8\text{--}1c)$$

where w_i is the weighting factor, σ_i is the standard deviation of the observed y_i, and $F(x_i)$ is the modeling function evaluated at x_i. The residuals, R_is, are the differences between the observed data and the modeling function. The summation is over the N data points fit. The weighting factor emphasizes or weights more heavily the more accurately known points. The proper weighting factors are given by Equation 8–1c (Bevington). Equation 8–1 assumes that all errors are concentrated in the y_is, which is frequently valid, and in fact is the only easily tractable case.

Explicit information on the σs is frequently unavailable, and it is common to assume that all w_is are equal. To simplify things, the w_is are all set equal to unity. This use of $w_i=1$, rather than some other constant, has no effect on the parameter values that minimize χ^2; a different constant merely scales the sum, but does not affect the best fit. We derive expressions using weighting factors; the unweighted case is obtained with all w_is = 1.

8.2 LINEAR LEAST SQUARES FITTING

We turn now to a specific case, the common problem of fitting a straight line:

$$F(x) = y = a_1 + a_2 x \qquad (8\text{--}2)$$

The least squares method selects a_1 and a_2, which minimize χ^2:

$$\chi^2 = \sum w_i R_i^2 = \sum w_i [y_i - (a_1 + a_2 x_i)]^2 \qquad (8\text{--}3)$$

For simplicity, we omit the indexes on the summations that run from 1 to N. Consider specifically the Stern-Volmer lifetime quenching data set of Figure A–7, where the y_is are defined as $(\tau_0/\tau) - 1$ and the x_is are the quencher concentrations. Figure 8–1 shows a contour map of the χ^2 surface plotted versus a_1 and a_2; all $w_i = 1$. Also shown is a surface map of the error surface. The a_1 and a_2 giving a minimum χ^2 could be estimated graphically, but these calculations are exceedingly tedious. From Figure 8–1, we estimate $a_2 = 0.2 \ \mu M^{-1}$ and $a_1 = -0.02$. Clearly, drawing error surfaces to estimate least squares parameters is an unacceptable option.

A much less complex process arises if one considers the necessary conditions for a minimum in the χ^2 surface; the partial derivatives of χ^2 with respect to both a_1 and a_2 must be simultaneously zero:

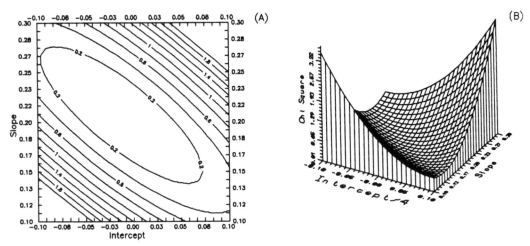

Figure 8–1. Contour **(A)** and surface **(B)** map of the errors for the linear least squares fit of the data of Figure A–7. The error contours are of $(\chi^2)^{1/2}$ rather than χ^2 to improve viewing.

$$\left[\frac{\partial \chi^2}{\partial a_1}\right]_{a_2} = 0 \qquad (8\text{–}4a)$$

$$\left[\frac{\partial \chi^2}{\partial a_2}\right]_{a_1} = 0 \qquad (8\text{–}4b)$$

Actually Equation 8–4 guarantees only that one is at a minimum, a maximum, or a saddle point in the surface; a linear fit yields only a minimum. Complex nonlinear fitting can give multiple minima, and the fitting method must discern between the desired global rather than local minimum.

Evaluating the necessary partial derivatives in Equation 8–4 and rearranging yields the two equations:

$$(\Sigma\, w_i)\, a_1 + (\Sigma\, w_i x_i)\, a_2 = \Sigma\, w_i\, y_i \qquad (8\text{–}5a)$$

$$(\Sigma\, w_i\, x_i)\, a_1 + (\Sigma\, w_i\, x_i^2)\, a_2 = \Sigma\, w_i\, x_i\, y_i \qquad (8\text{–}5b)$$

Equation 8–5 is two linear equations in the two unknowns a_1 and a_2. These equations are the system's "normal" equations and are readily solved for the desired a's by elimination, determinants, or matrix methods to yield:

$$a_1 = (\Sigma\, w_i\, x_i^2 \Sigma\, w_i\, y_i - \Sigma\, w_i\, x_i\, \Sigma\, w_i\, x_i\, y_i)\, /\, \Delta \qquad (8\text{–}6a)$$

$$a_2 = (\Sigma\, w_i\, \Sigma\, w_i\, x_i\, y_i - \Sigma\, w_i\, x_i\, \Sigma\, w_i\, y_i)\, /\, \Delta \qquad (8\text{–}6b)$$

$$\Delta = \Sigma\, w_i\, \Sigma\, w_i\, x_i^2 - (\Sigma\, w_i\, x_i)^2 \qquad (8\text{–}6c)$$

$$\sum 1 = N \text{ for } w_i = 1 \tag{8-6d}$$

This a_1 and a_2 give a minimum in χ^2. A common error is to forget that if all w_is are 1 then $\sum w_i = N$ (Equation 8-6d). Using Equation 8-6 for the data of Figure 8-1 with all w_is = 1 yields $a_1 = 0.20707 \ \mu M^{-1}$ and $a_2 = 0.04806$, which agree well with the graphical estimates.

We have made the important assumption that the weighting factors were constant, which is equivalent to assuming that the errors in the y_i are constant (i.e., σ_i = constant). This last assumption can lead to significant errors.

8.2.1 Linearized Complex Functions

We routinely encounter and use linearized functions. For example, we linearized the Stern-Volmer equation in Experiment 7-9 by using $y = (\tau_0/\tau) - 1$ and $x = [Q]$. All exponential fits so far have been done by the linearized semilogarithmic plot of intensity versus time. Many other nonlinear functions are also readily linearizable by a similar substitution of variables. We now show that common use of linearization schemes is a potential minefield.

8.2.2 Least Squares with Weighting

The common and apparently successful use of unweighted least squares fitting to many functions can produce a false sense of security. To show where you can get into trouble, consider the decay data of Figure 8-2 given by $D(t) = D_0 \exp(-t/\tau)$ where $D_0 = 10$ V and $\tau = 10$ with added constant Gaussian noise. The noise has a constant 0.05 V

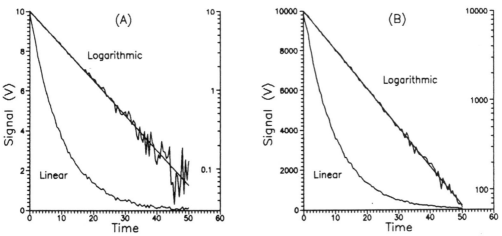

Figure 8–2. Linear and logarithmic plots of noisy exponential decays. (A) D(t)=10 exp(–t/10) with a time-independent constant noise of 0.05. (B) D(t)=10000 exp(–t/10) with Poisson noise. The straight lines are the unweighted linear least squares fit to the ln[D(t)]-versus-t plots.

standard deviation or only 0.5% of the peak. This decay might result from a high-quality signal and an amplifier with amplitude-independent noise and appears reasonable for data reduction. An unweighted linear least squares fit of the $\ln[D(t_i)]$-versus-t_i data over the 0–50 time range yields $D_0 = 10.173$ and $\tau = 9.799$. In view of the low noise level and the 101 points used in the fit, this agreement with the noise-free $D_0 = 10$ V and $\tau = 10.00$ is rather poor. The reason for this poor fit is revealed in the semilogarithmic data plot (Figure 8–2A); although quite noise-free at short times, $\ln[D(t)]$ is quite noisy at longer times and, especially for $t > \approx 35$, exceeds what one might have expected. The poor fit arises because the poor data at long times are weighted the same as the superior early data.

The solution is to give less weight to the less reliable data in the minimization of Equation 8–6. Proper determination of the w_i is not as obvious as it might seem.

For example, even though the σ_is on the D(t)s are constant, the w_is in Equation 8–6 are not constant; see the large increase in noise on the trailing portion of Figure 8–2A. This difference arises because the noise levels on $\ln[D(t)]$ and D(t) differ. To quantitate the differences between σ_y and σ_D, we ask what effect a small change or uncertainty in D(t) has on y. For $y = \ln[D(t)]$:

$$dy = d\ln[D(t)] = [1/D(t)]\,dD(t) \tag{8–7}$$

where dy and dD(t) are differential changes in y and D(t), respectively. Small fractional changes in D(t) (i.e., dD(t)/D(t)) produce D(t)-dependent changes in y (i.e., dy). For example, using incremental changes, if $D(t) = 10$ and $dD(t) = 10^{-1}$, then dy is 0.01. However, if $D(t) = 1.0$, then dy is 0.1 or ten times larger. Figure 8–2A clearly shows that the log data are good at short times and almost worthless for fitting near the end of the decay. Thus, in an unweighted fit the low S/N low-intensity points disproportionately affect the fit.

If we approximate the standard deviation in D(t) and in y by dD(t) and dy, we obtain:

$$\sigma_y = [1/D(t)]\,\sigma_D \tag{8–8}$$

The correct w_is for the semilogarithmic plot of Figure 8–2A are then:

$$w_i = 1/\sigma_i^2 = D(t_i)^2 / (0.05)^2 \tag{8–9}$$

For the example, the slope and intercept yield $D_0 = 9.992$ and $\tau = 10.025$, which agree much more closely with the correct answers. Thus, merely by using proper weighting factors, we have improved our accuracy by about an order of magnitude. If these calculations were repeated many times, the weighted fits would typically be more accurate and more precise than the unweighted fits. We will demonstrate shortly how to quantitate the quality of the fit.

Clearly, indiscriminate unweighted least squares fitting of transformed linearized functions must be done with great caution. At the very least, representative linearized plots and fits should be inspected. A properly weighted fit is always the best approach.

In the general case where the linearized function is $y = F(x)$, we have:

$$\sigma_y = [dF(x)/dx]\,\sigma_x \tag{8–10}$$

We consider another example of improper weighting. Assuming a linear fit and the Poisson statistics of nuclear or photon counting experiments, the standard deviation, σ_i, and weights for each point in the original data domain are:

$$\sigma_i = D(t_i)^{1/2} \tag{8-11}$$

$$w_i = 1 / D(t_i) \tag{8-12}$$

where $D(t_i)$ are the number of counts in each data channel.

Figure 8-2B shows a decay identical to Figure 8-2A, except that the noise is Poisson and D_0, before the addition of noise, was 10,000; the noise level at the peak is 1% ($10000^{1/2}/10^4$). While the effects are not as severe as for the constant noise case, data quality in the semilogarithmic plots does degrade seriously at long times and proper weighting will improve the results over an unweighted fit. For the semilogarithmic fit to Poisson data, use the following weighting factors in the linearized expression:

$$w_i = D(t_i) \tag{8-13}$$

The unweighted fit gave D_0=9979 and τ=9.995 ns, while the weighted fit gave 9986 and 9.998. Thus, with Poisson noise, weighting also improves results but not so pronouncedly as for the constant noise case above. This is a consequence of the slower variation of noise with amplitude in the Poisson case, a correspondingly slower change in the weighting factors, and, thus, less sensitivity to proper weighting.

To test the effects of weighting and not weighting, we carried out Monte Carlo simulations on 100 synthetic exponential decay curves with added Poisson noise (Demas, 1983). Weighted and unweighted least squares fits were made using the ln[D(t)]-versus-t plots. The average derived D_0 and τ, as well as the standard deviation for each set of decay curves, were calculated.

We summarize the results. The interested reader should consult the original reference. The weighted fits are consistently more accurate and precise than the unweighted ones. In a single experiment the chances of obtaining a nearly correct value can increase dramatically; we found up to a three times smaller standard deviation for weighted versus unweighted fits. The improvement was greatest where the data span a wide dynamic range; the w_is then varied more and unweighted fits gave less satisfactory results.

In order to quantitate noise levels for weighted linear squares fit to the semilogarithmic plots, we carried out a detailed calculation of the errors in the lifetime and preexponentials as a function of the fitting region and the total number of counts in the entire decay. Figure 8-3 shows the errors in D_0 and τ as a function of $D_0\tau$, the total number of counts that would be detected if the entire decay were observed, and the fitting period. We express the data in the form of the number of lifetimes that the data were fit over $\Delta t/\tau$ where Δt is the fitting period; the fit begins at t=0. For the calculations, we assumed 512 equally spaced points. Further, since the distribution for small counts (<20) deviates from Gaussian, we stop the fit when the data fell below 20 counts.

The results show that excellent precisions in both D_0 and τ can be obtained even for relatively low total count levels (i.e., 1% with only 10^4 detected photons). Precision degrades very rapidly as $\Delta t/\tau$ falls below 1; this is no surprise since for such short monitoring periods the data have not had a chance to decay appreciably.

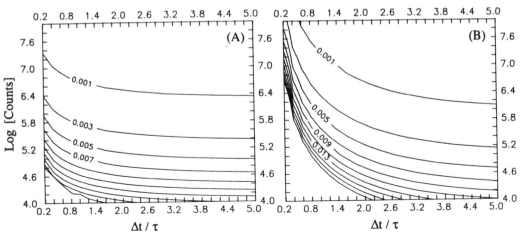

Figure 8–3. Error surfaces of the preexponential factors (A) and lifetimes (B) of weighted linear least squares fit of an exponential decay as a function of the total number of photons detected ($D_0\tau$) and the number of lifetimes used in the fit ($\Delta t/\tau$). Data courtesy of R. M. Ballew.

Another problem arises if the data to be fit are functions of two or more measured values each with uncertainty. For example, D(t) might be derived from a signal from which it was necessary to strip off a noisy baseline. How should the data be treated? In this case one uses standard formulas (Bevington, 1969) for the propagation of errors in the measured quantities to the σs of the derived quantities. For example, if the y that is fit is derived from $y = y'_i - B_i$, where y' and B are the measured signal and baseline respectively, then σ_y is given by:

$$\sigma_{y_i} = \left[\sigma_{y'_i}^2 + \sigma_{B_i}^2\right]^{1/2} \tag{8–14}$$

8.3 NONLINEAR LEAST SQUARES

Many functions, such as the sums of exponentials and other mixed transcendental functions, cannot be readily converted to a form linear in the parameters. For example, there is no linear form of the sum of two exponentials; if you follow through the least squares analysis for the linear case, you end up with a system of nonlinear equations that has no closed form solution. The problem, in effect, is how to solve these equations for the best-fit parameters. There are many different methods, along with FORTRAN programs for implementing them, given by Bevington (1969) and Daniels (1978). Press, et al. give Pascal programs. We describe briefly several strategies and develop several in detail. All methods are iterative. You make initial guesses of the parameters and use an iterative process which, you hope, improves on the guesses after each iteration.

Before discussing specific methods, we point out that caution is essential in interpreting the significance of parameters obtained by fitting. Many data sets can be fitted equally well by more than one function. Consider, for example, the following three functions:

$$D_0(t) = 1881 \sum_{i=6}^{22} \exp(-(\,(i-14)/3)^2) \exp(-t/i) \tag{8-15a}$$

$$D_1(t) = 7500 \exp(-t/12.7) + 2500 \exp(-t/17.9) \tag{8-15b}$$

$$D_2(t) = 2500 \exp(-t/10.5) + 7500 \exp(-t/15.2) \tag{8-15c}$$

The first is a distribution function of exponential decays with a mean of 14 and a standard deviation of 3. On a linear scale these apparently greatly different functions are indistinguishable within a pen's width over the time interval 0–50. All functions decay from 10^4 to about 10 at t = 100. Figure 8–4 shows the differences of $D_1(t)$ or of $D_2(t)$ relative to $D_0(t)$. Clearly discrepancies are minimal even though one "exponential" decay is actually a sum of 17 decays, and the other two are double exponentials, which have reversed amplitudes on the short- and long-lived components.

For comparison, assume that the data conform to Poisson statistics. The peak noise level of 100 falls to 3 at the end of the decay. The actual differences among all three functions are far smaller than the noise level of photon counting experiments with the indicated count levels. Clearly, the Poisson noise far exceeds the differences among the Ds. These examples demonstrate that some data sets are extremely insensitive to fitting parameter variations. It is possible to have statistically acceptable fits with large errors in the fitting parameters or even completely incorrect models.

The shapes of the error surfaces for nonlinear functions are also much more tortuous to search through than for the linear case. Figure 8–5 is the error surface for a 101-point decay of the form y=10exp(−t/20) (t=0.5i; i=0 to 100). Clearly, the error surface is much

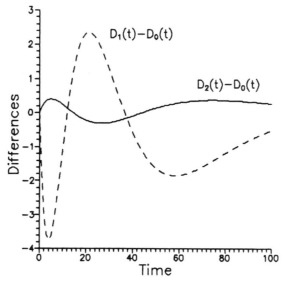

Figure 8–4. Differences between the distribution of decays and two different double exponential decays. Equation 8–15 describes the data.

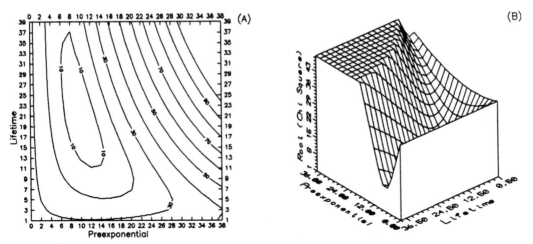

Figure 8–5. Contour map (A) and error surface (B) for the function D(t)=10exp(–t/20) as function preexponential factor and lifetime. Contours are for $(\chi^2)^{1/2}$ rather than χ^2. The error surface is truncated at 47 to improve viewing.

more complicated for a linear case; compare Figure 8–1 and 8–5. Now try to visualize an error surface that twists and turns in two other dimensions such as for a sum of two exponentials. Then add noise to the error surface to introduce irregularities. Now you have an approximation of what a nonlinear search algorithm has to tolerate.

We turn to nonlinear fitting schemes. A simple minimization approach is a grid search (Bevington, 1969). One makes initial guesses for the a_is and then varies each a_i by small amounts while holding the remaining a_is fixed. χ^2 is evaluated after each change. For example, a_1 is first varied until a minimum in χ^2 is found. Since it is unlikely that the search moved directly toward the minimum, this apparent minimum is probably not the true one. See Figure 8–1 where motion along only a_1 or a_2 does not usually directly approach the minimum. The search is then continued by varying a_2 while holding the remaining a_is fixed. The process of searching by varying each parameter in turn is repeated until all the parameters have been varied. This revised set of parameters yields a lower χ^2, but it is still unlikely to be the true minimum. The process is started over with a_1 and is repeated until the minimum is approached as closely as desired.

The grid search method is stable with the χ^2 improving or becoming no worse on each iteration. The derivative information needed by many other methods is not required, and programming it is trivial. The grid search is quite slow. The more efficient simplex search procedure that varies all the parameters simultaneously is described later.

The gradient or method of steepest descent is popular and efficient. The gradient of a function points in the direction of maximum rate of increase. The opposite direction is the path of maximum rate of decrease or the path of steepest descent. The gradient method searches from the current guess along the direction of steepest descent in χ^2 until a minimum is found. This minimum is rarely the true minimum, because the original search direction generally does not move directly toward the true minimum, although the search direction is better than the grid search. At this apparent minimum, a new search direction is evaluated, and the search is resumed in the new direction. The gradient search is stable, reasonably efficient, and easy to program. It is an excellent search method for steep-walled surfaces. However, near a minimum the χ^2 surface flattens and the gradient method becomes inefficient.

Other approaches use analytical Taylor series expansions of χ^2 or of the fitting function. Generally, these expansions are truncated after the first- or second-order terms. A normal least squares minimization is then carried out to determine the changes in each of the parameters that minimize χ^2. If the truncated expansion is a good approximation, the corrected guesses are better than the original ones. Near the minimum, the analytical approach can become very efficient because of the decreasing importance of the neglected higher-order terms. Analytical approaches require derivation information, but in return generally converge faster than brute force search techniques. Analytical approaches can, however, become unstable far from the minimum where the expansion is inaccurate. Indeed, it is common to combine a simplex or gradient search for the early portions of the search and then switch to an analytical solution as the minimum is approached.

In Section 8.3.2 a widely used analytical approach based on series expansion of the function is discussed. Convergence problems are demonstrated. In Section 8.3.3 the powerful and widely used Marquardt method is described. This method automatically changes from a gradient search far from the minimum to an analytical solution near the minimum. The Marquardt method is stable and fast, and is implemented with only minor modifications of the analytical method.

8.3.1 Simplex Method

The simplex nonlinear search method is basically an opportunistic empirical search through parameter space. Unlike the grid search, all parameters are varied simultaneously. The simplex method is stable, easy to understand, and easy to program. It requires no derivative information. For some problems it converges nearly as rapidly as more sophisticated approaches, but for three- or four-parameter problems it is invariably slower. Nevertheless, on a modern micro it makes a superb minimization method.

The basic and frequently modified simplex method is based on the one developed by Nelder and Mead (1965). Our treatment follows that given by Daniels (1978) using his recommended parameter variations.

The problem is to minimize $\chi^2(a_1, a_2 . . . a_n)$, where $a_1, . . .,$ and a_n are the n parameters varied to minimize χ^2. A simplex is a geometric figure. In an n-dimensional space, n+1 different points are needed to define the simplex. A two-dimensional simplex is a triangle, and a three-dimensional simplex is a tetrahedra-like figure. For n>3, the simplex cannot be visualized.

We develop the simplex minimization equations as follows: The points in the n-dimensional space are represented by vectors. To start the simplex procedure, we need a grid of n + 1 guesses which, we hope, are near the correct values. These guesses are $\mathbf{P}_1$, $\mathbf{P}_2, . . ., \mathbf{P}_n, \mathbf{P}_{n+1}$, where each $\mathbf{P}$ represents a set of parameter guesses. If we make initial guesses for the individual parameters a_1 through a_n, then in vector notation $\mathbf{P}_1$, our initial guess for the solution, is:

$$P_1 = P(a_1, a_2, \ldots, a_{n-1}, a_n) \tag{8-16}$$

P_2 to P_{n+1} are different points on the simplex and are a reasonable arrangement around P_1. For all a_is that are nonzero, the remaining n P_is can be generated from P_1 by:

$$P_2 = P(1.1a_1, a_2, \ldots, a_{n-1}, a_n) \tag{8-17a}$$

$$P_3 = P(a_1, 1.1a_2, \ldots, a_{n-1}, a_n) \tag{8-17b}$$

$$P_{n+1} = P(a_1, a_2, \ldots, a_{n-1}, 1.1a_n) \tag{8-17c}$$

One then evaluates the χ^2s at each P_i:

$$\chi^2(P_i), \quad i=1, \ldots, n+1$$

Now determine the P_i yielding the highest χ^2 (denoted by P_H), the next highest χ^2 (denoted by P_{NH}), and the lowest χ^2 (denoted by P_L).

The search through parameter space uses three operations: reflection, expansion, and contraction. Refer to Figure 8–6 during the following discussions of each operation.

Reflections. It is reasonable to assume that the best guess will be far removed from P_H, possibly on the other side of the remaining points. Calculate the centroid C (center of gravity) of all the points excluding P_H:

$$C = \frac{1}{n} \left[\sum_{i=1, i \neq H}^{n+1} P_i \right] = \frac{1}{n} \left[\left(\sum_{i=1}^{n+1} P_i \right) - P_H \right] \tag{8-18}$$

For a triangle, C is midway between P_L and P_{NH} and is the center of gravity of all points excluding P_H. Reflect P_H through C to form the reflected point P_R by:

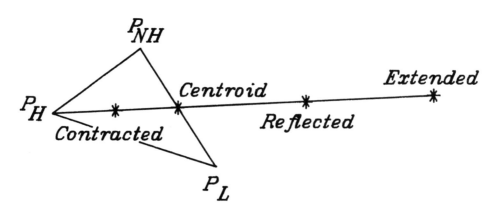

Figure 8–6. Basic operation on a two-variable simplex nonlinear search algorithm.

$$P_R = (1+\alpha)\,C - \alpha\,P_H \qquad (8\text{–}19)$$

where α is a reflection coefficient. Nelder and Mead (1965) used $\alpha = 1$, which places P_R directly opposite P_H through C and the same distance from C as is P_H. To avoid oscillations α is offset slightly from 1 (e.g., 0.9985).

There are three possible results of a reflection. First, the reflection may be moderately successful:

$$\chi^2(P_L) \le \chi^2(P_R) < \chi^2(P_H)$$

P_R is better than P_H but no better than P_L. In this case, we form a new simplex by replacing P_H with P_R. The process of reflection and testing is restarted using the new simplex.

Expansion. The reflection may be highly successful:

$$\chi^2(P_R) < \chi^2(P_L)$$

We appear to be moving in an advantageous direction and expand our search to form a new expanded point P_E:

$$P_E = \beta\,P_R + (1-\beta)\,C \qquad (8\text{–}20)$$

where β is the expansion coefficient. Nelder and Mead (1965) used $\beta = 2.0$, which moves P_E twice as far from C as P_R and in the same direction. To avoid instabilities β is slightly different from 2 (e.g., 1.95). If expansion is successful, that is:

$$\chi^2(P_E) < \chi^2(P_R)$$

we replace P_H with P_E. Otherwise we replace P_H with P_R. The process of reflecting and testing is then restarted. P_L is now P_E or P_R.

Contraction. If the initial reflection fails, or:

$$\chi^2(P_R) \ge \chi^2(P_H)$$

then the minimum may be on the same side of C as is P_H. Therefore, generate a contracted point P_C given by:

$$P_C = (1-\gamma)\,C + \gamma\,P_H \qquad (8\text{–}21)$$

For $\gamma = 0.5$, P_C is halfway along the line connecting P_H and C. Again, to avoid instabilities, $\gamma = 0.4985$. If contraction is successful:

$$\chi^2(P_C) < \chi^2(P_H)$$

then P_H is replaced and the reflection and testing procedure is restarted.

Contraction rarely fails, except as one closely approaches the minimum. If it fails, however, we can redefine the simplex by scaling and then trying again (Daniels, 1978). Every point P_i is replaced by:

$$P_i + k\,(P_L - P_i),\;\; i = 1, \ldots, n+1 \qquad (8\text{–}22)$$

where k is the scaling constant. P_L is left intact, but all other points change as follows: If $k = 0.5$, every point moves toward P_L and halves the distance. If $k = -2$, every point moves away from P_L and doubles its distance. If $k = 2$, every point moves toward P_L but overshoots and ends up as far away as originally but on the opposite side. In programs that run unattended, k is set to 0.5 (Nelder and Mead, 1965). In an interactive program, k is frequently an operator input. Generally, we decree that the solution has converged when scaling is required.

As the solution develops, the simplex tumbles through parameter space. When it finds an advantageous pathway, it stretches along it. When it finds a wall it backs away. Finally, as it homes in on the final parameter set, it contracts.

To give you a feel for the circuitous paths that a nonlinear search can take, we show the first twenty or so terms for a nonlinear simplex fit to the nonlinear single exponential decay error surface of Figure 8–5. The initial guess is (35, 35), which makes the three initial points on the simplex (35,35), (35,38.5), and (38.5,35). This is shown in Figure 8–7A. The solid lines start at the initial highest point and then connect together each succeeding point that improves χ^2. To aid in visualization, the first few simplexes are drawn in. It is clear that the first movement, as well as the second and third simplex, involves a reflection followed by a successful expansion. The next simplex uses only a reflection and rejects the next expansion. The next movement is to about (7,35); try to visualize how you got here. There are many moves before the χ^2 is successfully reduced.

To demonstrate the much more complex problem of a search in four variables, we fit the 100-point noise-free double exponential decay given by:

$$D(t) = 8000 \exp(-t/7) + 2000 \exp(-t/35) \qquad (8\text{–}23)$$

over the 0–100 time range. The preexponential factor gives a peak of 10^4 counts. The data were reduced using the four-parameter simplex fit with the function $F(t_i)$ given by:

$$F(t_i) = K_1 \exp(-t_i/\tau_1) + K_2 \exp(-t_i/\tau_2) \qquad (8\text{–}24)$$

Figure 8–8 shows a nonlinear search for several sets of initial guesses. We plot the current best τ_2 versus τ_1 and K_2 versus K_1. Unfortunately, there is no good way to

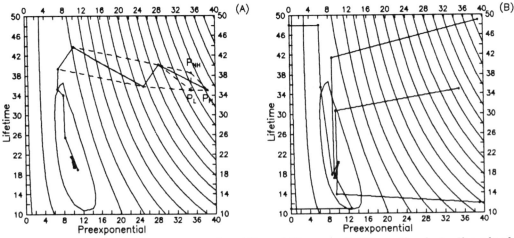

Figure 8–7. Search paths for simplex (A) and Marquardt (B) methods to the single exponential decay surface of Figure 8–5. In (A) the initial simplexes are dashed lines. The solid line starts at the initial P_H and follows the points of lowest χ^2. The initial guess is (35,35). (B) Different starting values are shown.

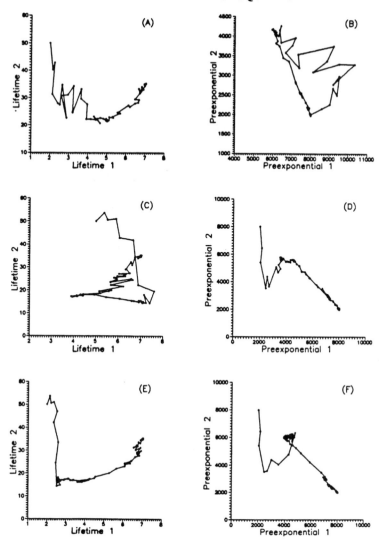

Figure 8–8. Nonlinear simplex searches for a double exponential fit to the decay of Equation 8–23. A and B are the τs and Ks for initial guesses of $\tau_1=2$, $\tau_2=50$, $K_1=8000$, and $K_2=2000$. C and D are for $\tau_1=5$, $\tau_2=50$, $K_1=2000$, and $K_2=8000$. E and F are for $\tau_1=2$, $\tau_2=50$, $K_1=2000$, and $K_2=8000$.

simultaneously see what is happening to the error surfaces. The first set of guesses uses reasonable estimates of the τs and the correct Ks. The failure to guess the correct τs, however, leads the estimates of the Ks well away from the correct value before they circle back to their starting point.

The two other sets of guesses make reasonable estimates of the τs, but the Ks guesses are reversed from the correct values. That is, K_1 is set equal to 2000 instead of the correct 8000 and K_2 was set to 8000 rather than 2000. The searches became enormously more tortuous than the first set of guesses. Inspection of Figures 8C–8F show that the simplex search first seems to try to invert the two lifetimes. When this fails, it then has to reverse the magnitudes of the two Ks. For the $\tau_1=2$ guess (E and F), the search then becomes incredibly slow. There are perhaps fifty points clustered tightly around $K_1=K_2\approx5000$; each movement makes a miniscule change in the parameters. The error surface must be very flat indeed.

We see this problem with all error minimization methods with sums of exponentials. If you guess the wrong relative magnitudes for the long- and short-lived components, the Ks must be reversed in the search and there is clearly no efficient search path through the complex χ^2 space.

We routinely use a general purpose program SIMPLEX for solving nonlinearizeable functions. SIMPLEX is adaptable to any nonlinear system. When used on a microcomputer, it is sluggish for large data sets with n>4, although we occasionally use it with n = 10.

Experiment 8–1. You learn to use the program SIMPLEX to fit nonlinear systems.

8.3.2 Analytical Solution by Taylor Series Expansion

We linearize the nonlinear equations formed from Equation 8–4 by expanding $F(x, a_1, \ldots, a_p)$ in a Taylor series around some initial guesses (Bevington, 1969; Demas, 1983). The guesses for a_1 to a_p are q_1 to q_p; then the a_is are:

$$a_1 = q_1 + \delta a_1$$

$$\cdot$$
$$\cdot \tag{8–25}$$
$$\cdot$$

$$a_p = q_p + \delta a_p$$

The unknown δa_js are the corrections to q_js and are assumed to be small enough to justify expanding F in a Taylor series in the δa_js and truncating all but the first-order terms:

$$F(x_i, a_1, a_2, \ldots, a_p) = F(x_i, q_1, \ldots, q_p) + \sum_{j=1}^{P} d_{ji}\, \delta a_j \tag{8–26a}$$

$$d_{ji} = (\partial F / \partial a_j)_i = \left[\partial F(x_i, a_1, \ldots, a_p) / \partial a_j\right]_{a_k, k\neq j} \tag{8–26b}$$

The a_is are given by Equation 8–25. Because of the truncation, Equation 8–26 works best for good guesses to the a_is.

Once we make initial guesses, everything in Equation 8–26 is known except the δa_js. We can now substitute Equation 8–26 into Equations 8–1 and 8–4 and apply a normal linear least squares solution to yield the δa_js. Then using Equation 8–25 we generate new a_js. If Equation 8–26 was exact, the new a_js would be correct. In general, Equation 8–26 is an approximation, and the new a_js are only better approximations. These new a_js are then treated as new guesses, q_js, and the entire procedure is repeated to generate new δa_js and then new a_js. For well-behaved functions, each iteration reduces χ^2. Near the minimum, convergence can become exceedingly rapid. Note that we are solving for corrections to these parameters, not the parameters themselves.

To demonstrate this technique we fit our familiar exponential decay using a nonlinear approach:

$$y = F(t) = K\exp(-t/\tau) = a_1 \exp(-t/a_2) \tag{8–27}$$

The initial guesses for a_1 and a_2 are q_1 and q_2, which yields:

$$F(t_i, q_1 + \delta a_1, q_2 + \delta a_2) = q_1 \exp(-t_i/q_2) + d_{1i}\delta a_1 + d_{2i}\delta a_2 \tag{8–28a}$$

$$d_{1i} = (\partial F/\partial a_1)_i = \exp(-t_i/a_2) \tag{8–28b}$$

$$d_{2i} = (\partial F/\partial a_2)_i = (a_1 t_i/a_2^2)\exp(-t_i/a_2) \tag{8–28c}$$

For N data points, there are N d_{1i}s and d_{2i}s.

To the level of approximation of Equation 8–26, χ^2 is given by Equation 8–1a with:

$$R_i = y_i - F(x_i, q_1, q_2) - d_{1i}\delta a_1 - d_{2i}\delta a_2 \tag{8–29}$$

As in the linear case, we minimize χ^2 with respect to both δa_1 and δa_2 by:

$$(\partial\chi^2/\partial \delta a_1) = (\partial\chi^2/\partial \delta a_2) = 0 \tag{8–30}$$

which yields the two linear equations in δa_1 and δa_2:

$$b_{11}\delta a_1 + b_{12}\delta a_2 = c_1 \tag{8–31a}$$

$$b_{21}\delta a_1 + b_{22}\delta a_2 = c_2 \tag{8–31b}$$

$$b_{kl} = \Sigma w_i d_{ki} d_{li} \tag{8–31c}$$

$$c_k = \Sigma w_i d_{ki} y_i \tag{8–31d}$$

This pair of equations has the following solutions:

$$\delta a_1 = (c_1 b_{22} - c_2 b_{12})/\Delta \tag{8–32a}$$

$$\delta a_2 = (c_2 b_{11} - c_1 b_{21})/\Delta \tag{8–32b}$$

$$\Delta = b_{11} b_{22} - b_{12}^2 \tag{8–32c}$$

The summations are over all points in the fit. We now apply Equations 8–31 and 8–32 to minimization of Poisson data similar to that of Figure 8–2B. We make initial guesses, q_1 and q_2, and calculate δa_1 and δa_2. We should verify that the χ^2 for the new a_1 and a_2 is an improvement. The new a_1 and a_2 are our guesses for the next iteration, and we repeat this process. Table 8–1 shows the results for fitting a decay curve; the parameters, before adding Poisson noise, were a_1= 10,000 and a_2 = 40. The fit was to 101 points over the 0–100 time range.

The first entry is for initial guesses of q_1=9500 and q_2= 55. Convergence was assumed when the fractional change in χ^2 between succeeding iterations was <10^{-5}, which required four iterations; the fourth iteration is omitted, since the discrepancies are too small to show up. After each iteration, the χ^2 was reduced. Similar results were obtained for any combination of 7500<q_1<12,500 and 10<q_2<60. Typically, convergence required four to five or, occasionally, six iterations. Thus, convergence was rapid for many outrageously bad initial guesses. The second set of initial guesses in Table 8–1

Table 8–1. Nonlinear Least Squares Fits for Different Initial Guesses[1,2]

Iteration	Simple analytical method			Marquardt method		
	K	τ	χ^2	K	τ	χ^2
0	9500.00	55.00	30983	9500.00	55.00	30983
1	9775.01	38.86	923.55	9767.93	38.91	902.57
2	10007.28	39.98	97.81	10007.50	38.98	97.81
3	10009.56	39.95	97.71	10009.56	39.95	97.71
0	3500.00	60.00	111841	3500.00	60.00	111841.
1	9657.66	0.75	355761	7870.26	33.32	40492.[3]
2	9334.20	3.21	321551	9886.76	41.80	585.0
3	5297.65	13.54	247456	10002.40	39.94	98.11
4	6194.83	58.86	25375	10009.56	39.95	97.71
5	9684.65	27.40	43922			
6	9475.84	40.79	700.71			
7	10008.26	39.90	98.29			
8	10009.56	39.95	97.71			
0	3000.00	60.00	138769	3000.00	60.00	138769.
1	9655.66	−9.13	1.3E15	7763.76	30.76	56050.[3]
2	1.03	−9.13	1.4E6	9972.06	42.71	1020.08
3	1.03	−9.98	2.5E5	9994.97	39.89	100.31
4	2.44	−12.37	5.5E5[4]	10009.55	39.95	97.71

[1] Fit to a decay with Poisson noise on D(t)=K exp(-t/τ) with K = 10,000 and τ = 40.

[2] Adapted from Demas (1983). Copyright © 1983. Used with permission of Academic Press.

[3] χ^2_T>χ^2_I. λ was increased until χ^2_T improved to give the indicated value.

[4] χ^2 continued to diverge for later iterations.

shows that some guesses may converge, but the χ^2 can increase during part of the search. Finally, the solution can be quite forgiving if one parameter is known accurately. For example, if $q_2=40$, then q_1 for $100-10^5$ rapidly converged, as did $q_1=10,000$ and q_2 in the range $5-130$.

The third set of guesses shows that too poor a starting point can diverge. Divergence can occur with only one inaccurate parameter (e.g., $a_1=10,000$, $a_2=135$). Thus, good initial guesses can be critical in this analytical method, especially for functions of more than two parameters.

We now generalize nonlinear least squares to more parameters. Using Equation 8-26 with p parameters and carrying through the setting of the p partial derivatives with respect to the δa_js equal to zero yields p equation in the δa_i unknowns:

$$b_{11}\delta a_1 + b_{12}\delta a_2 + \ldots + b_{1p}\delta a_p = c_1$$

$$b_{21}\delta a_1 + b_{22}\delta a_2 + \ldots + b_{2p}\delta a_p = c_2$$

$$\cdot$$
$$\cdot \qquad\qquad\qquad\qquad\qquad (8\text{--}33a)$$
$$\cdot$$

$$b_{p1}\delta a_1 + b_{p2}\delta a_2 + \cdots + b_{pp}\delta a_p = c_p$$

$$b_{kl} = \Sigma\, w_i\, d_{ki}\, d_{li} \qquad\qquad (8\text{--}33b)$$

$$c_k = \Sigma\, w_i\, d_{ki}\, y_i \qquad\qquad (8\text{--}33c)$$

The matrix is symmetric (e.g., $b_{kl}=b_{lk}$) and you need calculate only half the off-diagonal elements. Now solve for the δa_js and the new a_js. This process is repeated until convergence is obtained.

Convergence criteria are that χ^2s for succeeding iterations agree to within some error bounds (e.g., 1 part in 10^5) or that all $[\delta a_j/q_j]$ terms should fall below a certain level (e.g., 10^{-5}). While some programs demand that both criteria be satisfied, we generally assume convergence for either criterion.

Be forewarned. The more parameters, the more sensitive the solution is to the poor initial guesses. Searches can become very tortuous and false minima are increasingly bothersome. For good precision in multiparameter fits, the demands on data quality go up very rapidly.

8.3.3 Marquardt Method

Marquardt's (1963) method assumes a gradient-like search direction when far from the minimum and smoothly converts into the analytical method near the minimum. His method is easily adapted to our analytical solution. Marquardt left the off-diagonal elements of Equation 8-33a unchanged, but redefined the diagonal elements as follows:

$$b_{ii} = b_{ii}\,(1+\lambda), \quad i=1,\ldots,p \qquad\qquad (8\text{--}34)$$

If $\lambda=0$, we have our analytical solution. If λ is large, the diagonal elements dominate and the search direction is then along the path of steepest descent (Bevington, 1969).

The Marquardt method adjusts λ to ensure that after each iteration χ^2 decreases. If the χ^2 decreases, then λ is reduced. If χ^2 increases, however, λ is increased. In this manner, failure of the analytical-like solution causes λ to increase, making the solution more steepest-descent-like until χ^2 is reduced. As the minimum is approached, however, the analytical solution usually becomes more accurate and λ approaches zero.

The rules for carrying out the Marquardt minimization (Bevington, 1969) are as follows:

(1)   Make initial guesses for the a_is equal to $q_1,\ldots,q_p$. Calculate an initial χ^2 for these values to yield χ^2_I. Initially, set $\lambda=0.001$.

(2)   Generate the b_{ii}s using Equations 8–33 and 8–34.

(3)   Solve for the δa_j by Equation 8–33.

(4)   Using Equation 8–25, solve for the trial a_is and evaluate χ^2 to get a trial $\chi_T{}^2$.

(5)   If $\chi_T{}^2 < \chi^2_I$, then the trial solution was acceptable. Reduce the λ term by a factor of 0.1, replace the old q_is by the current a_is and χ^2_I by $\chi_T{}^2$, and go to step 2.

(6)   If $\chi_T{}^2 \geq \chi_I{}^2$, the trial solution was unacceptable. Increase λ by a factor of 10 and return to step 2.

Thus, λ increases as required to ensure that χ^2 decreases on each iteration and decreases to zero as convergence is approached. In a single iteration, it may be necessary to increase λ and solve for the δa_js several times before χ^2 decreases. As the b_{ij}s remain unchanged, the only extra computations are solving the linear equations for the δa_js and the χ^2 evaluation. Since for large data sets the b_{ij} evaluation is the most time-consuming part, the computation overhead for guaranteed monotonic convergence is quite modest. However, since there are never any false searches with increasing χ^2s, the Marquardt method frequently gives increased speed over the analytical method.

Table 8–1 demonstrates the results of the Marquardt algorithm applied to the same data that was used for the analytical method. For good initial guesses, both methods are virtually identical. However, for poorer guesses, the Marquardt approach converged monotonically and faster than the analytical solution; further, it solved the divergent cases of the analytical method.

Figure 8–7B shows the search paths for the Marquardt algorithm on the same data sets as for the simplex. The searches are direct and finish in no more than six iterations. Clearly, a dominant component of the initial search is usually a steepest descent. As a further point, a guess of zero for the preexponential is a bad choice since it blocks initial movement for the corresponding lifetime component.

We turn now to the formidable problem of fitting the sum of two exponentials. You have already had a chance to see how complex the surfaces must be from the simplex searches of Figure 8–8. In order to demonstrate the precision that can be realized with different parameters, we performed a series of Monte Carlo calculations (Demas, 1983).

Table 8–2. Double-Exponential Fits by Nonlinear Least Squares

Actual values[1]			Calculated values[2]			
K_1	K_2	Method[3]	K_1	τ_1	K_2	τ_2
500	9500	U	513 ± 62	34.8 ± 2.6	9501 ± 72	6.94 ± 0.10
		W	512 ± 28	34.3 ± 0.9	9501 ± 58	6.87 ± 0.08
1000	9000	U	1012 ± 65	34.9 ± 1.4	9004 ± 76	6.97 ± 0.11
		W	1013 ± 33	34.7 ± 0.6	9002 ± 61	6.97 ± 0.09
5000	5000	U	5010 ± 89	35.0 ± 0.4	5007 ± 102	6.9 ± 0.2
		W	5013 ± 56	34.9 ± 0.2	5004 ± 76	7.0 ± 0.2
9000	1000	U	8996 ± 110	35.0 ± 0.3	1026 ± 124	6.7 ± 1.4
		W	8987 ± 111	35.0 ± 0.2	1021 ± 107	6.9 ± 1.7
5000	5000[4]	U	5059 ± 771	34.8 ± 2.1	4854 ± 731	14.6 ± 1.5
		W	5090 ± 633	34.9 ± 1.8	4917 ± 599	14.7 ± 1.2

[1] Adapted from Demas (1983). Copyright © 1983. Used with permission of Academic Press.

[2] Unless otherwise indicated $\tau_1 = 35$ and $\tau_2 = 7$.

[3] U is unweighted; W is weighted.

[4] $\tau_1 = 35$ and $\tau_2 = 15$.

Table 8–2 summarizes some of the simulations. These were for $\tau_1 = 35$ and $\tau_2 = 7$ with K_1 from 500 to 9000 using $K_1 + K_2 = 10{,}000$. Also, simulations were performed with $\tau_1 = 35$, $\tau_2 = 15$, and $K_1 = K_2 = 5000$. In all cases Poisson statistics were used. Data reductions were carried out by the Marquardt nonlinear least squares fitting using weighted and unweighted fits. In all cases 100 data points in the range t=0–99 were fit.

As the 35 and 7 lifetimes are reasonably well separated, reduction is fairly straightforward. In contrast, the 35 and 15 lifetimes are sufficiently close to challenge the fitting problem.

We first discuss convergence problems. Unlike the single exponential case, convergence could be quite difficult to obtain. We describe a noise-free two exponential fit (Demas, 1983) with $K_1 = 9000$, $\tau_1 = 35$, $K_2 = 1000$, and $\tau_2 = 7$. We use a nonlinear, Poisson weighting fit with different initial guesses. Regardless of the weighting scheme or initial guesses, the solution should converge to the initial parameters. For initial guesses of $K_1 = 10{,}500$, $\tau_1 = 36$, $K_2 = 0$, and $\tau_2 = 0.5$, χ^2 reduces to 10^{-9} in six iterations. However, with the same guesses, except for $\tau_2 = 100$, the search is tortuous and inefficient. After 30 iterations $\chi^2 = 55.6$. At 50 iterations $\chi^2 = 44.6$ ($K_1 = 5490$, $\tau_1 = 26.0$, $K_2 = 4213$, and $\tau_2 = 44.6$). At 60 iterations $\chi^2 = 34.5$. Convergence then becomes very rapid, and $\chi^2 = 10^{-17}$ at 69 iterations with the correct parameters. Clearly, the reason for the slow convergence was the need to convert the high amplitude, short lifetime guess into the low amplitude, short lifetime component; this is exactly the same problem experienced with the simplex method for data similar to that in Figure 8–8. Of course, early visual inspection would reveal that the guesses were poor, and the program could be restarted with more appropriate values. The complexity of two exponential fit χ^2 surfaces is beautifully demonstrated by the contour maps of Hinde, et al.

This simple case reiterates the importance of good initial guesses. If convergence problems arise, change the guesses. For two-exponential fit, reverse the amplitudes of the long and short lifetimes. Visual inspection of the fits is invaluable for difficult cases. Alternatively, use a simplex fit with a coarse grid to locate reasonable starting parameters.

Table 8–2 summarizes the results of the double-exponential fits. Every entry is the result of 20 simulations; the mean and standard deviation are given for each parameter. Note several important points. The calculated Ks and τs all agree with the expected ones within statistical uncertainty (typically less than 1 standard deviation of the mean = $\sigma/20^{1/2}$). Except for the entries with large Ks associated with the long τ or for the close lifetime sets, proper weighting is a simple way to significantly improve the results. The $K_1 = 500$ and $\tau_1 = 35$ case is especially dramatic; the unweighted results give standard deviations for K_1 and for τ that are over two times greater than with weighting. The disparity is large here because the unweighted fit overweights the noisy low- amplitude $\tau=35$ component. In contrast, weighting has little effect for fast small K components; the short-component decay is completed at short times, where the amplitude is relatively constant and the weighting factors nearly constant.

Table 8–2 also justifies our earlier claim that reducing a component's contribution decreases the accuracy with which its parameters can be measured. Also, as the lifetimes approach each other, the accuracy suffers enormously. Compare the $K_1 = K_2 = 5000$ cases for the two lifetime sets.

8.4 JUDGING THE FIT

Having generated the best-fit parameters, how does one judge the quality of the fit? Is it statistically acceptable? Mathematical and/or visual methods are frequently used to test the fit. We discuss the residual plot and the chi-square test.

Residual Plots. The simplest and most common method is to view the simple residuals, R_is, or weighted residuals, R_{wi}s, versus time:

$$R_i = F(t_i) - D(t_i) \qquad (8\text{–}35a)$$

$$R_{wi} = w_i^{1/2} R_i = R_i / \sigma_i \qquad (8\text{–}35b)$$

where F(t) and D(t) are the calculated best fit and observed decay data, respectively. The w_i and σ_i are the normal weighting factors and standard deviations of the ith point. A good model yields randomly distributed residual plots.

To demonstrate the use of residual plots, we plot the results for the data of Figure 8–2B in Figure 8–9. Since the model is a good one, the Rs are randomly distributed.

Figure 8–9A shows a problem with the simple residual plot. This is the fit to the linearized form of the exponential decay for the decay with Poisson noise (Figure 8–2B).

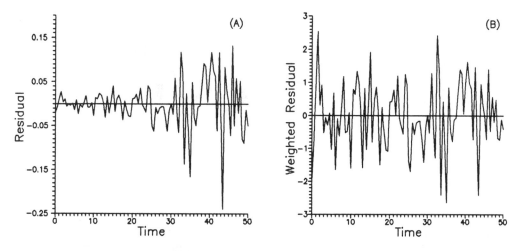

Figure 8–9. (A) Unweighted and (B) weighted residual plots for the data of Figure 8–2B with Poisson noise. The differences are for the weighted fits to the ln[D(t)] versus t plots.

At early times where the logarithm of the data are more noise free, the Rs are much smaller. It is easier to judge the fit at later times when the noise amplitude is larger.

A better way to view the fit is with the weighted residual plot. For direct fits to single-photon counting data, σ_i^2 is D(t), while for the linearized form, σ_i is $1/D(t)^{1/2}$. The weighted residual is:

$$R_{wi} = [F(t_i) - D(t_i)]/D(t_i)^{1/2}, \text{ direct fits to Poisson decay} \qquad (8\text{–}36a)$$

$$R_{wi} = D(t_i)^{1/2} [F(t_i) - D(t_i)], \text{ fits to ln plots of Poisson decay} \qquad (8\text{–}36b)$$

Figure 8–9B shows the R_{wi}s for the same data as Figure 8–9A using Equation 8–36b. Clearly, visualization of the low-amplitude region is much improved. Further, the errors are uniformly distributed around zero and all the weighted residuals fall in a band of about ±3 with most of the points falling in ±1. The quality of the fit is a result of the use of a correct model and weighting; normalization of the residuals by Equation 8–35b keeps the magnitudes comparable.

Figure 8–10 gives an example of the use of residual plots to detect model failure. A weighted nonlinear least squares single exponential fit was applied to a double exponential decay with Poisson noise. For all decays, $K_1 = 10^5$, $\tau_1 = 12$, and $\tau_2 = 40$. For three decays, K_2 was set to 100, 200, and 500. This is equivalent to adding small amounts of a long-lived component to a dominant, short-lived decay. Figure 8–10A and B show the unweighted and weighted residual plots for the fits with $K_2 = 100$. Figure 8–10C and D show similar data for $K_2 = 200$, and Figure 8–10E and F are for $K_2 = 500$. Since the fit was directly to D(t), the weighted residuals are given by Equation 8–36a. In contrast to Figure 8–9, the R_is are larger at the beginning because the fit is directly to D(t) rather than ln[D(t)]. Thus, the larger initial amplitudes yield larger residuals. Visually, the unweighted residual plots clearly show failure of the unweighted single-exponential

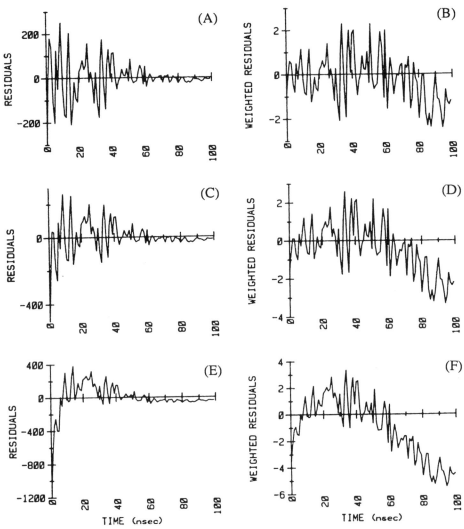

Figure 8–10. Comparison of unweighted (A, C, E) and weighted (B, D, F) residual plots for a single-exponential fit to a sum of two exponential decays: $D(t) = K_1 \exp(-t/\tau_1) + K_2 \exp(-t/\tau_2)$. $K_1 = 100,000$; $\tau_1 = 12$; $\tau_2 = 40$. For (A) and (B), $K_2 = 100$. For (C) and (D), $K_2 = 200$. For (E) and (F), $K_2 = 500$. Weighted nonlinear least squares were used in all fits. Demas (1983). Adapted with permission of Academic Press.

model for $K_2 = 200$ and 500; however, the extent of this failure is much better shown in the weighted residual plot. For $K_2 = 100$, both the unweighted and weighted residuals suggest a model failure, especially at long times; however, the discrepancies are not large enough to be sure.

This type of data examination should be used with caution; it is very sensitive to trivial artifacts. In our double exponential case with $K_2 = 200$, the single exponential model failure is rather extreme, yet the long-lived decay contributes only 0.7% of the total integrated signal. In luminescence work, one part in 10^4 of a highly luminescent material could produce such deviations if the main component had a 1% luminescence efficiency. Such levels of sample cleanliness are frequently impossible to achieve. Further, interpretations do not always require better data.

Chi-Square Test. The most common mathematical test is the chi-square test. One calculates the χ^2 of Equation 8–1, or the reduced chi-square χ_r^2, and compares it with the expected value:

$$\chi_r^2 = \chi^2 / v, \quad v = N - P - 1 \tag{8–37}$$

where v is the number of degrees of freedom in the fitting of N points with P parameters. Intuitively, if the fitting function is correct, R_i/σ_i should tend toward an average absolute value of unity. Thus, for a relatively large number of points, χ^2 is about N, or χ_r^2 is about unity.

To interpret the χ^2 or χ_r^2 results use Table 8–3. This is a greatly abbreviated table of χ_r^2 and is read as follows: For the indicated number of degrees of freedom, each entry corresponds to the χ_r^2, for which there is a probability, p, of measuring a χ_r^2 greater than, or equal to, the indicated value. Thus, for p = 0.10 and v = 100, χ_r^2 = 1.19. This means that for an experiment with 100 degrees of freedom there is a 10% chance of measuring a $\chi_r^2 \geq 1.19$. Extensive tables are available (Bevington, 1969). The current table is adequate for fitting computer-collected data with large numbers of data points, since the χ_r^2 distribution is not very sensitive to v for large values of v (>90), especially for p < 0.95.

Table 8–3 is used as follows: Evaluate χ_r^2 and determine the probability of observing this χ_r^2. If this probability is highly unlikely, then the fit is suspect. Too small or too large a χ_r^2 is equally unacceptable. Usually too small a χ_r^2 results if you select a model

Table 8–3. Distribution of Reduced Chi-Squares[1,2]									
p	0.99	0.95	0.90	0.60	0.50	0.40	0.10	0.05	0.01	0.001
v										
50	0.59	0.70	0.75	0.94	0.99	1.04	1.26	1.35	1.52	1.73
90	0.69	0.77	0.81	0.96	0.99	1.03	1.20	1.26	1.38	1.53
100	0.70	0.78	0.82	0.96	0.99	1.03	1.19	1.36	1.36	1.45
200	0.78	0.84	0.87	0.87	1.00	1.02	1.13	1.17	1.25	1.34

[1] For v degrees of freedom, each entry corresponds to χ_r^2, for which there is a probability, p, of measuring a χ_r^2 greater than, or equal to, the indicated value.

[2] Adapted from P. R. Bevington, *Data Reduction And Error Analysis For The Physical Sciences*, (1969), McGraw-Hill. Used with permission of McGraw-Hill Book Company.

with too many parameters or you improperly evaluate the σs.

We applied the χ^2 test to the data of Figures 8–9 and 8–10. Since 101 points were fit to a single exponential model, $v = 98$ ($N = 100$ and $P = 2$). For the single exponential data of Figure 8–9, $\chi_r^2 = 1.06$. From Table 8–3, the probability of observing a χ_r^2 greater than this is only slightly less than 40%; thus, the model appears to be a good one. Actually, the χ_r^2 would probably be smaller, but our use of a differential to estimate the transformed weighting factors is likely to be a little off for the very large relative errors near the end of the decay. For Figure 8–10B, $K_2 = 100$ and $\chi_r^2 = 1.26$, which corresponds to a probability slightly less than 5%. This result makes the model suspect but, as with the visual test, does not disprove it; after all, about one in twenty experiments would yield a χ_r^2 greater than this value for a correct model. However, for the $K_2 = 200$ and 500 cases (Figure 8–10D and F), the χ_r^2s are 2.06 and 6.52, respectively. Since in both cases there is much less than a 0.1% chance of observing this χ_r^2, the single-exponential model fails.

For counting data, $1/\sigma_i^2$ is just $1/F(t_i)$ or, more commonly, $1/D(t_i)$. For other instruments, rigorous knowledge of σs is not usually available and χ_r^2 must be approximated; with experience the expected noise level becomes known and the necessary w_is can be estimated. However, except for counting experiments, rigorous application of Table 8–3 is generally not possible. For a given instrument, one usually determines empirical χ_r^2s using well-characterized systems. Deviations from these values for unknown systems indicate a model failure.

8.5 ERROR ESTIMATION

Ideally, the best way to estimate experimental errors is to repeat the experiment many times and calculate the standard deviations. However, this is unacceptable with time-consuming experiments. One can, however, estimate the uncertainty in the least squares best-fit parameters directly from a single experiment. The following expressions come from Bevington (1969).

The normal equations, Equation 8–33, of the analytical solution of Section 8.3.2 can be expressed in matrix form as:

$$\mathbf{B}\,\delta\mathbf{a} = \mathbf{C} \tag{8–38a}$$

$$\mathbf{B} = \begin{bmatrix} b_{11} & b_{12} & \cdots & b_{1p} \\ & \cdot & & \cdot \\ \cdot & & & \cdot \\ \cdot & \cdot & & \cdot \\ b_{p1} & b_{p2} & \cdots & b_{pp} \end{bmatrix}, \quad \delta\mathbf{a} = \begin{bmatrix} \delta a_1 \\ \cdot \\ \cdot \\ \cdot \\ \delta a_p \end{bmatrix}, \quad \delta\mathbf{C} = \begin{bmatrix} c_1 \\ \cdot \\ \cdot \\ \cdot \\ c_p \end{bmatrix} \tag{8–38b}$$

To solve for the δas, multiply both sides by the inverse matrix of $\mathbf{B}$, $\mathbf{B}^{-1}$:

$$B^{-1} \, B \, \delta a = B^{-1} \, C \qquad \qquad (8\text{--}39a)$$

$$\delta a_j = B^{-1} \, C \qquad \qquad (8\text{--}39b)$$

B^{-1} is the error matrix, and the uncertainties in the a_js, σ_{a_j}, are (Bevington, 1969):

$$\sigma_{a_j} = \left[B_{jj}^{-1} \right]^{1/2} \qquad \qquad (8\text{--}40)$$

The standard deviation in a_js is the square root of the jth diagonal element of B^{-1} (denoted by B_{jj}^{-1}). The data must be properly weighted. If weighting is not used and unit weights are assumed, then the σ_{a_j}s are approximated by:

$$\sigma_{a_j} = s \, [\, B_{jj}^{-1}(w_i = 1) \,]^{1/2} \qquad \qquad (8\text{--}41a)$$

$$s^2 = \Sigma \, \frac{\left[y_i - F(x_i) \right]^2}{N - P - 1} \qquad \qquad (8\text{--}41b)$$

where s^2 is just the variance of the fit, and $B_{jj}^{-1}(w_i=1)$ is the jth diagonal element of B^{-1} evaluated for unit weights.

For the Marquardt method, these equations assume $\lambda=0$. If λ approaches 0 at convergence, then the last matrix inverted approximates B^{-1}. However, λ is frequently significant at convergence. Thus, the inverse of the modified B of Equations 8–40 and 8–41 can yield large errors in the σs. To circumvent this problem, generate B with $\lambda= 0$ after convergence and calculate the correct B^{-1} for Equations 8–40 and 8–41.

We evaluated the reliability of Equations 8–40 and 8–41 by Monte Carlo simulations with a double exponential decay using Poisson statistics. We then compared the estimated errors with the "true" errors determined from the standard deviations of twenty simulations (Demas, 1983). With proper weighting, Equation 8–40 gives very reliable error estimations. Thus, a single experiment can provide both the parameters and reasonable estimates of their uncertainties.

For the unweighted case, however, Equation 8–41 provided unrealistically optimistic uncertainties. For data with widely varying σs, this is a general problem of Equation 8–41. However, even in the absence of proper weights, Equation 8–41 still provides estimates of relative uncertainties that can be compared between different experiments. It should be used cautiously for stating true error limits. For a complex, rigorous, but fascinating treatment for two exponential fits, see the paper by Hinde, et al.

One of the very nice features of Equation 8–40 is that it provides error estimates even for data without noise as long as proper weights are used. In other words, if you want to know what errors to expect for a given data reduction, put in noise-free data built with suitable parameters and carry through the least squares reduction. Since the data are correct, you get the right answer, but the estimated parameters are what you would expect if the data really had noise on it. The alternative way to do this would be by Monte Carlo calculation, which can be enormously more time consuming. Figure 8–3 was constructed by this approach and confirmed by Monte Carlo calculations.

8.6 TESTING/APPLYING NONLINEAR LEAST SQUARES

If you have a nonlinear program or algorithm, you want to frequently verify its performance and compare it with other algorithms. We show how to do this, along with a frequently overlooked application of nonlinear least squares, solutions of nonlinear equations.

Testing Nonlinear Routines. The testing of nonlinear minimization routines is a fascinating topic. Several functions, along with contour maps and convergence data for different algorithms, are given by Daniels (1978). One of the most widely used is the Rosenbrock function:

$$E = 100 (x_1^2 - x_2)^2 + (1 - x_1)^2 \qquad (8\text{-}42)$$

The accurate location of the minimum at (1,1) for this deceptively simple function is remarkably difficult. It is a steep-walled, highly curved canyon with a relatively flat bottom. The usual starting point is at (−1.2.1). The grid search takes hundreds of iterations, and the simplex method takes forty trials to reduce E to below 10^{-6}, which gives x_1 and x_2 accurate only to 0.1 and 0.2%, respectively.

Solutions of Nonlinear Equations. Nonlinear least squares is valuable for solving nonlinear equations. Suppose we want the roots of the nonlinear equation:

$$F(x_i, x_2, \ldots, x_p) = 0 \qquad (8\text{-}43)$$

To find the roots, we can solve for the minimum of:

$$[F(x_1, x_2, \ldots, x_p)]^2 \qquad (8\text{-}44)$$

If, at our minimum, F is zero, the x_is are a root. For multiple roots, different starting points must be used. For programs that do not use derivatives, such as the simplex method, it is more accurate to minimize |F| rather than F^2. The method also works with systems of nonlinear equations. Consider two nonlinear equations:

$$F_1(x_1, x_2, \ldots, x_p) = 0 \qquad (8\text{-}45a)$$

$$F_2(x_1, x_2, \ldots, x_p) = 0 \qquad (8\text{-}45b)$$

The solution of Equation 8–45 is obtained by minimizing:

$$F_1^2 + F_2^2 \qquad (8\text{-}46)$$

Again, if the minimum is zero, the x_is are roots. This approach is clearly generalizable to any system of equations.

8.7 REFERENCES

Bevington is overpriced for a very old paperback, but it is essential for anyone interested in data fitting. Daniels has a delightful discussion of minimization algorithms and beautiful error surfaces. The classic book on numerical methods, including data fitting, is by Press, et al.

Problems

8–1 [8.2]. A common problem is when the fitting function is a constant:

$$y = a_0 \qquad (8\text{–}47)$$

Using a least squares criterion for N data points of the form (y_i), determine the best a_0. Include weighting factors. Your solution should look very familiar.

8–2 [8.2]. A common problem is when the fitting function is linear but the intercept is identically zero:

$$y = a_1 x \qquad (8\text{–}48)$$

Using a least squares criterion for N data points of the form (x_i, y_i), determine the best a_1. Include weighting factors. Note that the solution is not the same as for the general case of an unknown a_1 and a_2.

8–3 [8.2]. A set of N data points (x_i, y_i) are believed to be fit by an even function of the form:

$$y = a_0 + a_2 x^2 \qquad (8\text{–}49)$$

Develop a closed form solution for fitting data using Equation 8–49. Include weighting factors.

8–4 [8.2]. A common fitting function is a polynomial of order n:

$$y = \sum_{i=0}^{n} a_i x^i \qquad (8\text{–}50)$$

Surprisingly, while this is not a linear function, it has a closed form solution; you must, however, solve a system of n+1 linear equations in n+1 unknown coefficients. To convince yourself, consider a set of N data points (x_i, y_i) fit to the quadratic function:

$$y = a_0 + a_1 x + a_2 x^2 \qquad (8\text{–}51)$$

Solve the system for the coefficients including weighting factors. Proceed only as far as setting up the normal equations, since there is no simple form solution for the three linear equations; they are best handled by matrix methods.

8–5 [8.2]. A problem that arises in luminescence decay time measurement involves deactivation by both ground state association and by bimolecular quenching. The emission decay lifetime is related to the deactivator concentration by:

$$y = a_1 [Q] + a_2 [Q]^2 \qquad (8\text{–}52a)$$

$$y = \tau_0/\tau - 1 \qquad (8\text{–}52b)$$

where τ is the lifetime as a function of quencher (deactivator) concentration, [Q], and the subscript 0 denotes the lifetime in the absence of quencher. While this expression could be readily solved in closed form, commonly it can be rearranged to form a linear equation in [Q]. Find this rearrangement (i.e., the y' for $y'=b_0+b_1[Q]$). While aesthetically pleasing because it allows visual inspection of the linearity of the y' versus [Q] plot, it actually adds one additional layer of computation between the experimental data and the fit. A nonlinear fit is actually superior, although there is no linear plot for inspection. However, the residual plot is invariably a superior way to inspect the quality of the fit.

8–6 [8.2]. Another common fitting problem that readily lends itself to linear least squares fitting is one in which y is a linear function of two independent variables, X_1 and X_2. That is, the data are of the form (X_{1i}, X_{2i}, y_i). Assuming that the data are fit by:

$$y = a_1 X_1 + a_2 X_2 \tag{8-53}$$

derive expressions that solve for the a's in a least squares sense.

8–7 [8.2]. Using Monte Carlo methods, determine the accuracy and precision of the linear least squares method of evaluating an exponential decay. Generate your exponential decay wth the formula:

$$D(t_i) = 10000 \exp(-t_i / 100), \text{ where } t_i = 0 \text{ to } 511 \tag{8-54}$$

Add Poisson noise to each point and reduce the data by the linear fit to the semilogarithmic plot of D(t) versus t. Repeat the calculation 100 times and calculate the mean and standard deviation for K and τ. Do the calculations once assuming unity weights (i.e., unweighted) and with proper weighting (i.e., $w_i = D(t_i)$). Compare the two methods. In particular, if signal averaging could be used to improve the noisier of the two methods, how many more experiments would be required to make the poorer method equivalent to the better one?

8–8 [8.2]. The rapid lifetime determination method developed by Ashworth (see Ballew and Demas) is used for extremely fast evaluation of the preexponential factor and the lifetime exponential decays of the form:

$$D(t) = K \exp(-t/\tau) \tag{8-55}$$

K and τ are evaluated from:

$$K = \frac{D_0}{\tau(1 - D_1/D_0)} \tag{8-56a}$$

$$\tau = \frac{\Delta t}{\ln(D_1/D_0)} \tag{8-56b}$$

where:

$$D_0 = \int_{x=0}^{x=\Delta t} K \exp(-x/\tau) dx \tag{8-57a}$$

$$D_1 = \int\limits_{x=\Delta t}^{x=2\Delta t} K\exp(-x/\tau)dx \qquad (8\text{-}57b)$$

The RLD is 20 to 500 times faster than the normal linear least squares fit of the semilogarithmic plot of D(t) versus t depending on whether the integrals are available or must be calculated numerically from the tabular data. However, speed without adequate precision is worthless.

Using Monte Carlo methods, evaluate the precision of the method for τ. Use $\Delta t/\tau=2$ and $K\tau=10,000$. Assume Poisson statistics. Do the calculation 100 times and calculate the mean and standard deviation in both K and τ. Compare your results with the least squares method of Figure 8–3. For details, see Ballew and Demas.

8–9 [8.2]. Frequently there is a computational need for the evaluation of the series:

$$T_i = a_1\exp(-t_i/a_2), \quad t_i=(i-1)\Delta t, \quad i=1,\ldots,n \qquad (8\text{-}58)$$

The most direct approach is to evaluate it n times using Equation 8–58. Exponentials are slow functions to evaluate and the computation time can become significant. The following iterative formula greatly accelerates evaluations of Equation 8–58:

$$T_{i+1} = a_1\exp[-(t_i+\Delta t)/a_2] \qquad (8\text{-}59a)$$

$$T_{i+1} = a_1\exp(-t_i/a_2)\exp(-\Delta t/a_2) \qquad (8\text{-}59b)$$

$$T_{i+1} = T_iC, \quad i=2,\ldots,n \qquad (8\text{-}59c)$$

$$C=\exp(-\Delta t/a_2), \quad T_1=a_1 \qquad (8\text{-}59d)$$

Thus, each succeeding term can be calculated from the previous term and a constant C. In Equation 8–58, even if $-1/a_2$ was evaluated first, n exponential evaluations and 2n multiplications are needed to evaluate n terms. Equation 8–59 requires one initial division and exponential evaluation, and then n multiplications.

To compare the speeds of Equations 8–58 and 8–59 evaluate 1000 terms using $\Delta t = 0.25$, $a_1 = 10,000$, and $a_2 = 40$. Report the speed for both. Use an outer loop as required to get measureable times. You should find enhancements of 2–5 depending on the computer and whether or not a math coprocessor is used. This method is frequently used to improve the performance of nonlinear search methods using exponential functions.

8–10 [8.3.1]. The data set in the file dampexp.dat provided to you can be fit to the function:

$$a_1\cos(a_2 t)\exp(-t/a_3) \qquad (8\text{-}60)$$

Use SIMPLEX to fit the data set. Provide plots of the best fit and of the residuals. List the best fit parameters and their error estimates. All standard deviations are the same. This problem is an excellent one for demonstrating false minimum. If you guess too long a period, you end up plowing through the oscillations.

8–11 [8.3.2]. Work out the normal equations for a function of the form:

$$f(x) = a_0 \exp(-x/a_1) + a_2 \qquad (8-61)$$

8–12 [8.3.2]. Work out the normal equations for a function of the form:

$$f(x) = a_0 \exp(-x/a_1) + a_2 \exp(-x/a_3) \qquad (8-62)$$

Note that it is a simple matter to generalize your treatment to a sum of any number of exponentials.

8–13. [8.3.2]. Using an analytical expansion, fit the nonlinear function:

$$y = \tan(a_1 t) \qquad (8-63)$$

Derive the normal equation ignoring weighting. Fit the data set tan.dat provided to you; the noise level is constant, which justifies a constant weighting factor. Use a starting guess of 0.1. What is the least squares fit parameter? Turn in your normal equation and its derivation, a printout of the search, the program listing, and a residual plot.

8–14 [8.4]. This problem demonstrates the use of residual plots to test models.
(A) Generate a 101-point exponential of the form $D(t) = 10\exp(-t/10)$ over the range 0–50. Add Gaussian noise with an amplitude independent standard deviation of 0.05.
(B) Reduce the decay by linear least squares assuming unit weights. Plot the residuals of the linear fit (i.e., $\ln[D(t_i)] - \ln[D_{calc}(t_i)]$) versus t.
(C) Reduce the decay using proper weighting factors. Plot the weighted residuals versus t.
(D) Calculate the χ_r^2 for the fit of part C. Is the fit statistically acceptable?
Turn in your weighted and unweighted fit parameters, the unweighted and weighted residual plots, and the χ_r^2, as well as your justification of whether the fit is acceptable.

8–15. [8.6]. Use SIMPLEX to find the minimum of the Rosenbrock function of Equation 8–42. Use the standard starting points. How many iterations are required for convergence? What is the "final chi square" at convergence?

8–16 [8.6]. Use SIMPLEX to find the root in the first quadrant of the following two equations:

$$x^2 + y^2 = 1 \qquad (8-64a)$$

$$4x^2 + y^2/9 = 1 \qquad (8-64b)$$

9

Communications on the RS-232 Serial Port

9.1 INTRODUCTION

The RS-232 serial communications standard was designed well before microcomputers. In particular, it was intended to facilitate connections of terminals and computers to long distance communications equipment (e.g., modems used on phone lines). Because serial connections are so much cheaper than parallel ones, the RS-232 has more recently become the standard method for connecting computers to a host of peripherals and to other computers.

In principle, this connection of a computer and its peripheral seems like it should be simple. "My computer and the new peripheral are both serial devices and conform to the RS-232 standard. Therefore, I just connect them together and they work. Right?"

Wrong! The "simple" interconnection of serial devices has probably driven away more users and created more ulcers than any other single aspect of computers. Indeed, to the novice everything about the RS-232 seems designed to confuse and mislead, and the only thing standard about the RS-232 seems to be "Standard" in the title. There appears to be neither rhyme nor reason to the way in which manufacturers set up their hardware and write communications protocols. A wag once commented that the operational statement of hardware manufacturers must be, "How shall we implement the RS-232 standard today?". At times this seems discouragingly astute. For reasons that will become clearer, our alternative title for this chapter was "Why Did I Ever Buy this Stupid Thing?"

There is an historical explanation for this sorry state. As we have seen, proper communication between devices that operate at different speeds requires a suitable bidirectional handshake for regulating information flow. The RS-232 standard predated modern communication problems and has no defined bidirectional handshake. Thus, manufacturers are now forced to implement their own handshake schemes with the resulting chaos.

Incidentally, there is a more recent and much more complicated standard, the RS-449. The RS-449 does resolve some of the protocol problems of the RS-232. Unfortunately, it does so by addressing not only the relatively simple problems but also a number of much more complex ones; this results, for the average microcomputer user's simple problems, in a very cumbersome standard. To further cloud things, the RS-449 uses a completely different nomenclature, even for functionally equivalent lines on the newer and older standards. Connectors are not compatible and the electrical signals of one version of the standard are different from the RS-232. One version of the RS-449, however, is suitable for much higher baud rates and longer transmissions than is the RS-232. The RS-449 has not gained wide acceptance and is not routinely implemented on PCs.

The PC's serial port is invariably an RS-232, and we restrict all subsequent discussion to the RS-232. We show how the RS-232 is configured, give some basic nomenclature, show representative interconnecting communication schemes, and indicate how to program around some PC weaknesses.

9.2   RS-232 INTERCONNECTIONS

Originally, the RS-232 was designed to interconnect a computer or terminal to a modem (MOdulator/DEModulator). The modem is normally then connected to a phone line, which allows the computer to communicate with similarly equipped machines all over the world. The RS-232 standard provides for proper interconnection between the computer/terminal and the modem. The standard connector is the 25 pin DB-25 and more recently a 9 pin D shell connector. AT class machines and laptops (LT) typically use the 9 pin connector while older PCs and XTs use the DB-25. Nominally, the two devices connected are called the Data Terminal Equipment (DTE) and Data Communications Equipment (DCE). For a computer/terminal and a modem the computer/terminal would normally be called the DTE and the modem the DCE.

Remember from Chapter 3 that RS-232 lines are not TTL compatible. One level is +3 to +12 V and the other is −3 to −12 V. The logic on the external transmit and receive lines is inverted or negative true. That is, +5 V is a logic level 0 and −5 V is a logic level 1. However, to further confuse the issue, the control lines use positive true logic (i.e., +5V=logic 1 and −5V= logic 0).

Figure 9–1 shows the ideal interconnection of a DTE and a DCE. We show only the more commonly employed wires and associated pin numbers for the 9 and 25 pin connectors. The DTE accepts a female connector on the cable and the DCE accepts a male connector. RI is the ring indicator, DTR is the data terminal ready, DCD is the data carrier detected, DSR is the data set ready, RTS is the request to send, CTS is the clear to send, TxD is the transmit data, and RxD is the receive data. Electrical signals can travel

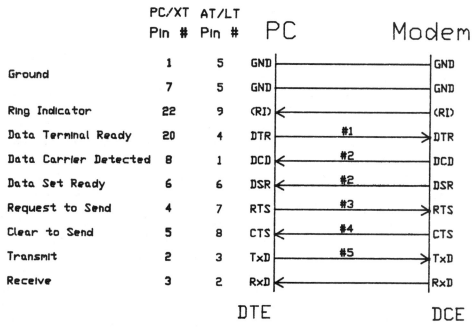

Figure 9–1. The ideal case: connection of DTE to DCE. The computer 9 pin connections are under AT/LT and the 25 pin one under PC/XT.

in only one direction on each wire and the arrows indicate the signal going from the source to the receiver.

Close inspection of Figure 9–1 reveals several points:

(1)   In the ideal DTE/DCE case the pins are connected in a one-to-one fashion on the pin of the same number on the other device. That is pin 1 of the DTE goes to pin 1 on the DCE, pin 2 of the DCE and DTE are connected together, and so on.

(2)   The labels on each pin number are the same for the DTE and the DCE. This means that the TxD line on the DTE is a transmit line on the DTE while the TxD line is a receive line on the DCE end. CTS is a receive line at the DTE end and a send line at the DCE end.

This last point causes no end of confusion. To know which way a signal is going on a labeled line you must know whether you are at the DTE or DCE end. Things get worse when we try to communicate between two devices that cannot agree as to which one is the DTE and which one is the DCE. Take, for example, two computers that both feel that they are DTEs. At the very least we have to cross-couple some lines so that the senders are paired with the receivers. Before we get into cross-coupling schemes, however, let us return to the ideal case and see how communication is actually established. For the purposes of this discussion, we consider the PC as the DTE. Because it is our experience that many people cannot keep DTE and DCE straight, we will refer to the computer end as the PC end and the secondary device as the DCE.

9.3 IDEAL CASE

We begin with the ideal case, a DTE connected with a straight across cable to a DCE. If the PC wishes to send data, it first raises, brings up, or sets the data terminal ready line. This DTR signal from the PC goes into the DTR line of the DCE. Hopefully, the DCE recognizes that the DTE is requesting a connection. If an open phone line exists for the DCE, it sets both the data set ready and data carrier detected. When the PC sees these two signals on its DCD and DSR input lines, the PC is free to set the request to send line. This is the announcement that the PC has data to send to the DCE. If the DCE is clear to accept data, it sets the clear to send line. The CTS line tells the PC that the DCE is free to receive, and the PC begins transmitting data over the TxD line where it is received on the corresponding line on the DCE.

The problem with the standard is that it assumed that once the communication link was established, it would not be broken and that there was no speed mismatch with the two partners. While this was usually true while someone was working at a terminal, it is not true with computers. For example, since the PC can transmit at more than 1000 characters per second (cps), and a printer rarely exceeds 200 cps, we have a problem. A handshake is needed to regulate the flow. Unfortunately, the solution is usually to assume a handshake since one is not defined in the standard. That is not to say that the presence of a handshake is not reasonable but, since it is not standard, there is a good chance that the two ends will not agree and the whole thing will come down.

One other point worth noting is that the sequence of events within the standard must occur in exactly the order specified. A violation of the order could result in failure to establish the PC to DCE link. Fortunately, most devices are much more forgiving than that, and as long as the right signals are available when the time comes to check them, the device does not care in what order they arrive. The PC serial communications is rather forgiving.

9.3.1 A Non-Ideal Case: DTE to DTE

Many serial computer peripherals (e.g., printers) are configured as DTEs. We must somehow fool the two devices since the correct signals are no longer available at the correct time.

Figure 9–2 shows one way in which this might be arranged. The particular example shown is for a PC to Qume Sprint serial printer. The printer is much slower than the PC (45 cps), and the printer manufacturer implemented a hardware handshake. When the printer's buffer becomes nearly full, it drops or lowers the DTR line (i.e., it says it is no longer ready). As long as the PC recognizes this and stops sending until the buffer empties and the DTR is set again, we are all right. We explore the interconnection in greater detail.

The first thing that must be done is to match the send lines with the receive lines on the other device. We accomplish this by connecting the RxD on one device with the TxD wires on the other. This is the minimal requirement of any DTE to DTE connection.

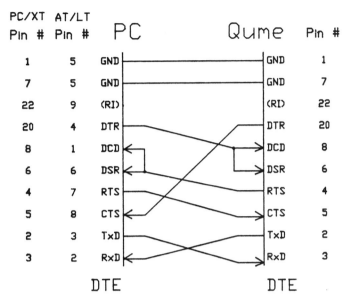

Figure 9–2. A typical nonideal case with a DTE to DCE. This is an interface to a Qume serial printer and the handshake is implemented in hardware. Adapted with permission from the AST Research Incorporated *Six Pack Plus Manual.*

The handshake lines get a little messier. Nominally, the PC and the printer come up with their DTR lines set. Consider the signals as seen by the printer. The PC's DTR line satisfies the printer's DCD and DSR input line requirements. The printer responds by setting RTS, which in turn satisfies the PC's need for a DCD and DSR signal. The PC also requires its CTS send line to be set before it can transmit, but notice that the printer's DTR is wired to the PC's CTS, so this requirement is satisfied. The PC is now free to transmit and receive and so is the printer. We have satisfied all of the standard's rules with the exception of the order in which the PC's CTS input line was set, which fortunately makes no difference in its function.

In actual operation, the printer happily receives characters until its receive buffer becomes nearly full. It then drops its DTR line, which drops the CTS input line on the PC. As soon as the PC sees this it stops transmitting until the CTS is set again, which only occurs after the printer has had a chance to catch up and empty its buffer.

We stress that this handshake is in fact a violation of the standard. Once DTR is set by the printer, it should never drop unless there is a total system failure. Fortunately, in this case the manufacturers were more flexible than the standard.

There are many handshake schemes other than the one just described. There are two ways to get your new peripheral working: 1) read the manufacturer's literature carefully and find out how the handshake is implemented and then make the necessary interconnections that will satisfy the rules listed above; and 2) find a ready-made solution for either your system or a closely compatible one. Ready-made solutions will frequently come out of the manufacturer's manuals or application notes, from your computer dealer, or out of "RS-232 Made Easy" by Seyer.

9.3.2 Null Modems

The problem of interconnecting DTEs is an extremely vexatious one, and there is a common solution that can be applied to a variety of situations: the null modem. In contrast to what the name might lead you to believe, the null modem is not a device at all; it is a cable that is wired so as to fool the DTEs into thinking there is a modem at the other end of the cable. Thus, each DTE will happily sit there and send to the other. Unless a suitable handshake is implemented, however, data can be lost. We show you two null modems in Figure 9–3 that satisfy a variety of problems.

In Figure 9–3A we show you the most stupid null modem. We merely connect the DTR line of each DTE back into its own DCD, DSR, and CTS. Thus, once the DTE's DTR line comes up, all the control lines are satisfied and the computer happily sends. The computer, in effect, is always telling itself that the other device is ready—which it had better be or you will lose data. We assume here that the DTE is not fussy about the order in which the lines are activated; fortunately, this is usually the case. This null modem is the one we used in Chapter 3 for displaying the serial port output on the oscilloscope. Since the oscilloscope has no handshake lines, we had to satisfy this need in some other way.

In Figure 9–3B, we show a more refined null modem. This one is suitable for connecting two computers together. It satisfies most of the order requirements except for the

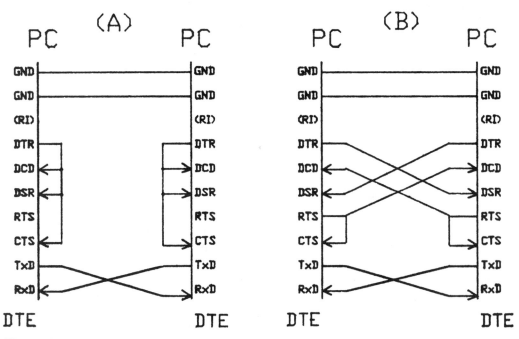

Figure 9–3. Typical null modems. (A) A very simple one without any handshake. (B) A more complex one with a bidirectional handshake to control information flow.

DCD line, and it satisfies this level before data are sent. In contrast to the previous null modem, this one allows the RTS line to be used to control information flow. Software can be used at each end to monitor the DCD line, which can then be used to start and stop information flow.

There are many other null modem schemes that you can envision; you will run across many of them if you have much RS-232 experience. Remember that what works in one system might not work in another.

9.4   IT DOESN'T WORK!

In the beginning, failure to achieve successful interconnections is the rule rather than the exception. Failures can be divided into three categories:

(1)   The received data are garbage.
(2)   The received data are fine for a while and then become garbage or the program gets lost.
(3)   No apparent communications at all.

We discuss the more common reasons for failures and methods of overcoming them. In addition, we will describe the breakout box, which is the most important hardware tool you can get.

Problem 1 is invariably caused by a mismatch in baud rate, stop bits, parity checking, or word length. Go back and check these very carefully. In many cases, they are dip switch settings on your devices, and the manufacturer's information is not always unambiguous. For example, some dip switches have "on" and "off" and others are "1" and "0", which may not agree with the manual. Do not be afraid to experiment. Another common problem with computers is the software changing of the default settings. On the PC, someone might have installed a MODE command in the AUTOEXEC.BAT file so that the computer will come up compatible with another device. Check the AUTOEXEC.BAT file by typing it out to make sure the serial parameters have not been reassigned.

Note. One very nice feature of the RS-232 is that it is essentially burn-out proof. The inadvertent connection of any signal line to another signal is most unlikely to damage the devices. The one possible exception to this is that some RS-232 connectors bring out ±12 V or other voltages. These power supplies are not standard, and inadvertently connecting them to ground, to each other, or to other lines might do damage. Other than that, you can make all kinds of miswiring errors without damage. Further, the only way to get many of these monsters to work is by experimentation, which means trying lots and lots of interconnections—many of which are wrong and would damage a less robust standard. So our advice is simple. While working on an interconnection, find out what the nonstandard lines are, stay away from them, and then experiment like mad without fear of damaging the interfaces.

Problem 2 is a handshake problem caused by miswiring or by failing to establish a software handshake. Since the data are transmitted correctly for a while, the serial port parameters are alright. The transmission failure occurs when the data receive buffer fills and data are overwritten before they can be processed. The failure here is that data are allowed to flow and not stopped in time. See problem 3 for debugging suggestions.

Problem 3 is also a handshake problem, but the handshake is preventing data from being transmitted at all. Check the wiring carefully. Remember that completely different functions have the same pin basing and labeling on the DTE and the DCE. Further, just because the connector on the back of your device is female does not mean that it is a DCE. Manufacturers are not above putting DTE connectors on a DCE or vice versa. Check the manual. If this does not help, bring out the big gun—the break-out box.

Break-Out Box. The break-out box is essentially a patchboard that you can splice into the cable between two devices. It allows you to connect any pin on one device to any pin on the other device or any pin on each device to any other pins on itself. Equally important, it has light emitting diodes that can be jumpered to any of the lines so that you can monitor the state of any of the signal and control lines.

A break-out box will cost between $80 and $150 and is available from numerous manufacturers. If you do not have one and do a significant amount of RS-232 work, then buy, beg, or borrow one.

The beauty of a break-out box is that it can tell you at a glance where your control and data signals are, whether the control signals are active and are properly set and changing, and whether data are being transmitted. You cannot tell much about baudrate (110 looks slow and 9600 looks fast) or anything about word length, parity, or stop bits. Nevertheless, after you have used a break-out box once to debug a serial problem, you will not attack another serial problem without it.

A second tool is also indispensable in any serial debugging kit: a gender changer cable for solving the sex mismatch problem. The gender changer is usually a ribbon cable with two male DB25 connectors and two female DB25 connectors. The wiring is straight through. With this cable you can connect any DB25 connector to any other one. Individual gender changers (i.e., male to male and female to female) are available, but the single four-connector cable solves all the problems. Also with the proliferation of 9 pin systems, a 25-to-9 pin adaptor is essential.

9.5 SOFTWARE HANDSHAKES

Once you are able to send and receive, there are two common software handshakes that you will use for regulating the flow of information between two devices. They work by sending ASCII codes over the line to let the other devices know when transmission is allowed. These are:

(1)   Xon-Xoff Handshake.
(2)   Enquire/Acknowledge Handshake.

Both methods require that the receiver have a buffer so that it can accept a block of data. The sender and receiver must agree on the size of the block of data so that the buffer does not get overwritten. In the following discussion we will refer to a transmitter and a receiver. The transmitter is sending data to the receiver. For both handshake modes, the receiver is sending characters back to the transmitter, but these are information control signals, not data.

Xon-Xoff Handshake. In this mode the receiver quietly receives data and processes it until its buffer reaches a certain percentage full, which is the Xoff threshold. At this point the receiver recognizes that it is in impending danger of losing data, and sends an Xoff character to the sender. This can be an actual Xoff character or some other character that the two devices have agreed upon. The transmitter, which is monitoring its serial input, sees the Xoff character and halts transmission. The receiver must be sure that there is some residual buffer space when it sends the Xoff character; it will usually take a few characters before the transmitter becomes aware of the Xoff signal.

Once the transmitter is shut off, the receiver can begin to process the data and catch up. The receiver has a second threshold called the Xon threshold. Once the buffer empties to this level, the receiver sends an Xon character to the transmitter. This is the signal to the transmitter that it is alright to resume transmission.

Thus, in operation the receiver controls data flow by stopping it with an Xoff character and turning it back on with an Xon character. As long as there is enough residual space in the buffer and the receiver monitors the input often enough not to drop characters during transmission, no data will be lost. This very attractive handshake should be high on your list of options.

Enquire/Acknowledge. In this handshake mode the transmitter asks the receiver whether it is ready to accept a block of data. Only when the receiver has enough buffer space to accept data does the receiver acknowledge. Then the transmitter sends over a block of data. Not surprisingly, the request for availability is made with an ENQ character and the acknowledge is made with an ACK character.

The Xon/Xoff and ENQ/ACK differ significantly in their concept. The Xon/Xoff handshake is basically a continuous transmission mode, which is interrupted when the receiver fills. The ENQ/ACK handshake is a block transmission mode in which data are sent in blocks that are kept small enough not to saturate the buffer.

We have glossed over some details. For example, in the ENQ/ACK there might be a terminator at the end of the ENQ signal, and the transmitter might echo characters back to the receiver. These are, however, system dependent features and the users will have to check the protocols for their peripherals to set up the right software.

9.6   GETTING INTO THE GUTS OF THE PC

We conclude with a very brief description of how to get into the PC serial communication hardware and program some things that previously thwarted us. Figure 9–4 shows a block diagram of the PC's serial communications port. This is based on an 8250 programmable serial communication chip or functional equivalent; programming is done via port read and writes. Inspection of the input-output pins shows that the PC is configured as DTE.

In principle, everything about the serial port is programmable via ports. Do not do it. As you will see in the next chapter, you can perform many of the communications port features via interrupts. If you can do it with an interrupt, then it is folly to program the chip directly. The manufacturers do not guarantee that the hardware will not change—including port assignments. They will only guarantee that the DOS calls and probably the BIOS calls will all continue to work the same way. Probably, the hardware

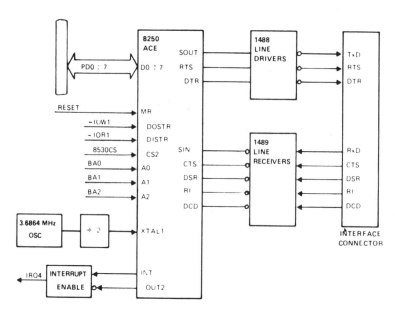

Figure 9–4. Block diagram of the PC's serial port interface. The 1488 and 1489 are RS-232 to TTL level converters.

ports and programming sequences will not change, but it is best not to bet on it if you do not have to. To discourage such tinkering, we will not even show you how to do it.

The one place where you do not have good control in DOS and BIOS, however, is the handshake lines. We show you how to program the modem control lines. This is an important point from the standpoint of Turbo Pascal usage of the serial ports. As we mentioned earlier, the DTR line on the COM ports does not come up reliably under DOS. If the DTR line is not set, however, the serial port will never respond to the outside world. We will show you how to turn DTR and RTS on and off and monitor CTS, DSR, RI, and DCD lines in software; this would allow you to implement your own hardwired handshakes and communications protocols.

The port assignments for serial ports 1 and 2 are shown in Table 9–1. We give only a partial listing, but the modem status port and the control register for setting the output lines are indicated in detail. For example, if we wanted to turn on DTR and RTS on serial port 1, we would write to the port 1 modem control register:

```
PORT[ $3FC ] := 3;    {Set DTR=1 and RTS= 1 for port 1}
```

Alternatively, if we wanted to check if both DSR and CTS were set to 1, we would read the modem status register:

```
SerialPortStatus:= PORT [ $3FE ] and $60 ;
If SerialPortStatus <> 0 then writeln('DSR and CTS Set');
```

Table 9–1. Serial Port Assignments and Significance of Bits

Port 1	Port 2	Name	Read/Write
3F8	2F8	Characters	R/W
3F9	2F9	Interrupt Enable	W
3FA	2FA	Interrupt ID	R
3FB	2FB	Line Control	R/W
3FC	2FC	Modem Control	R/W
3FD	2FD	Line Status	R
3FE	2FE	Modem Status	R/W

Modem Control Register

bit 0	Set Data Terminal Ready line to indicated value
Bit 1	Set Request to Send to indicated value

Modem Status Register

Bit 0	Delta Clear to Send. Modem has changed status since last read
bit 1	Delta Data Set Ready. Modem has changed status since last read
bit 2	Trailing Edge of Ring Indicator. RI has changed from a logic 1 to 0
bit 3	Delta Data Carrier Detected. DCD input has changed status
bit 4	Clear to Send
bit 5	Data Set Ready
bit 6	Ring Indicator
bit 7	DCD-Bits 0–1 reset to 0 when register read

Once you can read and have control of all the status bits, you can implement any type of hardware handshake or communications protocol. Note that although interrupt $14 (Chapter 10) can interrogate the modem port, it lacks any provisions for setting the DTR and CTS lines.

9.7 COMMERCIAL INSTRUMENTS

Numerous manufacturers make intelligent instruments that can be programmed and run under serial control. Generally, the commands are issued as ASCII English-like mnemonics, and data can be returned in ASCII, although more compact binary formats provide higher throughputs.

Our recommendations on these instruments are *caveat emptor* or buyer beware. Many are excellent with beautiful support software. The Stanford Research Systems' program for driving their lock-in is outstanding, although verbose at times. With their package you can do just about anything that you want with the lock-in; they also provide more intimate details for programming the lock-in.

Unfortunately, many manufacturers are less forthright. Their general purpose program frequently does not come with the serial interface but is an option, and their description of programming their instrument via your own software is sketchy to nonexistent. Frequently, there are bugs in their description or in the hardware that require major effort to work around. Their philosophy seems to be that if you cannot do it with their applications package, then you should not be using the instrument. What is worse, these problems arise on systems and software specifically designed for interfacing to PCs.

Thus, our recommendations are: always get a very good look at the software and instrument and use it on your system before purchase. Look closely at the instrument programming manuals. An alphabetic listing of commands is totally unacceptable. The commands probably interact with each other and must be used in very specific ways to work right, and you will spend days making the most trivial examples work correctly. Try serial programming the instrument to find out how it works. In this regard, we find TTY (Chapter 3) or PROCOM in the "chat" mode invaluable. You send codes to the device from the keyboard and see the responses displayed on the screen.

The following programming fragments show the code for programming our Tektronix 2221 digital storage oscilloscope:

```
Async_Send_String('INIt;');                  {initialize scope}
Async_Send_String('DATa CHAnnel:CH2;');      {setup chan 2 for data}
Async_Send_String('WFMpre ENCdg:ASCii;');    {set up ASCII display}

Async_Send_String('WFMpre?;');               {get scope parameters}

Async_Send_String('ACQ WEI:8;');             {on averaging do 8}
Async_Send_String('ACQ REP:AVE;');           {do a repetitive average}
```

All commands are three characters with extra characters being acceptable for readabilty. The Async_Send_String is in the Async Unit and just sends the quoted string through the specified serial port. The INI initializes the scope. DAT with the following argument sets the scope to digitize data on channel 2. The WFM command with the argument tells the scope to send data information back in a specific ASCII format rather than the default compact binary. The WFM? command asks the scope to send back its current setting including sweep speed, sensitivity, trigger mode, and so on. The ACQ command sets up and triggers data acquisition. The WEI:8 tells the scope when it does signal averaging to do 8 averages. The last command initiates signal averaging.

While such sequences of commands are not English, they do form a reasonable set of easily remembered mnemonic commands that allow relatively easy writing of data instrument control programs. The Tektronix code above is typical of the instrument-specific programming languages used by manufacturers of intelligent instruments.

Experiment 9–1. You use a break-out box to examine the operation of a serial interface.

9.8 REFERENCES

M. D. Seyer's little paperback is an extensive, although cutesy, description of the standard. It has a wealth of technical information including the exact pin-for-pin connections for interfacing an enormous variety of devices and is the bible of many who make serial connections. The AST *Six Pack Plus Manual* has a very lucid appendix that discusses the RS-232 and PC interconnections.

Problems

9–1. Write a pair of programs that transfers ASCII files between two computers. Connect the two computers with the null modem of Figure 8–3A. Use the Xon-Xoff protocol. For this problem, reassemble Async with a buffer size of 128 so that overflow is more rapidly achieved if the handshake fails. For simplicity's sake, you can use a filter with I/O redirection to read the input file on the transmitter. Send the ^Z when the end is detected and terminate the program. Display the transferred file on the receiver's monitor. Have the receiving program terminate when a ^Z is received.

Note that the receiver program must be running and waiting for data when the sender program is started. If the receiver is not working, characters are lost.

10

CPU Architecture and System Calls

10.1 INTRODUCTION

We have restricted ourselves to the high-level languages Pascal and BASIC. While quite powerful, easy to program in, and fast executing (especially the compiled forms), they have important limitations. Some functions still cannot be performed fast enough, or the high-level language lacks the intimate machine-level control for efficient implementation. For example, while it was easy to program the DT2800 boards in Pascal, performance was significantly degraded unless DMA was used. However, many functions did not lend themselves to DMA control. If we wanted to simultaneously drive stimuli (DAC or digital outputs) and examine analog inputs (ADC) at high rates, it was impossible in the slow high-level language because we could not mix DMA operations on the DAC and ADC. Finally, at least until Turbo Pascal 4, it was not possible to directly access such important functions as the clock or calendar with normal Pascal or BASIC.

To circumvent the limitations of high-level languages, we have several tools. One method is machine or assembly language in the processor's native instruction set. Alternatively, we might be able to access relatively primitive but fast machine language routines that are available in the operating system. Finally, we might want to examine or modify directly the contents of the computer memory which, in turn, provides the hooks for accessing a variety of hardware functions. Turbo Pascal provides all of these features.

Since the CPU understands only binary machine language codes, you need a way of depositing these patterns in the memory. However, even with a way to enter binary patterns, the human mind relates poorly to 8- or 16-digit strings of 1s and 0s. In many early computers, codes were entered for a primitive disk or tape loader program (boot strap loader) using a bank of toggle switches (see Figure 1–19). To avoid binary, octal, or hexadecimal formats, assemblers convert English-like instructions (mnemonics that describe each of the computer's fundamental instructions) into appropriate binary codes. The programmer's source program is translated by an assembler into true machine code. You see frequent references to machine language programming, but what is usually meant is assembly language programming. We will use both terms although we usually mean assembly language.

Assembly language programming has numerous disadvantages. It is a tedious, error-prone task. Even with the mnemonics, programs are difficult to read and maintain. Further, unlike high-level language programs, assembly language runs only on the CPU for which it was written. Finally, because machine language programs frequently tinker with the most fundamental elements of the computer, a program might not even run on different computers using the same CPU. For example, some software fails to work on even some very compatible IBM clones. We have the first rule of machine language programming:

If a function can be done satisfactorily in a high-level language, do not write it in assembly language.

Waive this rule if you are a masochist or enjoy Chinese puzzle boxes or other brain teasers—and have the free time. For most people, machine language programming is a court of last resort. Since one of us (J.N.D.) finds great pleasure in assembly language programming, we introduce you as painlessly as possible to this delightful topic.

In this and succeeding chapters we show you different ways to program in machine language or to carry out fundamental machine operations. First, we describe the CPU's architecture and memory. We show how to directly access computer memory from Pascal. Next we show you how to exploit the many powerful system subroutines in DOS or the basic input-output system (BIOS), without using machine language. Because the system routines and the assembly language are extensive and can be very complex, we describe a limited subset. In the next chapter we describe assembly language.

Finally, because machine language is so complex, only the most dedicated programmer considers carrying out an entire, substantial project in machine language. The most rational approach to writing programs is to use the following hierarchical approach:

(1)   If possible, write the entire project in a high-level language.
(2)   If some functions cannot be written in a high-level language, write only these functions in machine language and link them to the main high-level program. With Turbo Pascal there are few functions that cannot be achieved directly.
(3)   Now test the program performance. If it is acceptable in features and speed, stop!
(4)   If the program is too slow, determine where it wastes most of its time. A good analyzer program is very useful, as a subjective judgment of a bottleneck is

usually wrong. Infrequently called, very inefficient routines waste much less time than frequently used moderately efficient routines.

(5) Reduce bottlenecks in the high-level code by streamlining or using more efficient algorithms (e.g., a quick sort rather than a bubble sort).

(6) If you cannot solve the speed problem in the high-level language, then, and only then, rewrite the critical code in assembly language. Careful design of the original program will ease assembly language conversion.

(7) While this is not a programming solution, you can move to a faster computer or add an accelerator board. This might prove less expensive than writing much assembly language.

The tactic of writing the bulk of a program in a high-level language and incorporating machine language only in those places where the speed or exquisite control of machine language is required is a common and very sound programming strategy. Even if you know in advance that you will have to rewrite parts of it in assembly code, it is much easier to replace piecemeal parts of a working high-level program than to write and debug a machine language one from scratch. This marriage of two languages does raise problems of compatibility and communications, which we address later.

10.2 SYSTEM ARCHITECTURE

The heart of the IBM PC and clones are 80X86 CPUs including the 8088, 8086, 80286, i386, i386sx, and i486. With the exception of the i386 and i486, these CPUs use 16-bit data paths internally, which makes them all formally 16-bit microprocessors. The original PCs 8088 uses 8-bit external data paths; the 8086, 80286, and i386sx use 16-bit external paths; and the i386 and i486 use 32-bit paths. Wider external data paths mean that they can grab bigger chunks of data and instructions at one time and will execute faster at the same clock speed.

The speed enhancement of 32- versus 16- versus 8-bit external data paths is not as great as one might expect. The CPU has an efficient prefetch or queue that allows data or the next instruction to be fetched while the current instruction is being decoded and executed. In this way, the CPU has data or instructions when they are needed and the narrower external data paths exact no penalty.

The 8086 and 80286 are proving persistent building blocks, and should see wide use for some time in low-end machines. This is especially true of the 80286 because of its support for very large memories.

Excluding some of the more exotic features, and from a DOS standpoint, the internal architecture of the 16-bit 80X86s are the same. Figure 10–1 shows a schematic diagram of the organization of the CPU. The 8086 is a register-oriented device with numerous internal registers for data storage and manipulation. We now discuss the functions of the different registers.

General Purpose Registers. There are four general purpose 16-bit arithmetic logical registers, AX, BX, CX, and DX. These can be subdivided into 8-bit registers denoted by the first letter A, B, C, and D followed by an H or an L that indicate whether the high or low byte of the register is being referenced. Thus, CH refers to the high byte of the CX register. Many logical and arithmetic operations can be performed with all of these

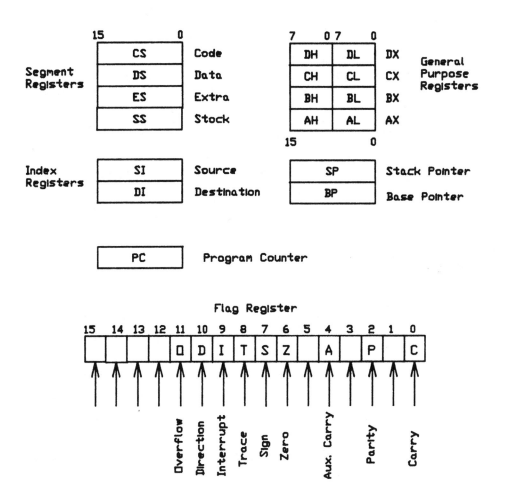

Figure 10–1. Schematic representation of the 8086 CPU. Flag bits without a notation are reserved for future expansion. Some others are used in the 80286, i386, and i486.

registers. Unfortunately, the AX, BX, CX, and DX registers are not equivalent for all operations. It is this irregularity of the 80X86 that makes it especially irksome for beginners to program—what works on one instruction for one register fails on another, and the programmer must remember the exceptions.

Program Counter. The Program Counter (PC) or Instruction Pointer (IP) points to the next instruction to be fetched from memory, decoded, and executed. Since the register is 16-bits wide, the maximum range of instructions that can be directly addressed without changes in the PC is 64K. However, the 8086 can address 1M byte (20 bits). We return to this problem shortly.

Flag Register. The Status or Flag register contains information pertaining to the result of arithmetic, comparison, or logical operations. For example, what was the result of comparing two numbers? Was there a carry to bit 17 when two 16-bit numbers were added? Was there overflow on a 2s complement operation? What is the parity or sign of a byte or word? Conditional branching or other control operations are usually made based on the results of an operation that changes the flag register. Several flags control CPU operations. Direction is set to control whether block operations are from high-to-low or low-to-high memory. Interrupt is set or cleared to control whether the CPU acknowledges hardware interrupts. Trace is set to allow a single step debugger operation.

Source and Destination Index Registers. The Source Index (SI) and Destination Index (DI) registers are used as 16-bit pointers for accessing data in memory. They also find use in special move and compare instructions. They cannot be subdivided into two 8-bit registers.

Stack and Base Pointers. The Stack Pointer is used for keeping track of the stack, which is a scratchpad memory used for storing data and for supplying return information when subroutine calls are made. If you have wondered how a program finds its way back after you make a series of nested subroutine calls, the answer is the stack. The Base Pointer (BP) is used for accessing information on the stack.

Segment Registers. There are four segment registers. These are the Code Segment (CS), Data Segment (DS), Stack Segment (SS), and Extra Segment (ES). The stack segments are what allows the 8086 to access a full megabyte of memory with only 16-bit registers. The actual address for a program instruction or data is the 20-bit address formed by combining the segment address and the effective memory address with a suitable algorithm. To form the actual 20-bit memory address, the segment address is left-shifted 4 bits and added to the effective memory address to give the actual address:

```
Segment Register (X's)        =     XXXXXXXXXXXXXXXX0000
Effective memory address (Y's) =    +0000YYYYYYYYYYYYYYYY
                                     ─────────────────────
Actual address                =     ZZZZZZZZZZZZZZZZZZZZ
```

Addresses are most readily expressed in hexadecimal (4 digits/16 bits or 5 digits/20 bits). We use hexadecimal arithmetic to perform the calculation. For example:

```
Segment Register    =   D001
Effective Address   =   37FE

                        D0010
                      + 37FE
                        ─────
Actual address          D380E
```

Any segment register can be combined with other 16-bit CPU pointers to access any portion of memory. However, if we hold the segment value fixed, we can address no more than 64K by varying the effective 16-bit address. Turbo Pascal allows up to 64K of data in static variables, although the heap can use all free memory. The 64K limitation is a consequence of the segment architecture. Also, each Unit can have no more than 64K of code. Storage is frequently referred to as paragraphs where a paragraph is 16 bytes.

The Code, Data, Stack, and Extra segments are nominally used for different purposes. The program code segment is started at a memory location determined by the CS register. Without changing this segment register, no more than 64K of program is available through the Program Counter. Each Unit has a different CS value, which sets the limitation of 64K of code in any Unit.

The Data Segment register also sets where variables are stored. Again, no more than 64K of data can be addressed by a 16-bit pointer without changing the DS register. Turbo keeps all program variables in one data segment.

The Stack Segment register positions the stack portion of memory. For reasons that will become clear later, the stack segment actually points to the end of the stack region rather than the beginning.

Finally, the Extra Segment points to another region that the programmer is free to use for any specialized purpose. It is also used for several specialized instructions.

Note two important things. First, the different registers do not have to point to different regions of memory. The regions can overlap in part or entirely. Frequently, several segment registers are the same. Second, different machine language instructions have different assumed or default segment registers. Thus, while a machine language instruction might not explicitly state the segment register used to generate the actual memory address, one is actually used automatically by the CPU. This implied addressing mode is one thing that makes 80X86 assembly language difficult for the novice. It is possible to override these assumed values in many cases, but this requires a special instruction.

Some programs do not have the 64K limit for either program or data. This is accomplished by bumping segment registers and the effective address so that larger blocks of data or program can be manipulated. However, the overhead associated with such manipulations can degrade performance. Some languages allow selecting the memory model to optimize for speed or data size.

10.3   REFERENCING MEMORY

Fortunately, Turbo provides the hooks for accessing and manipulating information directly in memory and for accessing input and output ports. Previously, we have shown how to input and output data through PC ports with Turbo Pascal; this is really a Pascal implementation of a machine language instruction. Turbo Pascal provides the following functions for manipulating data or programs in memory. These include the following predefined functions:

`Addr(var)` `@var`	Returns a pointer (segment plus offset) to the specified variable, procedure, or function var. The importance of procedures and functions will become apparent later when we set up our own interrupt routines. For example, if Bilge is a function, Addr(Bilge) returns a pointer to the function. The @ version is a convenient and widely used shorthand.
`Seg(var)`	Returns the segment address (integer) of variable, procedure or function var.

`Ofs(var)`   Returns the offset address (integer) of the variable var.

`Cseg`   Returns the value of the CS (integer) for the currently running Pascal code. Every Unit has a different value. Constants are stored in the code segment.

`Dseg`   Returns the value of DS (integer). This is the segment where the program and unit global variables are stored.

`Sseg`   Returns the base address (integer) of the Pascal stack segment as an integer.

Ofs and Seg can be combined to form the actual memory location of the first byte of the specified variable. The variable may be any simple type (i.e., char, string, integer, or real) or a more complex data structure such as an array, a specific matrix element, a record, or an element of a record. Thus, the following line writes out the segment and offset of the variable x:

```
Writeln('Segment of x = ',Seg(x),' Offset of x = ',Ofs(x),'
```

The following program HEXDIS.PAS shows how to get the segment and offset of a variable. It also shows the code and data segment addresses for the compiled code. If you run this, note that the segment addresses of the variable and the Pascal data segment are the same since data are stored in the data segment. Hex is our routine for displaying a number in hex (see Chapter 3).

```
PROGRAM HEXDIS;              {Display memory location variables }

CONST
   M:string = 'Hello';
VAR
   x,y,z:integer;
   str:real;

BEGIN                       {main}
   writeln('Segment: offset of x ', hex (seg(x),hex(ofs(x)));
   writeln('Segment: offset of y ', hex (seg(Y),hex(ofs(y)));
   writeln('Segment: offset of M ', hex (seg(M),hex(ofs(M)));
   writeln('Code segment ',hex(cseg), 'Data seg ',hex (dseg));
END.                        {main}
```

Run this program. Note that variables and typed constants are in the data segment.

Memory Arrays. In addition to port arrays, Turbo has a predefined array **Mem** that points to any byte in the 1M memory address space. It works much like Port except that the index is made up of both a segment and an offset. The two are separated by a colon. Valid examples would be Mem[0000:$0100], Mem[$1000:0000], and Mem[i:j] where i and j are integers. For example, to interrogate the byte at 0000:$0081, use:

```
Value:= Mem[0000:$0081];
```

If you want to assign this memory location to a variable value, use:

```
Mem[Seg(Var) : Ofs(Var)]:= Value;
```

Few things are as dangerous as indiscriminately stuffing bytes into memory, since you can inadvertently change variables, programs, disk update information, and so on. If you are lucky, the whole system will just freeze or crash. If you are unlucky and write to a disk after playing, you might clobber the entire disk.

If x and y are byte variables, the following fragment copies the contents of the memory location containing x into the memory location containing y (i.e., it assigns y the value of x):

```
y:=0;
x:=73;
y:= Mem[ Seg(x): ofs(x)];
writeln( y );   {display the first byte of the variable x}
```

Absolute Variables. Turbo Pascal makes provisions for declaring variables to occur at specific memory addresses. For example:

```
VAR
  Abc :integer absolute $0000:$00EE;
  Def :integer absolute $0000:$0081;
```

This is useful for pointing to specific system locations that you need to reference by label. You can also use this technique to declare variables "on top" of each other. This is sometimes done so that more than one name can be used to reference the same multi-function variable or so you can reference system variables by name.

10.4 RECORDS

Before we can cover system subroutines, we must introduce records. Records are more complex variables that are made up of multiple and frequently dissimilar elements. A record consists of a fixed number of components. Each component is called a field. Fields may be of different types and each field is given a name called the field identifier. The definition of a record type consists of the reserved Pascal word RECORD followed by the field list and terminated by END. Each section of the record definition is separated by a semicolon. Each record section consists of one or more identifiers separated by commas and followed by a colon and either a type identifier or a type descriptor. Each record section thus specifies the identifiers in the record and their types. While this sounds very messy when written out, it is not really very hard to use at all, especially for simple records. An example more clearly shows a record definition:

```
PROGRAM StudFile;

TYPE
  StudentRecord = RECORD
                     name:string[20];
                     SSnumber:integer;
                     Grade: array [1..10] of char;
                  END;
VAR
  Student: array [1..5] of StudentRecord;
  j:Integer;

BEGIN  {Assign names, SS#'s, grades on quiz 1 of 2 students}
  Student [1].name: = 'Jones';
  Student [1].SSnumber: = '4567';
  Student [1].Grade[1]:='A';
  Student [2].name: = 'Smith';
  Student [2].SSnumber: = '1111';
  Student [2].Grade[1]: = 'B';

  writeln; {output name, ss#, and first grade of student 1}
  writeln (Student[1].name, ' ', Student[1].SSnumber, ' ',
           Student[1].Grade[1]);

  writeln; {Output records for both students}
  for j:=1 to 2 do
  BEGIN
    WITH Student [j] do
      writeln (name,' ', SSnumber,' ', Grade[1]);
    END;
END.
```

This program shows both how a record can be set up and methods of accessing individual elements. We created a record type StudentRecord that contains a single student's name, social security number, and letter grades for up to ten assignments. The latter are the field identifiers. To set up a complete class record of up to five students, we create an array of StudentRecord. Basically, each student record is an array element, except now the entire record for each student is a single array element.

There are two ways to access individual elements within a record. The simplest is to reference a variable identifier within a record by using the variable identifier and the field identifier separated by a period. Thus:

```
StudentRecord[3].SSNumber
```

addresses the social security number of student number 3. One can either read this information out or assign new information to it. The period method of specification is used above to initialize the student's records. The period method of accessing individual record elements can get unwieldy to use, especially if there are records within records within records that have to be referenced.

Since we frequently work within a single record, the WITH statement allows accessing individual fields within a record as though they were simple variables. The WITH opens up a record, and then it is no longer necessary to specify the currently opened record name. The WITH statement consists of the reserved word "WITH" followed by a list of record variables separated by commas, followed by the reserved word "do" and finally a statement.

The WITH construction is used above to print out the student's identification and grades on the first quiz. The compactness of the notation compared to the period method is clear. Many programmers, however, feel clarity is lost in WITH and use only the period notation. Programs generated by both methods are functionally identical, and individuals must decide which is best for them. You will encounter both methods.

10.5 INTERRUPTS

The PCs have two types of interrupts: hardware and software. Hardware interrupts require external electrical signals to reach in and tap the CPU on the shoulder—so to speak—and ask it to do something. The keyboard, for example, has a hardware interrupt so that it can usually get the CPU characters that you type even when a program is running. Notice, for example, that you can type ahead of DOS by a few characters even when it is accessing the disk. Hardware interrupts can be quite complicated, especially on the PCs, and we will not deal with them further in this text. Async uses a hardware interrupt with the serial port chip to avoid losing characters.

The second type of interrupt is actually just a software instruction. It is equivalent to a subroutine call to a specific memory location. In a normal subroutine call the assembler or the compiler must specify the exact memory location of the subroutine; this could take up to 4 bytes just for the address (i.e., a segment and an offset).

Interrupt subroutine calls work in quite a different way. There are 256 possible interrupts that require only a 1-byte address number. The first 1K of memory is broken up into 256 4-byte groups; each group has a complete memory address consisting of an offset and a segment. The offset is given first, followed by the segment address. The first four locations are reserved for interrupt 0, the next four for interrupt 1, and so on. Each 4-byte address is called an interrupt vector, and gives the address of the subroutine associated with the specified interrupt. Thus, an interrupt 1 instruction is equivalent to a subroutine call to the memory location specified by the address held in memory locations $0000:$0004 to $0000:$0007. An interrupt instruction in assembly language would look like:

```
INT N  ;  N is the value of the interrupt
```

It is reasonable to ask why we use interrupts rather than direct subroutine calls. A simple answer is compactness. A subroutine call to any arbitrary location can take 5 bytes of machine language; that would be 1 for the call and 4 for the address. Once the vector is loaded, an INT N machine language instruction takes only 2 bytes, or a savings of 60 percent.

A more complex and significant reason has to do with versatility. The DOS and basic input output system (BIOS) are treasure troves of useful routines for the programmer and include all of the basic input and output routines, communications drivers and disk routines. For them to be useful, however, the user must know where they are. Unfortunately, every release of the operating system changes the absolute memory addresses. Not only that, their addresses are different for the BIOS on the IBM and for the clone manufacturer's software. Therefore, interrupt vectors provide a very convenient way to hide these changes from the user.

The way this works could not be simpler. The addresses of the various operating system routines are stored as interrupt vectors and the users are told their interrupt vector number rather than the absolute addresses of the routines. During initialization or when the operating system loads, the operating system, which knows where each routine is located, puts the appropriate addresses into the appropriate interrupt vectors. The user is now free to use any of these routines by calling the correct interrupt.

The interrupt vector method has other advantages. Suppose that you want to circumvent, either permanently or temporarily, one of the system's routines. All you have to do is replace the current interrupt vector with the address of your routine. Many keyboard enhancer routines do this. They redirect the standard keyboard routines to themselves. When a character is input, they check to see if it is something that they should enhance or modify. If the character is to be unaffected, the keyboard enhancer passes it on to the normal routine. If the input is to be modified, the enhancer alters the characters and then passes the information on to the regular routine.

Many interrupt routines need parameters and return information. This information is passed in the CPU registers. In assembly language, loading and examining these registers after an interrupt is straightforward (Chapter 11). While loading and examining CPU registers is not standard Pasacal, Turbo Pascal provides very simple ways to load and read registers. The format for a Turbo interrupt is:

```
Intr(Vector_Number, Register_Record) ;
```

where Vector_Number is the interrupt number and Register_Record is the record that includes all the registers. Before executing the interrupt, we would need to define a suitable type that contained all the registers and then a variable of that type. Further, we would need to load any necessary information into the appropriate record variables. The following type and variable definitions were required in Turbo 3:

```
TYPE RegisterRecord = RECORD   {Turbo 3}
       ax,bx,cx,dx,bp,si,di,ds,es,flags: integer;
     END;
VAR
  Reg  :  RegisterRecord;
```

Notice that the elements of the record have the same labels as the CPU registers. Setting these elements to specific values before an interrupt is equivalent to setting the corresponding CPU registers in machine code before executing an interrupt. Similarly, on returning from an interrupt, you can examine the CPU registers to see how the CPU registers were set during the call. Conspicuous by its absence is the CS register. If we changed CS, the program would begin executing in a place that we had not intended.

Interrupt calls are so important that Turbo 4 and 5 have a predefined record Registers:

```
Registers =
  RECORD
    CASE Integer of
      0: (AX,BX,CX,DX,BP,SI,DI,DS,ES,Flags: Word);
      1: (AL,AH,BL,BH,CL,CH,DL,DH: Byte);
  END;
```

If you use the Turbo 3 definition, you get errors. For Turbo 4/5 all you have to do is declare a variable of type Registers, and you are free to use the elements of the record to assign or read specific registers before or after an Interrupt.

The use of an interrupt is most clearly seen by an example. Suppose that we wanted to execute interrupt $14 with ax=222 decimal and then print out the contents of the dx register on return. The following code demonstrates this:

```
Reg.ax := 222;
Intr( $14, Reg );
Writeln (Reg.dx );
```

where we have used the "." method of accessing record elements and Reg is of type Registers.

MSDOS Calls. One of the interrupts is the main DOS interrupt and is the most commonly called system interrupt. This MSDOS interrupt is 33 ($21). Turbo Pascal gives this important interrupt a special name with the format:

```
MSDOS(Reg);   {Call interrupt $21}
```

The MSDOS interrupt is really only a convenience, since the following interrupt is exactly equivalent:

```
Intr($21, Reg) ;
```

There is a fundamental difference between the MSDOS interrupts and the others. The MSDOS interrupts are associated with the Microsoft DOS. The remaining interrupts are usually associated with the BIOS. The BIOS is one layer deeper in the onion of the operating system software and, in fact, many of the basic operations performed by the DOS interrupts in turn invoke the BIOS routines through their interrupts. Generally, if there is overlap between the BIOS and the MSDOS interrupts, the BIOS ones are more primitive. Compare, for example, the DOS and BIOS Time of Day functions in Norton's book. The BIOS routines give only the number of clock counts, which is about 18.2 ticks per second while the MSDOS routines give the actual time.

The BIOS routines are critical to every PC operating system, and there has been much legal wrangling over them. IBM stored their original BIOS in ROM and made the source code listing available to aid program developers. However, the code was copyrighted and could not be used without IBM's permission—which they did not give. Several computer manufacturers did not get permission, copied the BIOS verbatim, and either went out of business or fell on very hard times when IBM took them to court over copyright infringement.

Since the basic functions of the BIOS were not (and probably could not be) copyrighted, a new BIOS with the same functions that used none of the IBM code was perfectly legal. One of the most widely used BIOS on non-IBM machines was written by Phoenix. To avoid any possible legal entanglements, Phoenix had the BIOS written by a programmer who had never programmed an 8086 and had only worked on a Texas Instruments microprocessor, which was a stack rather than register-oriented CPU. Phoenix only interacted with the programmer through the mail and scrupulously kept all correspondence. The programmer was only allowed to see information on the BIOS that Phoenix supplied, which was all non-copyrighted. Therefore, he duplicated the functions of the BIOS without the slightest idea of how IBM actually wrote it.

Our AT&T 6300 operating system has two copyright messages: the Phoenix copyright on the BIOS when it loads and the Microsoft one when DOS loads.

10.5.1 System Calls

We have the machinery for using the system interrupts, and now we need to know what they do and their calling protocols. We now proceed to show you how to do such useful things as read the system time and date, measure elapsed time, do a screen dump to the printer, and set the baud rate on the communications port. There is actually an enormous number of functions, and we can cover only a few here. The interested reader is referred to Peter Norton's excellent *Programmer's Guide to the IBM PC* for a full discussion of all the interrupts.

Table 10–1 lists some useful BIOS interrupts. Table 10–2 shows details of the BIOS serial service setup codes and status. The interrupt number, the function, any necessary calling parameters, and the location of any returned results are shown. Table 10–3 shows some DOS interrupts. All use interrupt 21h. The indicated Service is the code passed in the AH register to tell DOS which function you wish.

We demonstrate the use of some of these interrupts with a print screen routine, a time-date program, a timer for measuring elapsed time, and the MODECOM1 program for setting up the serial port. Async uses a routine very similar to this for serial port setup. In the following examples we assume that you have a suitably defined register record.

Print Screen Routine. The print interrupt is simplicity itself. Set AH to 5 and execute interrupt 5:

```
Reg.AH:=$05;
Intr($05,Reg);
```

if you loaded GRAPHICS, this prints the current screen even in the graphics mode. The

Table 10–1. BIOS Interrupt Functions

Service	Interrupt (Hex)	Registers Input	Registers Output	Function
Serial Port Services				
Initialize serial port	14	AH=00 AL=setup code DX= port #	AX=success/ failure port status	Table 10–2 for setup
Send 1 Character	14	AH=01 AL=Character DX= port #	AH=success/ failure AL=modem status	
Receive 1 Character	14	AH=02	AH=success/ failure status code	Status bits (Table 10–2)
Output 1 Character	14	AH=01	AH=success/ failure	Status bits (Table 10–2)
Get serial port status	14	AH=03	AX=status code	Status bits (Table 10–2)
Printer Services				
Send byte to printer	17	AH=00 failure Al=Character	AH=success/ status code	Status bit settings: 0=time out 1,2=unused 3=1:I/O error 4=1:selected 5=1:out of paper 6=1:acknow. 7=1:not busy
Initialize printer	17	AH=01	AH=status code	Status bits See printer service 00
Get printer status	17	AH=02	AH=status code	Status bit setting see printer service 00
Miscellaneous Functions				
Print screen	05	AH=00		Print display
Reboot	19	none		No return

Table 10–2. BIOS Serial Port Setup Code and Status

AL Setup code:

Bit Position			
7 6 5 Baud Rate	4 3 Parity	2 Stop Bits	1 0 Word Length
000=110	00=None	0=1	00=Unused
001=150	01=None	1=2	01=Unused
010=300	10=Odd		10=7 Bit
011=600	11=Even		11=8 Bit
100=1200			
101=2400			
110=4800			
111=9600			

Status Word:

AH success/failure bit settings:	*AL success/failure bit settings:*
00=data ready	00=delta clear to send
01=overrun error	01=delta data-set-ready
02=parity error	02=trailing edge ring detected
03=framing error	03=change in receive line signal
04=break detected	04=clear-to-send
05=transm. buffer register empty	05=data-set-ready
06=transm. shift register empty	06=ring detected
07=time out	07=receive line signal detected

VIDGR4 Unit uses an even shorter machine language routine.

Date Function. A routine that displays the date is shown below. Turbo Pascal 4 and 5 have built-in GetDate and GetTime procedures that do this for you. However, they work by making a system call much like the program below:

```
PROGRAM datefunc;
USES Dos;

CONST
   months:ARRAY[1..12] OF STRING[4] =('Jan','Feb','Mar','Apr',
        'May','June','July','Aug','Sept','Oct','Nov','Dec');

   FUNCTION Date : STRING;              {Returns decoded date}
   VAR
     RegisterRecord : Registers;
     Month : STRING[8];
     Day : STRING[2];
     Year : STRING[4];
     DX, CX : Integer;
```

```
BEGIN
   RegisterRecord.AH := $2A;        {AH:=$2A for date call}
   Intr($21, RegisterRecord);       {Call to DOS int handler}

   WITH RegisterRecord DO
     BEGIN
        Str(CX, Year); {integer in CX to string format}
        Str(Lo(RegisterRecord.DX), Day);
        Month := months [ Hi (RegisterRecord.DX) ];
     END;
   Date := Month+' '+Day+', '+Year;
END;


BEGIN                  {main}
  WriteLn(Date);
END.                   {main}
```

Refer to Table 10–3 to see how this works. In Table 10–3 we see that the MSDOS Interrupt provides the Date-Time function that we want. Before calling it we set AH=$2A. On return, we have the year in CX, the month in DH, the day in DL, and the day of the week in AL. We break down the record using a WITH statement and convert the various values into strings using the Str procedure for the year and date. For the month, we have a typed constant array with the months as strings. We retrieve the month string from the array by using the number of the month as an index. A simple extension to the existing program gives the day of the week.

The clock routines require one comment. They claim 0.01 s precision. This is merely a human convenience. On the original PC the actual clock tick is about 1,573,040/64K, which corresponds to about 18.2 ticks per second. Thus, the real clock resolution is about 50 ms rather than the apparent 10 ms.

Serial Port. We turn now to setting up the serial communications port. This is quite a bit more complicated than the earlier functions, but given the port's complexity this should come as no surprise. Refer to Tables 10–1 and 10–2 under Initialization. The interrupt is 14, AH=00, and DX has the number of the port to be initialized (typically 1 or 2). AL contains the information on the values to be set. These are shown in Table 10–2, but we also reconstruct them in a somewhat different fashion here. The baud rate, parity, stopbits, and word length information are combined into one 8-bit value loaded into AL. The significance of the bits is given in Table 10–2. Thus, to set 150 baud, even parity, 2 stop bit, and 7-bit word length, we would load AL with 00111110 binary. The following procedure, MODECOM, emulates the DOS MODE command for the COM1: communications port:

```
{Modecom procedure -- mimics DOS mode command. Uses Dos unit}
TYPE
  ParityFlag = (e, o, n);

  PROCEDURE MODECOM ( COMn      : word;
                      BaudRate  : Integer;
                      Parity    : ParityFlag;
```

Table 10–3. MSDOS Interrupt Functions

Function	Service (Hex)	Registers Input	Output
Date-Time Services			
Get date	2A	AH=2A	AL=day of week 0=Sun.; 6=Sat. CX=year DH=month DL=day
Set date	2B	AH=2B CX=year(1980-2099) DH=month DL=day	AL=Return code
Get time	2C	AH=2C	CL=minutes CH=hours DL=0.01 of sec DH=seconds
Set time	2D	AH=2D CL=minutes CH=hours DL=0.01 of sec DH=seconds	
Serial Port Services			
Serial Input	3	AH=03	AL=Character
Serial Output	4	AH=04 DL=character	
Miscellaneous Services			
Printer output	5	AH=05 DL=output character	
Check Keyboard Status	B		AL=FF if a character ready AL=00 if no character ready
Display Output	2	AH=02 DL=Character	
Display String	9	AH=09 DS:DX= pointer to output string	
Terminate Program	4C	AH=4C	AL=Return Code

```
                    WordLength, StopBits : Integer);
VAR
  Reg: Registers;
  BaudBit, ParityBit, DataBit : Integer;
BEGIN
  If NOT (COMn in  [1..4]) then write(^G, 'Bad COMn Port');
  CASE BaudRate OF
    11, 110 : BaudBit := 0;
    15, 150 : BaudBit := 1;
    3,  300 : BaudBit := 2;
    6,  600 : BaudBit := 3;
    12, 1200 : BaudBit := 4;
    24, 2400 : BaudBit := 5;
    48, 4800 : BaudBit := 6;
    96, 9600 : BaudBit := 7;
  ELSE WriteLn(^G, 'Bad Baudrate');
  END;

  CASE Parity OF
    n : ParityBit := 0;
    o : ParityBit := 1;
    e : ParityBit := 3;
  ELSE WriteLn(^G, 'Bad Parity');
  END;

  CASE WordLength OF
    7 : DataBit := 2;
    8 : DataBit := 3;
  ELSE WriteLn(^G, 'Bad Word Length');
  END;

  IF NOT(StopBits IN [1,2]) THEN WriteLn(^G,'Bad Stopbit');
  writeln('COMn=', comn);
  Reg.DX := COMn - 1;
  Reg.AX := (BaudBit SHL 5)+(ParityBit SHL 3)+
  ((StopBits-1) SHL 2)+DataBit;
  Intr($14, Reg);
END;
```

This procedure, which requires the Dos Unit, is straightforward. We omit a few features such as time out. The call:

```
ModeCom(comport, baudrate, parity, wordlength, stopbits);
```

has the same format as the DOS mode command except that you cannot omit elements.

On return from MODECOM, the serial port status is reported in the AX register. The report is the same as if you had executed a Serial Port Status interrupt (Table 10–2). Data Ready indicates that a character is ready to be read. Overrun indicates that you failed to read a character before it was overwritten by a new one. Framing error indicates that the specified character length and/or parity did not match that set. Break indicates a Break was sent on the line. Transmission buffer register empty indicates the buffer for the output is free for a new character. Transmission shift register empty indicates that the last character has been shifted out. The modem control line meanings were explained in Chapter 9.

There is much more that can be done with the routines than we have given you at this point. In particular, we have barely touched on the serial port services. Async does almost everything we need.

10.5.2 Changing the Interrupt Vectors

There are times when it is extraordinarily useful to replace specific interrupt routines with your own. This turns out to be quite easy in Turbo. We have to be able to do three things to make this work: 1) we have to save the existing interrupt vector so that we can replace it when we are done; 2) we have to replace the vector with a pointer to our own interrupt routine; and 3) we have to restore the vector when we are done.

There are two interrupts that are used to get and replace a specific vector. However, Turbo 4/5 has the built-in procedures GetIntVec and SetIntVec, which get and set an interrupt respectively.

```
GetIntVec(InterNumber : Byte; Var Vector : Pointer);
SetIntVec(InterNumber : Byte; Vector : Pointer);
```

where InterNumber is the interrupt to be changed and Vector is a pointer variable that is used to either read the vector address or set it.

Interrupt procedures are not normal procedures. An interrupt has a different calling form than a normal procedure, and if you call a normal procedure or function as an interrupt, very bad things happen. At best, the system crashes. At worst, you lose data. To set up a procedure to be called as an interrupt, use the reserved word Interrupt immediately after the procedure name. For example:

```
PROCEDURE ProcedureName;
   Interrupt;
```

Never call an interrupt as a simple procedure and never call a normal procedure as an interrupt. Failure to obey this will invariably have catastrophic software consequences.

We now give you a specific example of substituting your own procedure for an existing one. The following contrived example prevents the Shift Print routine from working during the program execution:

```
PROGRAM stoprint;   {prevents print screen--intercepts vector}
USES Dos, Crt;

VAR
```

```
IntValue : Byte;
IntSave : Pointer;

PROCEDURE IntHandler;            {interrupt routine}
  Interrupt;
BEGIN
  WriteLn('Printer not available');
END;

BEGIN              {main}
  IntValue :=5;                    {set printscreen interrupt}
  GetIntVec(IntValue,IntSave);    {save old vector in IntSave}
  SetIntVec(IntValue, Addr(IntHandler));  {replace interrupt}
  WriteLn('Print Screen disabled');
  delay(5000);
  WriteLn('resetting print screen interrupt');
  SetIntVec(IntValue, IntSave);   {restore original interrupt}
END.              {main}
```

The first two lines of Main get the old Print Screen interrupt vector. The next line replaces it with the address of your interrupt routine IntHandler, which does nothing more than write a message that the Print Screen is disabled. The last line restores the original interrupt. If at any time during the delay you try to print the screen, Interrupt 5 is invoked, but the interrupt routine is now your interrupt routine and no printing is performed.

There is a real minefield here. If you do not restore the original vector, it continues to point at your routine. If your routine is overwritten, then any attempt to print the screen will execute whatever is in memory at that location. Disaster! Even if you restore the vector in your program, you might not get to the restoration code if the program crashes earlier (e.g., inputting letters for a number).

A similar problem existed with Async; you had to close Async before exiting programs that used it. Async has set up its own interrupt vector, and if you do not restore the original, any incoming serial character will cause the computer to try to execute whatever was where Async used to be—with the usual system crash.

10.5.3 Stealing the System Clock Interrupt

The PC system clock ticks at about 18.2 times per second. Each tick generates a hardware interrupt, which stops the system and executes a clock routine that, for example, updates counters used to keep track of the time. It would be quite nice if you could use this interrupt to do things of your own such as check various devices or acquire data. Since these are hardware interrupts, all of these activities could be performed in the background without conscious effort on the part of a currently running program. As it turns out it is very easy for you to attach your own parasitic programs to the clock interrupt.

One of the things that the hardware interrupt does is execute the timer interrupt $1c. As initially configured, interrupt $1c points at an interrupt return instruction and, thus, does nothing every time it is called. All you have to do is to replace the initial $1c interrupt vector with one that points at your routine.

TickTick demonstrates how this is done. It also convincingly shows you that hardware interrupts are being generated. The set up and exit are the same as before. Our interrupt service routine, Tick, increments the global variable Count. After initialization, the main body of the program sits in a tight loop and monitors Count until Count equals or exceeds 1000. However, since the loop does not alter Count, the program should be stuck in an infinite loop. After about fifty seconds, however, the program ends with Count equal to a 1000. The only way Count can change here is if a hardware interrupt is occurring, and since each interrupt increments Count the program ends after 1000 interruptions.

```
PROGRAM TickTick;
USES timer, Dos, Crt;

VAR
   IntVal  : Byte;
   IntSave : Pointer;
   Count   : Integer;
   EndTime : LongInt;

   PROCEDURE Tick;        {increment count on each system tick}
     Interrupt;
   BEGIN
     Count := Count+1;
   END;

BEGIN
   IntVal := $1c;
   Count  := 0;

   GetIntVec(IntVal, IntSave); {get/save original tick vector}
   SetIntVec(IntVal, @Tick);

   StartTimer(1);
       REPEAT UNTIL Count >= 1000; {escape after 1000 ticks}
   EndTime := ReadTimer(1);

   SetIntVec(IntVal, IntSave);      {restore original vector}

   WriteLn('Count ', Count:5, '    Rate ',
           (100.0*Count/EndTime):8:3);
END.
```

TickTick is not useful. However, suppose Tick was actually a data acquisition program. On each tick you could acquire one or more points, place them into a global data array, and update a global counter variable. Your main program could occasionally check the global counter variable and read the data out when the required number of points were acquired. Alternatively, you could save the data to disk in the background and not even use it with the currently running program. This time sharing by interrupt could obviously be carried to the extreme form where a number of independent programs were all run by an interrupt driven scheduler. This is actually the basis of a multiuser or multitasking system. Rather than creating new CPU time you are spreading it over several tasks with the clock interrupt and a scheduler rapidly switching between tasks to create the appearance of constant availability for all tasks. Since many programs, such as word processors, spend most of their time waiting for input, using the slack time to do other things can greatly increase performance.

There is one very interesting quirk that can arise with the system clock. The system clock on all PCs does not run at the same speed. Our AT&T 6300s run at 18.8 ticks per second. In spite of this, the time-of-day clock is correct. The DOS must be customized for the 6300 and adjustments made for the different clock. While we have not tried it, we suspect that the AT&T DOS run on an IBM PC would not give the correct time since it would assume a wrong system clock rate. Thus, it is essential to know the actual clock rate before taking precision data with interrupt $1c. TickTick was actually designed to do this, except that Counts was increased to 10,000 to give better resolution.

Figure 10–2 shows a case in which the system clock is used as a timing source. Here we wish to "simultaneously" record the transients on two capacitors. The DMA mode of the DT2800 only allows alternate points from each capacitor. However, after the transient starts, we can use the clock tick to vector to a routine that acquires, as quickly as possible, points from both capacitors. The discharge is slow enough that two ADC

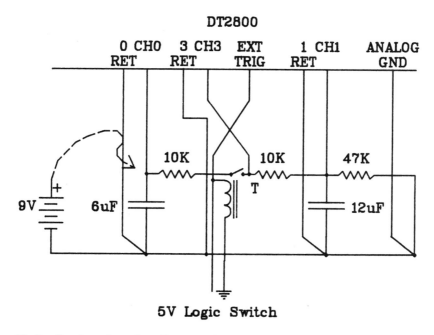

Figure 10–2. System for simultaneously measuring the decay of two capacitors. Discharge is initiated by a TTL level signal to the reed relay.

immediate reads are effectively simultaneous; this simplifies data reduction. Because the transients are slow, 18 points per second is adequate.

10.5.4   String Output Interrupts

There are two common MSDOS interrupts for outputting strings. Turbo's Write and Writeln are far more powerful, but we discuss interrupt output because it makes a good example of the use of system interrupts. There are times in machine language programming when you must output messages.

Referencing Table 10–3 we see that function $02h outputs a single character to standard output. The character is in the dl register. To output a series of characters scan sequentially through memory, fetch each character, and output it in turn.

Function 9h outputs an entire string at once. However, to tell the routine where to stop output, the string must be terminated with an ASCII $. With function 9 the AH register is set to 9. The beginning of the string is pointed at by the combination of the DS and DX registers, which form segment offset pairs (DS:DX), and the MSDOS interrupt is called. To use this function, you set up a Register record using the predefined Registers type of the MSDOS Unit, load AH with 9, DS:DX with the pointer to the character, and call the MSDOS interrupt.

The following program uses MSDOS interrupt functions 2 and 9 to display a string. Note that there are no CRLF sequences associated with either function. So they must be explicitly included:

```
PROGRAM prtstr;
USES Dos;
VAR
  i : Integer;
  Str : STRING;
  regs : Registers;

BEGIN
  Write('Enter string: ');        ReadLn(Str);
  WriteLn;
  Str := Str+Chr($0a)+Chr($0d)+'$'+Chr($0a)+Chr($0d);
  Write('Output using writeln:',Str);

  Write('MSDOS character by character output:');
  WITH regs DO
    BEGIN
      FOR i := 1 TO mem[DSeg:Ofs(Str)] DO
        BEGIN
          ah := 2;
          dl := mem[DSeg:Ofs(Str)+i]; {get next character}
          MSDOS(regs);
        END;
    END;

  WriteLn;   Write('MSDOS string $ method:');
```

```
WITH regs DO
  BEGIN
    ah := 9;
    ds := DSeg;
    dx := Ofs(Str)+1;          {skip length of string byte}
    MSDOS(regs);               {print out string}
  END;
END.
```

Note the use of MEM to locate the string position. The first byte of a string is its current length, and Ofs returns this string location. The string actually starts at the next byte of memory.

Experiments 10–1 – 10–3. You acquire the transients of a capacitor network decay and fit the decays using a simplex algorithm. Global fitting of multiple transients is demonstrated.

10.6 REFERENCES
The IBM BIOS reference manuals are the authoritative source. However, Norton has particularly lucid descriptions of the BIOS and DOS calls.

Problems

10–1 [10.3].   Write a function that uses direct memory addressing to read a string variable Bilge from memory, convert it into a real number, and store the result (a simple assign is adequate) into a real RealBilge.

10–2 [10.5]. The simple screen dump routine of Section 10.5 has a problem if you inadvertently call it on a computer that is not connected to a printer; the program hangs and you risk losing everything in the computer.

Write a print screen function that checks the printer status routine to see whether the printer is there. If it is not there (no acknowledgment), not ready, out of paper, not selected, or time outed, then abort the screen dump, announce what error occurred and return to the calling program. The significance of the status bytes bits is shown in Table 10–1.

The time-out error can be misleading. It suggests that the printer is hung up and will never respond. In fact, a particularly long operation such as page eject can yield a time out even though everything is working. Thus, under normal circumstances, a time out may simply mean that you should try again.

10–3 [10.5]. The printer routines place a status byte in memory 0000:$500. If this byte is $ff, then the previous print screen operation was not completed successfully, and something is seriously wrong. If the byte is 0, the previous print screen is finished and another one can be initiated. A 1 indicates that a print screen is in progress, and a request for another one will be ignored.

Add another portion to your print screen routine that checks the status byte before trying to print another screen. If there was an error, exit with an error message. If the routine is ready, go through with the printer status check and print the next screen. If the printer is busy printing the last screen, wait for it to finish.

10–4 [10.5]. Using the get time interrupt write your own GetTime procedure. Pattern it after GetTime in Turbo 4/5. Your routine should read the system clock and convert the hours, minutes, seconds, and hundredths of a second into a real number that returns the current clock reading in hundredths of a second.

10–5 [10.5]. Write a Pascal program that outputs a string to the printer using an interrupt. Most printers have a line buffer that will not print anything until a CRLF is received. So send a CRLF when you have completed sending your string.

10–6 [10.5]. Write a Pascal routine that uses an interrupt to emulate the keypressed function. Actually, keypressed appears to use this interrupt.

10–7 [10.5]. What day of the week will January 17, 1999 be? Use the Get date, Set date MSDOS functions to find out. Get the current data and save it. Set the data to January 17, 1999 and then get the date. DOS function 2Ah returns the day of the week in AL. Then use Set date to restore the current date.

10–8 [10.5.3]. Determine the number of 1ch ticks per second on your computer.

10–9 [10.5.4]. Write a procedure that accepts a string and prints it out in all capital letters. Use repeated calls to MSDOS interrupt function 2 to print the characters. You may use normal string operations to tear the string apart and capitalize the characters.

10–10. The following routine generates a directory similar to that given by the dir command of DOS:

```
PROGRAM direct;   {mimics DOS dir command from Pascal}
USES Dos;

CONST Space = ' ';
VAR Search : SearchRec;
  DateTimeRec : DateTime;
  PointPos, Blanks, i : Integer;
  Tmp : STRING;

BEGIN
  FindFirst('c:*', 0 , Search);
```

```
                              {find all files DOS normally sees}
   WHILE DosError = 0 DO
   BEGIN
     WITH Search DO
       BEGIN
         Tmp := name;
         PointPos := pos('.', Tmp);{insert blanks/ align .s}
         Blanks := 9-PointPos;
         IF PointPos > 0 THEN
           FOR i := 1 TO Blanks DO
             Insert(Space, Tmp, PointPos);
         WITH DateTimeRec DO
          BEGIN
           UnpackTime(time, DateTimeRec); {get timeentry}
           WriteLn(Tmp:0, size:20-Length(Tmp), ' ', year,'/',
             month:2,'/',day:2,hour:4, ':',min:2,':',sec:2);
          END;
       END;
     FindNext(Search);      {check for another directory entry}
   END;
END.
```

This routine is designed to generate a date output that allows sorting of files by date, which cannot be done with the normal DOS SORT.

In your Turbo Pascal manual or text, determine how this routine works. FindFirst procedure finds the first match for the indicated drive, subdirectory, and mask. FindNext is then called repeatedly to find the remaining files that match.

Rewrite direct so that you can pass it the path and mask from the command line. Hand in your source listing and be prepared to demonstrate its use.

11

Assembly Language

11.1 INTRODUCTION

We turn to the much more complex topic of assembly language. There are simpler assembly languages than the 80X86 with which we have to work (e.g., Motorola 68000). Much of the complexity of the 80X86 is historical. Intel's earlier processor was the 8-bit 8080 that had a very irregular architecture and instruction set. There was, however, an enormous established base of programs. Intel's two choices when they developed a 16-bit microprocessor were to generate a clean, new instruction set and architecture and lose all existing software, or to make their new 16-bit processor instruction set more minicomputer-like but still have it understand the 8080 instructions.

From a business standpoint Intel selected the latter, and the original and fantastically successful IBM PC resulted. Most of the PC's early success was due to the wealth of immediately available software that resulted from the ease of changing 8080 programs to 8086 ones. From the programmer's standpoint, Intel's decision was less satisfactory. Intel forced a rich, complex 16-bit minicomputer instruction set onto an irregular 8-bit one. The result was a complex and very irregular instruction set for which, at least to the novice, it seems that there are few rules—only exceptions.

The complexity of the 80X86 instruction set prevents us from doing more than scratching the surface. We present a useful subset of instructions that permits carrying out the majority of operations, albeit frequently neither in the fastest nor simplest manner. We ignore many complex instructions such as the block ones as well as some simple ones. See the references for omitted topics.

Microsoft did supply a debugger, DEBUG, with earlier versions of DOS. As a piece of software thrown in, it was not bad. It is a line-oriented debugger much like their EDLIN is a line-oriented editor. On an arbitrary machine, it may be the only debugger available; therefore, we recommend that you browse through the DEBUG section of the DOS manual.

However, there are much more powerful screen-oriented debuggers available; we like SST$^+$ (Scroll System Trace Plus). For learning pure assembly language routines, this is a lean debugger with delightful characteristics. Alternatively, Borland markets a source level debugger, Turbo Debugger, that interfaces not only their assembly language but their higher level languages including Pascal 5. Its command structure has many elements in common with the integrated debugging environment (IDE) of Turbo Pascal 5. While it is much more cumbersome than SST$^+$, its convenient interface of assembler and Pascal along with its common syntax with the IDE makes it the debugger of choice for larger problems.

Describing a debugger here would interrupt the flow of our assembly language presentation, but it is absolutely essential that you use one while learning machine language. The only way to understand how these things work is to try them out as you go along. Thus, you should read your instructor's handout on your debugger and begin using it immediately. It is now up to you to play with this treacherous and powerful new toy called assembly language.

11.2 ASSEMBLY LANGUAGE NOMENCLATURE

The basic instruction set of the 80X86 consists of several different classes of instructions.

(1) Data movement or copying instructions.
(2) Arithmetic, comparison, and logical instructions.
(3) Program flow control instructions.

We subdivide these different instructions into sections. In the next chapter we discuss interfacing Pascal to assembly language. Before we get into the instructions, we specify some conventions and assembler directives.

Register Mnemonics. In assembly language the source and destination are explicitly spelled out using the two-character shorthand of Figure 10–1: AX, AH, AL, BX, BH, BL, CX, CH, CL, DX, DH, DL, DI, SI, BP, SP, SS, DS, and ES. When referring to a generic register, we use **register$_8$** and **register$_{16}$** to indicate 8- and 16-bit registers respectively. Where a register may be either 8 or 16 bit, we use **register$_{8,16}$**. When specifying an indirect register pointer, we use [memory register pointer].

Numeric Conventions. For an assembler, there are several acceptable radix for the number bases. The default number base is decimal. A number specified without any other indication is decimal. Hexadecimal, octal, and binary numbers have the suffix H, Q, or B added on respectively. Thus:

```
125    =   125 decimal ;   1111B  =   1111 binary
0667Q  =   667 octal    ;   0ffffH =   ffff hexadecimal
```

The assembler and the debuggers are case-insensitive. Therefore, 0FFFFH, 0ffFFh, and 0ffffh are equivalent. Numbers for the assembler, but not the debugger, must begin with a numeric digit. Thus, FFFFH is not acceptable, and must have a leading zero added to yield 0FFFFH. The reason for this is that assembler labels begin with letters and the assembler cannot tell from the context whether you mean a label or a number. The debugger, however, does not require the leading numeric digit, because it does not know anything about labels.

Unfortunately, the assemblers and most debuggers use different conventions. The debuggers assume that all numbers are hexadecimal, do not require a leading number, and do not accept a trailing letter to denote radix. Acceptable numbers for the debugger and their corresponding hex values are: 125 (125H), 0ffff (0FFFFH), and FFFF (0FFFFH). Numbers unacceptable to the debugger are 0667Q, 1111B, and 0ffffH because of the trailing radix.

Forgetting your software's default radix is a common programming error. For example, "127" is 127 decimal to the assembler and 127H to the debugger. Yet in both programs, 127 raises no syntactic flags, and the programs execute. However, in one case it runs and in the other it fails.

In the following discussion, we will nominally assume the assembler notation unless we are explicitly using the debugger, in which case we default to the debugger's implied hexadecimal notation.

Assembly Language Format. A typical assembly language statement is divided into four fields:

`Label    Operator        Operands        Comments`

Label usually starts in column 1 and is optional. It is generally used only when we need to access the current operations or data by a symbolic label rather than an absolute memory address. In keeping with the irregular character of 80X86 assembly language, labels on lines without directives or instructions and labels that precede instructions must be immediately followed by a ":" (e.g., Outputstring:); otherwise the colon is omitted. The colon is not part of the label. Do not worry, the assembler complains if you violate these rules.

Operator is either the mnemonic for a machine language instruction or an assembler directive, which might be used to allocate data storage or initialize a section of memory. For clarity Operator is usually indented.

Operands are sources or destinations of operations or instruction modifiers. They might be constants, registers or memory addresses. They can be symbolic labels.

Finally, the line ends with an optional comment. Comments are preceded by a ";". Everything to the right of the ";" is a comment. A ";" is also allowed in column 1 if we want to make an entire line a comment.

Names are symbolic representations of values. If the name references an instruction, it is called a **label**. If it represents data, it is called a **variable**. If it represents a constant, it is a **symbol**. A name may include the legal characters A-Z (case-insensitive), 0–9, ?, %, _, and $.

Valid names cannot begin with numbers or they might be confused with a number. Names can be any number of letters and are unique to 31 characters in most assemblers.

Valid names are Data_Acquisition_Routine, CheckDTStatus, Acquired_Data, CRLF, ScratchPad, loop1, and loop2. While acceptable, the last two are poor choices since they are not very descriptive and there will be many loops.

Allocating Data Areas, Initialization, and Constants. Assembler directives can set aside and initialize variables or constants. These are equates (EQU), define byte (DB), define word (DW), define double word (DD), define quad word (DQ), and define 10-byte word (DT).

EQU is essentially a way of declaring constants or defining a string that will be substituted later. It tells the assembler that everywhere it sees a specific name it should replace the name with the assigned value or string. For example:

```
CR      EQU     0dh
J       EQU     [BP+8]
MaxNumberPoints     EQU     512
NumBytes            EQU     2*NumWords+1
```

Thus, every place that CR appears in the program it is replaced with 0dh and Max-NumberPoints is replaced with 512. NumBytes is replaced with the computed value of 2*NumWords+1 where NumWords must be numerically defined earlier. Every occurrence of J as part of an assembly language statement is replaced with [BP+8]. We show the utility of this later. The common arithmetic operations of multiplication, division, addition, and subtraction are supported. The EQU statement must appear before the defined symbol is used or the assembler will give you an "undefined value" error.

DB, DW, DD, DQ, and DT allocate variable space and define constants. All forms are similar:

```
name    DB <exp> [,<exp>,<exp>...] ;byte
name    DW <exp> [,<exp>,<exp>...] ;word
name    DD <exp> [,<exp>,<exp>...] ;double word (long
                                   ;integer or real)
name    DQ <exp> [,<exp>,<exp>...] ;quad word (double
                                   ;precision real)
name    DT <exp> [,<exp>,<exp>...] ;ten byte (BCD real)
```

where name and the terms in [..] are optional and <exp> may be:

(1)   The character ? in parentheses to indicate allocation without concern for value.
(2)   The (?) preceded by an expression or a constant and dup to yield <exp> dup (?). This defines an uninitialized data block of the specified type that is exp long.
(3)   A simple constant or an expression that evaluates to an appropriate type.
(4)   The expression <exp> dup (<exp2>[,...]) produces a data block that is initialized with <exp2>.
(5)   An address expression (word and double word only).

These are more clearly understood by examples:

```
data     db  0ffh    ; initialize 1 byte to 0ffh with label data
data2    db  0,1,2,3 ; initialize 4 consecutive bytes to 0,1,2,3
messf    db  'System Failure',0 ; Define ASCII message at messf
                              ; with a 0 terminator byte (15
                              ; bytes total)
Conversions dw (?) ;Allocate 1 uninitialized word at Conversions
                   ;Remember inverted storage (low-then high)
Results dw 512 dup (?)      ; Set aside 512 uninitialized words
NumXpoints dw 100           ; Initialize to 100
TotalXandY dw 2*NumXpoints ; Initialize with arithmetic
X dq 100 dup 0.000          ; Initialize 512 double precision 0s
Y dd 100 dup 1e0            ; Initialize 512 single precision 1s
Z dd 100 dup 1              ; Initialize 512 long integer 1s
```

The last definitions require comment. A double or quad word can be more than one data type. For example, a 32-bit quantity can be a 32-bit integer or a 32-bit single precision floating point number. By using a decimal (e.g., 0.0) or integer notation (e.g., 1), it is clear to the assembler that a floating point number or integer initialization is implied.

11.3 MOVE OR COPY INSTRUCTIONS

Move (MOV) or Copy Instructions are the most important single class of instruction. The move (MOV) instruction is used for moving data between registers and between registers and memory. It is also used for initializing registers or memory. It has several basic forms. In assembly language, the instruction mnemonic usually explicitly tells you whether an 8- or a 16-bit operation is involved. The form of a MOV instruction is:

```
MOV destination, source
```

where the information in source is copied into the specified destination. The source and destination may be registers or memory. Alternatively, the source may be explicitly data, which is known as an immediate instruction since the data are immediately visible in the instruction. The next section shows different addressing modes.

The unnatural backward direction of data flow copies data from right to left. Getting this reversed is a common programming error. The odd nature of the instruction arises from the bit mapping of the machine language instructions, which made it easier for programmers to read and write programs in octal. The historical reason for this convention is gone but we still use it. As an alternative way of viewing the move, think of it as a Pascal assign statement with the "," replacing the ":=".

11.4 ADDRESSING MODES

The addressing mode of the instruction is the way in which the source and the destination are specified. This is probably the most confusing aspect of assembly language programming. There are several different ways of addressing data and we demonstrate each mode using the MOV instruction as the template. However, most arithmetic and logical instructions use the same addressing modes and formats. The addressing modes include register operands, immediate operands, direct addressing, and the indirect addressing modes. We list the different modes with examples below.

11.4.1 Immediate Mode

Immediate operands are explicitly spelled out in the instruction as a numeric quantity or a numeric symbol previously defined as a numeric quantity. Immediate operands are used to initialize registers. The immediate operand is copied into the specified register:

MOV register$_{8,16}$, data$_{8,16}$

```
MOV AX,0            ;Copy 0 into AX
MOV BH,0FFH         ;Copy 0FFH into BH
MOV DX,0FFFFH       ;Copy 0FFFFH into DX
MOV BP,BaseAddr     ;Copy value of BaseAddr into BP
MOV AL,CR           ;Copy value of CR into AL
```

where BaseAddr and CR must be previously defined numeric symbols.

An irritating 80X86 irregularity is that you cannot move immediate data into any of the segment registers. Thus, the following is illegal:

```
MOV ES, 4000H    ; illegal instruction
```

The desired result must be achieved indirectly with a two-stage move:

```
;Load es with 4000h
MOV ax, 4000H   ; load any free general purpose register
MOV es, ax      ; move the contents into the segment register
```

All symbols must have been previously defined with an EQU in the assignment.

11.4.2 Direct Modes

In direct addressing, the register or memory location specified contains the quantity to be acted on. This contrasts with the immediate mode in which the data are explicit or the indirect modes in which the indicated register contains a pointer to the data.

Register Operands. Register operands use a specific register for the source or destination. The easiest to understand is one in which both the source and destination are register operands. The basic form and examples are:

MOV register$_{8,16}$, register$_{8,16}$

```
MOV AX,BX      ;Copy BX contents into AX
MOV CL,AH      ;Copy AH contents into CL
```

The source and the destination sizes must match. A 16-bit quantity will not fit into an 8-bit register, and the software cannot tell whether you want to assign an 8-bit quantity to the upper half or the lower half of a 16-bit register. Thus, MOV ah,bx and MOV ax,bl are both illegal.

Memory Operands. Direct memory addressing explicitly spells out the address (i.e., memory location) of the data. The valid direct memory accesses with examples are:

MOV register$_{8,16}$, memory$_{8,16}$
MOV memory$_{8,16}$, register$_{8,16}$
MOV memory$_{8,16}$, data$_{8,16}$

```
MOV dx, [200H]        ;Copy contents of 200H,201H memory
                      ;to dx ;([200]--->dl and [201]--->dh)
MOV [200H], AH        ;Copy contents of AH into
                      ;memory location 200H
MOV [count],77        ;assign 77 to memory location
                      ;specified  by count
MOV BP, temp          ;copies the contents of memory
MOV BP, [temp]        ;location pointed at by temp into BP
```

The square brackets around a quantity refer to the data in the specified memory address rather than the data itself. The square brackets prevent the instruction from being confused with an immediate one (i.e., MOV dx, 200H or MOV dx, [200H]). Thus, the first instruction listed above assigns dx to the 16-bit data stored at memory location 200H and not the value 200H.

The use of symbol labels for memory locations is a minefield. With this format, you must have defined a memory location with that label. The normal way to do this would be the db, dw, dd, and dq directives with an associated label. The last two forms require special comment. Both copy the contents of the location specified by temp into the BP. With [temp], the square brackets make it clear that we are using a memory reference. However, the valid form without the "[..]" can be misleading. On reading this it is unclear whether we are using a memory reference or are loading immediate data temp into BP. It depends on how temp was previously defined. The assembler accepts the "[..]" notation and we strongly recommend that you conform to it.

11.4.3 Indirect Mode

Register Indirect Addressing. In indirect addressing, a register is used to point at the memory location containing the data. The 16-bit register, which may be BX, BP, SI, or DI, contains the offset (address) of the data in the appropriate segment. The format and examples are:

MOV [memory register pointer], register$_{8,16}$

MOV register$_{8,16}$, [memory register pointer]

```
MOV CL, [BX]              ;Copy the contents of the memory
                         ;location given by the contents of
                         ;BX into CL
MOV [SI], DX             ;Copy DX contents into the memory
                         ;locations given by SI and SI+1
                         ;   DL--->[SI]
                         ;   DH--->[SI+1]
```

Displacement and Index Modes. The instruction is even more powerful. The specified address can be formed by adding a constant to it (displacement or offset) and the contents of an index register, which can be BX or BP. Thus:

```
MOV CL, [BX+SI-3]    ;Copy the contents of the memory
                     ;location given by the contents of
                     ;memory location BX+SI-3 into CL
MOV [SI+indent], DX  ;Copy DX contents into the memory
                     ;locations given by SI+Indent
                     ;where indent is a defined constant
MOV [BP+2], CX       ;Copy CX into the memory location
                     ;pointed at by the contents of BP+2
MOV CL, [BP+DI-77H]  ;Copy the byte at the memory location
                     ;pointed at by the sum of BP, SI and
                     ;-77H into CL
MOV AX, [BP+SI]      ;Copy the word in memory location
                     ;given by sum of BP and SI into AX
                     ;[BP+SI]--->AL
                     ;[BP+SI+1]--->AH
MOV [BP+DI-6], DX    ;Copy DX contents into memory
                     ;locations starting at BP+DI-6
```

Since we need a 20-bit address, the actual address is made by combining an appropriate segment register and the specified register to form a memory pointer. Each form of register instruction has an assumed or default segment associated with it. The default segment registers are shown in Table 11–1. Later we show you how to override these default segment registers.

Table 11–1. Default Segment Registers

Indirect Pointer Register	Default Segment Register
BX	DS
BP	SS
SI, DI without a base register	DS
SI, DI with base register BX or BP	Base register BX (DS) or BP (SS)

Thus, any indirect accesses of data using BP employ the stack segment register to complete the 20-bit address. [BX] or [SI] or [DI] point into the data segment or use the DS register. [BP+SI] points into the stack segment since the BP is the base register.

You cannot combine BX and BP to form new addresses. Thus, MOV AX,[BX+BP+3] is illegal and is flagged as an error by the assembler. The problem is that BX forms its effective address with DS while BP uses SS. Thus, the assembler cannot tell which one you meant.

Also, another way of expressing these combinations of pointers and constants is:

```
[BX+DI-6] is equivalent to [BX][DI][-6]
```

Indeed, some debuggers accept only the second form.

11.4.4 Immediate Data Memory Modes

We can combine immediate data with either direct or indirect memory references. These have special problems of notation not present in the register modes.

Data to Memory (Direct). Examples of direct immediate include:

```
MOV [memory], data₈,₁₆
```

```
MOV [1000], Word 0FH        ;Move 000F
                            ;into memory 1000 and 1001
                            ; [1000]<---0F
                            ; [1001]<---00
MOV [result], Byte 0FDH     ;Move byte 0FDH into
MOV byte ptr [result], 0FDH ;byte at location result
MOV [result], word 0FDH     ;Move 16-bit 000FDH into
MOV word ptr [result], 0FDH ;word at location result
```

The complication is that memory can contain anything. Thus, the assembler is not sure whether you mean to move a byte or a word into memory. For example, you must tell the assembler that 0FH is a 16-bit quantity rather than an 8-bit one. There are two ways to do this. The reserved words WORD or BYTE before a constant tells the compiler to treat the following quantity as 16- or 8-bit quantities, respectively. Alternatively, you can use the reserved phrases **byte ptr** or **word ptr** before the memory reference to specify that we are loading 8- or 16-bit quantities respectively.

Data to Memory (Indirect). Similar indirect movements of immediate data are possible:

```
MOV [memory register pointer], data₈,₁₆
```

```
MOV  Byte PTR [BX], 7      ;Move 7 into memory
                          ; location pointed to
                          ; by [BX]
MOV WORD PTR [BP], 0FEH    ;  Move 00FEh into
MOV [BP], WORD 0FEH        ;    [BP] and [BP+1]
```

```
;     [BP]<---FE
;     [BP+1]<---00
```

Again, to avoid confusion we must use either WORD or BYTE (on the data) or WORD PTR or BYTE PTR in the pointer to remind the assembler whether you mean an 8- or a 16-bit datum.

11.4.5   Offset and Seg Pseudo Ops

A problem related to addressing is setting up a register to point to specific data. That is, you want to load a register with the address of a variable rather than the variable itself.   Suppose we have variable message1 and want to load BX with the address in order to use an indirect addressing mode to get at the data. We will be tempted to write:

```
MOV BX, message1   ;This does not work
```

This actually loads the 16-bit quantity at message1 into BX with no warning that anything is wrong; it is equivalent to MOV BX, [message1]. Indeed, this cannot work, because the 20-bit segment:offset address cannot fit into a 16-bit register. So we must specify whether we are talking about the segment or the offset of the variable message1. We use the **offset** or **seg** pseudo ops to break down the address into its component parts. The correct way to do the above example is:

```
MOV BX, offset message1 ; offset address of variable message
                        ; is moved into BX
```

Similarly, seg extracts the segment value of a variable.   Offset and seg in assembly language are identical to Turbo Pascal's Ofs and Seg when applied to a variable.

11.5   INTERRUPTS

Assembly language directly provides the software interrupts that we found so useful in the last chapter. The interrupts have the form:

```
INT n              ; where n is any valid interrupt number
```

Thus, the MSDOS call of Turbo Pascal is:

```
INT 21H            ; equivalent to MSDOS of Pascal
```

in which you would previously have loaded all the registers; usually this loading would be done with MOV instructions.   The following is an assembly language print screen routine:

```
PrintScreen EQU 5      ; define print screen interrupt

MOV AH, PrintScreen    ; set AH register as required
INT 21H                ; invoke interrupt
```

We have not dealt yet with the dirty little business of how to get to this routine or how the return process actually works. We cover calling machine language routines from a high-level language in the next chapter and the mechanism of subprogram calling later.

You will also encounter two other instructions concerning interrupts:

```
CLI ; clear interrupt flag: disable maskable interrupts
STI ; set interrupt flag: enable maskable interrupts
```

CLI disables the CPU acknowledgement of all hardware interrupts. For example, if you executed this instruction while running Async, no incoming characters would be recognized. However, the CPU will recognize the pending interrupt and service it should interrupts become enabled. STI enables interrupt recognition. In addition to maskable interrupts, which are affected by CLI and STI, there is a nonmaskable hardware interrupt. If activated this will always interrupt the CPU. Without very intimate knowledge of system architecture and software, do not play with the hardware interrupts.

11.6 FLAGS

Before going on to mathematical and logical operations, we reiterate the functions of the arithmetic and logical flags in the flag register.

Carry reflects carry from the high-order bit of arithmetic addition or a borrow status from a subtraction.

Zero reflects whether or not the result of the last operation was a zero. A zero result sets the flag to 1 and a nonzero result resets it to 0.

Overflow indicates an overflow in a signed binary operation.

Sign bit is the high-order bit following an arithmetic operation. Assuming signed arithmetic, a 0 status shows a positive result and a 1 shows a negative result.

Auxiliary Carry is a special bit used for BCD arithmetic.

Parity flag is 1 if the low order 8 bits of any data operation contains an even number of 1s; otherwise the flag is reset.

In practice, the two most important flags are the Carry and the Zero flags. The Zero flag is a regular source of confusion since a 1 implies a zero result and a 0 implies a non-zero result. Fortunately, most instructions that make decisions on the basis of the flags have assembly language mnemonics that minimize misinterpretation.

11.7 REGISTER INCREMENTATION AND DECREMENTATION

The increment (INC) and decrement (DEC) instructions increment or decrement 8- or 16-bit registers or memory:

INC/DEC register$_{8,16}$

```
INC   AX        ;Increment 16-bit register AX
DEC DL          ;Decrement 8-bit DL register
```

INC/DEC [memory]   ; direct

```
INC [Counter]          ; Increment Counter in memory
```

INC/DEC [register memory pointer]   ; indirect

```
INC [BX] WORD          ;Increment 16-bit value in
INC   WORD PTR [BX]     ;  [BX] and [BX+1]
DEC [BP+DI-3] BYTE      ;Decrement byte at location
DEC BYTE PTR [BP+DI-3] ;  BX+DI-3
```

DEC and INC affect all arithmetic flags **except the Carry**. This seems odd until we see how INC and DEC are used in loop control for loops that contain arithmetic operations that affect the carry. If the INC or DEC in the loop control affect the carry, calculations become hopelessly scrambled.

11.8 LOOP INSTRUCTION

The LOOP instruction implements a primitive FOR NEXT capability. The form is:

```
LOOP    destination
```

Each time the LOOP instruction is encountered, the CX register is decremented. No flags are affected. If, after the decrementation, the CX ≠ 0, the program branches to the instruction destination; otherwise it executes the instruction after the LOOP one. The following program fragment can be used as a delay:

```
delay:
    MOV   CX, 100h
    LOOP  delay
```

This program executes the loop instruction 100H times before falling through.

The loop instruction affects no flags. Chaos would reign if our loop control affected the flags changed by the statements in the loop.

The maximum range for the loop is −127 (i.e., delay in the previous case). The loop jump is made relative to its current location and the range of the jump is limited by a 2s complement 1-byte integer. This is a **relative jump**. While this range may seem restrictive, the vast majority of loops are relatively short and this range is rarely a problem.

11.9 ARITHMETIC AND LOGICAL OPERATIONS

There are many arithmetic and logical operations in the 80X86 instruction set. We restrict ourselves to a subset:

```
ADC destination, source     ; Add with carry
ADD destination, source     ; Add
CMP destination, source     ; Compare
SBB destination, source     ; Subtract with borrow
SUB destination, source     ; Subtract
AND destination, source     ; Logical AND
OR  destination, source     ; Logical OR
XOR destination, source     ; Exclusive OR
NOT operand                 ; Complement operand
CLC                         ; Clear the carry flag
```

We omit the multiply and divide instructions, the shift operations, and the block instructions. The add and subtract instructions are useful arithmetic operations. The AND and OR instructions are useful for bit testing. The NOT is useful for bitwise complementing, and the carry clear instruction is useful for clearing the carry before beginning sequences of operations.

As a representative instruction of all of the two operand instructions, we will use the add instruction, ADD. This has several basic forms:

(1) Immediately, where the data are explicitly spelled out in the instruction.
(2) Register to register.
(3) Direct memory referenced, where the address is explicitly spelled out.
(4) Indirect, where a register's contents points to the data.
(5) Immediate to memory.
(6) Byte or word data, where the two are differentiated by BYTE or WORD on the data or BYTE PTR or WORD PTR on the pointer.

For all of these forms, all arithmetic and logical flags are affected. All of the standard addressing modes and 8- or 16-bit operations are supported. As with the MOV instructions, all logical and arithmetic operations use the backwards notation. Thus:

```
ADD   CX, SI
```

adds the contents of the SI register to the CX register; the sum is in the CX register and the SI register is unchanged. Other examples of arithmetic and logical operations are:

```
ADD    AL,        33
ADD    [result],  AL
ADD    [BP+SI],   DX
ADD    WORD PTR   [DI],  10B
```

The add with carry is a slight variation on the ADD. The source is added to the destination and the carry bit is added on. The carry bit and the other arithmetic-logical flags are all set to accommodate the result of the composite operation.

The ADD and ADC are used to handle the addition of multiple word numbers. For example, suppose we had two 32-bit numbers, one stored at dword1 and the other at dword2, and we wanted to sum these to give a 32-bit sum at result. We assume that the least significant bytes are stored first. An awkward program is:

```
dosseg
.model tiny

; ADDDW  Simple minded version with direct addressing
; Add double words at dword1 to dword2. Put sum at result

.data
dword1 dw 3333h,4444h         ; data initialization
dword2 dw 4444h,6666h
result dw 2 dup(?)

.stack 100h

.code
adddw  proc near
    mov ax,@data
    mov ds,ax                 ; point ds at data region
    clc                       ; clear carry
    mov ax,[dword1]           ; fetch first word of dword1
    adc ax,[dword2]           ; add first words together
    mov [result],ax           ; store first word result
    mov ax,[dword1+2]         ; fetch second word of dword1
    adc ax,[dword2+2]         ; add second word of dword2
    mov [result+2],ax         ; store second word in result

    mov ah,4ch                ; terminate program
    int 21h                   ;
adddw endp

end adddw
```

Study this program closely. The ADC is necessary to propagate a carry from the first word addition to the second. The direct addressing uses symbolic variable names. We could have used a simple add for the first addition; however, we are anticipating a loop version of the program that uses a single adc instruction.

ADDDW4 below is a much more powerful program using indirect addressing. We use BX to point at the first argument, SI at the second argument, and DI at the result. While appearing to be more complex, it is much more versatile. We use a loop statement to repeat the calculation for each word. Further, note that we have set up the number of words as a variable, which we can retrieve with mov cx, [numberwords]:

```
; ADDDW4  Improved version of ADDDW by using a loop
; supplies word length of data to be added with data

dosseg
.model small
.stack 100h

.data
   numberwords dw 2
   dword1 dw 4321h,8765h
   dword2 dw 2222h,3333h
   dresult  dw 2 dup (0)

.code
adddw4 proc near
  mov ax,@data               ;set up data segment
  mov ds,ax
  clc                        ; clear carry
  mov bx,offset dword1       ; initialize indirect pointer to
word1
  mov si,offset dword2       ;initialize si to point to word2
  mov di,offset dresult      ;initialize di to point to result
  mov cx, numberwords        ;cx =  number of words to add

addone:
  mov ax,[bx]                ; fetch first word of first argument
  mov dx,[si]                ; fetch first word of second argument
  adc ax,dx                  ; add first words together
  mov [di],ax                ; store first word dresult
  inc bx                     ; bump memory pointer to word1
  inc bx                     ; bump twice because of word length
  inc si                     ; bump memory pointer to dword2
  inc si
  inc di                     ; bump memory pointer to dresult
  inc di
  loop addone
  mov ah,4ch
  int 21h                    ; terminate program normally

adddw4 endp
end
```

As shown you could add any number of words up to a maximum of a third of 64K bytes merely by changing numberwords and putting in more data.

Before we get into conditional jumps, we introduce some invaluable comparison instructions. These have the standard form:

```
    CMP   register,  data
    CMP   register,  register
```

```
CMP    register,    memory
CMP    memory,      register
CMP    memory,      data
```

where all the normal addressing modes are used.

A CMP sets the flags by in effect subtracting the second value from the first, then restoring the first argument but leaving the flags. Thus, you have the advantage of determining the relative size of two quantities without changing either.

11.10 JUMPS

Normally program flow is straight through memory; jumps and conditional jumps are used to modify program flow. The easiest to understand is the absolute jump:

```
JMP address
```

This causes an unconditional branch to the specified address; usually address is a label. This may be forward or backward. It may be inter- or intrasegment. An intersegment jump requires that CS be changed to reach the destination. An intrasegment jump keeps CS fixed and only changes IP. While intra- and intersegment jumps look the same in assembly language, they are different instructions. Normally, the assembler takes care of determining which is required and selecting the right instruction.

The conditional jumps act on the current state of the flags. In good programming, the flags are invariably set as the result of an arithmetic, logical, or comparison operation. The conditional jumps are given in Table 11–2. The slash indicates that there are two acceptable abbreviations. For example, JA address and JNBE address are equivalent.

Above and below apply to unsigned binary numbers, while greater than or less than refer to signed 2s complement numbers. More than one mnemonic can stand for the same instruction. Thus, "not below" or "above or equal" are equivalent. While less obvious, "equal" and "zero" are the same. If the flags are set by a comparison instruction, then the zero flag will be set if the subtraction results in zero, which only occurs if the two values being compared are equal. We generally use only a small subset of these instructions.

As an example of the use of a conditional jump, we could have replaced the LOOP instruction of the previous example with:

```
NEXTPASS:      DEC   CX
               JNZ   NEXTPASS
```

However, there are two good reasons for using the LOOP instruction, if the CX register is free. Decrementation and jump is slower, takes more bytes, and affects more flags.

Another thing that the novice should notice is that a comparison instruction is frequently not required. Consider the two following code segments:

Table 11–2. Conditional Jumps	
JA/JNBE address	Jump if above/ if not below or equal
JNB/JAE address	Jump if not below/ if above or equal
JNC address	Jump on no carry
JB/JNAE address	Jump if below/ if not above or equal
JBE/JNA address	Jump if below or equal/ if not above
JCXZ address	Jump if CX=0
JE/JZ address	Jump if equal/ if zero
JG/JNLE address	Jump if greater/ if not less or equal
JGE/JNL address	Jump if greater than or equal/ if not less than
JL/JNGE address	Jump if less/ if not greater than or equal
JNP/JPO address	Jump on no parity/ if parity odd
JNS address	Jump on not sign
JO address	Jump if overflow
JP/JPE address	Jump if parity/ if parity even
JS address	Jump if sign status one
JNE/JNZ address	Jump if not equal/ if not zero

Segment 1:
```
    sub ax,bx
    cmp ax,0                ; Compare result with 0
    je resultzero
```

Segment 2:
```
    sub ax,bx               ; Set flags
    jz ResultZero
```

Both segments jump to ResultZero if the contents of ax and bx are equal. In the first case the code is perhaps more readable, although experienced assembly language programmers might disagree. The second uses no CMP, is more compact, and is faster.

Another delightful limitation of the 80X86 conditional jumps is that their range is limited to a 2s complement byte from the next instruction, which is about 128 bytes on either side of the instruction. This is not usually a burden since most of the time the range of a conditional jump is short. If the range is too great the assembler flags the error with a destination out of range error.

When you have a destination out of range you use an inverted construction. Consider the following, which goes to NOTZERO if a not zero test is true:

```
; If not zero go to NOTZERO
    jz  afternotzero
    jmp NOTZERO
afternotzero:
```

If the test is zero, then the code skips over the absolute jump to NOTZERO; otherwise it executes the jump to NOTZERO. Since a jump can be to anywhere in the 1M address space, this construction allows a conditional jump to anywhere.

11.11 ANATOMY OF AN ASSEMBLY LANGUAGE PROGRAM

Before going on to more instructions, we show you how an assembly language program is structured. For use of the assembler, consult Appendix A. Programs for the assembler have to obey certain rules. As the assembler formats can be very complex, we only give you templates on which to pattern your own routines. For further details, consult the references. Below is a template of a simple routine for generating an EXE file. It contains a main body and two subroutines:

```
    dosseg              ; Tell assembler how to set up pieces
.model tiny             ; Tell assembler what memory model to use

.stack 100h             ; Set up a return stack for EXE file

.data
    .......data here

; set up the program
.code

MainProg proc near      ; Indicate start of procedure mainprogram
                        ; This also starts program

        mov ax,@data    ; Point ds at data segment
        mov ds,ax       ; Note indirect initialization of ds


        .......program goes here


Routine1 proc near    ; beginning of Routine1
        .......Routine1 code here
        ret             ; Generally a return here
Routine1 endp           ; Ends procedure Routine1


Routine2 proc near    ; beginning of Routine2
        .......Routine2 code here
        ret             ; Generally a return a subroutine
Routine2 endp           ; Ends procedure Routine2
```

```
End MainProg          ; Ends entire block of program MainProg
```

The organization here is somewhat cryptic, but sufficiently stylized to use easily. Not all features can be used in a single program. DosSeg tells the assembler to set up a specific segmentation order in the final program—an issue which need not concern you.

The .data directive is equivalent to the var, type, const declaration portion of a Pascal program. You tell the assembler how much data space to reserve for constants and variables, what their names are, and, where appropriate, what their initialization is.

The .code directive is equivalent to telling the assembler that we are entering the program portion of the program. This includes the main program and ancillary routines.

The .model directive tells the assembler how you want to organize the different data and code segments, or which higher-level language will be used with the assembly language routine; more of this later. For many stand-alone programs we can use "tiny" or "small." Tiny allows one data and code segment that overlap in memory (i.e., code plus data must be less than 64K). Small allows one code and one data segment, each of which must be no more than 64K. Later we show directives for interfacing to Pascal.

The @data is the segment address of the data when the assembled program is loaded into memory. The mov ax,@data coupled with mov ds,ax sets the data segment at run time to point at the data. The need for the double mov is a consequence of the absence of a direct way to load segment registers with constants. Failure to do this in a stand alone program leaves the data segment pointing at some random location with cryptic side effects.

The End MainProg is equivalent to Pascal's END. construction. However, in contrast to Pascal, it has a name associated with it. For stand-alone EXE programs, this name is the procedure that will be executed initially when the program is run. Generally, this will be your first routine, but it is not essential.

Unless you use the simpler directives given later, each procedure including the main program MainProg must have a beginning and an end, which are supplied by the paired constructions:

```
name proc near (far)          ; start of name
name endp                     ; end of name
```

The near or far directive tells the assembler what type of call will be used to reach the program, and only one type can be used at a time. If this directive is omitted, the assembler will make its own decision.

These two directives are analogous to the "BEGIN {main}" and "END. {main}" of a Pascal program. In this template, we assumed that all procedures were lumped into the main.

The .stack directive tells the assembler how much stack space to set up for data storage and for return information in subroutine calls. This is generally required only for EXE files. For anything that we write here, 100H bytes is more than enough. For interfacing assembly language to other languages, .stack is not required as the high-level language manages the stack.

For simple programs, there is an even more compact format:

```
dosseg                      ; Tell assembler how to set up pieces
.model tiny                 ; Tell assembler what memory model to use

.stack 100h                 ; Set up a return stack for EXE file

.data
    .......data here

; set up the program
.code

mainprog:                   ; Indicate start of procedure mainprogram
                            ; This also starts program

        mov ax,@data        ; Point ds at data segment
        mov ds,ax           ; Note indirect initialization of ds

    .......program and any subroutines go here

Routine1:                   ; Beginning of subroutine Routine1
    .......Routine1 code here
        ret                 ; Return here

Routine2:                   : Beginning of Routine2
    .......Routine2 code here
        ret                 ; Return from Routine2

    End                     ; Ends entire block of program MainProg
```

In this case note that the entire body of the code portion of the program is bracketed by MainProg: and End statements. Two subroutines are shown.

11.12 INPUT AND OUTPUT

Port input and output is performed with IN and OUT:

```
IN ac₈,₁₆, port#   ; Input data from port# to accumulator
OUT port#, ac₈,₁₆  ; Output data in accumulator to port#
IN, ac₈,₁₆, DX     ; Input data from port addressed in DX
OUT DX, ac₈,₁₆     ; Output data to port addressed in DX
```

The first two forms are similar to direct addressing while the second two are indirect. Port# is a byte that limits this form to port 0 to 255. The second form is essential to be able to write ROMable code in which we can change I/O addresses in response to changes in the need of the system.

The next program, Ramp, is an assembly language linear ramp ADC routine. We assume that you are using an 8255A driving an 8-bit DAC via port A. The comparator input is bit 0 of port B. The base address of the 8255 is 300h. We first show a Pascal version:

```
PROGRAM Ramp;                          {Linear Ramp 8-bit ADC routine }

VAR
  Val, Flag : Byte;
BEGIN
  Port[$303] := $8b;                   { Set port A for output test byte}
  REPEAT
    Val := $ff;                        { Initialize counter }
    REPEAT                             { Inner increment-test loop }
     Val := Val+1;                     { Increment test byte }
     Port[$300] := Val;                { and output to DAC }
     Flag := (1 AND Port[$301]);{Test comparator B for too big}
    UNTIL Flag = 0;                    { Repeat until too big }
  UNTIL False;                         { Convert forever }
END.
```

An identical assembly language version would be:

```
; TADC
; 8-bit linear ramp ADC routine
dosseg
.model tiny
.stack 100h
.code
TADC proc near
     mov dx,303h          ;initialize 8255 at base 300h
     mov al,8bh           ;with A input B output
     out dx,al
Init:
     mov bx,0             ;initialize bx
AddOne:
     mov al,bl            ;output current text value in bl
     mov dx,300h
     out dx,al
     inc bl               ;increment test value
     mov dx,301h          ;input B comparator port
     in al,dx
     and al,1             ;test lsb
     jnz AddOne           ;if not zero need bigger value
     jmp Init             ;done—do another one
endp TADC
end
```

This program is stuck in an infinite loop and the only way to break out is with Ctrl-Alt-Delete. The worst case conversion time for the Pascal routine is 5 ms and for the TADC it is 3 ms, which is a significant but not impressive enhancement.

Significant improvements in performance can be realized by fine tuning ADC. Fine tuning is common for people who had to resort to assembly language in the first place. The biggest delays come from the need to keep reloading dx with immediate addresses, which is inherently slow. The following routine reduces this overhead by doing all port address calculations in CPU registers:

```
; TADC1 tasm version of TADC.
; All memory references are eliminated; Only CPU registers used
dosseg
.model tiny
.stack 100h
.code
TADC1 proc near
      mov dx,303h         ;initialize 8255 at base 300h
      mov al,8bh
      out dx,al
      mov dx,301h         ; set up dx for I/O
      mov cl,1            ; comparator mask in cl
Init:
      xor bl,bl           ; initialize bl with 0
AddOne:
      mov al,bl
      dec dx              ; dx=300 (port A)
      out dx,al
      inc bl
      inc dx              ; dx=301  Point at port B status
      in al,dx            ; get comparator status
      and al,cl           ; test bit 0 for done
      jnz AddOne          ; repeat if not done
      jmp Init
endp TADC1
end
```

These simple changes increase the speed to 2.3 ms per conversion in the worst case. This is roughly 25 percent faster than before. Note the use of the faster xor bl,bl to initialize bl to 0 rather than the mov bl,0 of the previous example.

11.13 SPECIAL MEMORY INSTRUCTIONS

Frequently, you want to load both a segment register and a general purpose register with a two word address in memory. LES and LDS load either the ES or DS segment registers and a general purpose register from memory using a single instruction. They are used for pulling parameters from the stack after calling an assembly language routine from Pascal:

```
LES reg, mem        ; load es and reg from memory
LDS reg, mem        ; load ds and reg from memory
```

These instructions load the contents of the specified memory word into the specified register and then load the contents of the memory word following the first word into the ES or DS registers respectively. For example, if the data section of memory looks like:

```
ds: 300        1A
ds: 301        1B
ds: 302        1C
ds: 303        1D
```

Then the following instruction:

```
LES  BP, ds:[300]
```

yields:

```
BP = 1B1A
ES = 1D1C
```

We show examples of this in the next chapter when we pluck parameters passed to an assembly language routine called from Pascal.

11.14 SUBROUTINE CALLS AND RETURNS

The key to a subroutine call (including software interrupts) is that the calling portion of the program must leave information somewhere so that when the subroutine is finished, the program can resume where it was interrupted. The place where this information is left is called the stack. It is a scratchpad portion of memory where return addresses are pushed. A subroutine merely pops these addresses into the IP to return from a subroutine call.

The stack works in conjunction with the stack pointer register (SP). One first initializes the SP to point to a region of free memory—usually at the top of the free memory. The reason becomes clear when we see how it works.

The assembly language name for a subroutine call is:

```
CALL address
```

CALLs can be either NEAR (intrasegment) or FAR (intersegment). We only worry about NEAR calls for the moment.

A CALL transfers program control to a specified address after saving the return address on the stack. The return address is the instruction immediately after the CALL. The saving is done as follows:

(1) Decrement the stack pointer by 2.
(2) Move or write the return address to the location pointed at by the modified stack pointer. Use the standard of the low byte first, then the high byte.

For example, consider the stack state for the CALL 1000 instruction in the following code segment:

```
                  CALL   1000
    0110          next instruction
```

The stack state before and after the call are:

```
                    Before CALL                    After CALL
                    ───────────                    ──────────
                    FFFD XXXX                       10  ←  SP_final=FFFD
                    FFFE XXXX                       01
    SP_in=FFFF  →   FFFF XXXX                       XXXX
```

where SP is the stack pointer value.

After the execution of the subprogram, the return address is used to return control to the instruction at 0110. This is done by the RET instruction. The return:

(1) Reads the return address off the stack.
(2) Increments the stack pointer by 2.
(3) Loads the return address into the program counter.

After a RET in our subroutine, our stack looks like:

```
                    FFFD      10
                    FFFE      01
    SP=FFFF    →    FFFF      XXXX
```

Notice that the RET address is not removed from the stack; that takes time and is unnecessary. We are simply no longer pointing at it with the stack pointer.

What happens if we have nested subroutine CALLS? Consider the following main program with two subroutines:

```
            A                1000                     2000
 0110   CALL 1000              .   B                    .  C
 0113       E                      CALL 2000               RET
                             1020   D
                                    .
                                   RET
```

At the following points A-E the SP and the stack memory look like:

Location:	A	B	C	D	E
Memory	FFFF	FFFD	FFFB	FFFD	FFFF

	A	B	C	D	E
FFFA	XXXX	XXXX	XXXX	XXXX	XXXX
FFFB	XXXX	XXXX	→ 20	20	20
FFFC	XXXX	XXXX	10	10	10
FFFD	XXXX	→ 13	13	→ 13	13
FFFE	XXXX	01	01	01	01
FFFF	→ XXXX	XXXX	XXXX	XXXX	→ XXXX

where Xs indicate uninitialized values and the → indicates the memory location pointed at by the stack pointer. After the call, the SP points at the low byte of the return address. The stack can be built up to any level of returns as long as you have left enough stack memory. In actuality, SP_0 is set to 0. Why?

There is also an intersegment or FAR CALL:

```
CALL  segment:address  ; true form
CALL  OutputStr        ; common usage with symbolic
                       ; destination
```

The formal form gives a destination complete with segment and offset. Generally, the symbolic labels are used. This instruction allows a call to a routine anywhere in the 1M-byte address space. This instruction pushes 4 bytes onto the stack: the CS and then the offset address of the return. This is necessary so that the CPU can find its way back.

Differences Between an INT and a Far CALL. INT is a special case of the CALL instruction. It differs in two important points. First, the location of the subroutine is the interrupt vector rather than an address in the CALL. Second, unlike a normal subroutine CALL, INT automatically pushes the flag register onto the stack followed by the 20-bit return address. A special interrupt return, IRET, pops the return address and then restores the flag register by poppng it off. A normal RET would leave the flag word on the stack and fail to restore the flag register. For this reason RETs must be used with CALLs and IRETs with INTs.

11.14.1 PUSH and POP—Using the Stack as a Scratchpad

In addition to handling the bookkeeping associated with subroutines, the stack is used as a general scratchpad region. While at first you feel that you have too many registers, you quickly find that there are not enough for serious programming. Alternatively, you might also find that you have arrived at a point where you need a specific register (e.g., the ax for port output), but you have something critical in that register. The 80X86 has two stack management operations, PUSH and POP, that allow you to use the stack as a general purpose scratchpad. PUSH and POP work with registers and memory. These have the form:

```
PUSH register  ; copy register onto the top of the stack
```

```
POP register      ; read top of stack into register
PUSHF             ; push the flag register
POPF              ; pop the flag register
PUSH indirect pointer   ; copy memory location pointed at
                        ; by register onto stack
POP indirect pointer    ; copy top of stack into memory
                        ; location pointed at by register
```

A PUSH copies the contents of a register onto the stack and decrements the stack pointer by two so that it points at the next free stack word. A POP reads the last entry off the stack and copies it into the specified register; the stack pointer is incremented to point to the next entry on the stack. Note that we can also use the powerful indirect addressing modes for moving data between memory and the stack. PUSH and POP only work with words. Note the special notation used with the flag register.

There is some confusion in nomenclature. The top of the stack is the latest entry, which is the lowest occupied memory location. The stack actually works much like one of those automatic plate dispensers in cafeterias. The dishes are set onto the spring-loaded holder and sink into the dispenser. The first one on is the deepest and least accessible. This is a so called first-in-last-out stack (FILO). Later we show ways to reach in and read items from anywhere on the stack.

To understand scratchpad use of the stack, suppose that we wanted to output 0ffh to port 3fh, but all registers contained important data. The following solves the problem:

```
push ax          ; save ax on stack
mov al,0ffh      ; load ax with output byte
out 3fh,al       ; output al register
pop ax           ; restore ax
```

Another common problem might be saving and restoring all the accumulator registers. The following code does this:

```
;save registers
    push ax
    push bx
    push cx
    push dx
 { .....your code here  }
;restore registers
    pop dx
    pop cx
    pop bx
    pop ax
```

The order is critical. The FILO nature means that if the last item PUSHed was the dx, then the first POPed off should be into the dx register.

Another use of PUSH and POP is exchanging registers. Suppose that we wanted to exchange the di and si registers. The following code solves this problem:

```
;switch di and si register
    push di    ; push di on first
    push si    ; push si (si now on top of stack)
    pop di     ; pop last item (si) into di
    pop si     ; pop next (di) into si
```

Since it is a FILO stack, taking data off in the same order it was put on has the effect of exchanging two registers.

Caveats. There are several common errors. The first is POPing data off in the wrong order. Examine closely the register save-restore and the register switch routines above. The second error is PUSHing items and not POPing the same number of items off. This causes the stack pointer to fail to be restored to its original value after your routine. Suppose, for example, you PUSHed five items but POPed only four in a routine. This leaves one extra item on the stack. If this routine was used 1000 times, the stack would grow 1000 words toward lower memory. Eventually, it is likely to collide with your program, which grows upward, or some other critical piece of information.

Mixing subroutine calls and PUSHs and POPs complicates things; you have the return addresses and data on the stack. The following disaster is common:

```
; A subroutine that blows up
; you are in a subroutine here
    ....
    push ax
    out 3f,al
    ret
```

DISASTER! You saved ax, which is good. However, you have failed to POP it off. When you return, you POP the top item off the stack, which should be the return address. It is not. It is the contents of the ax register. So your subroutine returns to the value of the ax register, and your program runs wild.

Stack errors can lead to inexplicable bugs. Depending on how many items are added, when they are added, and how far the stack can grow before it clobbers something critical, a program can fail immediately, after several runs, or in a totally random fashion. Such strange behavior in assembly language is a red flag that suggests that you carefully check to see that your stack is under control.

11.14.2 Segment Overrides

Each indirect addressing instruction has a default segment register to complete the 20-bit address. There are times, however, when you will want to point at data with other than the default extension. A segment override can be used to access data pointed at by any of the segment registers. For example:

```
    es:[bp]      ;points to data pointed at by extra segment
             ;    and base pointers
```

```
cs:[bx]        ;gets data from the code segment using
               ;    the bx register
```

We use this trick later to fetch data from memory when we interface assembly language with Pascal. The data are frequently not in the proper segment for the instructions that you want to use. Using a segment override takes time. Therefore, if you want the fastest code, select indirect register pointers that do not require an override.

Experiment 11–1 and 11–2. You learn to use Borland's Turbo Assembler.

11.15 REFERENCES

Lafore (1984) gives an excellent low-level introduction to 8086 assembly language and DOS calls with a very nice integration of the use of DEBUG in the learning process. Lemone and Yeung give readable, but more detailed, discussions of the full 8086 instruction set. Swan's book is excellent and directly covers Borland's TASM and debugger. Rector and Alexy give a good overview of the 8086.

Problems

The following problems should be written using Borland's TASM or Microsoft's MASM. Turn in assembled listings of your program (i.e., the .LST files). Indicate whether it worked and, if not, what it did. Be prepared to demonstrate correct operations using the debugger.

11–1. Write an assembly language program that takes a string of characters and prints it to the screen. However, remove all non-letter characters (including spaces) before printing. Use a DOS interrupt to print the characters. The character string should be stored in the data segment. The length of the string is held in the first byte (i.e., a 10-byte string takes up 11 bytes with the first one being 10d).

11–2. Modify Problem 11–1 so that it prints all characters in your string but capitalizes all letters that immediately follow a space character. Thus, "this is a string3 3t" becomes "this Is A String3 3t". This is a significantly more challenging problem.

11–3. Modify 11–1 to remove all letter characters before printing.

11–4. Write an assembly language program that reads a character from the keyboard and outputs the character ten times to the video display. Begin and end your output with a CRLF sequence.

11–5. Write an assembly language program that writes the lower case alphabet to the video in inverse order and omits every other character (i.e., z, x, v, . . . b). Begin and terminate your output with a CRLF sequence.

11–6. Write an assembly language routine that repetitively inputs data from ADC channel 0 of the DT2800 and promptly outputs it to DAC0. Do this as fast as possible. For maximum speed do not have provisions for breaking out of the program; you will have to reboot. Go back and carefully review the operation of the DT2800 board. How does the speed of the routine compare with the analogous Pascal program using the DTUtil Unit? This program is a straightforward exercise in input/output instructions with logical bit testing.

11–7. Rewrite the Pascal servo routines for analog-to-digital conversion: (A) Tracking ADC. (B) Successive approximation. Compare the speeds with your Pascal routines.

The successive approximation program requires shifting; the 80X86 has a wealth of shifting and rotating instructions including 2s complement division or multiplication by 2, and 8- and 9-bit circular rotations. We discuss only the simple 8-bit circular rotation needed here:

```
ROR register/memory   ; rotate word or byte right one bit
ROL register/memory   ; rotate word or byte left one bit
```

These are circular shifts. For example, a ROR of a byte shifts bit 7 to bit 6, bit 6 to bit 5, . . ., bit 1 to bit 0, and bit 0 to bit 7. Bit 0 is also copied into the carry flag. A ROL moves everything to the left one bit with bit 7 shifting to bit 0 and into the carry flag. Thus:

```
mov ax, 128
rol ax
mov bl, 1
ror bl
```

leaves 256 in ax and 256 in bl. The ror bl sets the carry flag.

12

Coupling Pascal
and Assembly Language

12.1 INTRODUCTION

While we now have a good handle on writing Pascal programs and assembly language routines, we lack the machinery for marrying Pascal and assembly language and for passing information between the two. We now eliminate this deficiency.

Turbo Pascal provides two mechanisms for incorporating machine language routines. The most primitive is inline machine code in which you must write out the machine language program as a string of hexadecimal digits. This is a throwback to the bad old days of programming with octal (not symbolic) debuggers. However, it does work and you see it frequently, although we do not recommend it for more than the simplest applications. It does allow accessing and modifying variables; it is relatively straightforward; and there are tools to ease the tedium of development.

The most powerful way uses assembly language .ASM files that are assembled to .OBJ files and linked directly into the run time machine code by the compiler. A new directive EXTERNAL is used. For major machine language program development this is the most reasonable approach. Parameter passing is the heart of interfacing Pascal and machine code, and we devote some time to the topic. As an added benefit, understanding parameter passing provides considerable insight into the operation of high-level languages.

The format for linking an assembly language program to Pascal is shown below:

```
PROCEDURE AsmProc  (parameter list); external;
  {$L asmproc.obj}

FUNCTION AsmFunc  (parameter list); external;
  {$L asmfunc.obj}
```

where *parameter list* represents any normal Pascal parameter list with the necessary type definitions. The asmproc.obj and asmfunc.obj are assembled assembly language routines. The {$L } compiler directive instructs the compiler to link the assembled .obj files into the completed code. The .obj extension is optional, but it must match the file name that, in turn, must be an assembled function or procedure.

One of several formats for a suitable assembly language routine is:

```
CODE SEGMENT BYTE PUBLIC
asmproc proc near
    public asmproc
    ....
asmproc endp

asmfunc    proc far
    public asmfunc
    ...
asmfunc endp
code ends
```

Public tells the assembler to make the labels asmproc and asmfunc externally visible for use by other routines. Note that the procedure is defined as a near procedure and the function as a far one. This means that they must be called by near and far calls, respectively. Failure to do this invariably crashes the system. There are two ways to specify whether calls from Pascal are near or far. You can set the option in the compiler Options to force far call. Alternatively you can use the directives:

```
  {$F+}          {turn far calls on}
  {$F-}          {turn far calls off}
```

to mix and match near and far calls. A common error is to have the compiler set wrong for the types of calls used.

12.2 SHARING INFORMATION WITH PASCAL (PUBLIC/EXTRN)

The assembler PUBLIC directive makes labels declared in an assembly language routine visible to Turbo Pascal. Thus, if you plan to use an assembly language routine in Turbo, you must declare its name public in the assembly language module.

Every PUBLIC label must have a corresponding procedure or function declaration in the Turbo Pascal program. Failure to do this results in a compiler error.

Assembly language can access any Pascal function, procedure, variable, or typed constant declared in the outermost level of a program or Unit to which it is linked. Pascal labels and constants are not visible to assembly language. The variable must be specified as EXTRN in the assembly language so that the assembler knows to look for them elsewhere rather than in the current assembly language code. Suppose our Pascal program has the following variables:

```
a : byte;          b : word;          c : shortint;
d : integer;       e : longint        f : single;
g : double;        h : real;          i : comp;
j : pointer;       k : extended;
```

then the following EXTRN declarations in the assembly language module makes them visible to the assembly language program:

```
EXTRN a : byte  ; { 1 byte  }
EXTRN b : word  ; { 2 byte  }
EXTRN c : byte  ; { 1 byte  }
EXTRN d : word  ; { 2 byte  }
EXTRN e : dword ; { 4 byte  }
EXTRN f : dword ; { 4 byte  }
EXTRN g : qword ; { 8 byte  }
EXTRN h : qword ; { 8 byte  }
EXTRN i : qword ; { 8 byte  }
EXTRN j : dword ; { 4 byte  }
EXTRN k : tbyte ; { 10 byte }
```

Assembly language is only concerned with how big a variable is at this level. It does not care what type it is. Thus, Turbo 8087 reals, doubles, and comps are 8 bytes and use the same EXTRN definition. Similarly, shortint and byte are both byte length.

The following Pascal program demonstrates this by calling an assembly language program addjk.obj to add two global Pascal integers j and k to yield the sum in an integer variable sum, and also add unsigned longints dj and dk to yield a longint dsum. The Pascal program is below. Note that external procedures and functions do not require a return. This is handled in the assembly language routine:

```
PROGRAM paddjk;    {calling assembly language routine to add
                    integers and longint}
VAR
   j,k,sum :integer;
   dj,dk,dsum : longint;
  PROCEDURE addjk; external    {PROCEDURE name must match }
   {$L addjk.obj};             {public asm name}

BEGIN
```

```
    j:=17;           k:=13;
    dj:=300002;      dk:=450002;
    addjk;
    writeln('Sum= ',sum,'    Dsum= ',dsum);
END.
```

The necessary assembly language routine addjk.asm is shown below. In particular note that all variable names are declared as EXTRN, and the data and code segments are PUBLIC as is the name of the procedure addjk called by the Pascal program:

```
; Assembly routine using Pascal GLOBAL variables
; addjk          manipulates Pascal variables
; sum:=j+k       where j,k,sum are integers
; dsum:=dj+dk    where dj,dk,dsum are longint

data segment word public
      assume ds:data
      extrn j, k, sum : word         ;make Pascal variables
      extrn dj, dk, dsum : dword     ;visible to addjk
data ends

code segment public
assume cs:code

addjk   proc far
          public addjk      ; make addjk visible to Pascal
          mov ax,j          ; get j
          add ax,k          ; compute j+k
          mov sum,ax        ; replace sum=j+k
          mov si, 0         ; initialize si to index into element
          mov cx,2          ; cx=number of words in longint
          clc               ; clear carry to allow a loop addition
                            ; si points at 1st word on 1st pass
      addnext:
          mov ax, [dj + si]  ;  move word of dj into ax
          adc ax, [dk + si]  ;  add word of dk  (use carry)
;    must use word ptr to override dword nature of dsum
          mov word ptr [dsum + si],ax  ;store word in dsum
          inc si             ;    point at next word
          inc si
          loop addnext       ;    add more words as required
          ret
addjk endp
code ends
      end
```

Note the use of two inc si's to bump the index pointer. An add si,2 instead is wrong and leads to some very subtle bugs. The add si instruction clears the flags even if it was set to propagate a carry from the low word to the high word. The need for a word ptr on the [dsum + si] arises from TASM's objection to putting a word into a double word.

However, TASM makes the correct assumption about the mov ax, [dj+si] construction; it takes a word from the dword dj and places it in ax. This is one of the many small quirks that you find in TASM.

While useful, passing information via the EXTRN statement is equivalent to using global variables with all their inherent limitations. You cannot set up general routines with dummy parameters. We turn now to more flexible parameter passing methods.

12.3   PARAMETER PASSING AND RETURNING RESULTS

You have been passing value and variable parameters regularly in Pascal. We show how Pascal parameter passing works and utilize the same method for communicating with machine code. In Pascal parameters are passed on the stack. Results are returned in the CPU registers, on the stack, or as modified Pascal variables. The general problem of parameter passing is straightforward but not simple. This is because each different type of variable is passed somewhat differently and functions have their own quirks.

We begin by considering the return of function results. Table 12–1 summarizes the method of returning function results. Note that an integer, byte, or character result is returned by loading it into the ax or al register; ah is zeroed if not used. Booleans are returned by setting the zero flag. The flag is set for a false (i.e., the result of an operation was zero). This is not surprising since with procedures a false is a 0 and a true is nonzero.

Real functions are placed into several CPU registers or onto the CPU stack in Turbo 5 (see next chapter). Parameter passing and the conventions for returning function results are major areas of inconsistency among different versions of Turbo Pascal. Even the very similar 4 and 5 versions use a different convention for 8087 reals. Turbo 4 returns the result on the 8087 stack and Turbo 5 uses the CPU stack. Thus, assembly code for one might not run when compiled with the other Pascal. The method of passing information on the stack will become clear shortly.

Table 12–1. Method of Returning Function Results

Type	Method of Return
Reals	80X87 Real on top of 80X87 stack or CPU stack Turbo 6 byte reals: most significant word in DX middle word in BX, least significant word in AX
Integer, Char, Byte	Word in AX, byte in or AL. If unused, AH=0.

Booleans	CPU Zero flag.
	    If false set to Z.
	    If true set to NZ

Pointers	DX:AX (seg in DX, ofs in AX)
Strings	A far pointer is pushed on stack before other parameters. The routine must point to result with pointer. Pointer is not part of parameter list.

For the moment, we alter our previous program for summing two global longints to a function. As shown in Table 12–1, the result must be placed in dx:ax with the high word in dx. The necessary calling Pascal program is:

```
PROGRAM pfaddjk;   {use asm lang. function to add longints}
                   {returns sum as a function}
VAR        dj, dk : longint;

  FUNCTION faddjk: longint;
   external {function matches public asm name}
   {$L faddjk.obj}};
BEGIN
  dj:=300010;     dk:=34502;
  writeln('Sum= ',faddjk);
END.
```

The assembly language routine is shown below. Note the use of si as an index register as well as the addition of 2 (e.g., [dj+si+2]) to the index to get the high word for the addition.

```
; Assembly function for adding two GLOBAL longints dj and dk
; call:  faddjk
; returns dj+dk  in dx:ax

data segment word public
      assume ds:data
      extrn dj, dk : dword      ;visible to addjk
data ends

code segment public
assume cs:code

faddjk  proc far
      public faddjk             ; faddjk now visible to Pascal
      mov si, 0                 ; set index to first element
      mov ax, [dj+si]           ; move word dj into ax
      add ax, word ptr [dk+si]  ; add word of dk  (NO carry)
      mov dx, [dj+si+2]         ; get high word dj into dx
      adc dx, word ptr [dk+si+2]; add high word dk with carry
      ret
faddjk endp
code ends
      end
```

Parameters are passed on the stack in two ways:

(1)   The parameter is passed directly on the stack.
(2)   The address of the memory location holding the parameter is passed on the stack.

Table 12–2. Method of Passing Value and Variable Parameters on Stack	
Value Parameters	
Byte, Integer, Boolean, Char, shortint, longint	1 word use the normal low-byte then high byte mode True=0001, false=0000 If unused, MSB is undefined
Real and Comp	8087 Reals-8 bytes on CPU stack[1] Normal Real-6 bytes on CPU stack
Arrays, Records	1, 2 and 4 long arrays/records duplicated directly on stack All other value parameters are passed by address on stack.
Strings, sets	Address is pushed on stack
Variable (Var) Parameters	
All types	Segment address is PUSHed onto stack first. Offset address is PUSHed next. Thus, the offset is at lowest memory (top of stack) and the segment is at higher memory.

[1] Turbo 5. Turbo 4 uses a different method. See text.

This is analogous to value versus variable parameter passing in Pascal subprograms.

Table 12–2 summarizes the passing methods for different types of value and variable parameters. Parameters or their addresses are PUSHed onto the stack. The order in which parameters are PUSHed works from left to right in the parameter list. Thus, starting at the top of the stack (lowest memory) and working towards higher memory we see the 16-bit return address of the calling Pascal program, then the last parameter, then the next to the last parameter, and so on. This is shown schematically below:

```
SP (on entry in subprogram)   →       Return Address
                                      Last Parameter
                                      Next to Last Parameter
                                       . . . .
                                      First Parameter
SP₀                           →       xxxxxx
```

where xxxxxx is the last word or stack before the call. Parameters can be either a parameter or an address.

Procedures or functions pull parameters or their addresses off the stack by using the BP. If parameters are stored explicitly on the stack rather than as addresses, they appear exactly the same on the stack as they are stored as variables in Pascal's memory, which makes examining them with a debugger easier.

Both variable and value strings or records are present on the stack as pointers. For value parameters, Pascal subprograms make a local copy of them on the stack and any changes to the string in the subprogram do not affect the original. This is tricky to use, and it takes a long time to load the stack. If you push too many items on the stack, you risk a stack-code collision and crash. Therefore, if you are passing arrays or records, we recommend using parameter passing by address.

For variable parameters, parameter addresses are always stored as 4-byte offset plus segment:

Low byte of offset address of variable parameter
High byte of offset address of variable parameter
Low byte of segment address of variable parameter
High byte of segment address of variable parameter

Including the segment address is convenient because you might not always be sure which segment data are stored in. Remember that Turbo uses only one data segment for all static variables and typed constants.

To more fully understand how an external call works, we alter our earlier function call to subtract two unsigned longints passed as value parameters rather than as global variables. This is an especially easy case, although the double word length of the parameter poses some interesting problems. The two arguments are passed on the stack and the result, a longint, is returned in dx:ax as before. Pascal automatically makes the assignment of this value to your function.

Before we give the program, we show the stack region and explain a few necessary bookkeeping problems. The function call looks like:

```
{$F-}
FUNCTION ParFsub(var1, var2: longint):longint;external;
```

where the {$F-} compiler directive forces a near call. Value parameters are pushed on the stack in their order in the list. Thus, var1 is pushed first followed by var2. Then, as in any subroutine call, the return address is pushed (the offset word here for a near call) and a jump to the subroutine is made. On entry into ParFsub, the stack pointer is at 10 less than its original value and the stack looks like:

$SP_0-10 \rightarrow$ Return address word
$SP_0-8 \rightarrow$ Low word of var2
$SP_0-6 \rightarrow$ High word of var2
$SP_0-4 \rightarrow$ Low word of var1
$SP_0-2 \rightarrow$ High word of var1
$SP_0 \rightarrow$ xxxx

where SP_0 is the stack pointer value before the call to the external routine. Thus, the stack pointer on entry into this machine language routine is 10 lower than the value in the calling Pascal program (two data double words and one return address word).

There are several rules that must be obeyed for successful subprogram use:

(1) External subprograms must not change the BP, CS, DS, and SS registers.
(2) Any external subprogram must restore the stack pointer to its original value on return. In other words, SP must equal SP_0 when you get back to the main Pascal program. All other registers can be changed with impunity.

If you disobey these rules the system might well crash. In particular, if you do not obey rule 2, the main Pascal program returns to the address of one of your parameters.

Now we address the problem of getting at the stack variables. This is quite easy if we use the BP as an indirect index register for pointing at stack parameters. Since the BP is also one of the registers that we cannot change, however, we must first save it, generally by pushing it onto the stack with a PUSH BP. The stack now looks like:

```
SP0-12  →     BP value word
SP0-10  →     Return address word
SP0-8   →     Low word of var2
SP0-6   →     High word of var2
SP0-4   →     Low word of var1
SP0-2   →     High word of var1
SP0     →     xxxx
```

The current value of BP does not necessarily point at the stack region, so we take care of this with:

```
MOV BP, SP              ; point BP at stack
```

The BP register now contains the current value of the stack pointer, which is SP_0-12. In other words, BP points at the last entry on the stack (i.e., low byte of BP).

We can now get at any value on the stack with offset-indirect indexing. For example, var2 starts 4 bytes above the present value of the BP. Thus, var1 starts at [BP+8]. Similarly, var2 is at [BP+4]. The following is a Pascal driver program for calling the assembly language function:

```
PROGRAM PParfsub;   {uses asm lang. function}
                    {Parfsub(j,k) returns j-k}
VAR
  dj, dk : longint;

  {$F-}    {enable near call}
  FUNCTION Parfsub(x,y:longint): longint ; external
  {$L Parfsub.obj};

BEGIN
  dj:=600000;    dk:=40000;
```

```
    writeln('Difference= ',parfsub(dj, dk));
END.
```

The assembly language program is given below. Note the absence of any EXTRN directive; there are no global parameters. Parameters are passed on the stack and the result is returned in the CPU dx:ax registers.

```
; Assembly function for adding two longints on stack
; call:  Parfsub(x,y)
; returns longint result x + y in dx:ax

code segment public
assume cs:code

Parfsub proc near              ; must be a near procedure
     public Parfsub            ; make Parfadd visible to Pascal
     push bp                   ; save current bp
     mov bp,sp                 ; point bp at stack
     mov ax, [bp+8]            ; move word of x into ax
     sub ax, [bp+4]            ; sub word of y   (NO carry)
     mov dx, [bp+8+2]          ; get high word of x into dx
     sbb dx, [bp+4+2]          ; sub high word of y with borrow
     pop bp
     ret 8
Parfsub endp
code ends
     end
```

We have one sticky little problem if we execute a normal near subroutine return. We leave 8 bytes on the stack and the stack pointer is 8 bytes lower than the original value. If you failed to clear them off, the stack would grow with each succeeding call and eventually collide with the program. The solution is the RET N instruction, which has the form:

```
    RET n      ; Return and drop n bytes from the stack
```

The RET n is similar to RET except that after returning (but before we resume execution of our main program) the stack pointer is increased by n. This has the effect of dropping n bytes off the stack. Our subprogram has 8 parameter bytes on the stack (two quad words), which a ret 8 removes, restoring the stack pointer to its original state.

Thus, the general layout for an assembly language routine is shown as:

```
    push bp       ; save bp
    mov bp,sp     ; point bp at stack data

    ...           ; your program
```

```
pop bp          ; restore bp
ret N           ; return/remove N parameter bytes from stack
```

There are some tricks that simplify stack maintenance and make documentation clear. The simplest is to use EQU to define stack elements with more meaningful labels. Thus, the computational part of the above code becomes:

```
x EQU bp+8
y EQU bp+4

mov ax, [x]         ;  move word of x into ax
sub ax, [y]         ;  sub word of y  (NO carry)
mov dx, [x+2]       ;  get high word of x into dx
sbb dx, [y+2]       ;  sub high word of y with carry
```

Note how nicely we can replace references to stack entries with symbolic labels. We still have to do all the bookkeeping, however, and if we change the parameter list, the positions change and we need to change our EQUs to reflect the changes.

We conclude with a more complicated example. We have an array of unsigned integers. We want a function that sums the elements starting at one index and ending at another. The function form is:

```
FUNCTION sumit(firstpt,lastpt:integer;
                    var data1:arrayint) : longint;
```

where firstpt and lastpt are the indices of the first and last point and data an integer array type. A suitable Pascal routine is:

```
PROGRAM psumit;
CONST
TYPE arraydata=array[1..1000] of integer;
VAR
  j,k,startpt,endpt,numpts:integer;
  sum,dummy:longint;
  data1 : arraydata;

  {$f+}
  FUNCTION sumit(first,last:integer;var dataarray:arraydata):
                  longint;
                  external;
  {$L sumit.obj}
  {$f-}

BEGIN
  startpt:=1;   endpt:=1000;
  for j:=1 to endpt do data1[j]:= j;
  for k:=1 to iterations do
```

```
      dummy:=sumit(startpt,endpt,data1);
      writeln(' sum ',dummy,' ','numpts ',numpts);
END.
```

The assembly language routine is shown below. For demonstration purposes we have set a global variable Numpts in the program. Closely inspect the EQUs. The labels are local to the subprogram and need not match any names in the calling Pascal program. The address of the array is passed since var arrays are alway passed as pointers on the stack. After pushing BP onto the stack, data1's address is at BP+6 (2 for BP and 4 for the long return). Endpt is at BP+10, since the pointer to data1 takes 4 bytes, and Firstpt is BP+12, since Endpt is a word. A double word is returned in the dx:ax registers with dx holding the high word. Thus, dx:ax is the logical register pair for doing the summation. Since we are adding words, we need only add each carry into the high word as it occurs. This is done with the conditional JNC over the line that increments dx. The indexing is performed by reading the address of data1 off the stack with a LES instruction. If we were certain that the data to be referenced were in the data segment, we would not have to use the es register and a segment override. However, if our routines were called from subprograms that did not use global variables, the data segment would address the data. Thus, the precaution of using the es register:

```
; sumit.asm
; function sumit( startpt, endpt : integer;
;                 data : intarray ) : longint;
; returns longint sum of elements of any array of integers
; from startpt to endpt
; Also, sets GLOBAL variable Numpts in calling Pascal to
; number of points summed

data    segment word public
        assume ds:data
        extrn numpts : word
data    ends

code    segment
        assume cs:code

startpt equ [bp+12]     ; 2 above endpt since endpt a word
endpt   equ [bp+10]     ; 2 (bp) + 4 (long ret) + 4 for data
data1 equ [bp+6]        ; 2 (bp) + 4 return

sumit proc far
        public sumit    ; make sumit available to Pascal
        push bp         ; save bp
        mov bp,sp       ; and point bp at stack region
        xor ax,ax       ; initialize sum=0 in dx:ax
        xor dx,dx       ; faster, smaller than a mov dx,0
        mov cx,endpt    ;  get last point
        mov si,startpt  ;  calculate number of elements
```

```
        sub cx,si
        inc cx            ; numpts in cx
        mov [numpts],cx   ; save in numpts
        dec si            ; calc startpt offset in array in si
        add si,si         ; must double numpts-1 because words
        les di, data1     ; get base of data1 array in es
        add si,di         ; add offset into array to base
addone:
        add ax,es:[si]    ; need es override to point at data
        jnc nocarry       ; if carry into high word or longint
        inc dx            ; sum then increment high word
nocarry:
        add si,2          ; point to next word
        loop addone       ; repeat as required
        pop bp            ; restore bp
        ret 8             ; return removes 8 parameter bytes
sumit endp                ;    from stack
code ends
    end
```

For a sum of one thousand elements, 1000 times the assembly language code takes 9.2 s. The corresponding Pascal code takes 24.2 s.

We can simplify our compiler directives by using the tpascal model as shown below:

```
.model tpascal
.data
      extrn numpts : word

.code

sumit proc far startpt,endpt: word,data1: dword returns sum: dword
      public sumit
      xor ax,ax             ; initialize sum=0 in dx:ax
                  (... remainder of code the same)
```

Note that the parameters are declared in the same order as in the function definition. Returns tells Pascal to expect a dword result and sum is a dummy variable. All parameters and the Returns must be defined on a single line, which is awkward for long parameter lists.

12.4   INLINE MACHINE STATEMENTS

With inline machine code one explicitly spells out the actual machine language (i.e., the bytes that correspond to the assembled code) in a format that tells Turbo Pascal to include these bytes in memory and pass control to them. The list is preceded by INLINE. Each byte element is separated by a "/"; the beginning of the list is initiated with a "(" and terminated with a ");".

For example, if we wanted to print the screen, INT 5 would perform this service, and no parameters would be passed. As described earlier, we set up a record and used an MSDOS call. Since no parameters need be passed, however, a simple machine language INT 5 is adequate:

```
INLINE
     ($CD/$05              {INT 5}
     );
```

INLINE code allows Pascal style comments using the standard delimiters. To include such inline code in a Pascal procedure, we could write:

```
PROCEDURE printscreen;
  VAR j:integer;
  BEGIN
    inline ($CD/$05); {INT 5}
    for J:=1 to 32 writelin (lst); {advance to next page}
  END;
```

Indeed, this was a procedure used in an early VIDGR4.

Warning. The requirements of inline code are that BP, SP, DS, and SS registers must not be changed on exiting an Inline section. If you need to modify these registers, they must be saved on the stack and restored just before you exit to Turbo.

Turbo also provides mechanisms for reading or altering Pascal variables from inline machine code or for obtaining parameters passed on the stack during a function or procedure call. Turbo Pascal permits you to include variable identifiers or procedures and function identifiers. When we altered a system interrupt, we saw an example in which being able to obtain the offset of a subprogram would be useful. When a symbolic identifier is used, the compiler replaces the label with the offset address of the variable, procedure, or function. For example:

```
    $bb/string1           {mov bx, =string1}
```

moves the offset of the variable string1 into the bx register. The comment is the machine language code that was assembled to the inline instruction on the left using a special INLINE assembler rather than the standard one. In standard assembly language mnemonic, this is mov bx, offset string1.

A more subtle example involves passing a variable parameter to a subprogram on the stack, and we cover this in greater detail later. For now, the base pointer register indexes into the stack and the following instruction:

```
    $C4/$BE/string1        {les di, [bp]string1 }
```

reads the stack, extracts the segment address of string1 and places it in the es register, then extracts the offset address of string1 and places it in the di register. Since the di register is one of the indirect address registers, it can be used to point to the data in string.

Some care is required. There are default segment registers for the different pointers and you must use the right one. For example, normal variables and typed constants in Pascal are stored in the data segment. The base segment of local variables (i.e., variables declared within the current subprogram) is the stack segment. The variable offset is relative to the base page (BP) register. The default segment for the BP register is the stack segment; use of the BP automatically causes the stack segment to be selected.

12.4.1   INLINER Program

There are two ways to generate the above inline code. You can develop the programs on a debugger or assembler using dummy addresses for the labels. After assembly, take the hex listing (lst file in TASM) and copy the program into your Pascal program after suitable editing.

The second and more convenient procedure is to use a mini Turbo assembler for writing inline code. This public domain program is INLINER (by A. M. Marcy). It is not terribly friendly (but then we generally do not find inline assembly that obvious) and does not support all assembler possibilities. Our old version does not support math coprocessor instructions. It usually works and can greatly reduce your work load if you like assembly language development but do not want to invest in, or do not like, an assembler. INLINER gives the tidy output shown in the previous section with the inline code side-by-side with your assembly language listing (commented out).

We describe briefly INLINER. INLINER is available from PC-SIG Library on disk #428 "Turbo Pascal Program #8". The source code along with the documentation are provided. INLINER is written entirely in Turbo Pascal and assembles inline code quite rapidly, which again provides you with a taste of the flexibility of Pascal. As we have not worked extensively with INLINER, much of the subsequent description of INLINER is extracted from Marcy's documentation.

According to Marcy, INLINER 1.00 works fully with Turbo Pascal 1 and 2 but might not generate proper code with Pascal 3, especially if one has label and constant identifiers. With simple programs, we have not had any problems. Our version was for Turbo 2 recompiled under Turbo 3. Marcy states that under 3, INLINER does not always properly handle complex expressions with labels, although we have never had a problem. We have not used it extensively with Turbo 4 and 5, but it would not surprise us if there are quirks. Nevertheless, it beats hand assembly.

INLINER accepts source code similar (but not identical) to TASM and MASM. INLINER does not support assembler pseudo ops, although all 8086 and 80286 instructions are supported. Also, there are some syntax differences. INLINER, for example, makes fewer judgments about near and far control statements and you must explicitly spell these out. Thus, a program from one of these assemblers will have to be edited to INLINER format before assembly. You can begin running several ways:

```
INLINER
INLINER source filename
```

```
INLINER source filename        destination filename
INLINER TRM:
```

In the first form, INLINER prompts for a source file and a target file. If no source filename extension is given, .ASM is assumed. The default destination file is your source filename with extension .PAS; a carriage return accepts the default, or you may enter any legal filename. In the second case, the default value is assumed. That is the source filename with a PAS extension. In the third case, you can specify the source and destination filenames.

The last form is useful for playing. You, in effect, type the file directly into INLINER. It will not be saved, however, and no editing is available. End your input with ctrl-z. Entering NUL as the target file will not generate an output file but you can still see the output on the screen.

Instruction Format. An INLINER source line takes the general form:

label: opcode operand,   operand   ; comment

where each component is optional.

A LABEL can be any legal Turbo identifier with a maximum length of twenty characters. The colon is mandatory.

OPCODEs are the standard Intel mnemonics. LOCK and the various REP prefixes (see any of the assembly language books for details) are supported. The segment override prefixes apply only to operands, not before the opcode.

OPERANDs can be register, address, and immediate. Register operands are the usual mnemonics—AX,BX, and so on. Address operands have the following form:

```
prefix: (type) [base] [index] offset
```

Each component is optional, but the order shown is mandatory:

```
prefix is a segment override—DS, CS, SS, or ES
type is a single letter-- N    Near
                          F    Far
                          S    Short
                          W    Word
                          B    Byte
base is a base register—BX or BP
index is an index register—SI or DI
offset is either a literal constant or Turbo identifier
```

Turbo identifiers (i.e., variables and constants) are copied into the INLINE code. Any identifier that does not occur as a label is assumed to be a Turbo identifier. If it is not, you will get an undefined label when you try to compile the Pascal program. During compilation, Turbo Pascal replaces each variable name with its offset within its appropriate segment and each constant identifier with its value. The location counter, *, is also legal. See the Turbo manual for details. Some valid examples:

```
ADD  AL,var1      ;var1: a global variable in the data segment
ADD  AL,[BP]var2  ;var2: a local variable in the stack segment
ADD  AL,CS:var3   ;var3: a typed constant in the code segment
```

Immediate operands are indicated with an equals sign prefix:

```
MOV AX,=2     ;loads the value 2 into AX
MOV AX,2      ;loads AX with the word at offset 2 in DS
MOV AX,var1   ;loads AX with the integer variable var1
MOV AX,=var1  ;loads the offset of variable var1 into AX
```

The equals sign is optional in the INT, RET, IN, and OUT instructions, and before character literals.

CONSTANTs can be decimal integers (positive or negative), Turbo hex constants ($ prefix), constant identifiers, or character literals enclosed in single quotes. Examples: 10, –998, $DDFF, pi, or 'x'. As with regular assembly language, byte or word ptr information must be supplied if it is not implicit in the statement.

```
ADD AX,[BP]2  ;AX is a word, so no B or W needed
INC (W)[BP]2  ;requires (W) or (B)
```

Immediate numeric constants default to (B)yte if in the range –128 . . 255, otherwise they are (W)ord. It is a good idea to always write out byte or word specifiers.

JMP is special since it can be either near or far. A (F)ar jump to an absolute address may be coded with two operands, both immediate constants, representing the segment and the offset: JMP =$0060,=$0100, where the absolute address is 0060:0100. A (N)ear jump to an offset in the CS requires a single immediate operand:

```
JMP =$0100   ;address CS:0100
JMP =*-1     ;this instruction jumps to itself
```

An indirect jump takes either a register or an address operand. In the latter case, the type must be specified:

```
JMP AX              ;must be (N)ear
JMP (F)[BP][SI]
JMP (N)var1
```

We include the above information so that you can recognize it in other programs. INLINER supports standard jumps to INLINER label. For backward jumps INLINER uses short jumps where possible. Forward jumps are always long unless you override them with a short jump. Thus, on forward references use a short jump override for more efficient code:

```
    JMP lab1     ;forward references use long jmp (4 byte address)
    JMP (S)lab2 ;forces a fast short jump (2 byte address)
```

CALL is similar to JMP, except that (S)hort cannot be used. Conditional jumps (e.g., JNZ, JC, JA, and so on) take a single operand, which may be either an immediate constant (−128 .. 127) or more clearly an INLINER label.

A great weakness of INLINER 1.00 is its failure to support 8087 mnemonics. Pascal variables or constant declarations must be used for data definition to replace DB, DW, EQU, and so on. However, these are Turbo Pascal variables, and INLINER cannot verify that you are addressing them properly. You must provide segment overrides where needed.

Below are more INLINER examples:

```
    PUSH BP
h2: CMP var1,=-1     ; byte immediate data assumed
    CMP var1,(W)=-1 ; word override to give word constant
    MOV var2,=var4  ; offset of var4 into var2
    JE (S)h5         ; a short forward jump
    mov es:4, '&'    ; INLINER is case and space insensitive
h5: SUB (W)var3,=$40
    NOP
    MOV [BX][DI],CS
    RET (N) 4        ; (N) or (F) required
```

We now provide examples of uses and misuses of inline code using INLINER format. The following inline code was written to add two integers x and y and assign the result to the integer z:

```
; INLINE code adds global integers x and y
; sum in z
    mov ax,x
    add ax,y
    mov z,ax
```

Assembling this code with INLINER and incorporating it into a suitable Pascal driver yields:

```
VAR
    x,y,z : integer;

BEGIN
    x:=77;
    y:=66;
Inline(
            { ; INLINE code adds global integers x and y }
            { ; sum in z                                 }
   $A1/x    {        mov ax,x                            }
```

```
/$03/$06/y     {          add ax,y                              }
/$A3/z  );     {          mov z,ax                          }
     writeln('Sum = ',z);
END.
```

The interesting point about this routine is the execution time. Half a million iterations take 9.4 s on our 8 MHz 8086 machine. The analogous Pascal statement "z:=x+y;"
executes in exactly the same time. If you disassemble the machine code (i.e., convert the
machine code into assembly language) from the compiler, you discover that the compiler
generates exactly the same machine code as the assembly language routine. Therefore,
for this simple example all we have done is make more work by going to assembly
language with absolutely no gain in performance. Machine code should be used selectively and you should not assume *a priori* that assembly language will improve performance; for certain types of constructions the compilers are very efficient.

The places where assembly language will give the biggest gains are where Pascal
subprograms would be called (there is considerable overhead with a call), for looping
operations, and where there is array or data indexing. The Pascal compiler does not
recognize when the CPU register will be free for special operations and always errs on
the side of saving too much rather than too little.

The following INLINE routine capit.asm is designed to be incorporated into a function or procedure. It converts every lower case character in a string into upper case. It
expects the address of the string on the stack (i.e., parameter passing as a variable parameter).

```
;capit.asm
;Inline machine code program for converting the variable strg
;in a subprogram into all caps.  Program is in INLINER
;assembly mnemonics.  The code must be used in a procedure or
;function that passes information about the location of the
;string on the stack.
        les     di, [bp]strg    ;strg address in es:di
        mov     ch, =0          ;load cx with string length
        mov     cl,es:[di]
l1:
        inc     di              ;point to string byte
        cmp     es:[di],'a'     ;if not a..z, get next char
        jb (s)  l2
        cmp     es:[di],'z'
        ja (s)  l2
        sub     es:[di], (b)=$20   ;otherwise cap it
l2:     loop l1
```

LES pulls the address of the string off the stack. All comparisons and arithmetic are
done on the characters stored in memory; nothing is routed through the CPU registers.
Lower case letters are converted to capitals by subtracting 20H. Again the es register is
used in case we call the routine from a subroutine in which the data are not in the data
segment.

To use capit.asm, assemble it with INLINER and read it into a suitable Pascal program. The assembled code, less the comments for brevity, coupled to a Pascal drive program is shown below:

```
PROGRAM ucapit;
VAR
x: string;
j,k:integer;
PROCEDURE capit(var strg:string);
BEGIN
Inline(
  { ;capit.asm }
   $C4/$BE/strg    {les di, [bp]strg    ;strng address in es:di}
   /$B5/$00         {mov     ch, =0       ;load cx with length    }
   /$26/$8A/$0D     {mov     cl,es:[di]                           }
                    {11:                                          }
   /$47             {inc     di           ;point to string byte }
   /$26/$80/$3D/$61{cmp      es:[di],'a' ;if not a..z, get next}
   /$72/$0A         {jb (s)  12                                   }
   /$26/$80/$3D/$7A{cmp      es:[di],'z'                          }
   /$77/$04         {ja (s)  12                                   }
   /$26/$80/$2D/$20{sub      es:[di], (b)=$20 ;otherwise cap it}
   /$E2/$ED  );     {12: loop 11                                  }
END;


BEGIN
for j:=1 to 10000 do
  x:='12345 !@#$%^&*()_+=NoW Is tHe TiMe FoR aLl men';
  capit(x);
  writeln(x);
END.
```

How does the speed of this inline program compare with a high-level program? The assignment of x to a long string (70 characters) and capitalization with 10^4 iterations took 9.5 s on an 8 MHz 8086. The assignment alone took 2.5 s. A high level routine using the UpCase function written directly in place of capit(x) took 28.2 s. Thus, here inline code is 3 times faster.

In the program below UOUTSTR.PAS uses an MSDOS interrupt to output a Pascal string. Note the use of the =worldmessage to obtain the offset of the string worldmessage in the Pascal data segment. The (n) on the jmp instruction insures that a fast, compact near jump is used. INLINER has few error checks and will happily assemble disasterous errors. Note, for example, the use of both a near call and near return for the subroutine. If one of these was a near and the other a far, the program crashes.

```
PROGRAM uoutstr;
VAR
   worldmessage : string;
BEGIN
```

```
worldmessage:='Hello World'+char($0a)+char($0d)+char($0);

Inline(
 $BB/worldmessage          {     mov bx, =worldmessage }
 /$43                      {     inc bx                }
 /$E8/$03/$00              {     call (n) printstring }
 /$EB/$0F/$90              {     jmp(n) finis          }
                          { PrintString:          }
                          { PrintStringLoop:       }
 /$8A/$17                  {       mov dl,[bx] }
 /$22/$D2                  {       and dl,dl }
 /$74/$07                  {       jz EndPrintString }
 /$43                      {       inc bx                }
 /$B4/$02                  {       mov ah,=2         }
 /$CD/$21                  {       int $21         }
 /$EB/$F3                  {       jmp PrintStringLoop }
                          { EndPrintString:            }
 /$C3                      {       ret (n)            }
   );                      { finis:                 }

END.
```

As you can see from the above discussion, INLINER is delightfully sophisticated and with it you can do just about everything in machine language. However, for anything very large use EXTERNAL machine language routines.

We conclude with a slightly more complicated example. We copy one string into another. Remember the first byte of the string is the actual number of bytes occupied by the current string. This must also be copied into NewString or we will corrupt our new copy. We will assume that the maximum length of the source and destination are the same and that no errors can occur. A suitable Pascal program with inline machine code is shown below:

```
PROGRAM picpstr;
VAR
   a,b:string;
   j: integer;

{$F-}  {must be a near call}
PROCEDURE icpstr(var x,y:string);
BEGIN
Inline(
{ ;         ICPSTR.ASM }
{ ;          icpstr(string1,string2:string); }
{ ;            copies string1 into string2 }
{ ;          MUST be a NEAR call i.e., $F- }
{ ;          si = pointer to source string }
{ ;          di = pointer to destination string }
{ ;          es:= segment register for pointing to both strings}
 $C4/$7E/$04  {les di, [bp]4 ;get addr dest string in di}
 /$C4/$76/$08 {les si, [bp]+8 ; get addr source string in si}
              { ;You can overwrite ES: register here because}
```

```
                    { ;it is the segment register for both strings}
/$8A/$2E/$00/$00  {   mov ch,0          }
/$26/$8A/$0C      {   mov cl, es:[si] ; get # of bytes to move in cx }
/$41              {   inc cx     ; set total number of bytes to move}
                  { nextchar:                                        }
/$26/$8A/$04      {     mov al, es:[si] ; fetch a byte               }
/$26/$88/$05      {     mov es:[di], al ; move it destination         }
/$46              {     inc si          ; bump both memory pointers  }
/$47              {     inc di                                        }
/$E2/$F6  );      {     loop nextchar   }
END;

BEGIN
  a:='01234567890abcdefghijklmnopqrstuvwxyz7890123456789012345 67890';
  b:='';
  icpstr(a,b);
  writeln(a);  writeln(b);
END.
```

While this makes a nice example of assembly language program, parameter passing, and inline code, it is a disaster in terms of speed. The time for assigning 20,000 long strings was 12 s with the inline machine code. If we replace the block of inline code with the Pascal "x:=y;", the execution time was 5.0 s! The reason is that there are very fast block copy instructions in the 80X86 instruction set. The compiler uses these instructions and runs circles around our code. Again, this points out the dangers of blindly writing machine code without thought of bottlenecks or the speed of compiled code for certain operations. It also suggests that if you want to get the most from assembly language, do more reading on this rich instruction set.

12.5 INLINE PROCEDURES AND FUNCTIONS

An inline procedure or function is a clever way of inserting a single machine language statement or group of statements into your programs in a more meaningful form. Basically you define a named function or procedure that is made up of machine language instructions. Wherever you explicitly need this string of machine language instructions, you merely insert the procedure or function name. This is an exact replacement and not a procedure or function call.

The following example makes this clearer. The two instructions that are used to enable and disable hardware interrupts are CLI and STI, which are 1-byte instructions with the values $FA and $FB, respectively. Rather than remembering the values and inserting them as inline statements, make the following definitions:

```
PROCEDURE ClearInt;  INLINE ($FA);
PROCEDURE SetInt;    INLINE ($FB);
```

When you incorporate the procedure statements ClearInt or SetInt in your program, the actual inline code shown is incorporated directly into the program. Every occurrence of ClearInt or SetInt is replaced by "INLINE($FA);" or "INLINE($FB);". The advantages are clarity and speed, since a call to a procedure is not made with its associated overhead. The disadvantage is that if you use longer INLINE procedures or functions many times, the code gets expanded every time you use it and can take up a lot of space. Therefore, inline procedures and functions are generally used for short routines.

Parameter Passing and Returning Results. Parameter passing is done exactly the same as normal procedures or functions. The parameters in the parameter list are extracted going left to right in the procedure or function call, and either their value or their address is pushed on the stack. The inline code in the function or procedure definition is executed.

Function results are returned in the normal fashion either on the stack or in CPU registers. The following is an inline function routine in a program that adds two longint and returns a longint result:

```
PROGRAM alongint;
VAR
   x,y,z: longint;

FUNCTION addlongint(a,b:longint) : longint;
Inline(
    { ; funcion addlongint }
    { ; adds two longints passed on stack return longint }
    { ; result.   No error checking                     }
   $58          {  pop ax                                     }
   /$5A         {  pop dx     ; Get 2nd param into dx:ax      }
   /$5B         {  pop bx                                     }
   /$59         {  pop cx     ; 1st param into cx:dx     }
   /$03/$C3     {  add ax,bx  ; add low word          }
   /$13/$D1     {  adc dx,cx  ; add high word        }
    );          {; done: sum in dx:ax--required for 2-word result}

BEGIN
  x:=40000;    y:=60001;
  z:=addlongint(x,y);
  writeln('Sum = ',addlongint(x,y));
END.
```

Note that the stack pointer must be returned to its original value before the function. This is done by popping both parameters off the stack. Failure to adjust the stack pointer will lead to system crashes or very erratic, hard-to-find bugs.

In this particular case the Pascal assignment z:=x+y is significantly faster. However, this assignment uses fixed variables rather than a flexible function with variable parameters.

12.6 REFERENCES
The Borland TASM manuals are essential reference material. Swan's book on the Turbo assembler and on Pascal has useful examples of interfacing assembly language and Pascal.

Problems

12–1. Write an assembly language/Pascal program with the following characteristics. The assembly language routine should be called from Pascal and should record 256 points at maximum speed in assembly language. For your ADC routine you can use one of the routines developed in the last chapter for either the 8-bit DAC servo converter or the DT2800. Store the data as it is acquired in a 256-element Pascal array. After completing the data acquisition, return to Pascal and confirm the acquisition by displaying the results.

12–2. Enhance 12–1 by permitting execution of an assembly language routine that displays the 256 points of data on the DAC to an oscilloscope display. First output the most negative DAC value followed immediately by the most positive to trigger the display. Then output the complete waveform as fast as possible. After a software delay to allow your scope to reset, repeat the low, high, waveform sequence. After 100 complete cycles, return to the calling Pascal routine, and check for a key stroke. Repeat the display routine until a key is pressed.

12–3. Make a copy of DTUtil. Rewrite the following DTUtil routines in assembly language OBJ file and link them into a new Unit:

(A) DTCommandStatus
(B) DTCommand
(C) DTDataWrite
(D) DTDataRead
(E) DTReadADCIm

Sequentially replace each of the Pascal routines with the assembly language ones. After each change, evaluate the speed by measuring the time required to input a suitably large number of points. What is the input rate in conversions per second after each change? Which was the worst bottleneck, and could you have judged that by inspecting the code? You will probably not be able to achieve the maximum rate of the board. Why not? What would you do to overcome this bottleneck?

12–4. Do Problem 12–3 using inline machine code. Use INLINER to assemble the necessary code. The performance should be identical to 12–3 if you use the same routines.

12–5. A more functional variation of DTUtil is to replace the procedure pairs DTSetDACPar/DTWriteDAC or DTSetADCPar/DTReadADC with assembly language versions. Do this. What is the maximum throughput? Write an assembly language routine that calls one routine immediately after the other. Does this improve the performance? Why or why not?

12–6. The signal averaging routine, SIGAV, of Chapter 8 is slowed by the time necessary to add the new data to the running total. Rewrite this addition in assembly language. Is there a noticeable improvement in the rate of acquisition of the average using fast, rapidly repetitive, transients (maximum acquisition rate)? Slow transients (i.e., 1 ms /point)? Use 100 points. Adjust the number of averages to give measureable times.

13

80X87 Math Coprocessor

13.1 INTRODUCTION

To date we have seen two things that can really speed up your programs: 1) using software that supports the 80X87 math coprocessor for math intensive calculations; and 2) replacing high level language routines with well-crafted assembly language. In math-intensive computations, the obvious next step is to do the computations in a well-crafted assembly language that directly addresses the 80X87 rather than going through an indirect high-level language.

In this chapter we discuss the architecture and instruction set of the 80X87. We provide examples of how to directly control the 80X87 in assembly language. Since you know how to interface assembly language to Turbo Pascal, you can then greatly accelerate high-level calculations by replacing mathematical bottlenecks with assembly language patches.

First, we describe the nature of the beast. The math coprocessors are the 8087, the 80287, and the i387. The 8087 interfaces directly to the 8086 or 8088 CPUs. The 80287 interfaces directly to the 80286 and the i387 interfaces to the i386. The i486 has the math coprocessor built into it. There are minor differences in basic architecture. The 8087 must run at the same clock speed as the mother 8086. The 80287 and i387 run off a separate clock that can be either faster or slower than the parent 80287. Early IBM ATs used a 4MHz 287 in a 6Mhz machine since 6 MHz 287s were not available. This combination could actually run more slowly on some computations than when the 80287 was not used. The i387 is largely compatible with the 8087 and 80287, but with a somewhat more powerful instruction set. It is still common for the math coprocessor to run more slowly than the CPU. Since we deal only with instructions common to all processors here, subsequent discussions will refer to the generic term 80X87.

The 80X87 is a very specialized microprocessor that is optimized to do just one thing extremely fast—arithmetic. It has a complexity of at least 70,000 transistor equivalents, which makes it far more complex than the 8086 CPU and also a lot more expensive.

The 80X87 is a true coprocessor. That is, it runs its computations in parallel with the CPU. This has important ramifications. We point one out now and discuss the others later. The 80X87 can do numerical computation while the CPU is concurrently calculating something else. More often than not, this something else is an address or some other quantity that will be used to store data or extract data from the 80X87. This concurrency allows far faster operations than would otherwise be possible.

The 80X87 has it own assembly language instruction. On the 80X86's bus all 80X87 instructions begin with an ESC. The 80X86 uses the ESC as a flag to tell it to ignore the next instruction, while the 80X87 picks these instructions off and executes them as they fly by. The 80X87 instruction set is complex, although much less so than the 80X86s, and we will restrict ourselves to a useful subset of the full instruction set. In particular, we omit the transcendental, the comparison, and the status reporting functions. Interested readers can consult the references.

13.2 80X87 HARDWARE ARCHITECTURE

The 80X87 is a stack-oriented processor and is shown in Figure 13–1. It has eight arithmetic registers that can hold 80-bit temporary reals (Chapter 1). These registers form a push down stack (first-in-last-out). The registers are referred to as ST(0), ST(1), . . , ST(7) or as ST0, . . ,ST7. ST(0) is also labelled ST and is known as the **top of the stack (TOS)**. There is also a 16-bit status word that supplies information on the results of 80X87 operations including any computational errors. Finally, there is a control word that is used to set different control options. The status and control words are beyond the

Register	Stored Quantity
ST(0), ST or Top of Stack (TOS)	80 bit temporary reals
ST(1)	80 bit temporary reals
ST(2)	80 bit temporary reals
ST(3)	80 bit temporary reals
ST(4)	80 bit temporary reals
ST(5)	80 bit temporary reals
ST(6)	80 bit temporary reals
ST(7)	80 bit temporary reals
Status Word (16 bit)	Status Register (16-bit)

Figure 13–1. 80X87 internal architecture.

Table 13–1. Different 80X87 Number Representations

Name	Length and Type	Bytes in Memory
Short Integer	32-bit 2s complement	4
Long Integer	64-bit 2s complement	8
Short Real	32-bit single precision floating point	4
Long Real	64-bit double precision	8
Temporary Real	80-bit floating points	10
BCD Decimal	80-bit decimal	10

scope of our elementary discussion. Turbo Pascal has already set the 80X87 to acceptable values.

Those familiar with a stack-oriented calculator, such as the reverse Polish notation (RPN) Hewlett-Packard ones, will feel right at home. The 80X87 has several data types, which we discussed in detail in Chapter 1. You should review them. These are shown in Table 13–1.

We deal largely with reals here, but we will give you appropriate integer instructions. We ignore the BCD decimals since they are of little use to scientists.

Each data type takes up several bytes of contiguous memory with the usual convention of starting with the least significant byte at the lowest memory. Fortunately, the 80X87 instruction set works automatically on these and we rarely need to know any more about their format than how many bytes each takes up in memory.

13.3 80X87 INSTRUCTION SET
The 80X87 has instructions that fall into the following general classes:

(1) 80X87 initialization.
(2) Register initialization.
(3) Moving data between stack registers.
(4) Moving data between registers and main memory.
(5) Arithmetic operations on stack elements.
(6) Comparison operations.
(7) Loading or reading the control or status registers.

Except for the last two, we discuss these different operations in greater detail below.

13.3.1 Processor and Register Initialization
80X87 Initialization. The 80X87 is initialized to the power up state by issuing the instruction:

```
FINIT        ; Reset the 80X87 to the power up state
```

This aborts any operations in progress, empties all registers, and sets the 80X87 to a useful state. This rarely needs to be done unless you lose control.

Register Initialization. There are several important quantities that we would like to be able to load into the registers. There are instructions for loading 0, 1, pi, ln(2), and $\log_{10}(2)$. The assembly language instructions are:

```
FLDZ       ; push 0 onto the top of the stack
FLD1       ; push 1 onto the top of the stack
FLDPI      ; push pi onto the top of the stack
FLDLG2     ; push ln(2) onto the top of the stack
FLDN2      ; push log  (2) onto the top of the stack
                     10
FLDL2T     ; push log (10) onto top of the stack
                    2
FLDL2E     ; push log (e) onto top of the stack
                    2
```

Every time a number is pushed onto the top of the stack, each datum in the stack is pushed down another element. Thus, as we executed the following program:

```
           ;      point A
FLDZ       ;      point B
FLD1       ;      point C
FLDPI      ;      point D
FLDLG2     ;      point E
FLDN2      ;      point F
```

then the state of the stack after each instruction would be:

	After Instruction:					
Register	A	B	C	D	E	F
ST(0)	Empty	0	1	PI	ln(2)	$\log_{10}(2)$
ST(1)	Empty	Empty	0	1	PI	ln(2)
ST(2)	Empty	Empty	Empty	0	1	PI
ST(3)	Empty	Empty	Empty	Empty	0	1
ST(4)	Empty	Empty	Empty	Empty	Empty	0
ST(5)	Empty	Empty	Empty	Empty	Empty	Empty
ST(6)	Empty	Empty	Empty	Empty	Empty	Empty
ST(7)	Empty	Empty	Empty	Empty	Empty	Empty

All variables on the 80X87 stack are stored as temporary reals. All values are converted into this format as they are brought in, or converted to other formats as they are stored in memory.

Warning. The stack is not circular. If you put more than 8 elements on, the deepest ones fall off the far end and are permanently lost. If you are lucky, this error will result in exceptions (interrupts) that terminate your program. Much software is set up to accommodate this.

13.3.2 Register and Memory Moves

Register Moves. Several instructions move data around within the registers. These include:

```
FLD  ST(i)   ;    push ST(i) onto the TOS
FST  ST(i)   ;    copy ST(0) into ST(i)
FSTP ST(i)   ;    copy ST(0) into ST(i) and pop TOS
FXCH ST(i)   ;    exchange ST(0) with ST(i)
```

The FLD ST(i) load is a variation of the load instruction that copies any register onto the top of the stack. This adds one more element to the stack. If we were to perform an FLD ST(3), the contents of the stack before and after the operation are:

ST (i)	Before FLD ST(3)	After FLD ST(3)
0	A	D
1	B	A
2	C	B
3	D	C
4	Empty	D

where we omit references to higher stack elements. To duplicate the top of the stack, use:

```
FLD  ST(0)      ;  push ST(0) onto top of stack
```

The store instruction, FST ST(i) copies (stores) the TOS into register ST(i) without changing the number of items on the stack. For example:

```
FST  ST(1)    ; copy ST(0) into ST(1) (lose current ST(1))
FST  ST(7)    ; copy ST(0) into ST(7) (lose current ST(7))
```

The FSTP ST(i) instruction is the same as the FST ST(i) instruction except that the TOS of the stack is popped off after the copy. When we pop an element off the stack, we merely remove it and move every other element to a stack position one lower than before. This reduces by one the number of occupied registers.

To demonstrate the differences between the FST and FSTP instructions, compare the effects of an FST ST(3) and an FSTP ST(3) below:

ST (i)	Before	After FST ST(3)	After FSTP ST(3)
0	A	A	B
1	B	B	C
2	C	C	A
3	D	A	Empty

The exchange instruction exchanges any register with the TOS (ST(0)). For example:

```
FXCH register    ;exchange ST(0) with register
FXCH             ;exchange ST(0) and ST(1)
```

The second form, without arguments, assumes ST(1) and is, thus, equivalent to FXCH ST(1). Examples include:

```
FXCH  ST(5)    ;    exchange ST(0) and ST(5)
FXCH  ST(7)    ;    exchange ST(0) and ST(7)
```

There is no instruction to exchange any arbitrary pair of registers, but you can do it with three instructions. To exchange ST(1) and ST(5), use:

```
FXCH ST(1) ; original ST(1) in ST(0), original ST(0) in ST(1)
FXCH ST(5) ; original ST(1) in ST(5), original ST(5) in ST(0)
FXCH ST(1) ; original ST(5) in ST(1), original ST(0) in ST(0)
```

13.3.3 Register Memory Transfers

Ignoring BCD and temporary reals, there are three types of integer moves (word, short, and long) and two types of floating point moves (single and double precision). The reals have one instruction and the integers have another instruction:

Real Transfers

```
FLD source          ; load (push) real from memory onto TOS
FST destination     ; store TOS in memory (leave on stack)
FSTP destination    ; store TOS in memory and pop TOS
```

Integer Transfers

```
FILD source         ; load (push) integer from memory onto TOS
FIST destination    ; store TOS in memory (leave on stack)
FISTP destination   ; store TOS in memory and pop TOS
```

A critical and frequently forgotten point is: **All memory loads or stores using the TOS as the destination or source, respectively.**

Two obvious questions are: How do we specify the source and destination? How do we differentiate between long and short integers and single and double precision reals?

First, the standard 80X86 direct and indirect memory addressing modes are used to point at the memory holding variables. Immediate data cannot be used. Second, we can specify the precision (length) of the data to be moved by an assembly language pointer specification. For example, word pointer specifies a 16-bit word, dword pointer specifies a 32-bit argument (i.e., short real or integer), and qword pointer specifies a 64-bit quantity (i.e., long integer or real). Alternatively, for direct memory moves the length of the variable is defined; therefore, the assembler knows its length, and automatically uses the correct size move. Confusion would arise about real and integer variables of the same size if the 80X87 instructions did not explicitly differentiate between reals and integers. This is most clearly seen by examples:

```
FLD qword pointer [BX]      ; load 64-bit (double prec.) real
                            ; from memory pointed at BX
FIST dword pointer cs:[BP]; store a 32-bit integer from TOS
                            ; to location pointed at by CS:[BP]
FSTP dword pointer [BP]     ; store TOS in [BP] as a single
                            ; precision real and pop TOS
FLD qword pointer [BX+SI+2] ; load real at memory location
                            ; pointed at by BX+SI+2
```

The following direct mode instruction is also legal, but it troubles some assemblers. TASM does it correctly.

```
FLD DATA   ; load real data from location DATA
FLD [DATA] ; load real data from location DATA
```

where DATA is either a long or short real. The type is determined in the original assembly language or Pascal routine.

13.3.4 Mathematical Operations

Single Operand Operations. The 80X87 has several single operand mathematical operations, which all work only on the TOS. These are the square root, the absolute

Table 13–2. Summary of 80X87 Two Operand Mathematical Operations

Instruction Type	Mnemonic Form	Operand Form Destination, Source	Example
Register	F*op*	ST(i),ST or ST, ST(i)	FADD ST(7),ST
Register pop	FI*op*P	ST(i), ST	FSUBP ST(3),ST
Real Memory	F*op*	ST, short/long real	FDIV Quotient
Integer Memory	FI*op*	ST, word/short integer	FMUL Scaling

Permissible Instructions:

op =

ADD	destination	←	destination + source
SUB	destination	←	destination - source
SUBR	destination	←	source - destination
MUL	destination	←	destination * source
DIV	destination	←	destination / source
DIVR	destination	←	source / destination

value, and the change sign operations:

```
FSQRT        ; take square root of TOS (ST(0) or ST)
FABS         ; absolute value of TOS
FCHS         ; change sign of TOS
```

Double Operand Mathematical Operations. The mathematical operations of addition, subtraction, multiplication and division have several forms. We show these in Table 13–2 where op stands for addition, subtraction, multiplication, and division. In keeping with the usual 80X86 organization the instructions have the form:

```
Fop destination, source
```

Table 13–2 shows the common operations including direct and reversed division and subtraction. **However, the source or the destination of a register-register operation must be ST(0).** If you did not have the reversed instruction, how many operations would it require to subtract ST(3) from ST(0)? Several combinations are absent. A FLopP ST, ST(i) is meaningless since the result is popped and lost. A reverse addition is not required.

The clearest way to understand the different register modes is to consider examples. Below we show three registers before and after different versions of a subtraction:

| | | After | | | |
| | | FSUB | FSUB | FSUBR | FSUBR |
Register	Initial	ST(2),ST	ST,ST(2)	ST(2),ST	ST,ST(2)
0	1	1	−2	1	2
1	2	2	2	2	2
2	3	2	3	−2	3

We omit the pop versions, which remove the top value from the stack. Any pop instruction that alters ST(0) is useless.

Implicit Operands. The 80X87 instructions have implicit or explicit forms. We have shown several implicit forms in which we could omit a register specification (e.g., FXCH). There was usually little ambiguity.

However, in the mathematical operations there is a potential minefield. The following class of mathematical operations with two implicit operands is allowed:

```
fop          Example: FADD
```

Your logical interpretation is that this is equivalent to a FADD ST(1), ST(0). It is not. It is equivalent to a FADDP ST(1),ST(0). Every time you do an operation with two implicit arguments, it is actually the equivalent pop operation. Use of this shorthand notation is a major bug source, and we strongly recommend against use of implicit mathematical expressions. Use of the explicit mode adds only a few bytes to the source code, assembles to the same size machine codes, and is clear and unambiguous.

13.3.5   Synchronization and the Wait

Because the 80X87 and 80X86 are true coprocessors, there is a subtle error that arises when you write programs with a debugger. We show two versions of the program to add ten ones. The result should be ten. One was written with the debugger and the other with the assembler.

Debugger version:

```
:100       mov cx, 9
            finit
            fld1
            fst ST(1)
:xxx       fadd st(0),st(1)
            loop xxx
            int 20
```

Assembly language version:

```
            mov cx, 9
            finit
            fld1
            fst ST(1)
Addone:     fadd st(0),st(1)
            loop Addone
            int 20
```

If you enter the debugger version, step through it, and examine the 80X87 registers, you get the right answer. If you go through it in one pass with the g=100 instruction, you get the wrong answer.

If you assemble the assembly language version to a COM file, load it with DEBUG, run it with the G=100 command, and examine the 80X87 register, you get the right answer! Here we have two apparently identical programs, one created with DEBUG the other with the assembler, that give completely different results. What is going on? Clearly our "identical" programs are not. Disassembling the correctly assembled assembly language version yields:

```
:100       mov cx, 9
            wait
            finit
            wait
            fld1
            wait
            fst ST(1)
:xxx       wait
            fadd st(0),st(1)
            loop 10A
            int 20
```

This is not what we entered with debug. Before every 80X87 instruction we see a new instruction WAIT. The WAIT is also referenced by the FWAIT mnemonic. The WAIT instruction allows synchronization of the 80X86 and the 80X87 and prevents the 80X87 instruction register from being overwritten with another 80X87 instruction before the first one is finished. The 80X86 can carry out many operations such as data fetch or deposit and address calculations faster than the 80X87 can compute results. Thus, if the 80X86 tells the 80X87 to operate on a memory location and then reads the result from that location before the 80X87 has updated it, the result used by the 80X86 is wrong. Further, if a new 80X87 instruction comes along before the 80X87 finishes its current calculation, the 80X87 gets lost. The WAIT instruction permits the 80X87 to complete what it is currently doing before it accepts another instruction. It also allows the 80X87 to finish a calculation before the 80X86 moves data from memory locations that might be addressed by the 80X87.

The introduction of a WAIT with every floating point calculation is very conservative. In many cases an overlap will not occur and no errors would have arisen. However, standard assemblers always add WAIT to be absolutely sure.

13.4 EXAMPLES

We now give examples to make the exercise more concrete. After the convenience of a high level language, you will find the register restrictions bothersome, but we give some examples that should convince you of the computational capabilities of the 80X87.

In the first example, we compute the sum of all the square roots between 1 and 30,000. This entire calculation can be done on the 80X87 stack and no memory references are necessary. The assembly language source is:

```
; SUMROOT    Use the 80X87 to calculate the sum of the
; square roots of the integers 1 through 30,000.

NumberRepetitions equ   20
MaxInt            equ 30000

dosseg

.model small
.stack 100h
.data
    sum dq (0.0)

.code

sumroot proc near
        mov ax,@data        ; Critical must do to point at data
        mov ds,ax

; Initialize
  mov dx, NumberRepetitions

outerloop:
        finit               ; Clear 80X87
        fld1                ; Put 3 1s on stack
```

```
        fld1
        fld1
        mov cx, maxint        ; maximum value to root/add
        dec cx                ; first one already on stack
another:                      ; "a"
        fadd st,st(1)         ; "b" +1 to get next value to root
        fld st(0)             ; "c" dup it
        fsqrt                 ; "d" take root
        faddp st(3),st        ; "e" form partial sum
        loop another

        dec dx
jnz outerloop                 ; repeat outer loop as required
        fst [sum]             ; store in sum

        mov ah,4ch
        int 21h               ; Exit gracefully from exe file
sumroot endp
end
```

The outer loop increases the computation time to a measureable value.

To understand how the calculation works, let us look at the stack on the first entry into the "another" loop. We show the stack on the first pass and part of the second pass through the loop.

			Point in program				
Register	"a"	"b"	"c"	"d"	"e"	"b"	"c"
ST(0)	1	2	2	1.414	2	3	3
ST(1)	1	1	2	2	1	1	3
ST(3)	1	1	1	1	2.414	2.414	1
ST(3)	Empty	Empty	1	1	Empty	Empty	2.414

A 1 is always kept on the stack to add to the current index. The index is formed by adding a 1 on each successive pass through the loop, and it is duplicated before taking the square root so that it is not lost. The partial sum is the bottom of the stack.

The real question is, how fast is the calculation? All of this bother with assembly language is not worth much if the computations are not noticeably faster. In Turbo 3, a sum of 30,000 square roots takes 6.9 s on our AT&T 6300s. In the assembly language version given above, it takes 1.3 s for 30,000 iterations—or about a factor of six speed enhancement. However, Borland claims that Turbo 5 uses the 80X87 more efficiently than Turbo 3. The execution time for Turbo 5 was 2.4 s—justifying their claim. Nevertheless, assembly language speeds the calculations even against the more efficient Turbo 5 compiler.

We turn now to a more useful example. In statistics and fitting equations to sets of x,y pairs, we frequently need the following results:

$$SUMX = \Sigma\ x_i, \qquad SUMY = \Sigma\ y_i, \qquad SUMXY = \Sigma\ x_i y_i,$$

$$SUMX2 = \Sigma\ x_i^2, \qquad SUMY2 = \Sigma\ y_i^2$$

where the summations are over all the points in the fit. In least squares fitting, much of the time in the calculation is spent here. We demonstrate a simple 80X87 routine that reads each x,y pair in turn out of memory and generates all necessary sums. The final sums are stored back in memory. The routine demonstrates the power of stack operations, the difficulty of visualizing what is going on in a stack architecture without writing out everything in excruciating detail, and the 80X87's speed. In particular, the calculations can be done with only two memory reads per x,y pair. The assembled routine is shown in LSRSQR.ASM:

```
; program lstsqr.asm
; calculates sumx, sumy, sumx2, sumy2, and sumxy in 80X87

;Values on stack during calculation:
;       Highest (TOS)    sumxy
;       Next highest     sumy2
;       Next             sumx2
;       Next             sumy
;       Next             sumx
dosseg
NumberRepetitions equ 50
n                 equ 3000
.model small
.stack 100h
.data
    sumx    dq   ?
    sumx2   dq   ?
    sumy    dq   ?
    sumy2   dq   ?
    sumxy   dq   ?
    x       dq n dup (2.0)
    y       dq n dup (3.0)
.code
lstsqr proc near
        mov ax,@data
        mov ds,ax
        mov dx, NumberRepetitions
outerloop:
        finit
        fldz
        fldz
        fldz
        fldz
        fldz
        mov cx,n          ;number of elements
        xor si,si         ; zero offset
start:
        fld x[si]         ;load x[i]
        fadd st(5),st     ; add to sumx
        fld st(0)         ; dup x on TOS
```

```
      fmul st,st(0)      ; from x*x on TOS
      faddp st(4),st     ; add to sumx2
      fld y[si]
      fadd st(5),st      ; add to sumy
      fld st(0)          ; dup y on TOS
      fmul st,st(0)      ; form y*y
      faddp st(4),st     ;form sumy2
      fmulp st(1),st     ; form x*y
      faddp st(1),st     ; form sumxy

      add si,8           ; bump point by 8 since double
loop start
      fstp sumxy
      fstp sumy2
      fstp sumx2
      fstp sumy
      fstp sumx

      dec dx
      jnz outerloop
      mov ah,4ch
      int 21h
lstsqr endp
end
```

We have artificially set up two 3000 element 80X87 arrays, each filled with a constant. The SI register is used as an indirect index pointer into the data arrays. Note the convenient method of referencing array elements with the notations:

```
      x[si]
```

This is equivalent to taking the offset of x and adding it to the current contents of SI to point at quad word data. In this program, it points at a quad word automatically since x is a quad word. Now to index through the array, we merely add 8 to SI after every iteration. The value is 8 since every 80X87 long real takes up 8 bytes.

We return to the question of performance. A Turbo 3 Pascal program with all variables declared as REAL takes 2.8 s per calculation with an 8087. The same program in Turbo 5 takes 2.0 s with the 8087 enabled and 8.0 s without. However, using all variables declared as DOUBLE and using the 8087 takes 0.8 s in Turbo 5. The reason for this striking discrepancy is that variables of TYPE REAL must be converted into 80X87 reals for the 8087, while DOUBLE variables are a direct match for the 80X87 and no conversion is required. This stresses the need to use SINGLE or DOUBLE reals as opposed to REAL reals for optimum 80X87 performance. The tradeoff here is speed versus memory storage. REALs take 6 bytes and DOUBLEs take 8. While singles take only 4 bytes, the reduced numeric storage precision may not be acceptable.

The assembly language program takes 0.35 s or over a factor of two enhancement. This is significant in tight calculations. Further, the assembly language routine could be patched to a Pascal program using SINGLE variables with the result that the calculations would all be done at full precision even though the results were stored as single precision.

To put this all into perspective, interpreted GWBASIC at 37 s is about a factor of ten slower than the non-coprocessor compiled Pascal program. The best 8087 Pascal version is about a factor of four faster, and the assembly language 8087 version is another factor of two faster. Thus, the overall improvement from a primitive interpreter is two orders of magnitude; a one hour math-intensive calculation in GWBASIC is half a minute with assembly language.

13.5 REFERENCES

Palmer and Morse give a very nice overview of the 8087 and its programming. Among other things, they explain how to rethink the 8087 as a register rather than a stack processor with little loss of efficiency. Startz gives a complete discussion of the 8087 with particular emphasis on useful data reduction subprograms and their interface to BASIC. Examples include matrix multiplication and solution of linear equations. Conversion to Pascal would be a "doable" but non-trivial exercise.

Problems

13–1. Write an 80X87 assembly language routine that calculates the value of a sixth order polynomial for any value of x:

$$y = a_0 + a_1 x + a_2 x^2 + a_3 x^3 + a_4 x^4 + a_5 x^5 + a_6 x^6$$

The memory allocation immediately after your program will look like:

```
x     argument
a 0   coefficients
a 1       "
a 2       "
a 3       "
a 4       "
a 5       "
a 6       "
y     result
```

There are two ways to do the calculation and on a stack-oriented processor; both are fairly efficient. The first is the bullmoose left-to-right way while keeping the partial x^n for the next calculation. The second works backward:

$$y = a_0 + x (a_1 + x (a_2 + x (a_3 + x (a_4 + x (a_5 + a_6 \, x)))))$$

The first approach takes twelve multiplications and six additions. The second takes six multiplications and six additions. If each floating point operation takes the same time, then the expansion method executes in about two-thirds the time. Obviously, the second method is the method of choice, but you may use either one.

Repeat a large number of the calculations so that you can time the calculation. It will be necessary to use an assembly language outer loop.

13–2. The operation of lst.asm is not obvious. With a sample set of numbers, go through one complete cycle of the calculation showing the registers after each instruction.

13–3. Rewrite lst.asm so that it calculates the slope and intercept of the data. Use a much smaller value for the number of points (i.e., 5–10) and enter them in the dq statements. Be sure to change N. Since N is an integer, you must load it in the coprocessor with FILD. You can either store the result in memory and examine it with the DEBUG e command or leave it in the 80X87 and examine it with your debugger's register display mode.

Note that since this is a simple, fast portion of a least squares calculation, you do not need to keep everything in the 80X87 to speed up the calculations. External scratchpads are acceptable.

13–4. Rewrite LSTSQR.ASM to interface with a Pascal program. Have it accept the addresses of the x and y arrays, sumx, sumy, sumxy, sumx2, and sumy2 as variable parameters on the stack from a calling Pascal program. Change the appropriate sum variables in the calling Pascal program.

13–5. Rewrite 13–4 so that Slope and Intercept are also passed on the stack as variable parameters. Calculate the slope and intercept and return the result via address.

13–6. A trickier problem is if the first and last points for the least squares fit are not the beginning and end points in the arrays. Write a least squares routine that accepts x and y arrays (var parameters) and the indices of the first and last point to be used in the fit (the indices can be value parameters). You must calculate the starting addresses of the first point and the last point. The Pascal and the assembly language portions will have to agree in advance whether your array index starts at 0 or at 1.

Calculating the address of the first point is not as bad as it might at first seem. See sumit.asm, the sum of integers program, in Chapter 12. If x_0 is the offset of the first element of array x, then the offset address of x_n is:

$$x_0 + 8n$$

8n is very easy to calculate since it will be a 16-bit number and 8 is a power of 2. Any arbitrary power of 2 can be calculated by adding the number to itself n times. Thus, if the element number is in ax, multiplication by 8 is achieved by:

```
add ax, ax      ; 2 times original ax in ax
```

```
add ax, ax      ; 4 times original ax in ax
add ax, ax      ; 8 times original ax in ax
```

The number of elements is the difference between the first and last +1.

13–7. Write an assembly language routine that solves a quadratic equation for real and imaginary roots. Pass your routine the three coefficients and the address of two solution vectors. The vector should be a two dimensional array where:

S(1,1)= real part of first solution
S(1,2)= imaginary part of first solution
S(2,1)= real part of second solution
S(2,2)= imaginary part of second solution

Reminder: Under most circumstances write only code time-critical portions in assembler. The solution of a quadratic is not a major bottleneck and would not justify the work.

14

Miscellaneous

14.1 INTRODUCTION

It is impossible to cover all important topics in a book this size and cuts have been necessary. For valid reasons, others would have selected a different distribution of topics. We devote this chapter to pointing out some of our omissions and some relevant literature. We discuss some aspects of software and hardware.

In an area moving as rapidly as computer technology, we cannot be absolutely up to date. The reader should visit the book store for current monographs and technical magazines. Our favorites are *Byte*, *PC Magazine*, and *InfoWorld* for general information on computers and software; frequently, hardware and software are reviewed. *Dr. Dobb's Journal* (originally *Dr. Dobb's Journal of Computer Calisthenics and Orthodontia— Running Light Without Over Byte*) is an entertaining, hardcore software-only journal. *Radio Electronics* is one of the best general electronics magazines. *Electronics* and *EDN* are professional electronics hardware magazines. For scientific applications, *Review of Scientific Instruments*, *Journal of Physics E*, *Analytical Chemistry*, *Analytica Chimica Acta*, and *Computers in Physics* make enjoyable browsing.

In summary, follow the literature and write away freely to the manufacturers for their literature. Much of it is highly informative and free.

14.2 SOFTWARE

While software represents a major cost of your computer system, there is very well written software that is either inexpensive or free. Much of it will do useful and important things better than some highly priced commercial software; indeed, some of this free or inexpensive software does things for which there is no expensive commercial package. Much of this software is shareware or public domain.

Public domain software is open to the public to be freely used and distributed. Much of it is restricted to non-commercial use only; commercial users must negotiate with the authors. Usually, copies must always bear the original authorship credit, and if any changes are made they must be fully documented. Indeed, much of this software has been debugged and greatly enhanced by many able users.

Shareware software is more commercial, although in many cases marginally so. Distribute it to as many people as possible along with the author's credits. If you like it, send the author or company the suggested donation or price. To sweeten the pie, some of these come with only partial manuals on the disk, and if you wish to realize the full power, you pay to get the latest update and the full manual. Alternatively, some have irritating little bugs like a long initialization sequence or messages that periodically pop up on the screen asking you to pay. Paying gives you a clean copy. Given that these packages are usually very modestly priced ($5–100), and you get to test drive before you buy, these sources are excellent ways to get some high-performance software for a very modest price.

In another trick, every purchased copy has a unique owner's serial number. When owners want to purchase a copy, they send in their current bootleg copy with payment. The company then sends a small royalty to the original authorized owner. The new purchaser is then encouraged to distribute his or her copy widely to collect royalties.

Where do I find all these nice packages? PC Software Interest Group is one of the biggest distributors of public domain software. Their copying and mailing fee is about $7 per disk (less in quantity). Many computer clubs and users are ready sources. Computing centers frequently supply utilities. Computer bulletin boards have a cornucopia of software. We list a few packages below.

Word Processors. A quality shareware program is PC-Write. PC-Write was extremely popular at our University, since it supports central laser jet printers. Many students wrote their theses on it.

CHIWRITER is a shareware scientific version of PC-Write. It gives a "what you see is what you get" (WYSISWYG) display that shows equations, tables, and Greek symbols on the screen in the format that they will be printed.

RAM Utilities. RAM utilities are like cockroaches. Once you find the first one, you can never get rid of the things. RAM utilities are usually programs that you load on booting up. They stay resident and invisible in the background until you need them. To activate them, you use a special key combination (so-called "hot keys") that does not conflict with anything else (e.g., ALT and / simultaneously). Examples include spelling checkers, thesaurus, calculators, calendars, dialers, memo pads, and keyboard enhancers.

We comment briefly on how these work. As you might guess, the utility installs itself for permanent RAM residency, and then usurps control of the keyboard DOS interrupt function. Usually the way this is done is to note the current value of the interrupt and replace it with the address of the utility. Now, whenever a key is struck it is processed through the keyboard interrupt, which is the utility. The utility checks to see if it is a function that the utility should process. If the utility should ignore the keystroke, the character is passed on unchanged to the standard routine.

Side Kick is one of the first pop-up RAM utilities that includes a memo pad; an appointment calendar; a four function calculator complete with hex, octal, and binary arithmetic; and an automatic modem dialer with a phone library.

Utilities have several problems. First, they take up memory. After you allocate a RAM disk and load up several utilities, there may not be enough memory to run your programs, especially on 640K PCs. When we started to use our first 1K system, the thought that 640K might not be enough never occurred to us. The 80286 and 80386 machines with DOS 3.0 and greater support larger memories, at least for RAM disks and some utilities that were designed to work with it.

The second problem is that there really is not a completely clean way to intercept the DOS calls. This means that many utilities end up doing non-standard things and tripping over each other. With multiple utilities from different manufacturers, it is common for the system to fail, behave erratically, or freeze. Frequently, installing them in a different orders solves the problem. If this, or calls to your dealer, do not help, figure out which utility you need most and delete the others.

Keyboard Enhancer. Keyboard enhancers are RAM utilities that filter your key strokes and redefine keys. The enhancer can delete certain keys and convert one keystroke into a sequence of keystrokes that are passed to the operating system.

The utility of a keyboard enhancer is probably best shown by an example. The Borland WordStar-like editor has no transpose-two-letters command, so we implemented one by redefining one of the special function keys. This can be done with six commands of ten key strokes. Can you determine what they are? With our enhancer, we redefined a special function key with this ten key stroke sequence. Then, to transpose two letters, we hit the special function key. Done! Also, we use many long complicated chemical formulas with a lot of superscripts and subscripts (translate: a lot of typing errors). By properly defining them once, we can call them up by a single keystroke.

A good enhancer allows easy creation of new macros on the fly if, at any time, you tire of typing something and wish to abbreviate. It should also have provisions for editing your definitions and for deleting old macros or loading new ones.

Prokey was the original keyboard enhancer and is still quite popular. The authors use Borland's SuperKey.

Enhancers can also keep track of your commands and allow you to pull them up to see what you did or to issue the same command again. Our group uses the public domain CED (Command Editor) or DOSEDIT.

CAD (Computer Aided Design). CAD is to drawing figures as a word processor is to writing manuscripts. A good CAD allows you to draw figures on the screen, move pieces around, delete sections, rotate, expand, or contract pieces, and label. You can save pieces to disk and call them back later to insert them into figures. When you have it the way you want it, you can print it on a plotter, or a dot matrix or laser jet printer. Some allow automatic insertion of measurement angles and dimensions. High level CAD allows display and rotation of three dimensional figures.

Probably the best part of CAD is the cut and paste feature. Many figures are just composites made up of pieces that you used before. By saving these pieces or by cutting them out of existing drawings, you can frequently build very complicated figures with little effort. For example, we have major electronic components and units (e.g., operational feedback configuration) stored in files and can incorporate even the most complicated into a figure in seconds.

Prices range from about a hundred dollars for GenericCAD to "if you have to ask, don't bother." The *de facto* standard is AUTOCAD, which is available from a few hundred to a few thousand dollars. Most of the other CADs have utilities that permit inter-conversion of AUTOCAD and their files. Except for data plots, all figures here were drafted with AUTOCAD.

You need a mouse or digitizing tablet as well as a hard disk, at least EGA graphics, and a math coprocessor for reasonable results. Most CADs configure for a variety of different pointing devices and plotters.

Disk Utilities. There are numerous disk utilities on the market. Generally these allow the users to examine disk organization, to patch files, to eliminate file fragmentation to speed up your disk, and to recover damaged or erased files. These programs are particularly useful when you are trying to learn how a disk is really organized and how the operating system manipulates data on it. Although it is only one of many excellent products, we find the Norton Utilities to be extremely useful.

Also, moving around on a fully tree structured disk is no fun if you type poorly. Many utilities show a disk map and allow changing directories by merely pointing at the desired destination and entering return. Some allow marking files in a group with a single key stroke for later block operations, and carry out block operations such as deletions or copies. If you have not moved a number of files on a hard disk, you will not appreciate how useful this is. We like PCBOSS, which is a very tidy utility that does most things very cleanly.

Miscellaneous, Miscellaneous Software. Many of our figures were plotted on a dot matrix printer with Golden Software's SURFER and GRAPHER. GRAPHER plots x,y data. SURFER is a delightful contour or three-dimensional surface mapper (Chapter 8).

POWER (Turbo Power Software) is a fantastic collection of utilities that sells for about a hundred dollars. The source code (largely in Turbo Pascal) is also available. POWER includes a Pascal formatter and structure analyzer that allows you to consistently format all of your programs, track down a variety of sneaky bugs, or clean up a program by removing unused variables. POWER has a utility that gives your disk tree structure along with the size of each subdirectory. POWER also has a profiler that allows you to tell where your programs spend their time, which is invaluable for speeding up bottlenecks.

UNIX-Like Software. The AT&T operating system is UNIX. It was developed to run their computer systems and the phone networks. It is a multiuser, multitasking system; more than one user can independently use the computer and each user can be running more than one task at a time. OS/2 is Microsoft's version of this.

Without a shell, UNIX is flexible, powerful, cryptic, and positively user-hostile; in short, dangerous. This book was typeset using the UNIX troff typesetter with the Berkeley me macros. Many UNIX utilities are so useful that they have been implemented on PCs. The most useful are the editors, the sort, and the search-pattern recognition routines. We would not be without several of them. The two you really should have are the pattern search (GREP) and the sort (SORT) routines.

Borland supplies a GREP program with Pascal. GREP is like FIND but infinitely more powerful. Most UNIX routines use regular expressions, which are DOS wild cards run amok. You can specify any combination of any number of letters, numeric digits, and punctuation. You can specify location in the line and surrounding syntax. Commands look like a chicken dipped in ink ran across the page, but they are powerful. In one command you can find all READLNs without regard to capitalization, all lines on which the first non-space character is ";", all lines ending with "external;" without regard to capitalization, and so on. Read about it and use it; you'll love it.

UNIX sort allows sorting on primary and secondary keys. You can sort a DOS directory alphabetically by extension and, within extension, alphabetically by name. Try that with DOS!

SED (Stream Oriented Editor) is useful for making changes in ASCII files. If you messed up a variety of things you can write a series of sed commands that can be executed from a single file to go back and make all the corrections at once. Since regular expressions are supported and you can limit the action of certain commands to specific pieces of the file, it is much more flexible than most word processors.

We have used UNIX utilities from Mortice Kerns Software. This can provide more of a UNIX-like command structure and closer UNIX compatibility.

14.3 IEEE-488 INTERFACE BUS

The Institute of Electrical Engineers (IEEE) 488 standard (IEEE-488) is their standard for Hewlett-Packard's Interface Bus (HPIB). It is a byte parallel, serial interface for local instrument control. Virtually every computer-interfaceable instrument is equipped with an IEEE-488 or has that option. The system uses open collector logic so that the multiple instruments can sit on the same set of lines without risk of burnout. A three-wire handshake is used to insure that all systems being addressed are ready before information is transmitted.

Commands are generally issued in ASCII, much like the Tektronix scope example of Chapter 9; indeed that scope accepts either an RS-232 or IEEE-488 interface with identical commands. The maximum transmission rate is 400K bytes per second, which makes it much faster than the RS-232.

There are numerous PC IEEE-488 cards ($400–500) on the market. A favorite with instrument manufacturers is the one from National Instruments. For example, the Tektronix interface card is a National card, which is much cheaper from National. National supplies support software in all the major languages including GWBASIC, QuickBASIC, assembler, and Turbo Pascal.

The standard was designed to be all things to all people and it is very complicated. The IEEE standards manual contains it all and is a typical opaque standards reference. If you just want to see how the IEEE works, see Liebson.

The manufacturer's claim that their instrument is IEEE-488 compatible may mean very little if you have to write the control software yourself. One of our students spent an entire summer interfacing an absorption spectrometer to a PC via its IEEE-488 port; the interface control was very quirky and poorly documented. Success came only with incredible diligence and the extensive assistance of one of the manufacturer's engineers.

Our recommendation is to avoid, if at all possible, having to write PC instrument control software. Insist on a package from the manufacturer. If they cannot supply one, go with another manufacturer. Also, be sure to test drive it before purchase. Increasing numbers of manufacturers are making their instruments RS-232 compatible for direct use on a PC, so the need for IEEE-488 interfaces is becoming less severe.

14.4 PLOTTERS

While many software packages such as GRAPHER use digital plotters, we have not touched on plotter graphics. Plotters have their own graphics language, and the *de facto* standard is HPGL (Hewlett-Packard Graphics Language). Most manufacturer's plotters use HPGL. Each HPGL command is two letters followed by parameters as required. The language is the same for RS-232 or IEEE-488 interfaced plotters. For example, IN is initialize, PA is plot absolute, and PR is plot relative. The language is not difficult to learn. The Hewlett-Packard plotter manuals give exceptionally lucid descriptions along with GWBASIC programs.

To aid in learning and using HPGL, we have developed two tools (Carraway, Xu, Ballew, and Demas, submitted). One is a Pascal program, HPGL, which allows you to issue keyboard commands directly to the plotter and visualize the effect. Parameters can be sent and returned results displayed (e.g., current pen position, status, or digitized value). Error checking prevents you from issuing a syntactically incorrect command that would mess up the plotter, although you can override error checking to view the result of a bad sequence. HPGL is quite useful for learning HPGL and for developing simple program sequences.

The other program, PLOT5, is a graphics command interpreter. It allows you to create a file of even higher level graphics commands. PLOT5 reads the file, converts the commands into an appropriate series of HPGL commands, and drives the plotter. PLOT5 allows reading in data files in GRAPHER format, generating numbered X and Y axes with titles, and displaying Greek and other symbols. Because PLOT5 is modular, you can define and add your own high-level graphics commands.

14.5 SENSORS AND MECHANICAL MOVEMENT

Sensors form the core of most physical measurements. Sheingold gives an excellent description of temperature, pressure, force, and flow sensor, as well as the necessary electrical considerations for interfacing them. Horowitz and Hill, as well as Malmstadt, et al., give good overviews of sensors. In particular, for temperature sensing, National Semiconductors, Analog Devices, and Motorola make nice solid state devices that give linear outputs with temperature. The latest RCA phototube manual is an excellent description of phototubes and photomultipliers. Sprague (1987) makes a cute line of magnetic and optoelectric sensors.

For mechanical movement, the stepping motor is the work horse. Stepping motors have several winding and magnetic poles. When the appropriate series of pulses is applied to the different windings, the motor will move clockwise or counterclockwise a fixed number of degrees; the step size depends on the motor configuration and pulse sequence. Step size ranges from 0.1 to 30° with 1.8 to 7.5° being typical. Smaller resolutions require gear trains. For details see Malmstadt, et al., and literature from Philips and Sprague. For a nice discussion and a list of manufacturers see the article by Lancaster. Note that most manufacturers supply single chip drivers for their motors. You need only supply power, a TTL compatible direction level and a single pulse for each step. Wilkins, et al., give a nice example of a stepping motor driven titrator.

A digital plotter makes a convenient system for certain types of movement. One of our students built a conductive film on an 8.5"x11" piece of paper with two electrodes. When a voltage is applied between the two points, an electric field distribution results on the sheet. A plotter pen was converted into an electrode. By scanning the "pen" over the surface and measuring the potential at each point, we generated a surface electric field contour map.

Optical scanners are useful for moving light around. They are frequently nothing more than a mirror mounted on the shaft of meter type movement. Current is applied to the coils, the shaft twists, and any light beam falling on the mirror is deflected. The laser optical scanners in many stores use galvanometer deflectors for scanning the beam over the product bar graph. Frequencies of up to about a kiloHertz can be achieved for small mirrors. Deflections of about 30° are possible.

Appendix A

Experiments

A.1 Chapter 2 Experiments: DOS and BASIC

The following experiments were briefly described in Chapter 2. In particular, many of the things that you do are potentially very dangerous to the existing disk contents. Be especially careful not to erase anything on the system or hard disks. Should you inadvertently format a hard disk or erase any files that you need, stop immediately and **do not** do anything further. These files can probably be recovered by your instructor. The same is true of a hard disk that has been formatted—although this is generally tedious. FORMATing a hard disk does not reinitialize the entire surface, as it does with a floppy disk.

Experiment 2–1. Boot the computer from the supplied system disk. Use the directory command to see what files are on this disk. Play with the wildcard features of DIR. Print the directory. Use CHKDSK to verify the system disk integrity and to determine memory use.

Experiment 2–2. Format a disk. Copy several files from the system disk over to your disk. Use wildcards to copy groups of programs selectively to your disk.

Experiment 2–3. Erase all the files on your disk and set up a bootable disk. Since it is already formatted, you can use either the SYS or the slower FORMAT/S methods.

Experiment 2–4. Using the COPY command, create the following file called DEMO.BAT on your disk:

```
DIR/W
REM Hit any key to continue
PAUSE
REM You have just seen a demonstration of a batch file
```

Do not forget to close the file with ^Z and <CR>. When finished execute the file by typing DEMO. What happens?

Experiment 2–5. Using TYPE, display the AUTOEXEC.BAT and interpret what it does. Type other files. Some files print and some give garbage or a mixture of garbage and text (i.e., GWBASIC.EXE or COMMAND.COM). Print your batch file or some other text file to the line printer using the COPY method. Also, use the PrtSc method.

Experiment 2–6. Compare the speed of several disk operations using a physical drive and a RAM disk. A good test is to first copy GWBASIC.EXE to your working disk and to the RAM disk. Then use COPY to generate a new file (e.g., MYBASIC.EXE) from GWBASIC using both the physical and the RAM disks as sources and destinations. Time the operations when the copy is entirely on the RAM disk, entirely on the physical disk, and between the physical and the RAM disks.

On our AT&T 6300, we find the times to be about 12 s and 6 s for floppy to floppy and floppy to RAM disk, respectively. The transfer from RAM disk to RAM disk is too fast (<1 s) to be timed accurately.

Experiment 2–7. In this experiment you use different directory management commands. As it is easy to do an enormous amount of damage with very little effort, use a floppy disk.

Make a formatted system disk. Set up several subdirectories and sub-subdirectories. Change between directories. Move files around within your hierarchy. Type and delete files in different subdirectories.

Move some of the DOS utilities into a subdirectory using COPY and ERASE. Demonstrate that the only way to run programs from a subdirectory is by being in that subdirectory or by using a complete path specification (DOS 3 or higher). Now use the PATH command to set a path to this subdirectory so that you can execute programs from any place in the disk structure. You can invoke the path command directly from DOS rather than in an AUTOEXEC.BAT file.

A.2 Async Serial Communication Unit

For the serial experiments of Chapter 3, we provide a Unit Async that has powerful serial routines. Async is a public domain package originally written by M. Quinlan with correction of bugs and upgrades to Turbo Pascal 4 and 5 by A. Dealey, K. Hawes, W. M. Miller, R. Ballew, and J. N. Demas.

Async is interrupt driven. Once opened, it catches and saves in a buffer any incoming characters regardless of what your program is doing elsewhere. Then, at your leisure, you can extract the characters from the buffer. For pedagogical reasons we have moved the Implementation variables Async_Head, Async_Tail, Async_Buffer_Used into the Interface section so that they can be displayed by your Pascal programs. The more important routines and their functions are listed below:

```
PROCEDURE Async_Init;
```

This routine initializes all variables. It must be called before any other Async routine.

```
FUNCTION Async_Open(Comprt    : word;
                    Baudrate  : word;
                    Parity    : Char;
                    WordSize  : Word;
                    StopBits  : Word)   :  Boolean;
```

Async_Open works much like the mode command of DOS. It initializes the communication port (COM1 or COM2), sets the baudrate, the parity, the word size, and the stop bits. In addition it sets up and enables the interrupt driver routines. It is a function that returns a TRUE if the initialization was successful and a FALSE if it failed. If you try to open COM2 and it is not available, Async_Open tries to open COM1 instead. Async_Open must be called before using any other function.

```
FUNCTION Async_Change(Comprt    : word;
                      Baudrate  : word;
                      Parity    : Char;
                      WordSize  : Word;
                      StopBits  : Word)   :  Boolean;
```

This routine allows you to change all the communications port routines on the fly. It uses the same protocol as Async_Open, but can only be called after Async_Open.

```
FUNCTION Async_Buffer_Check(VAR C : Char):  Boolean
```

If a character was received by the communications software and is currently available in the buffer, a TRUE is returned and the character is returned in the variable parameter C. The extracted character is removed from the buffer queue. The standard buffer size holds up to 4,096 characters.

PROCEDURE Async_Send(C : Char);

This routine sends the character C passed. There is no error trapping except to return a time out message if the character was not sent.

PROCEDURE Async_Send_String(S : String);

This routine sends the string S passed. There is no error trapping except to return a time out message if the string was not sent.

PROCEDURE Async_Close;

This routine exits gracefully from Async. If you fail to use it and exit your program, then the first serial character that is received activates the receive character routine in memory. Unfortunately, this routine will no longer be there and the system will crash. Always call Async_Close before exiting a program that called Async_Open.

A simple program, TTY2, that uses Async is shown below. This reads the keyboard and serially outputs each character, but does not echo or display the keyboard character. An ESC character terminates program execution. This program also monitors the serial input buffer and displays the characters received serially. It ignores CRs and converts LFs into CRLF sequences. Further, it displays the Async_Head, Async_Tail, Async_Buffer_Used, and Async_Overflow at the end of every line so that you can monitor the operation of the circular buffer and see when overflow occurs. If you remove the display of the variables, this program is quite useful for controlling and monitoring the operation of ASCII character-oriented serial instruments.

```
PROGRAM  tty2;
USES Crt,Async;
CONST  BAUD = 9600;      {Set the baud rate as a constant}
VAR
  c : char;
  k : integer;

BEGIN
  Async_Init;   { initialize  variables }
  {open com1 to BAUD rate, no parity, 8-bits, 1 stop}
  if not  Async_Open(1, BAUD, 'N', 8, 1)  then
    BEGIN
      writeln( '** ERROR:  Async_Open  failed') ;
      halt
    END;

  writeln( 'Serial Input-Output begins now...' );
```

```
writeln ('Baud rate : ',BAUD);
writeln('Press    ESC key  to terminate...');

repeat
  if Async_Buffer_Check(c)   then
    case  c of
    #013 : ;   {ignores CR}
    #010  : BEGIN    {treats LF as CRLF sequence}
              write('  HEAD ',Async_Buffer_Head,'  TAIL  ',
                Async_Buffer_Tail);
              write ('  ', Async_Buffer_Overflow,'   ',
                Async_Buffer_Used);
              Writeln  { handle carriage  return as CR/LF }
            END
  else
      write(c)  {  else write incoming char to the screen }
    END; { case }

  if KeyPressed then
    BEGIN
      c := readkey;
      if c = #027   then  { Trap Esc Key }
        BEGIN
          Async_Close;     { reset the interrupt  system, etc.}
          Writeln ('End  Serial I/O...' );
          halt;            { terminate the  program }
        END
      else
        Async_Send(c)
    END;
until FALSE;              {repeat forever}
END.
```

Note that closing the routine is critical. If you fail to do it, the system may suddenly crash at a later time should a serial character be sent to your computer.

A.3 Chapter 3 Experiments: Serial-Parallel Interfacing
For the first time you play directly with computer hardware using both serial and parallel interfacing. These two techniques are extremely important and are the basis of virtually everything that is done later.

Warnings. While making connections, it is possible to damage seriously the devices or the computer. Therefore, careful attention to wiring is essential. **Never** connect a ground or voltage source to an output line; this may burn out the computer. Connecting a display to an input pin will do no harm, and allows you to monitor the signal being input.

With programmable I/O devices it is especially possible to have outputs where you intended inputs—with potentially damaging consequences. Thus, not only must you be careful about your wiring, you must also be careful about your software.

Experiment 3–1. In this experiment, you explore serial output using Async. Use the configuration shown in Figure 3–2.

Write a Pascal program that outputs characters to the serial port. First, initialize to the COM1 communications port with 300 baud, no parity, and one stop bit. Check the keyboard for a character input. If there is no character, continue to output the last character read from the keyboard to the COM1 serial output port. Terminate program execution on an ESC character. Remember to use Async_Close.

Use the oscilloscope to monitor the transmission. Try to pick out the start bit, the stop bits, and the character. This is almost hopeless. There are just too many high-low transitions for the oscilloscope to trigger reliably if the UART sends the data out as fast as it can. However, the receiving UART gets in step at the beginning and stays there. You and the oscilloscope are not clever enough to lock on.

To circumvent this problem, modify your program by inserting a delay (Delay function) of about one character transmission time (1/30 s) after each character transmission. This permits the line to settle to the idle state long enough for the oscilloscope to trigger properly on the next start bit.

Once you get a good display, try outputting different characters. Convince yourself that they are being output correctly by comparing the outputs with Table 3–1.

By modifying the Async_Open parameter, explore the effect of variations in the baud rate, parity, the number of stop bits, and the number of data bits on the display. You might want to modify the program so that the changes can be entered from the keyboard in response to the computer queries.

An important question is how fast the computer can output data and keep the serial data transmission line fully occupied. This will, of course, be a function of the program, but one answer to the question is given by the following program. Set the baud rate to 9600. Rewrite the program so that it outputs the same character repeatedly in a loop with 1,000 iterations, and then goes back and checks for a new keyboard character. Does the display show that the UART is being used continuously or are there spaces between characters? If there are gaps, the program is slower than the serial data transmission software. By the size of the gaps, estimate what baud rate would not exceed the processor speed. Try it. Many modern PCs show no gaps even at 9600 baud.

Experiment 3–2. Examine the parallel input and output connectors brought out, the display, and the patch board. Using jumpers, we configured it as shown in Figure 3–5. Using the S8255 Unit, set PORT C to output and A to input; the output on C can be read on A. The LEDs show the data.

Write a program that continually tests the keyboard for a key press. When a new key is pressed, have the program read in the new character and output it to the parallel output port. The LED display shows the binary pattern of the last input character. Try typing different characters and examine the displays. Do they match the ASCII codes?

If you have not already made provision to escape, rewrite the program so that you can break out. Terminate the program by testing each character as it comes in and end the program on an ESC.

Experiment 3–3. An informative variation on the previous problem generates a reproducible pattern and sends it out to the parallel port. The easiest pattern is to initialize a byte variable to 0, increment it, and output it after every incrementation. The pattern will repeat itself. In principle, you should be able to watch the eight LED displays count up from 0 to 255, reset to zero, and repeat. Try it. All except the most significant LED bits seem to be on all the time. The software is so fast that your eye perceives an average value. Examine the output of the least significant bit (0) on an oscillosope (Figure 3–5) or measure the frequency on a counter. The maximum rate is what the program can sustain.

Experiment 3–4. Using bit set/reset operations for the C port, write a program that first zeros all C bits, then sequentially turns bit 0 on and off, bit 1 on and off, and so on. Hold the bit set for 100 ms before going on to the next bit. After bit 7 has been turned off, start over with bit 0 and repeat until any key is pressed.

Experiment 3–5. Wire up the NAND gate tester of Figure 3–6.
(A) Write a program to test Gate #1 for full functionality. That is, it must give the correct output for all four possible input combinations. You may use a look-up table if desired. It is only necessary to make one test of the gate.
(B) Write a program to test the entire gate for full functionality. It is not adequate to test each gate separately. You must test all 256 possible input combinations and verify that the correct four outputs are obtained. The reason for this more extreme test is that there can be interactions between different gates, and a gate may fail only for a specific combination of other inputs. This is known as pattern sensitivity.
You may not use a look-up table, but must compute the correct answer and compare it with the observed NAND outputs. The wiring has been set up to make this computation as simple as possible. This is an excellent exercise for familiarizing you with bit level logic and shifting operations. The actual testing portion is only a few lines of Pascal code.

Experiment 3–6. Wire up the parallel interface for the Intersil universal counter (Figure 3–7). Use a TTL oscillator to give frequency readings. Play with the ranges and the different functions until you are comfortable with their operation.
Write software that triggers the counter and holds the reading on the display. Now write a program that reads the counter display and displays it on the video; include the decimal point. You can get the data either in an ASCII format or as a number. If you get it as a string, convert it to a real number. If you get it as a real, convert it to a string. This non-trivial program allows for much creativity in the handling of the address and the digit processing.
You should be aware of several points. First, the digit address provided by the encoder is the inverse of the actual digit address. Secondly, once you start reading digits, do not count on succeeding reads giving succeeding digits. The window of opportunity for reading each digit is only 200–300 µs. If your software is not fast enough, you might miss the next digit. Indeed, it is possible with a slow enough machine to get an accidental locking of your software to the scan rate; you might have to try dozens of times and still never get all the digits.
We have not told you whether the counter scans from most significant digit to least or the inverse. Can you determine whether it scans forward or backward using only

software? It is easy with a scope. For maximum speed of transfer, does the direction have any effect on how fast you can update your data? Demonstrate this experimentally.

Note: In spite of the potential problems with getting all the digits across, we never had difficulty using an 8 MHz 8086 based machine (faster than the first PC, but slower than an 80286 machine) with the counter and either Turbo Pascal 3 or Turbo Pascal 4.

A.4 Chapter 4 Experiments: Graphics and Digitizers

This series of experiments leads to a useful digitizer and data reduction program. You will find the problem much easier if you read through all of the exercises first and then develop procedures that can be used later. Pascal readily lends itself to modular programming, and you should begin to think this way. Failure to think through the overall problem in advance means trying to integrate parts that should have been designed initially to work together harmoniously. If you do not exploit the strengths of Pascal, you might as well have programmed in the worst style of BASIC.

All experiments work well with the HiPad, the Summagraphics digitizer, or a variety of other digitizers. When we use the HiPad we have switches on its side that permit changing the baud rate, the resolution (0.01 inch or 0.005 inch), and the resettable zero. We configure our Summagraphics for autobaud and no parity. The default resolution of 500 lines per inch (lpi) is adequate for this experiment, but the 1000 lpi resolution gives the cursor coordinates in 0.001 inch directly.

In order to play with the digitizer and to demonstrate the operation of the buffer, we use the interrupt driven Unit Async described above. Our version declares Async_Buffer_Used and Async_Head and Async_Tail in the INTERFACE rather than in the IMPLEMENTATION. This allows you to display the value as each line of digitizer input is displayed and as the circular buffer pointers chase each other while the buffer fills and empties.

Experiment 4–1. Familiarize yourself with your digitizer. Examine the digitizing platen and the cursor. If possible, note the coil and the embedded wires.

Set the program's baud rate to 9600 baud by changing the constant and change the baud rate on the digitizer to match. Run SerIO to confirm satisfactory operation. Play with the cursor in the different modes and note the effect. Place the digitizer in the stream and switch stream mode. If you have a Summapad, use the request by sending a D, then force digitizations by sending P characters.

Experiment 4–2. Write a Pascal program to initialize the digitizer, set it to the point mode (if possible), and display each string as it is output from the digitizer.

For the Summagraphics you must initialize the baud rate by first sending a space character and waiting. If something goes wrong or you want to change the baud rate, you can only reset the digitizer by unplugging it and plugging it back in.

Unless otherwise indicated use Point in subsequent problems.

Experiment 4–3. Modify the previous program to pull apart the strings and convert them into two integers that give the X and Y cursor coordinates. Use string operations such as VAL, Copy, and Delete to tear the strings apart and convert them into integers. Store the resultant (x,y) pairs in a data array of reals in anticipation of later changes. Exit the acquisition loop if the number of points exceeds 500 or the user presses a keyboard key or a specific cursor button.

Experiment 4–4. A useful variation of the basic program is to digitize and draw figures. Scale the PC's screen to match the full scale coordinates of the digitizer (e.g., [0,0] to [6000,6000] for the Summapad in the 500 lpi mode). Rather than print points, display your points on the video as each one is digitized. Use the following rules: 1) draw a line to the next point if the 1 button is pressed; and 2) move to the next point if a specific other button is pressed.

Experiment 4–5. Modify the program of Experiment 4–3 so that you can initially digitize the lower left-hand corner of the data that you wish to digitize and then the upper right-hand corner. Provide the program with the user coordinates of these points. For example, if you were digitizing an absorption spectrum, the lower left corner might be 300 nm and 0 absorbance units and the upper right 700 nm and 1 absorbance unit. This portion of code provides the program with the necessary information to convert digitizer output, which comes across in digitizer units, into user units. With the Summagraphics you might use different digitizer number buttons to signify different functions.

Experiment 4–6. Modify your program so that the remaining data are converted to user units before storage. After termination of data input, plot the data in user units.

Experiment 4–7. This problem and the next one concern digitizing and obtaining the lifetime for the luminescence decay of the oscilloscope trace of Figure A–1. The trace is a luminescence decay curve measured from a laser-excited sample. The emission intensity was determined with a photomultiplier tube. There are several complications:

(1)   The decay curve of interest falls outside the area that has calibration lines.
(2)   There is a baseline that must also be determined and removed from the decay curve before data reduction.
(3)   The decay has increasing emission intensity as the signal becomes more negative; this is a consequence of the increased electron flow in the phototube as the light intensity increases.

We describe how to deal with each problem. It is irrelevant that the calibration lines are in an area smaller than the curve of interest. Your lower left and upper right user points do not have to be the actual corners of the plot as long as you specify their actual user coordinates. For example, you might use the circled points as (50,1) and (400,6) for your digitized corners; the units would then be nanoseconds and scope screen divisions. Of course, for plotting you must make provisions so that the data stays on the screen.

Rewrite your program, if necessary, so that you can digitize the decay curve. Plot the data on a scale with units of time and height in screen units as it is digitized.

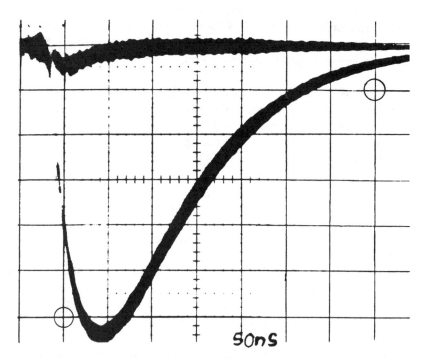

50nS

Figure A–1. Oscilloscope photograph of a laser-excited luminescent decay of a tris(4,7-diphenyl-1,10-phenanthroline)osmium(II). Every major division is 50 ns. Demas (1983). Copyright© 1983. Adapted with permission of Academic Press.

Experiment 4–8. In order to fit the exponential portion of the curve by least squares, you must baseline correct the data. To simplify your determination, assume that the baseline is constant with a value equal to those at the latest times. Set your software up so that you can enter one baseline point on request. With the Summagraphics you could use one button to enter data and another for the baseline. If you then subtract every point on the decay from this baseline, you end up with positive baseline corrected intensities, which are convenient for plotting and logarithmic fitting.

Rewrite your program to permit entering a baseline point. Strip the baseline, plot the baseline corrected intensities versus time, and plot the semilogarithmic plot of intensity versus time. Allow specifying the range of points to be fit by linear least squares and fit the data to obtain the lifetime. Use your earlier log fit procedure.

Finally, after you calculate the best parameters, point plot the data with a symbol. Superimpose on this plot the theoretical curve for your least squares fit. Note that you will have to guard against calculating negative numbers or selecting too wide a range for the log axis.

The finite rise time of the curve is a consequence of the finite laser excitation pulse width. The early portion of the curve is not free from continued laser pumping and is not exponential. When you do your fitting, examine the semilogarithmic plot and determine where the decay becomes exponential before selecting the fitting region.

Experiment 4–9. To make the program truly useful, have provisions for saving data to disk files. Use a sequential Text file. The file should have a line that contains a string that describes the contents, a line that gives the number of x,y pairs stored, and the data as x,y pairs with one pair to a line. A much more elegant and compact way to store the data is a record, but that is not necessary to achieve a useful program.

Once stored, data from these files could be recalled and any type of calculation and graphics could be performed. Note that the recall program would look exactly like your write program except that you would use Readln statements instead of Writeln statements.

Experiment 4–10. A useful option is to modify the program so that it only displays results if the x coordinate has changed by more than some delta x that you specify in a dialog or as a program constant. There would be no sense in storing digitized points that are too close together. This modification is particularly useful for eliminating the data glut in Stream or Switch Stream.

Experiment 4–11. If you have a Summagraphics, write a program that uses the Remote Request mode to read data. If you set this up correctly, you can manually sweep across a curve and digitize it continuously. Use of a threshold level between points is essential so that you do not store too many points.

Notes: If you do not have multiple cursor buttons, you could define an area on the platen for commands. The HiPad, for example, has a premarked area. If you write software that recognizes whether or not a point is digitized in a specific block, you can use this to control program flow. Digitizing in different blocks might signal begin Point digitization, begin Switch Stream digitization, enter baseline, save to disk, read data from disk, strip baseline, plot raw data, plot baseline corrected data, and so on.

General Comments. Without telling you how to write the oscilloscope program, we suggest one approach. Write the main program to get a keyboard command and then carry out the command with a case statement that invokes procedures to do all the dirty work. For example:

```
BEGIN                {main body}
ControlCode:='';     {Initialize so works first time}

Repeat

  If Keypressed then
      ControlCode:=ReadKey;       {Get a keyboard character}

  Case ControlCode of
       '1'    :        DigitizeCurve;
       '2'    :        SwitchStreamDigitizeCurve;
       '3'    :        PlotCurve
       '4'    :        DefinePlottingField;
       '5'    :        DefineAxes;
```

```
      '6'      :        StripBaseline;
      '7'      :        LogPlot;
      '8'      :        SavetoDisk;
      '9'      :        LoadfromDisk;
      '0'      :        CalcLifetime;
      'e'      :        ControlCode := 'E';
  END; {case}

until ControlCode ='E';   {end of main loop repeat}

END.
```

This approach is not unique but is easy to follow or modify. Individual functions can be written and debugged separately and combined into the final version.

There are other equally acceptable designs. However, one unacceptable solution is to write the program as one giant body without procedures. This is a nightmare to write, debug, read, and modify.

Alternatively, you may write two or more programs with different functions. For example, one might digitize and save the data while another could read the data off the disk and do the fitting.

Experiment 4–12. There are many commercial graphics packages and you should have available and know how to use at least one of them. We use GRAPHER from Golden Software, which is a highly rated, modestly priced scientific graphics package. As with many commercial packages, it will format and print quality graphs on dot matrix and laser jet printers as well as on digital plotters. GRAPHER requires data in ASCII files with each line containing an x,y pair and one or more spaces separating the pair. The file extension must be DAT. As there are so many packages and preferences, we do not go into the details of using GRAPHER, but provide this information to our students in handouts and a lecture demonstration.

Write a Pascal program that generates two data files containing data conforming to the following functions:

$$D_1(t) = 10000 \exp(-t) \qquad\qquad (A–1)$$

$$D_2(t) = 10000 \left[\exp(-t) - \exp(-2t) \right] \qquad\qquad (A–2)$$

Put 100 pairs for each function $(t, D_1(t))$ and $(t, D_2(t))$ in two files with .DAT extensions. Use the range t=0 to t=5. Delete the t=0 point in the D_2 file. These equations describe serial kinetics or RC electrical networks.

Using GRAPHER or an analogous program plot both functions on a common figure. Include clearly labeled axes. Turn in a linear presentation of the data and a logarithmic presentation (i.e., log[D(t)] versus t). If you have available both a digital plotter and a printer for hard copy, turn in one plot from each.

Experiment 4–13. An alternative to 4–12 is to output your data from the digitizer in GRAPHER format files and plot the background-subtracted data and its logarithmic presentation. Also, GRAPHER will do least squares fitting.

A.5 Chapter 5 Experiments: Analog Considerations

These experiments demonstrate principles of analog-to-digital conversion and the Nyquist sampling theorem.

Experiment 5–1. Use the configuration of Figure 5–9 with an 8255A and an 8-bit DAC to demonstrate different ADC conversion schemes. For demonstration purposes an 8-bit DAC suffices and the programming via only one output port simplifies the problem. Write software to implement (A) a linear ramp ADC; (B) a tracking ADC; and (C) a successive approximation ADC.

The only tricky one is the successive approximation. One possible algorithm is:

(1) Initialize a byte RESULT to zero and another one TESTBIT to 10000000_2 (128_{10}).

(2) Exclusive OR TESTBIT with RESULT to set the new bit to be tried. Output RESULT to the DAC.

(3) Test the V_{in} to see whether $V_{in} > V_{DAC}$.

(4) If $V_{DAC} > V_{in}$, the test byte was too large, and the bit just set should not be kept. Delete it from RESULT by Exclusive ORing TESTBIT and RESULT.

(5) If bit just tested was not the least significant bit, shift TESTBIT right one bit and repeat steps 2–5.

RESULT contains the digitized result after the last test.

Measure the conversion times for different amplitude input voltages. Input a sine wave and monitor the V_{DAC}. Increase the frequency until at least several good points are obtained on each cycle. Find the maximum frequency at which the ADC fails to accurately sample the sine wave. For a monopolar 10 V DAC, you need a sine wave generator that can be offset to appear in the 0–10 V range.

Experiment 5–2. This experiment is designed to demonstrate the Nyquist theorem both on an oscilloscope and with a speaker. Using the preassembled system of Figure A–2, demonstrate the Nyquist sampling theorem. A variable frequency sine wave is digitized at a fixed rate of about 1000 Hz by a computer program and each digitized point is output through a DAC to a speaker. The ear is quite sensitive to the frequency of the waveform, and you can hear the occurrence of aliasing by sweeping the signal generator from below the Nyquist frequency to above it.

Vary the frequency of the input sine wave from well below the Nyquist frequency of 500 Hz to well above. Watch the waveforms and listen to the sound on the speaker. As you approach the Nyquist frequency the tone rises and then falls. Near the Nyquist frequency the tone beats (comes on and goes off). This appears to be due to the fact that at the Nyquist frequency the digitized output must be constant. However, the system clock interrupts acquisition and alters the phasing. Thus, it can be constant or outputting a frequency depending on when the clock interrupts data acquisition.

The RC network acts as a low pass filter and cuts off the higher frequency harmonics that would otherwise be present. The cutoff for the indicated filter components is about 500 Hz, so the digitization rate should be 1000 Hz. Using an oscilloscope monitor

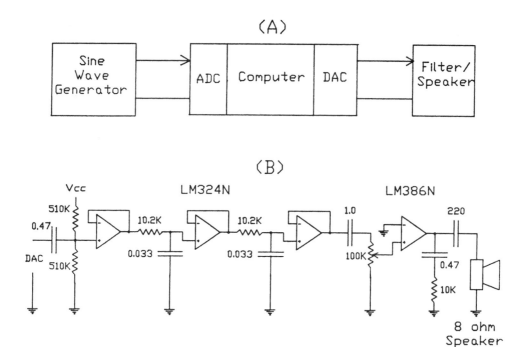

Figure A–2. (A) System to demonstrate the Nyquist sampling theorem. (B) The filter/amplifier is for driving the speaker. The power supply voltage V$_{cc}$ can be 9–15 V. All capacitances are in µF. The peak-to-peak DAC voltage must be about 2 V less than V$_{cc}$ and the variable resistor is adjusted to prevent the speaker driver from overloading. The filter is optimized for about a 1000 Hz sampling rate. Design, construction, and testing courtesy of S. Vincent and M. Grubb.

the input waveform, the DAC output, and the filtered signal.

The filter system uses followers to prevent loading and a two-stage low pass filter with a high frequency cut off to remove frequencies above 500 Hz. Thus, the digitization rate must be close to 1000 Hz. The filter is essential since the DAC output is rich in higher harmonics. We will discuss low pass filters later.

Experiment 5–3. Use a simulation program NYQUIST to show the effect of digitizing different waveforms at different frequencies and the effect of undersampling. The data of Figures 5–14 and 5–15 were generated using NYQUIST.

A.6 Chapter 6 Experiments: Analog-Digital I/O System

These experiments are designed to give you familiarity with a commercial data acquisition system and to apply basic data acquisition approaches to several problems. A digital breadboarding station such as DigiDesigner simplifies setting up the digital exeriments and supplies the necessary TTL oscillator, logic switches, and debounced pushbuttons.

Experiment 6–1. Examine the parallel port input and output connectors. Wire up the system as shown for the 8255 (Figure 3–5) except that Port 1 is output and Port 0 is input. Repeat Experiments 3–2 and 3–3. Determine the relative speed of the DTUtil routines versus those for the 8255.

Note carefully the warning for the experiments for Chapter 3. The 8255 parallel card is relatively easy and inexpensive to repair; the DT2800s use expensive, specialty I/O chips that are soldered in place. Thus, burnout of a DT2800 card is serious.

Experiment 6–2. We provide a configuration with the 3 most significant bits of Port 0 and Port 1 connected together. It is actually the unused portion of the transient recorder of Figure 6–3. Write a program that outputs to Port 1 the seven possible combinations of these bits, reads the information on Port 0, and displays the output and the input.

Use DTSetModifiers to set external triggering in your program before you enter the loop. Connect External Trigger to the debounced push button, which is normally in the 1 state. Rerun the program. Nothing happens until after each press of the push button. Then one digital operation is executed. Thus, two pulses are required to complete one cycle. Note that releasing the button has no effect because the trigger is on the high-to-low transition.

Note that a debounced push button makes exactly one state change when it is pressed and one when it is released. Thus, when you press it, you get a $1 \rightarrow 0$ transition and when you release it you get a $0 \rightarrow 1$ transition. Ordinary switches give tens to hundreds of transitions on one switching because of the mechanical scrapping and bounce of mechanical devices.

Now connect the breadboard TTL oscillator to Ext. Trigger. Start at the lowest rate and increase it. Note that the output rate only increases initially, but eventually stops increasing. The software driving the DT2800 has reached its limit. After running at the highest clock rates, exit the output routine with a key press and check for errors with DTCheckErrors. Even though you were getting more triggers than the program could handle, the DT2800 did not detect the extra trigger pulses and gives no error message. Be forewarned that this is one error that is not trapped.

Experiment 6–3. Using the digital transient recorder of Figure 6–3 collect a 200-point transient for the decade counter. Set up an array and record 200 points from the counter using the External Trigger mode. Plot the decade counter input clock and the outputs on a simple stacked plot (i.e., one above the other) so that you can see the relationship between the outputs and the clock.

Experiment 6–4. Wire the output of DAC0 to the input of an oscilloscope (Figure 6–4). Write a program that outputs a linear ramp as fast as possible. Remember that it is a 12-bit DAC, which means that the acceptable digital inputs are 0 to 4095. How fast does the ramp repeat itself? How many points per second does the software output? If you use larger steps (i.e., 100), you will actually be able to see the steps in the output.

Experiment 6–5. Set up a 100-point array in memory that contains a full cycle of an exponentially damped cosine wave. It should be scaled to integers in the range of 0 to

4095. Using DTDACWriteIM, output it to DAC0 as fast as possible. Examine the result on the oscilloscope. What is the rate in cycles per second?

Experiment 6–6. Run ADCDMA and DACDMA to get a feel for the DMA modes.

Experiment 6–7. Repeat 6–5 using the DMA mode. How fast can you go (μs/point) before you get errors after displaying the data or the output becomes trashed?

Experiment 6–8. Use the X-Y plotter configuration of Figure 6–5 to draw a circle—or ellipses if the axes do not match. The pen control is connected to the digital output port. A logic high lowers the pen and a logic low raises it. Again, remember that the DAC range is 0 to 4095. Remember how fast your software is and how slow the plotter is.

The easiest way to draw a circle is in polar coordinates:

$$x = R * \sin(M * ANGLE) \qquad\qquad (A–3)$$

$$x = R * \cos(N * ANGLE) \qquad\qquad (A–4)$$

where R is the radius and ANGLE is an angle. M and N are integer constants. For M=N a circle of radius R with a center at (0,0) results. You will have to carefully select the range of angles and remember that sin and cos require angles in radian. Use M=N=1. Centering is not included and for the DAC you must have the center at (2048,2048).

More interesting figures arise when M and N are not equal. Try M=2 and N=1 or M=3 and N=2. Attractive multipetalled flowers result for different combinations. You might want to experiment using VIDGR4 before using the DAC.

Experiment 6–9. Wire the output of DAC0 into the ADC 0 input channel. Using immediate modes, output a full scale linear ramp one point at a time and digitize the results as you go along. Display differences between the DAC digital output and the corresponding digitized value. These differences should agree very closely (<2–3). Are there differences and can you account for them?

Experiment 6–10. In this experiment you record and reduce RC charging and discharging curves. The circuit of Figure 6–6 is used to demonstrate the operation of a simple RC network. The op amp follower prevents the DT2800 from drawing current from the capacitor and distorting the measurement. The pushbutton allows you to accelerate the charging and discharging to get to the terminal values.

Write software to record the charging and discharging transients. The software should have a user-selectable full scale sweep and should record at least 100 points during the decay. The DMA mode must be used. Use channel 1 to monitor the input voltage and trigger the data acquisition. Have provision in your software for acquiring a single discharge or fully charged voltage.

For the charging experiment, discharge the capacitor completely. Measure the baseline voltage. Select a suitable sweep time. Manually initiate the sweep by moving the switch to the charge position. Monitor channel 1. When the voltage leaps above 1 V, start the recording and store the transient. After the capacitor is fully charged record the terminal value.

For the discharging experiment, fully charge the capacitor. Set the switch to discharge. By monitoring channel 1, you can initiate recording when you see the switch in the discharge position (i.e., <<9 V). Select a suitable sweep speed. Start the sweep, and after a full charge reference line has been established, switch to discharge. You should get the signal to discharge to less than 5% of its original value for a complete trace. Make provision for recording the terminal baseline value.

After each recording, plot the data. Then plot the linearized form of the data and fit it by linear least squares to get the fit to the RC time constant. Typical data are shown in Figure 6–6.

Obtain the value of RC from the discharging data using a ln[V(t)] versus t plot. The data fits:

$$\ln V(t) = \ln V(0) - \frac{t}{RC} \qquad (A–5)$$

Since the charging data fits the equation:

$$\frac{V(\infty) - V(t)}{V(\infty)} = \exp(-t/RC) \qquad (A–6)$$

also evaluate RC from a plot of ln {[V(∞)–V(t)]/V(∞)} versus t. Do the two values agree?

Measure the 1 M resistor with a digital multimeter or a bridge and calculate C. Submit your raw data plots, the linearized plots, and your two calculated RCs and Cs. Does the calculated C agree with the stated value? Would this technique be useful for evaluating unknown capacitance?

Experiment 6–11. The shortcoming of Experiment 6–10 is that it lacks graphics. Add on-the-fly graphics so that you can follow the transient as it evolves. You can use tight block coded ADC mixed with graphics. However, this has the problem of possible point missing if you take too long on a graphics operation.

Alternatively, use the DMA mode. Fill each point of the data array with an illegal 12-bit number (i.e., $ffff). Start data acquisition. Begin testing the first array element after each graphics operation. If the point is $ffff then it has not been digitized yet. Once it is a legal (i.e., digitized value), plot it and check the next array element. Repeat this checking and plotting until the last point is digitized. With this scheme, you do not have to worry about losing points. If you get behind, the points are still stored in memory waiting for you to plot them.

A.7 Chapter 7 Experiments: Signal-to-Noise Enhancement

The following experiments demonstrate different methods of S/N enhancement. Some of the experiments require a noisy signal. We use the instrument simulator of Wohltjen and Dessey. This has digitally stored signal waveforms, a clock and DAC for outputting the waveforms at different rates, and a noise generator. In the free run mode, the simulator provides a trigger pulse at the initiation of each waveform. It can also be triggered externally by your computer for initiating output.

Experiment 7–1. (A) Using a high frequency oscilloscope (at least 15 MHz bandwidth), connect a wire to the probe. Without touching anything that is electrically hot, explore your environment using the probe as an antenna for noise reception. In particular, move the probe around and touch different potential noise sources such as the case of your computer, your calculator, incandescent and fluorescent lights, and yourself (yes, you make an excellent extended antenna). Turn the room lights on and off. Turn the computer monitor on and off. This last measurement will help you isolate the difference between monitor noise and computer noise.

Warning. Do not touch anything that is electrically hot such as the inside of your computer or a power socket.

Repeat the measurements with an AM or FM radio as the detector. Tune it off a station, and turn the volume up all the way. The AM receiver is generally more susceptible to interference than the FM. Each transmitter has a different characteristic noise pattern or sound. Note, in particular, the low frequency hum as you approach the power supply portion of your computer. This is 60 cycle or ac pickup. Notice that the pickup strength is a function of relative orientation of your devices and detector. Also, you may find that certain portions of the computer case leak interference more than others. Seams are a common problem, and we find that some of our machines leak more severely through the open floppy disk region.

(B) Hang a long wire antenna in the room. Use a scope to maximize pickup and pass the data through a 500 Hz low pass filter (an active filter or a follower on the antenna is required). The filter is necessary because of the Nyquist sampling theorem. Digitize 512 points over a 0.1 s interval using the program POWERSP. POWERSP uses a fast Fourier transform (FFT) to compute and display a power spectrum of the results. Trigger the ADC asynchronously from the line using any TTL oscillator. Compare the averaged spectrum with the unaveraged one. Now trigger the averager with a 60 Hz power line derived TTL square wave. Compare the averaged spectrum with the asynchronous one. Hand in PrtSc copies of all the measurements.

Experiment 7–2. Use the instrument simulator and the circuit of Figure A–3 to show the effect of a variable RC on S/N. Note the improvement with increasing RC as well as the distortions that occur for larger values. To fully appreciate the distortions, turn off the noise generator. The dual trace scope allows viewing the input and filtered waveforms simultaneously.

Experiment 7–3. This experiment is based on the article by Xu, Demas, and Grubb (1989). With the setup of Figure 7–5, record transients from the simulator using different gate widths. At a fixed noise level, note the variations of S/N with different gate widths and the distortions for too wide a gate. Hand in hard copies of transients for 0.01, 0.1, and 1 s gates.

Experiment 7–4. This experiment requires a commercial lock-in amplifier. Using the circuit of Figure A–4, noise can be derived from the instrument simulator. We could have used a summer, but for demonstration purposes the three-resistor network makes a

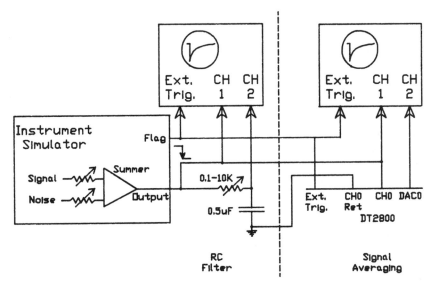

Figure A–3. Instrument simulator configurations used to show noise reduction by RC filtering and by ensemble averaging.

perfectly respectable mixer. Any stable oscillator will work for the signal source. However, since you must not change the reference level during measurements, a generator with an independent TTL reference is useful. The switch is used to simulate a square wave signal.

Record transients at different S/N ratios and with different RC time constants. Estimate the S/N for different RCs. If you have a computer controlled lock-in, use the

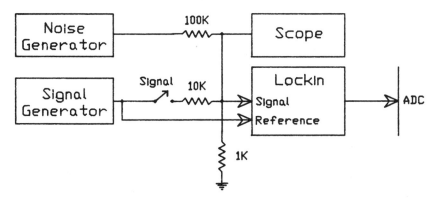

Figure A–4. Circuit for demonstrating S/N enhancement with a lock-in amplifier. A signal is simulated by switching in a signal source.

manufacturer's software. Otherwise, use an ADC on the lock-in output. Record data at even time intervals. For the same input signal, turn in plots for RCs of 0.03, 0.1, 0.3, and 1 s. From the digitized data calculate the S/N enhancement. To obtain the original noise level digitize the input waveform and calculate its standard deviation.

Experiment 7–5. You measure the phase and attenuation factors for an RC filter by implementing a dual channel lock-in amplifier in software.

Much information can be determined for many systems by characterizing their response to a sinusoidal excitation. This characterization can consist of measuring the attenuation and phase shift of some output property relative to the applied waveform for different frequencies. A few of the many scientific applications of these measurements are electrical networks, magnetic hysteresis, luminescence lifetimes, phase transformations of proteins and polymers, and heat transfer. In this experiment we characterize an electrical high pass filter by the phase shift and attenuation of an applied ac sine wave as a function of frequency. The methodology is, however, general.

You will use two input ADC channels, the block ADC commands, and clocked data acquisition to simultaneously acquire both the applied input waveform and the attenuated and shifted output waveform. To extract the attenuation and phase shift, you will digitally simulate the operation of a two channel lock-in amplifier on the stored waveforms.

A schematic diagram of the network and the measurement circuit is shown in Figure A–5. The analog ground connection between the signal generator and the DT interface

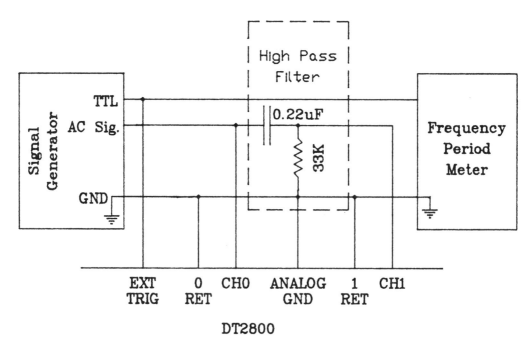

Figure A–5. Schematic diagram of circuit and interface connections for measuring the characteristics of a high pass RC electrical network.

board is critical; it is not enough to connect the signal returns of the ADC channels to the source grounds. You can get away with this only when your signal generator makes a common ground connection with the computer via the power line ground. Note carefully the connection of the differential input ADC lines to the signal sources. Remember this interconnection is important for minimizing ground loops.

For proper data collection, you need the period of the sinusoidal signal. You measure this with a period meter. We use the same Intersil Demonstration Universal Counter-Timer Kit that was used in the parallel interfacing experiment. You can either read the period visually and enter the data in response to a program request or read the period with the software that you developed in the earlier experiment.

You use the block ADC mode on the DT2800 to simultaneously collect a series of points on both waveforms. Use the TTL-compatible output of your generator to externally trigger data acquisition. If the amplitudes of the signals are too low, use a higher gain on the programmable preamplifier.

For this experiment you need to collect data over exactly one complete sine wave. To do this, set the clock period to:

$$\text{Clock Period} = \Delta t = T / (2 * N) \tag{A-7}$$

where T is the period of your sine wave and $N+1$ is the number of points that you plan to collect on one complete waveform. The reason for the $N+1$ is that you need both a beginning and an end point to complete one waveform. The factor of 2 comes in because you will record two channels of information—one each for the input and output waveforms.

If $W(t)$ is the input waveform and the W_is are the input waveforms taken at t_i (i=0 to N), then the average synchronously rectified in-phase signal for the adder-subtractor circuit is:

$$I = \text{Average In-Phase Signal} = (I_1 - I_2) \tag{A-8}$$

where:

$$I_1 = \int_{t_0}^{t_{N/2}} W(t)dt \tag{A-9a}$$

$$I_2 = \int_{t_{N/2}}^{t_N} W(t)dt \tag{A-9b}$$

Using the trapezoidal rule integration, we have:

$$I_1 = (\Delta t/2) (W_0 + 2W_1 + 2W_2 .. + W_{N/2}) \tag{A-10a}$$

$$I_2 = (\Delta t/2) (W_{N/2} + 2W_{N/2+1} + 2W_{N/2+2} .. + W_N) \tag{A-10b}$$

Similarly, if we wish to find the rectified output that is 90° out of phase with the first one, Q, which is the *quadrature* signal, we evaluate:

$$Q = \text{Average Quadrature Signal} = (I_2 - I_1 - I_3) \tag{A-11}$$

$$I_2 = \int_{t_{N/4}}^{t_{3N/4}} W(t)dt \qquad\qquad\qquad\qquad \text{(A--12a)}$$

$$I_1 = \int_{t_0}^{t_{N/4}} W(t)dt \qquad\qquad\qquad\qquad \text{(A--12b)}$$

$$I_3 = \int_{t_{3N/4}}^{t_N} W(t)dt \qquad\qquad\qquad\qquad \text{(A--12c)}$$

Again using the trapezoidal rule we obtain:

$$I_2 = (W_{N/4} + 2W_{N/4+1} + 2W_{N/4+2} \ldots + W_{3N/4}) (\Delta t/2) \qquad \text{(A--13a)}$$

$$I_1 = (W_0 + 2W_1 + 2W_2 \ldots + W_{N/4}) (\Delta t/2) \qquad \text{(A--13b)}$$

$$I_3 = (W_{3N/4} + 2W_{3N/4+1} + 2W_{3N/4+2} \ldots + W_N) (\Delta t/2) \qquad \text{(A--13c)}$$

In order to simplify the calculations and to improve accuracy, we have selected an N that is evenly divisible by four. This makes a 90° phase shift very easy to determine since it is then exactly one quarter of the data points.

Using Equation 7–6 calculate the average amplitude, I_{av}, and the phase shift ϕ_{li} where ϕ_{li} is the phase shift of the input waveform relative to your lock-in amplifier's square wave. A positive phase angle means that the signal waveform leads the square wave (i.e., appears before it) while a negative phase angle means that the signal lags (i.e., appears after) the square wave.

We are assuming that we have a pure fundamental with no harmonics. If the input is not a pure sinusoidal wave, there will be errors in the phase and amplitude calculations. While most sine wave generators will have some small components at the harmonics, these are too small to affect your results.

Remember that the DT2800 board only takes a datum point every clock cycle, even when it is taking data from two or more channels. Thus, if we are reading the input signal S from channel 0 and output signal O from channel 1, then the clock period is Δt, and the first reading is at t=0, then we read points in the following way:

S points are read at 0, 2Δt, 4Δt, 6Δt, and so on.
O points are read at Δt, 3Δt, 5Δt, 7Δt, and so on.

Thus, even if S and O are the same waveform, O is phase shifted relative to S. This shift of O relative to S in degrees is given by:

$$\text{phaseshift}=360° (\Delta t/T) \qquad\qquad\qquad \text{(A--14)}$$

where T is the waveform period. The phase shift is positive since the O waveform appears to lead the S waveform.

The simplest way to handle this phase shift in the ADC acquisition is to ignore it while calculating the phase shift for the delayed waveform. Then, correct the phase data for the timing error. Alternatively, you can interpolate the points from one transient to give data at the same times as the other.

Wire up the circuit of Figure A–5. Use two consecutive ADC channels for the input and output sine waves so that you can use the block DMA input mode for clocked dual channel input. Write a program that allows you, either manually or under software, to input the sine wave period, T, and then acquire N+1 points across one complete waveform cycle (i.e., 2N+2 points). N must be a multiple of 4. At higher frequencies you will be limited to the number of points that you can digitize across a waveform, but use no fewer than sixteen points on each waveform. At lower frequencies you can use more points for a more accurate integration.

Make provisions for displaying the digitized waveforms. You can either display them by plotting them on the computer or use the DAC outputs to view them on an oscilloscope. This is useful for diagnostics to insure that the data acquisition went properly and need not be pretty. The things to look for are: 1) did you get exactly one complete waveform? and 2) are the waveforms clean sine waves? Failure to satisfy the first is an indication that you have mismatched the number of points acquired or have an error in the clock calculation. A noisy signal is frequently caused by improper grounding.

You can either use the ADC in a free-running mode or externally trigger it. External triggering gives a reproducible starting point on each recorded waveform and possibly higher reproducibility. We have had excellent results either way.

When you get an acceptable set of waveforms, calculate the phase and amplitude of each one. Then calculate the phase shift of the output waveform relative to the input waveform. Correct for any phase shifts caused by the digitization offset on the second channel. Calculate the gain of the circuit from:

$$\text{Gain} = I_{av-out}/I_{av-in} \qquad (A-15)$$

where I_{av-out} and I_{av-in} are the amplitudes of the input and output waveform respectively.

To insure that everything is working well, apply the input waveform to both ADC channels. The gain should be very close to 1 and the phase shift very close to 0. Repeat this determination several times at several different frequencies to get an estimate of the precision and accuracy of the measurement.

Once you are satisfied with everything, measure the filter characteristics as a function of frequency. Use the range of about 2–5 Hz to the highest frequency that allows N=16 or until the output amplitude is too low to measure accurately.

Make a plot of gain and phase shift versus the logarithm of the sine wave frequency f. On the same plot include the theoretical curve calculated from the nominal values of the components used in the high pass filter.

$$\text{Attenuation} = \frac{(\omega\,R\,C)}{\sqrt{1 + (\omega\,R\,C)^2}} \qquad (A-16a)$$

$$\text{Phase Shift} = 90^\circ - \arctan(\omega\,R\,C) \qquad (A-16b)$$

$$\omega = 2\,\pi\,f \qquad (A-16c)$$

Your plots need not be pretty with lots of points. The primary goal is to demonstrate interfacing and a valuable data reduction principle.

We find this system extraordinarily sensitive and reproducible. If we connect an oscilloscope to the output of the filter via a 6-foot length of coaxial cable, the phase shift and amplitude of the output waveform are noticeably changed by the 150 pF of scope-cable capacitance now in parallel with the 33K resistor.

An alternative way to extract the phase shift and attenuation is to perform a Fourier transform to the input and output waveforms and measure the attenuation and phase shift of these waveforms relative to each other. For an essentially pure sinusoidal input waveform the Fourier transform and lock-in amplifier approaches yield virtually identical results.

Experiment 7–6. Using the setup of Figure A–3 and the program SIGAV record transients with different degrees of averaging. Turn in hard copies of an unaveraged noisy transient and ones with 4, 64, 256, and 1024 averages. Estimate the S/N improvement by averaging noise only and calculating its standard deviation. Does S/N improve by the predicted amount? If not, why not?

Experiment 7–7. Use the program QUANT to examine the effects of quantization noise on S/N. Turn in copies of the plots for noise equal to 0.5 of a quantization level with no averaging, 10 averages, and 100 averages. Provide a table of rms noise for 100 averages with a noise level of 0.05, 0.1, 0.25, 0.5, 1.0, and 2 times the quantization levels.

Experiment 7–8. Use the instrument simulator in the configuration of Figure A–3 to show the elimination of quantization noise by ensemble averaging of noisy data. Use the program 2bitav, which turns your 12-bit ADC into a 2-bit ADC by throwing away 10 bits. Turn in plots of the digitized waveform with no noise and 1 and 100 averages. Also, provide for noise estimated to be near the optimum with no averaging and after 400 averages.

Experiment 7–9. This experiment measures fast luminescence decay times with a xenon flashlamp based lifetime apparatus. Luminescence measurements are common and powerful tools in many physical and biological sciences. In particular, lifetime measurements and time resolved techniques are becoming increasingly important (Lakowicz [1983] and Demas [1983]). This experiment uses a $25 photographic strobe lamp to measure luminescence lifetimes to about 200 μs. We describe a Stern-Volmer quenching experiment that gives a bimolecular quenching rate constant of 10^8 $M^{-1}s^{-1}$, which easily falls in the range of fast chemical kinetics. The computer interfaced portion of the experiment demonstrates S/N enhancement by ensemble averaging, qua..tization noise, and reduction of quantization noise by averaging.

The system selected is the $Ru(phen)_3^{2+}$ (phen=1,10-phenanthroline) quenching of $Tb(dpa)_3^{3-}$ (dpa=pyridine-2,6-dicarboxylic acid). $Tb(dpa)_3^{3-}$ has an unquenched lifetime on the order of 2 ms at room temperature in water.

Excited state decay kinetics can be described using the following equations:

$$D + h\nu \rightarrow D^*$$ (A–17a)

$$D^* \overset{k_1}{\rightarrow} D + h\nu \text{ or } \Delta$$ (A–17b)

$$D^* + Q \xrightarrow{k_2} D + Q^* \tag{A-17c}$$

where D is the ground state species, D^* is the excited species and Q is the quencher. The k_1 is the first order rate constant for decay of the excited state (1b) and k_2 is the bimolecular rate constant for deactivation. The k_2 is the sum of all processes depleting the excited state including catalytic deactivation, energy transfer, and electron transfer. We show only energy transfer, which is the sole path in the current system.

To determine k_2, the excited state lifetime, τ, is determined as a function of quencher concentration. The data are normally treated using a Stern-Volmer equation:

$$\frac{\tau_0}{\tau} = 1 + K_{SV}[Q] \tag{A-18a}$$

$$K_{SV} = k_2 \tau_0 \tag{A-18b}$$

$$\frac{1}{\tau} = \frac{1}{\tau_0} + k_2[Q] \tag{A-18c}$$

where [Q] is the quencher concentration and τ_0 is the lifetime in the absence of quencher. K_{SV} is the Stern-Volmer quenching constant and equals the reciprocal of the quencher concentration that would deactivate half the excited state species. Plots of τ_0/τ or $1/\tau$ versus [Q] should be linear with slopes of K_{SV} or k_2, respectively. The bimolecular quenching constant can be computed from K_{SV} and τ_0 (see Lakowicz [1983], Demas [1983], and Ballew, et al. [1990]).

Data Reduction. The two methods for data reduction of baseline-corrected luminescence decay data that have been employed are a Linear Least Squares (LLS) fit of the semilogarithmic plot of the decay data versus time and the Rapid Lifetime Determination (RLD) Method (Ballew and Demas).

Apparatus. A schematic representation of the complete apparatus is shown in Figure A–6. The luminescent molecule is excited with the ultraviolet component of a simple auto exposure photographer's strobe. Filters isolate the excitation and the emission.

The flash is fired from a TTL oscillator after a 250 µs delay. Data acquisition is initiated by external triggering of the data acquisition board to provide about 250 µs of baseline before the lamp fires.

Typical data taken with the program FASTKIN are shown in Figure 7–19. Figure A–7 shows a typical Stern-Volmer plot. The expected linearity is good and k_2 agrees well with the value measured on a much more expensive system.

FASTKIN is menu driven. It allows the user to set the number of averages; choose a reduction method and fitting region; and display the raw data, the semilogarithmic plot of intensity versus time (useful for selecting the fitting region), the best fit, and the residuals. It allows saving data and recalling previously saved data.

Experiment. Measure the lifetime of an unquenched and several quenched samples of aqueous $Tb(dpa)_3^{3-}$ with various concentrations of $Ru(phen)_3^{2+}$. We provide 0, 2, 4, 6, and 8 µM $Ru(phen)_3^{2+}$ in 10 mM $Tb(dpa)_3^{3-}$.

Prepare and turn in a Stern-Volmer quenching plot. Provide your measured K_{SV} and k_2. Also turn in a print-out of an unaveraged decay and one that is averaged at least

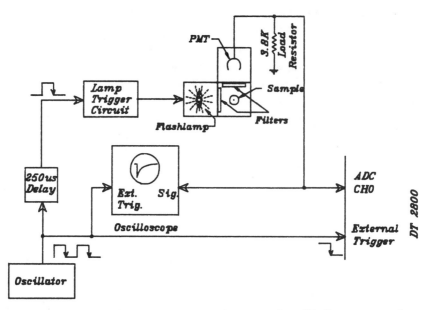

Figure A–6. Schematic representation of the complete lifetime apparatus.

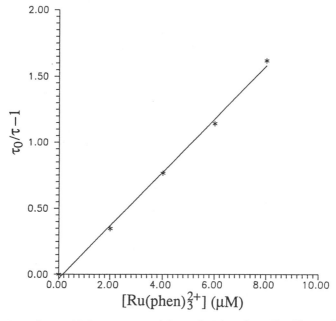

Figure A–7. Typical Stern-Volmer quenching plot for deactivation of Tb(dpa)$_3^{3-}$ by Ru(phen)$_3^{2+}$. Data courtesy of R. M. Leasure.

ten times. Select a quencher concentration that shows quantization noise and its reduction.

Experiment 7–10. Use the program SMOOTH to show the improvement of S/N and signal distortions using a Savitzky-Golay filter. SMOOTH really requires a color graphics card to do justice to the different plots. Hand in printouts for the screens with the noise-free data and a 3-point smooth, and the noise-free data and a 25-point smooth. Repeat the measurement with a noise level of 5% of full scale. Is the distortion unacceptable for the 25-point smooth? Estimate the optimum number of points in the smooth for the provided data set.

A.8 Chapter 8 Experiment: Nonlinear Data Fitting

The experiment is based on the program SIMPLEX written by S. W. Snyder. It was adapted to a PC and enormously expanded from a version for a Hewlett-Packard 85 desktop computer (Demas, 1983). SIMPLEX uses the basic simplex algorithm given in Chapter 8. It has several built-in models, and by altering the model file YOURMODL.PAS and recompiling, you can add your own custom model. The program supports pull-down menus, point and shoot for loading files, a variety of file utilities, and automatic detection and installation of graphics drivers. SIMPLEX has integrated graphics with direct viewing of the course of the simplex search as well as the best fit and the residuals plot. It will perform weighted or unweighted fits. Further, you can restrict the search region to preclude physically impossible parameters. It will save the data fits and the residuals plots in GRAPHER format files for later plotting. It makes error estimates of the parameters. In short, SIMPLEX is an extremely flexible and powerful data fitting program and serves as one of the primary data fitting programs for our research.

We describe briefly the use of the program and how to customize it with your own functions. It is menu driven, and many of its features are self-explanatory and will not be discussed here. SIMPLEX requires a PC with an 8K RAM disk on D, a graphics card, and a math coprocessor.

Using SIMPLEX. The following discussion assumes that we are trying to fit data to the equation:

$$D(t) = K [\exp(-t/\tau_1) - \exp(-t/\tau_2)] \qquad (A-19)$$

This corresponds to the exciplex model of luminescence or the discharge of one RC network into another RC network.

We provide you with a version of SIMPLEX that incorporates the exciplex model of Equation A–19; it has been renamed FITEXCIP. We show you how to generate this program later. A data file exciplex.dat is provided where K is about 18800, τ_1 about 35, and τ_2 about 7; Poisson noise has been added to the decay. It is best to work through the description that follows while using this example. Start the FITEXCIP by typing its name. The following menu comes up:

```
Copyright (c) 1989, Seth Snyder, University of Virginia
                        2-13-1984
                      File:
```

```
                                         Fit:  FALSE
                                         Path:  C:\TP\TPU
```

```
    F1)    Read data
    F2)    Simplex fit
    F3)    Test fit
    F4)    Plot results
    F5)    Reprint results
    F6)    Scale factor
    F7)    Logged drive
    F8)    Disk directory
    F9)    Continue fit
    F10)   Done


    Which option:
```

Commands are issued by using either the special function keys or the numeric keys. No return is required. You must first load data, so type F1 or 1. The following menu comes up:

```
Rampath = D:\        Driver location =              Available memory = 376 kB
Graph driver = ATT  Graph mode = 640 x 400 AT&T  Horiz = 640  Vert = 400

Alt M=new mask, P=new path,  K=new directory, L=print file, V=view file,
D=delete file,  C=copy file, R=rename file,    Esc=new window

-------------------------------------------------------------------
| Directory of path: C:\TP\TPU\*.dat        Disk space:  272 Kb.  |
|                                                                 |
|  95200570.DAT   EXCIPLEX.DAT                                     |
|  DB1545.DAT                                                      |
|  DBERR.DAT                                                       |
|  DBERRSUR.DAT                                                    |
|  DBEXP.DAT                                                       |
|  DBEXP2.DAT                                                      |
|  GTAU.DAT                                                        |
|  SI15.DAT                                                        |
|  GTAU3.DAT                                                       |
|       Esc to return, arrows to move, ret to choose              |
-------------------------------------------------------------------

              File read

-------------------------------------------------------------------
| File:  95200570.DAT    Size:  3618  Mod:  9: 3, Jan 12, 1989|
-------------------------------------------------------------------
```

Ancillary commands at the top are issued with the Alt key and the indicated letter. A file is highlighted. Use the arrow keys to move the highlight to the file that you wish to load. Hit return to load it. Subdirectories, \, and .. are colored differently. If you select a subdirectory, you change to the indicated directory. Note that the size and creation date of the file picked is shown in the box at the bottom of the screen.

Frequently, the file listing is cluttered and fills more than one window. To page forward, type Esc. There is no page backward option. The number of files displayed can be reduced by setting a DOS mask. Type Alt M, supply the requested DOS mask (i.e., *.dat for only .dat files), and return.

After the file is loaded, the first menu comes up again. You can view the data graphically by pressing F4 to confirm that it is what you wanted or to aid in parameter selection. To begin fitting, press F2, which brings up the following menu:

```
Which option:  2:  Simplex fit
F1)    Gem:km,kc
F2)    Gem:k(diff)
F3)    CPL:km,kc
F4)    CPL:k(diff),kq
F5)    TL
F6)    racemization
F7)    Exciplex
F8)    Exit
Which option:
```

Note that in this version of SIMPLEX, there are six preinstalled models that were written for Mr. Snyder's research. Your version will have different models. After striking F7 or 7 for the custom exciplex model, the following dialog ensues:

```
7:  Exciplex
Variables:  Exciplex
Parameter(1) ( 0.00000E+00):  10000
Float Parameter(1)?  Y
Parameter(2) ( 0.00000E+00):  70
Float Parameter(2)  Y
Parameter(3)  ( 0.00000E+00):  1
Float Parameter(3)?  Y
Enter fit start (1):
Enter fit end (501):
```

You respond with an answer to each requested numeric parameter; use either a new value or a return if the listed one is acceptable. After entering each parameter, you are then asked if you want the parameter to be varied during the simplex search. Answer with Y or N accordingly. If you answer no, the parameter is held fixed at the initial value. This feature is very convenient for fixing parameters that you know from other measurements. The indicated values are 10000 for K and 70, and 1 for the first and second lifetimes respectively. The default start and end points for the fit are shown and are selected by typing return. You can alter either by entering a number. The default is all points or 1 to 501 for the data set; the length is calculated automatically. After completing the last entry, the following menu is printed:

```
F1)    New simplex model
F2)    New fit range
```

```
F3)    Change variables
F4)    Plot results
F5)    Reprint old fit
F6)    Change weighting
F7)    Limit variable range
F8)    Load new data
F9)    Exit fit routine
F10)   Fit data
Which option:
```

You have the option of selecting one of the other models to fit the data (F1), changing the fitting range (F2), changing the initial guesses (F3), plotting the data (F4), reprinting the results of the previous fit (F5), changing the weights to either weighted or unweighted where default is weighted (F6), limiting the range of permissible parameter variations (F7), loading new data (F8), exiting the fitting routine to the main menu (F9), or fitting the data (F10). Pressing F10 brings up the screen of Figure A–8.

Figure A–8 shows the initial fit and the first four fits. Note that each fit is displayed in addition to all the preceding ones. Clearly, we guessed too short for the short lifetime. You could stop the fitting, change the parameters, and restart it. More often, if the fit is not too bad, just let it go.

The space bar controls program flow. Pressing it stops the fitting. X stops/starts all graphics displays. Y stops simplex fitting completely. P clears the graphics display and

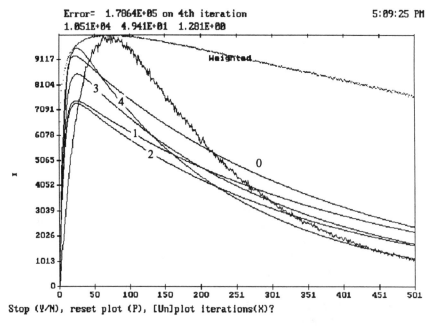

Figure A–8. Simplex fits for first four iterations of a simplex fit to the exciplex model. The current error and parameters are shown across the top. The dotted line is the logarithm of the data. Numbers indicate the iteration for each fit.

begins updating the display with the next iteration. N resumes without altering the graphics screen. Do not type a return. Graphics rarely slows the program up enough to justify hiding the plots. For example, fifty-two iterations of exciplex took 4:15 min with graphics and 3:15 min without. Being able to visualize the iterations is extremely useful for early detection of poor initial guesses, false minima, or inadequate models.

After the simplex progam has converged, it estimates the errors—the same is true if you pressed Y; this might take a while, so do not panic. The final results are displayed:

```
C:\TP\TPU\EXCIPLEX.DAT
7 Double Exp Fit
          Range:  1 - 501
  TRUE Parameter(1)=  1.8676E+04  σ=  1.0734E+01
  TRUE Parameter(2)=  3.5001E+01  σ=  1.1528E-02
  TRUE Parameter(3)=  6.9961E+00  σ=  6.1580E-03
          Error=  5.0264E+02 Weighted
    Relat Error=  1.0093E+00 Chi}(R)

Hit any key to continue, S to save, P to print
```

Since we used a weighted fit, the relative error is actually a true χ_r^2, which for the 500-point fit is very nearly one and perfectly acceptable. Since the data was simulated with Poisson noise, this is no surprise. You are given the opportunity to print or save these results to a disk file. Any other key brings up the main menu. To reprint the results use F5 and to see the graphics display of the fit use F4. Figure A–9 shows the graphics screens for data with the best fit and the weighted residual plot. As expected, the residuals are random around zero with respect to sign and show the proper range of less than −3 to +3.

Customizing SIMPLEX. The key file for customizing SIMPLEX is YOURMODL.PAS. The listing of YOURMODL set up with the exciplex equation of Equation A–19 and Poisson weighting is shown below:

```
unit YourModl;

interface
USES utility, simpvar;

CONST
  YourModelName : STRING[20] = 'Exciplex Fit';

VAR
  YourVariable : mat10d;
  FlashName : STRING;
  Flash : datarec;
  {Fix YourParams at end of this unit or vary it in yourvarsetup}
  YourParams : Integer;        {number of parameters in fit}

  {any other of your parameters here}
```

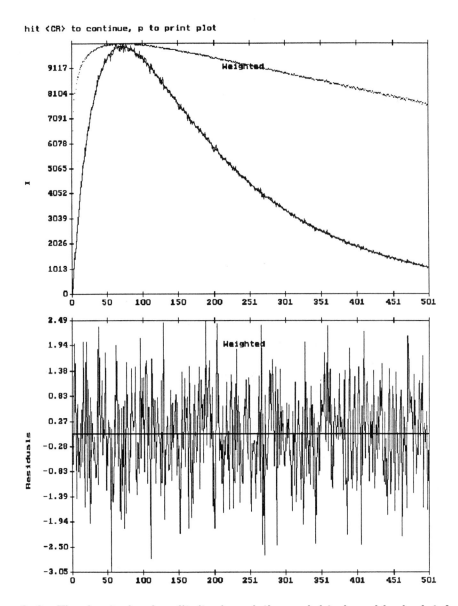

Figure A–9. The best simplex fit (top) and the weighted residual plot for the exciplex model of exciplex.dat.

```
PROCEDURE YourVarSetUp(VAR variable : mat10d);
PROCEDURE YourReprint;
FUNCTION yourmodel(VAR variable : mat10d) : double;
FUNCTION yourweight(index : Integer) : single;

implementation

USES simpproc, simmodel;
```

```
{Your local variables here}

FUNCTION yourmodel(VAR variable : mat10d) : double;
VAR i, j : Integer;
  sum : double;
BEGIN
  FOR i := 1 TO YourParams DO setfloat(i, variable,
    YourVariable[i]);
  sum := 0;
  WITH tl DO FOR j := fitstart TO fitend DO
    BEGIN
      {your model here}

      {ycalc[j]:= f(xobs[j],yourvariable(1..yourparams)}

      {Example model}
      ycalc[j] := YourVariable[1] *
                  ( Exp(-xobs[j]/YourVariable[2]) -
                  Exp(-xobs[j]/YourVariable[3]) );

      ydev[j] := (yobs[j]-ycalc[j])*Sqrt(weight(j));
      sum := sum+Sqr(ydev[j]);
    END;
  yourmodel := sum;
END;

PROCEDURE YourVarSetUp(VAR variable : mat10d);
VAR i : Integer;
  s : STRING;
BEGIN
  {Your input}
  FOR i := 1 TO YourParams DO
    BEGIN
      s := 'Parameter('+Chr(i+$30)+')';
      float[i] := checkfloat(s, YourVariable[i], variable);
    END;
END;

PROCEDURE YourReprint;
VAR i : Integer;
BEGIN
  {Your output}

  FOR i := 1 TO YourParams DO
    WriteLn(f, float[i]:5, ' Parameter(', i, ')= ', expouts(
    YourVariable[i]), u(i));
END;

FUNCTION yourweight(index : Integer) : single;
BEGIN
  WITH tl DO
```

```
        {Your statistical data weighting function}
        yourweight := 1/(yobs[index]);   {Poisson weighting}
  END;


BEGIN
  modelnames[yournum] := YourModelName;
  YourParams := 3;
  darks := 0;
END.
```

The only things that absolutely require your attention are shown in boldface. The variable YourParams, which is set three lines from the end, must match the number of variables in your model equation; a mismatch in these two produces very obscure or catastrophic behavior.

The array elements YourVariable[1]...YourVariable[YourParams] are the parameters used in your defining equation. The (x,y) data points are contained in the arrays xobs and yobs. The function YourModel returns χ^2, and you must insert your own function for the calculated y in this expression. In general, you need only invoke xobs in YourModel to generate ycalc, which in turn is used to calculate the residual; the error is already caculated and you will usually not change this equation. To implement the function of Equation A–19, insert the following definition for ycalc:

```
ycalc[j] := YourVariable[1] *
                  ( Exp(-xobs[j]/YourVariable[2]) -
                  Exp(-xobs[j]/YourVariable[3]) );
```

where YourVariable[1] is K, YourVariable[2] is τ_1, and YourVariable[3] is τ_2.

If Poisson weighting is unacceptable, change the Procedure YourWeight to generate a different YourWeight for each yobs. Remember one of the options of the program is unweighted (i.e., yourweight=1), so you do not have to write a separate unweighted routine.

The constant YourModelName is the identifier that is displayed in the Model List menu. Change it to match your custom model.

To write a new version of SIMPLEX with your custom model, carry through the following procedure:

(1) First, copy the backup copy of YOURMODL.PAS (YOURMODL.ORG) to YOURMODL.PAS.
(2) Edit the defining equation in YOURMODL.PAS, and change the variable YourParams and the constant YourModelName to reflect the new model. Make a copy of this under another name, so that you can retrieve it later if you alter YourModl.
(3) Compile YourModl to disk to give a new Unit YourModl.
(4) Load the file SIMPLEX.PAS and compile it to disk to give the new custom program SIMPLEX.

(5)   Rename SIMPLEX.EXE to another name so it will not be altered the next time you make a custom simplex routine.

You need the following files on your disk when you compile SIMPLEX:

```
DATAVAR.TPU      SIMPPROC.TPU      PLOTUNIT.TPU
DIRUNIT.TPU      SIMPVAR.TPU       SIMMODEL.TPU
UTILITY.TPU      SIMPLEX.PAS       YOURMODL.PAS
```

For best results all these files should be in your working directory and compilation should be to the same directory. This organization prevents other copies of the Units from inadvertently being used.

Quirks. SIMPLEX is reasonably forgiving as to input errors, and resists crashes from most common typing errors, misinterpreted input, or incorrect operations. Snyder makes no claims to a completely bulletproof program; the amount of code required to do that would probably make the program twice as big as it is (greater than 100K on disk). Since it only takes a few seconds to reload, the rare crashes were not considered a major bug.

More insidiously, we find that on our 8086/8087 based AT&T 6300s compilation can yield a program that, if run directly, will freeze the system. The point where it freezes is erratic and problems may not always arise. Sometimes rebooting with Alt-Ctrl-Del does not eliminate the failure of the EXE file; the program still freezes at different stages. Turning the computer off and back on eliminates the problem, and the EXE file that failed earlier runs flawlessly. Our AT 80286/287 systems suffer from the problem or crash much less frequently. We assume that this is a compiler/math coprocessor bug that may disappear in later releases.

To simplify plotting, the plot is of dependent variable versus data point number rather than dependent variable versus independent variable. For computer-collected data where constant times were used, this presents no display problem. However, if the independent variable is at irregular intervals, then the plot can look rather strange indeed, although the fitting is perfectly correct. Also, as SIMPLEX does no sorting, out of order data gives a plot that is a jumble of crisscrossing lines; again the fit is unaffected. The GRAPHER format best fit and residual plot files contain all the information for generating a proper plot with other plotting programs.

Experiment 8–1. (A) Using the precompiled program EXCIPLEX, load and reduce the data file EXCIPLEX.DAT using the model of Equation A–19. Play with the various options of EXCIPLEX. Turn in the best fit parameters for weighted and unweighted fits. Also, turn in a best fit plot and a residual plot for the weighted fit.

(B) Generate a version of SIMPLEX called FIT2EXP that fits a sum of two exponentials. Use it to fit the data file FUN2EXP.DAT. Use the starting guesses 2500, 12, 7500, and 17. Also, use the starting guesses 7500, 13, 2500, and 17. Allow only the lifetimes to float. Hand in the residual plots, the best fit parameters, and the χ_r^2 for both. Comment on the discrepancies between the two "good fits."

(C) With the data file FIT2EXP.DAT, repeat the fit, but fix the two preexponential factors at 4000 and 6000. Find the best fit lifetimes and the χ^2 for the fit. Turn in the residual plot for the best fit. Comment on this fit versus those of part B.

A.9 Chapter 9 Experiments: Serial Interfacing

The following experiments require a break-out box, and Experiment 9–1 uses two computers running TTY. All the serial parameters must be matched between the two computers.

Experiment 9–1. Use a break-out box to connect the two computers together serially. On the break-out box, wire up the null modem of Figure 9–3B. Note that the break-out box has twenty-five switches on it; if closed, they directly connect the corresponding pins of the two computers together (i.e., 1 to 1, 2 to 2, and so on). Since both computers are DTEs, make sure the switches are open or disconnected. Then use jumpers to wire up the modem.

Send data from one computer to the other. If the break-out box is wired properly, transmission will occur and you can watch the TxD lead flicker. Note that the DTR and RTS are both set.

Experiment 9–2. Using only one computer, wire up the null modem of Figure 9–3A. Write a short program that turns DTR on and off at about half-second intervals. Verify that your program is working with the break-out box.

Experiment 9–3. Using only one computer, wire DTR to DSR and CTS. Toggle the state of DTR about every five seconds. Read DSR and CTS via a port read to the Modem Status register. Verify that DTR matches the states of DSR and CTS. Confirm your conclusion by monitoring DTR with the break-out box and your computer display, which should show the current state of the two inputs.

Experiment 9–4. If you have a commercial serial programmable instrument, send commands and receive data or status information from it. Details will be supplied by your instructor.

A.10 Chapter 10 Experiments: Timer Acquisition and Fitting

In this experiment you record the discharge of a series-connected RC electrical network. You then fit the resulting decay curves by nonlinear least squares to obtain the decay parameters of the network. You use the timer interrupt to acquire the data and simplify data treatment.

We demonstrate the concept of global fitting of parameters to several data sets. For example, in the current experiment you record two experimental decay curves described by the same physical parameters. Each decay gives a different set of best fit parameters, even though the parameters should be the same. Since the same parameters apply to both data sets, how can you get the best overall or global set of parameters for all the data? By a very slight change in our fitting procedure, we show you how to get the best set of parameters.

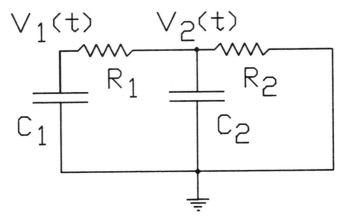

Figure A–10. Schematic of dual RC discharge network.

Figure A–10 shows a simple ganged series RC network. This network has the following equations for the time dependence of the voltages:

$$V_1(t) = c_1 D_1 \exp(\lambda_1 t) + c_2 D_2 \exp(\lambda_2 t) \qquad \text{(A–20a)}$$

$$V_1(t) = c_1 \exp(\lambda_1 t) + c_2 \exp(\lambda_2 t) \qquad \text{(A–20b)}$$

$$\lambda_1 = 0.5 - (k_1 + k_2 + k_3) + [(-k_1 + k_2 + k_3)^2 + 4k_1 k_2]^{1/2} \qquad \text{(A–20c)}$$

$$\lambda_2 = 0.5 - (k_1 + k_2 + k_3) - [(-k_1 + k_2 + k_3)^2 + 4k_1 k_2]^{1/2} \qquad \text{(A–20d)}$$

$$D_1 = k_1 / (k_1 + \lambda_1) \qquad \text{(A–20e)}$$

$$D_2 = k_1 / (k_1 + \lambda_2) \qquad \text{(A–20f)}$$

$$c_1 = [V_1(0) - V_2(0)] / [D_1 - D_2] \qquad \text{(A–20g)}$$

$$c_2 = V_2(0) - c_1 \qquad \text{(A–20h)}$$

$$k_1 = 1 / (R_1 C_1) \qquad \text{(A–20i)}$$

$$k_2 = 1 / (R_1 C_2) \qquad \text{(A–20j)}$$

$$k_3 = 1 / (R_2 C_2) \qquad \text{(A–20k)}$$

where $V_1(t)$ and $V_2(t)$ are the capacitor voltages as a function of time, t, the V(0)s are the initial capacitor voltages at t=0, and the Rs and Cs are the circuit's resistances and capacitances.

This system of equations is analogous to the kinetics of a chemical system of the following type:

$$A \Longleftrightarrow B \to C$$

where the formation of B from A accounts for B's rise time and feedback from B into A prevents A from decaying with a simple exponential decay.

Except for special limiting sets of ks, neither capacitor decay voltage is exponential. Thus, to solve for the ks, nonlinear least squares must be used.

There are several ways to configure the system for measurements. We chose the configuration of Figure 10–2. We initially discharge C_2 while it is disconnected from C_1 (relay open) using a clip lead. After charging C_1 to a suitable voltage with a clip lead, we connect C_1 to C_2 by closing the relay. Data recording of the voltages on both capacitors is begun at the same time. C_1 discharges more slowly than a simple exponential because of the back potential developed by C_2. C_2 shows the most interesting behavior; it starts at zero, rises to maximum, and then decays. A much more elegant arrangement can be built using relays to control charging and discharging of the various capacitors.

Experiment 10–1. Wire up the circuit shown in Figure 10–2. Open the relay so that C_1 and C_2 are disconnected from each other. Using a clip lead, discharge C_2. Connect C_1 directly to a 9 V battery to charge it to about 9 V. Disconnect your clip leads and then close the relay.

Write software to record the discharge of both capacitors simultaneously. There are several ways to determine when the discharge starts.

You can use an immediate ADC mode to monitor the voltage T. V_T is essentially equal to V_1 until the relay closes, and then it drops to about $V_1(0)/2$. This happens because the voltage at #2 is initially 0 and the two resistors function as voltage dividers once the relay closes. Put your program in a loop monitoring point T until its voltage suddenly falls, then begin recording both capacitor voltages.

Alternatively, you can assume that the decay starts at the instant you issue the close command to the relay. Monitor the relay line with an ADC channel or your inverted TTL relay control signal to trigger the DT2800. Because the relay is mechanical, there is some delay before it closes. With a good relay and tight software, the delay is minimal here (a few hundred microseconds).

You now need to record the data. There are two ways to do this:

(1)   The clocked input block ADC mode.
(2)   Using the 1ch timer interrupt to drive your data acquisition routine.

The simple, but less instructive, way uses the clocked modes. If instructed to use this simple way, try clock rates (e.g., 10–50 ms/point) until you get good traces. Be sure to get data well past the maximum voltage on V_2. Also, be certain to record the potential at #1 just before you close the relay. Remember that the V_1 and V_2 data are taken on alternate clock cycles.

The more interesting approach uses a 1ch timer interrupt routine similar to Tick-Tick. Set TickTick to acquire a point from both capacitors as close together as possible on every tick. Use global variables that are monitored by TickTick to determine how many pairs of points should be acquired and when TickTick should initiate acquisition. Have TickTick provide a variable that can be monitored by your main program to allow it to determine when acquisition is finished. Notice that unlike the DT2800 routine, each point has a simultaneous (at least for such slow signals) point for both C_1 and C_2.

Include a built-in plotter routine so that you can look at the data. Store your good traces to disk files in a format compatible with SIMPLEX.

10–2. Fit each transient with SIMPLEX to get the best estimates of the ks. Fit for the ks, and fix $V_1(0)$ to the voltage just before the relay was closed. As estimates of the ks, use the RCs calculated from the values given on the Rs and Cs where RC is in seconds if R is in ohms and C is in Farads.

Turn in the best fits and residual plots for the V_1 and V_2 data. Do the discrepancies indicate systematic errors? If so, suggest possible explanations. How well do the estimates obtained for the ks match for the V_1 and V_2 data sets? Are the differences within your estimated experimental errors?

10–3. In 10–2, you found differences between the ks for the two data sets. Modify SIMPLEX so that it minimizes the sum of the χ^2 for both data sets. That is, for a single parameter set calculate χ^2 for V_1 to yield $\chi^2{}_1$ and for V_2 to yield $\chi^2{}_2$. Then from the error routine return:

$$\text{Error} = \chi^2{}_1 + \chi^2{}_2$$

When you minimize this error, you are generating the best set of parameters for fitting both V_1 and V_2 simultaneously. This is referred to as a global minimization of the data.

The bookkeeping can be tricky here. The following approach is convenient and not difficult to code. Build an augmented file with the sequential (t, V_1) points followed immediately by the (t, V_2) data. In your error routine, when the time decreases the data have changed from V_1 data to V_2 data. Before beginning each summation, set a flag that says you are on the V_1 data. Before calculating the residual determine whether the time has decreased. If it has, then you are beginning V_2 data, so change the flag. When you calculate the contribution, use Equation A–20a for the first data set and Equation A–20b for the second. A simple if-then-else clause works fine.

We have applied this approach to fitting emission decays monitored at two different wavelengths. Since the materials are the same at both samples, we expect that the lifetime will be the same for each wavelength but that the preexponential factors will vary. Thus, a two exponential fit to two wavelengths has six parameters; two lifetimes and four preexponential factors (one for each component at each wavelength). Clearly, this strategy could be applied to several linked data sets.

A.11 Chapter 11 Experiments: Using Turbo Assembler

We outline the use of Borland's TASM assembler. Microsoft's MASM version 4 or later can be used with its CodeView debugger, but it does not offer the convenient user interface to mixed assembly language-Turbo Pascal programs that TASM does. Therefore, we restrict our discussion to TASM. TASM and MASM work like the command line QBASIC compiler. First they generate a .OBJ file that must be linked separately to yield an executable program. Unlike the higher level version, the linker is not usually combining libraries; it merely combines your specified assembly language routines and puts the package into an EXE format.

We show a simple assembly language routine that is to be assembled to an EXE file. It displays a sign-on message and exits to the operating system. The complete program is shown below:

```
;   Program HELLO
;   Displays a string using function 2 MSDOS interrupt
dosseg
.model small
.stack 200h

.data
WorldMessage db 'Hello  World!',0dh,0ah,0

.code
programStart PROC near
             mov ax,@data
             mov ds,ax
             mov bx,offset WorldMessage
             call printString
             mov ah,4ch   ; standard interrupt for dos return
             int 21h
ProgramStart  ENDP

PrintString Proc near
PrintStringLoop:
     mov dl,[bx]
     and dl,dl
     jz EndPrintString
     inc bx
     mov ah,2
     int 21h
     jmp PrintStringLoop
EndPrintString:
     ret
PrintString ENDP

     End ProgramStart
```

To assemble it with Borland's TASM, use one of the following lines:

> **TASM filename**   "Generate only an OBJ file"
> **TASM /zi filename**   "Generate an OBJ file, include debugging information"
> **TASM filename,,**   "Generate an OBJ and LST files"
> **TASM /zi filename,,**   "Generate an OBJ and LST file include debugging information"

These commands will generate new files with the name filename and extensions. These will be OBJ and, with the third form, a LST file. For example, if you use the third form on TEST.ASM, you generate files TEST.OBJ and TEST.LST. As with QBASIC, the assembler assumes that if you do not specify an extension, you mean an ASM file. Thus, if the file is TEST.ASM, the commands TASM TEST or TASM TEST.ASM are acceptable. The debug option includes information if you later plan to debug the program with Borland's Debugger. The OBJ form contains all the information needed for linking. The LST form shows the actual mapping of source code onto machine language code. It also shows any error messages in context.

When TASM runs it lists errors and their line numbers on the screen. The two types of errors are "Warning" and "Fatal." Warning errors indicate that the assembler found something that it believes might be incorrect, but it is not sure. Because of the large number of options, some types of correct programs always generate Warnings. Beyond this exception, however, a Warning must be fixed. Fatal errors are just that. The assembler cannot generate an OBJ file. It does complete assembly and tells you about any other errors it finds, but it does not generate any OBJ file.

If you omit the LST option, you get only a list of error messages on the screen with their associated line numbers. This is rarely very useful. It is much better to generate an LST file, which has the errors embedded in it. Below we show the screen:

```
Turbo Assembler  Version 1.0  Copyright (c) 1988 by Borland International

Assembling file:   PANIC.ASM
**Error** PANIC.ASM(14) Illegal instruction
**Error** PANIC.ASM(16) Undefined symbol: PRINTSTRNG
**Error** PANIC.ASM(25) Illegal indexing mode
Error messages:    3
Warning messages:  None
Remaining memory:  204k
```

Clearly, this is not very useful. To be useful, it must note the error messages, load the source file into the editor, move to the specified lines, and compare the error message with the code to determine what happened.

An LST file, if generated, is directly useful. We show an abbreviated PANIC.LST file below:

```
Turbo Assembler  Version 1.0        11-05-88 11:40:07        Page 1
PANIC.ASM

    1                                    dosseg            ; Normal segmentation
    2 0000                               .model tiny
    3
    4 0000                               .stack 100h       ; Allocate stack
    5
    6 0000                               .data             ; Message
    7        = 000D                      CR EQU 0dh        ; Define a CR and LF
symbol
    8        = 000A                      LF EQU 0ah
    9 0000   44 6F 6E 27 74 20 50 + mess db "Don't Panic",CR,LF,0    ; Message
   10        61 6E 69 63 0D 0A 00
   11
   12 000E                                      .code
```

```
13 0000                          Panic:                  ; Begin of program
14 0000  B8 0000s                         mov ax,@data   ; Point ds at data
15                                         movv ds,ax
**Error** PANIC.ASM(14) Illegal instruction
                                 ; Load bx with pointer to message
16 0003  BB 0000r                         mov bx,offset Mess
17 0006  E8 FFF7                          call PrintStrng     ; Print it out
**Error** PANIC.ASM(16) Undefined symbol: PRINTSTRNG
18 0009  B4 4C                            mov ah, 4ch         ; Return to DOS
19 000B  CD 21                            int 21h
20
21                               ; PrintString:
22                               ; Print out string pointed at by bx.
                                 ; Terminate when 0 byte encountered
23                               ;
24 000D                          PrintString:
25 000D                          printStringLoop:
26 000D  8A                               mov dl,[ax]         ; Fetch next byte
and see if terminator
**Error** PANIC.ASM(25) Illegal indexing mode
27 000E  22 D2                            and dl,dl           ; set flag
28 0010  74 07                            jz EndPrintString   ; if a 0 terminate
29 0012  B4 02                            mov ah,2            ; display character
is dl with DOS
30 0014  CD 21                            int 21h
31 0016  43                               inc bx              ; Point to next
character
32 0017  EB F4                            jmp PrintStringLoop; Get another char-
acter
33 0019                          EndPrintString:
34 0019  C3                               ret                 ; Return when done
35
36                               End                  ; End of entire pro-
gram
```

Each error message is placed after the line on which the assembler discovered the error. In context, it is easy to see what the errors are. The first uses the unknown movv instead of the correct mov. In the second, an i was omitted in PrintStrng, which means the assembler cannot tell what routine to call. The third is also a typing error where ax replaced the correct bx; the ax register cannot be used for indirect addressing.

The first column of the listing is the line number, the second is generally the address of the instruction in memory, and the next block is hexadecimal equivalents of the code or data. Note that Mess is a list of the ASCII codes for the message. The final EXE file will look a little different, but you can see the basic idea. In the mov bx, offset Mess instruction, you might note the r after the memory address 0000. This tells you that it will be relative to the beginning of the data segment, and in this case is the first item.

While we do not wish to become ensnared in the details of the machine code, note several things. Many instructions are single byte instructions with address or immediate data modifiers. C3 is a return. INT 21h translates into CD 21 where the first byte is the code for the INT instruction while the second byte is the immediate data.

In line 32, the EB is a jump and the F4 denotes the destination. The destination is close, and a short displacement from the next instruction places you at the goal. The F4 is a 2s complement displacement that tells you the destination is −12 from the next (RET) instruction; counting backward this places you at the expected PrintStringLoop location. Addresses are expressed as four-digit hex numbers. Further, the address is expressed as the actual address in the normal sense rather than as the inverted order in which it is actually stored in memory.

Once you make the corrections and can generate a good OBJ file, you must link it. Borland's linker is TLINK while Microsoft's is LINK. To link a file use:

```
>TLINK filename       "Link specified file to executable code"
>TLINK /v filename    "Link/incorporate debugging information"
```

The first form merely links it to executable code. The second appends the debugging information generated by the assembly step. If you omit either of the debugging flags you will be unable to do symbolic debugging with Turbo Debugger.

To circumvent problems with the inclusion of debugging information and the output of a list file, we use the following batch file:

```
echo off
if not "%1"=="" goto ASSM
echo
echo Usage: ASM filename    (without extension)
echo  Generates filename.OBJ and .LST--if no errors, also EXE
echo  Includes Turbo Debugger information
goto END
:ASSM
if exist %1.obj erase %1.obj
c:tasm /zi %1,,
if not exist %1.obj goto END
c:tlink  /v %1
:END
```

This batch file assumes that TASM and TLINK are properly pathed, that the file to be assembled is in the current directory, and that it has an ASM extension that is not typed as part of the command line name. An old OBJ file with the same name is first erased and the file is assembled to an OBJ file. If there are no fatal errors, the OBJ file is linked to an executable file.

Experiment 11–1. Assemble the program HELLO to an EXE file and execute it. Deliberately insert syntax errors into the original and reassemble. Use your editor to inspect the HELLO.LST file and note the nature of the error messages.

Experiment 11–2. Change the PrintString procedure of HELLO to the following:

```
PrintStringLoop:
     mov dl,[bx]
     xor dl,dl
     jnz EndPrintString
     inc ax
     mov ah,2
     int 21h
```

```
    jmp PrintStringLoop
EndPrintString:
    ret
```

where the changes are shown in boldface. Assemble and link it. If you are using TASM and Turbo Debugger, enable debugging on both steps. Run the program from DOS; it fails. Using your symbolic debugger, single step through the final EXE file. Follow the registers as the program executes to determine where it fails. Turbo Debugger, for example, allows you to view the code with the current instruction highlighted; you see the registers including the flags, the data region, and the output display screen. You immediately find that the flags are set wrong. Correct the error. While most debuggers allow patching the code, it is generally easier to exit, edit the source, and reassemble. Repeat the debugging session. It quickly becomes clear that you are repeatedly outputting the first character. The indirect pointer is not being changed. Inspection shows that the ax rather than the correct bx is being incremented.

Play with the debugger to get a feel for its operation and become comfortable with its capabilities. It is invaluable for debugging insidious assembly language problems such as the failure to increment the correct register in the above example. In particular, note the ability to set breakpoints and to change registers (useful for setting a counting register near the end of its range to allow early termination). For full details, see your instructor's handout for your particular debugger.

Appendix B

Editing in QuickBASIC and Turbo Pascal

B.1 QuickBASIC

Table B–1 summarizes the QuickBASIC editing commands described in the text. As in the text, we adopt the shorthand of using a ^ to indicate that the next character is struck with the control key. The list is not intended to be exhaustive. As you will see, many of the commands are patterned after the Turbo Pascal editing commands, which in turn were derived from the very popular WordStar commands.

B.2 Turbo Pascal

Since we will be using Turbo Pascal, we describe its program editor in greater detail. The commands are summarized in Table B–1. We expand on some of the details below and explain the underlying logic.

All edit commands are operated by pressing the CTRL key in combination with another key; this alters the letter key's functions. The editing commands in the Turbo Pascal are compatible with most of those in WordStar.

Beginning Editing. To begin editing you must first enter Turbo Pascal by typing TURBO and then a carriage return. Then, type Alt F to enter the editor.

Table B–1. Turbo Pascal and QuickBASIC Editing Commands

Function	Pascal	BASIC
DELETE/INSERT		
Toggle Insert Mode	Ins or ^V	Ins
Delete Character under Cursor	Del or ^G	Del or ^G
Delete from Cursor to Next Word	^T	^T
Delete from Cursor to End of Line	^QY	^T
Delete Current Line	^Y	^Y
CURSOR MOVEMENT		
Move Forward to Next Word	^F	^F
Move Backward to Last Word	^A	^A
Move Left a Character	Left Arrow or ^S	Left Arrow or ^S
Move Right a Character	Right Arrow or ^D	Right Arrow or ^D
Move Up a Line	Up Arrow or ^E	Up Arrow or ^E
Move Down a Line	Down Arrow or ^X	Down Arrow or ^X
Move Up a Screen	PgUp or ^R	PgUp or ^R
Move Down a Screen	PgDn or ^C	PgDn or ^C
Move to End of Line	^QD	End or ^QD
Move to Beginning of Line	^QS	Home or ^QS

Additional Pascal Editing Commands

EXTENDED MOVEMENT	
Move to Beginning of File	^QR
Move to End of File	^QC
SEARCH AND SEARCH/REPLACE:	
Find and stop at specified string	^QF
Find string and replace it	^QA
Find next occurrence of string	^L
Continue search	^L
Undo Deletions	^QL
BLOCK COMMANDS:	
Mark block beginning	^KB
Mark block end	^KK
Delete block	^KY
Copy block to cursor	^KC
Move block to cursor	^KV
Hide markers	^KH
Write block to disk	^KW
Read block (file) from disk	^KR

Cursor Movement. The control E-S-D-X keys control small cursor movements. For example, ^E moves the cursor up one line and ^D right one character.

Inspections of the keyboard show the logic. The diamond pattern of the E-S-D-X keys logically matches the movement of the cursor. You reach up for the E in order for the cursor to go up and you reach down to the X for the cursor to go down.

Full word move commands (^A and ^F) are further to the right and the left of the single character movement keys. Grander forward and backward movements use ^R and ^C for page up and page down movements.

If you are intimidated by this flood of CTRL codes, use the cursor movement keys on the right hand key pad. The cursor arrows point in the direction of cursor movement and move by one character space at a time. PgUp and PgDn keys are equivalent to ^R and ^C. While the cursor keys are easy to learn, touch typists find that use of the CTRL keys minimizes lifting their hands from the keyboard.

For bigger movements, ^Q modifies the basic movements. ^QD moves the cursor to the end of the current line, ^QS to the beginning of the current line, ^QR moves the cursor to the file beginning, ^QC to the file end, ^QE to the top of the screen, and ^QX to the screen bottom.

Typing and Correcting. The keyboard is a regular typewriter keyboard. Text does not fold over automatically when you reach the end of a line. The line simply shifts off the screen to the left as you type. Turbo accepts lines up to 127 characters; however, we recommend limiting lines to 80 characters. Longer lines confuse 80 column printers and are hard to read.

Corrections can be made as you type by backing up and deleting with the back arrow key (above the <CR>). Other errors can be corrected by overwriting the error correctly in the overwrite mode or by inserting the correct material and then deleting the incorrect.

Deleting. As with cursor movements, delete functions operate on characters, words, or lines (Table B–1). You can also delete large blocks of material.

Inserting. The initial state of the system is with the insert mode on. EVERY-THING you type will be put in where the cursor is, and existing material is retained and shifted to the right. Pressing the Insert key or ^V toggles the editor into the overwrite mode. Hitting the Insert key or ^V again toggles the editor back to the insert mode. The state of the insert mode is shown in the upper right hand corner of the editor screen.

Block Handling. The block commands are used to delete, move, or copy blocks of material. The block commands only work on marked blocks. To mark a block, set the cursor at the beginning and strike ^KB. Then, move the cursor to the end and press ^KK. Until both beginning and end marks are in place, a ^B and ^K are visible. Once both marks are in place, the block is highlighted. We call a highlighted section a block.

Once marked you can delete the block (^KY), copy it to a new location with the original intact (^KC), move the block to the current cursor position with deletion of the original (^KV), and hide the block (^KH) to prevent accidental deletions or movement. In addition, you can write a copy of the block to disk (^KW)—the editor prompts you for the file name. ^KR reads a file from a disk and inserts it at the cursor; the editor asks for the file name.

The block read and write functions are especially convenient for saving or loading common routines to or from disk. As you build up a library of valuable procedures, you might want to put them into files that you can read into programs.

Search and Search/Replace. To search for a character, word or phrase in the file press ^QF. The system asks you to enter the string you are searching for and then allows you to indicate search options or to replace the last options. Possible options are:

B   Searches back through the file as opposed to its normal searching from the cursor forward.

W   Locates your letter combination only when it is a whole word (for example, avoids finding "the" in "theory").

U   Locates combinations regardless of case. A U search for "the" finds "THE", "thE", "The", and so on.

G   Globally searches the entire file regardless of cursor position. The cursor stops at each occurrence of your letter combination allowing you to change it or check on it, or whatever. ^L resumes the search.

To have the system search for something, find it, and then replace it with something else, you press ^QA. Again, you enter the search string and then the system asks for the replacement. Once that is entered you will be offered the above options. In addition:

N   The No Ask option automatically makes a replacement without your approval. A global replacement with No Ask can rapidly decimate a file if you are not careful.

A ^U stops any search and replace should it begin doing something catastrophic to your file. Since a search and replace is potentially damaging, we suggest you save your work before you begin replacing.

Undo Function. If you hopelessly garble a line during editing, ^QL restores any line to its preedited state as long as you have not left the line. It does not work if you move off the line or if you use the ^Y line delete.

Appendix C

Software Availability

C.1 DISCLAIMER

All software described in this book and supplied by the author is provided as is and with no guarantee for a specific purpose. The authors would appreciate any problems being reported to them.

C.2 AVAILABILITY

As a service to users, most of the routines described in this book (including VIDGR4, Async, INLINER, DTUtil and DTDef, S8255, QUANT, SMOOTH, and SIMPLEX) are available on 360K or 1.2M 5.25" diskettes or 720K 3.5" diskettes. To cover duplication and mailing costs, pricing is $7.00 for the 1.2M format and $12.00 for the others. Address all correspondence to

Professor James N. Demas
Chemistry Department
McCormick Rd.
University of Virginia
Charlottesville, VA 22901

BitNet jnd@virgina.bitnet
Other networks jnd@virginia.edu

Be sure to specify format and make checks payable to the University of Virginia Fund. Foreigners with currency exchange problems please correspond with the above post office or E-Mail address.

Note that some of the provided software is copyrighted. Users are expected to abide by any stipulations of shareware software. The copyrighted software from this book can be given to other individuals as long as there is no charge, but **any** distribution, free or otherwise, by commercial companies must have the express prior written approval of the authors.

The authors reserve the right to provide more recent versions of software; the function and use may not match exactly the description in this book. However, sufficient details will be provided to fully utilize it.

References

Auslander, D. M. (1981). *Microprocessors for Measurement and Control."* Berkeley, CA: Osborne/McGraw-Hill.

Ballew, R. M., and Demas, J. N. (1989). "An Error Analysis of the Rapid Lifetime Determination Method for the Evaluation of Single Exponential Decays." *J. of Analytical Chemistry* **61**, 30.

Ballew, R. M., Demas, J. N., Ayala, N. P., Grubb, M., and Snyder, S. W. "Computer Interfaced Fast Kinetics Luminescence Decay Experiment." Submitted to *J. of Chemical Education.*

Bevington, P. R. (1969). *Data Reduction and Error Analysis for the Physical Sciences.* New York: McGraw-Hill.

Borland International (1988). "Turbo Assembler Reference Guide." Scotts Valley, CA.

Borland International (1988). "Turbo Assembler User's Guide." Scotts Valley, CA.

Borland International (1988). "Turbo Debugger User's Guide." Scotts Valley, CA.

Bradley, D. J. (1984). *Assembly Language Programming for the IBM Personal Computer.* Englewood Cliffs, NJ: Prentice-Hall.

Butterworth, J., MacLaughlin, D. E., and Moss, B. C. (1967). "Use of Random Noise to Improve Resolution in Analogue-to-Digital Conversion." *J. of Scientific Instrumentation,* **44**, 1029.

Carraway, E., Xu, Q., Ballew, R. and Demas, J. N. "Graphics Tools and Simple Language for Interfacing Hewlett Packard 7400 Series Digital Plotters to IBM Compatible PCs." Submitted to *J. of Chemical Education.*

Crawford, J. H., and Gelsinger, P. P. (1987). *Programming the 80386."* Alameda, CA: Sybex, Inc.

Daniels, R. W. (1978). *An Introduction to Numerical Methods and Optimization Techniques.* New York: North-Holland.

Data Translation, Inc. (1985). "User Manual for DT2801 Series." Marlborough, MA.

Demas, J. N. (1983). *Excited State Lifetime Measurements."* New York: Academic Press.

Demas, J. N., and Keller, R. A. (1985). "Enhancement of Luminescence and Raman Spectroscopy by Phase-Resolved Background Suppression." *J. of Analytical Chemistry,* **57**, 538.

Dettmann, T. R. (1988). *DOS Programmer's Reference.* Carmel, IN: Que Corporation.

Eggebrecht, L. C. (1983). *Interfacing to the IBM Personal Computer.* Indianapolis, IN: Howard W. Sams & Co.

Engstrom, R. W. (1980). *Photomultiplier Handbook.* Lancaster, PA: RCA Solid State Division, Electro Optics and Devices.

Enke, C. G., and Nieman, T. A. (1976). "Signal-to-Noise Ratio Enhancement by Least-Squares Polynomial Smoothing." *J. of Analytical Chemistry,* **48**, 705A.

Foster, C. C. (1982). *Real Time Programming—Neglected Topics.* Menlo Park, CA: Addison-Wesley.

Gonzalez, R. C., and Wintz, P. (1977). *Digital Image Processing*. Reading, MA: Addison-Wesley Publishing, Co.

Hewlett-Packard (1984). *Interfacing and Programming Manual/HP 7470A Graphics Plotter*. San Diego, CA.

Hinde, A. L., Selinger, B. K., and Nott, P. R. (1977). "On the Reliability of Fluorescence Decay Data." *Australian J. of Chemistry*, **30**, 2383.

Horowitz, P., and Hill, W. (1989). *The Art of Electronics*. New York: Cambridge University Press.

IEEE, Inc. (1983). *IEEE Standard Digital Interface for Programmable Instrumentation—IEEE Recommended Practice for Code and Format Conventions for Use with ANSI/IEEE Std 488-1978*. New York.

Inman, D., and Albrecht, B. (1988). *Using QuickBASIC*. Berkeley, CA: Osborne/McGraw-Hill.

Intel Corporation (1987). *80387 Programmer's Manual*. Santa Clara, CA.

Jamsa, K. (1988). *DOS: Power User's Guide*. Berkeley, CA: Osborne/McGraw-Hill.

Johnson, K. J. (1980). *Numerical Methods in Chemistry*. New York: Marcel Dekker, Inc.

Lafore, R. (1984). *Assembly Language Primer for the IBM PC & XT*. New York: The Waite Group, Inc.

Lakowicz, J. R. (1983). *Principles of Fluorescence Spectroscopy*. New York: Plenum Press.

Lancaster, D. (1974). *TTL Cookbook*. Indianapolis, IN: Howard W. Sams & Co., Inc.

Lancaster, D. (1989). "Hardware Hacker." *Radio Electronics*, **November**.

Leibson, S. (1983). *The Handbook of Microcomputer Interfacing*. Blue Ridge Summit, PA: Tab Books, Inc.

Lemone, K. (1985). *Assembly Language & Systems Programming for the IBM PC and Compatibles*. Boston: Little, Brown & Co.

Madden, H. H. (1978). "Comments of the Savitzky-Golay Convolution Method for Least-Squares Fitting Smoothing and Differentiation of Digital Data." *J. of Analytical Chemistry*, **50**, 1383.

Malmstadt H. V., Enke, C. G., and Crouch, S. R. (1981). *Electronics and Instrumentation for Scientists*. Reading, MA: The Benjamin/Cummings Publishing Company, Inc.

Marquardt, D. W. (1963). "An Algorithm for Least-Squares Estimation of Nonlinear Parameters." *J. of Society for Industrial and Applied Mathematics*, **11**, 431.

Microsoft (1987). *Microsoft QuickBASIC 4.0 BASIC Language Reference*. Redmond, WA: Microsoft Corporation.

Microsoft (1987). *Microsoft QuickBASIC 4.0 Learning and Using Microsoft QuickBASIC*. Redmond, WA: Microsoft Corporation.

Norton, P. (1985). *Programmer's Guide to the IBM PC*. Bellevue, WA: Microsoft Press.

Norton, P. (1986). *Inside the IBM PC*. New York: A Brady Book.

Nelder, J. A., and Mead, R. (1965). "A Simplex Method for Function Minimization." *Computer J.*, **January**, 308.

Ott, H. W. (1976). *Noise Reduction Techniques in Electronic Systems*. New York: Wiley-Interscience.

Palmer, J. F., and Morse, S. P. (1984). *The 8087 Primer*. New York: John Wiley & Sons, Inc.

Pearson, T. D. L., Demas, J. N., and Davis, S. (1982). "An Autozeroing Microcomputerized Boxcar Integrator." *J. of Analytical Chemistry*, **54**, 1899.

Press, W., Flannery, B., Teukolsky, S., and Vetterling, W. (1989). *Numerical Recipes in Pascal.* Cambridge: Cambridge University Press.

Rector, R., and Alexy, G. (1980). *The 8086 Book*. Berkeley, CA: Osborne/McGraw-Hill.

Rutkowski, G. B. (1984). *Integrated-Circuit Operational Amplifiers,* 2d ed. Englewood Cliffs, NJ: Prentice-Hall.

Sargent, M., III, and Shoemaker, R. L. (1986). *The IBM Personal Computer From the Inside Out.* Reading, MA: Addison-Wesley.

Savitzky, A., and Golay, M. J. E. (1984). "Smoothing and Differentiation of Data by Simplified Least Squares Procedures." *J. of Analytical Chemistry*, **36**, 1627.

Seyer, M. D. (1984). *RS-232 Made Easy.* Englewood Cliffs, NJ: Prentice-Hall.

Sheingold, D. H. (1980). *Transducer Interfacing Handbook—A Guide to Analog Signal Conditioning.* Norwood, MA: Analog Devices, Inc.

Sprague Electric Company. Semiconductor Group (1987). "Hall Effect and Optoelectronic Sensors." Concord, NH.

Startz, R. (1983). *8087 Applications and Programming for the IBM PC and Other PCs.* Bowie, MD.: Robert J. Brady Co.

Summagraphics Corp. (1984). "Technical Reference Publication 84-DM11-440." Fairfield, CT.: Summagraphics Corporation.

Swan, T. (1989). *Mastering Turbo Pascal 5.5,* 3d ed. Indianapolis, IN: Hayden Books.

Swan, T. (1989). *Mastering Turbo Assembler.* Indianapolis, IN: Hayden Books.

Taylor, D. G., Turley, T. J., Rodgers, M. L., Peterson, S. H., and Demas, J. N. (1980). "Microcomputer Controlled Boxcar Integrator with Subnanosecond Rise Time." *Review of Scientific Instruments*, **51**, 855.

Toney, J. H. and Demas, J. N. (1982). "Low-frequency Computerized Lock-in Amplifier." *Review of Scientific Instruments*, **53**, 1082.

Vassos, B. H. and Ewing, G. W. (1972). *Analog and Digital Electronics for Scientists.* New York: Wiley-Interscience Inc.

Wakerly, J. F. (1981). *Microcomputer Architecture and Programming.* New York: John Wiley & Sons.

Wilkins, C. L., Perone, S. P., Klopfenstein, C. E., Williams, R. C., and Jones, D. E. (1975). *Digital Electronics and Laboratory Computer Experiments.* New York: Plenum Press.

Wohltjen, H. and Dessy, R. (March 1979). "An Instrument Simulator for Use in Computer Interfacing Laboratories." *J. of Chemical Education*, **56**, 153.

Wood, C. M. (1987). "Strain-Gage Transducers." *Radio-Electronics*, **December**.

Woods, R. J., Scypinski, S., Cline Love, L. J., Ashworth, H.A. (1984). *J. of Analytical Chemistry,* **56**, 1395.

Xu, Q., Demas, J. N., and Grubb, M. (1989). "Computer Interfaced Digital Counter-Analog Data Acquisition System S/N Enhancement." *J. of Chemical Education*, **66**, A199.

Yeung, B. C. (1984). *8086/8088 Assembly Language Programming.* New York: John Wiley & Sons.

Index